TO THE MOUNTAINS

TO THE MOUNTAINS

A collection of
New Zealand alpine writing

Selected by

LAURENCE FEARNLEY
& PAUL HERSEY

OTAGO

Published by Otago University Press
Level 1, 398 Cumberland Street
Dunedin, New Zealand
university.press@otago.ac.nz
www.otago.ac.nz/press

First published 2018

ISBN 978-1-98-853120-5

Published with the assistance of Creative New Zealand, the Mountain & Forest Trust and the New Zealand Alpine Club DOW Hall Fund.

A catalogue record for this book is available from the National Library of New Zealand.

Jacket photographs: Main photograph, Tony Rac; Paul Hersey by Derek Morrison
Internal photographs: pp. 26–27, Troy Mattingley; pp. 84–85, Shelley Hersey; pp. 190–91, Troy Mattingley; pp. 276–77, Paul Hersey

Printed in China through Asia Pacific Offset.

CONTENTS

PART 2: CLIMB

LAURENCE FEARNLEY

A Writing Climber: An introduction to New Zealand alpine literature

Disembarking in Port Chalmers in 1882 after a long and eventful journey, Irish mountaineer William Spotswood Green was met by his two Swiss climbing companions: guide Ulrich Kaufmann and hotelier and keen mountaineer Emil Boss. Green, who hoped to make the first ascent of Aoraki/Mt Cook, questioned his friends about how they had occupied their time while waiting for him. They explained they had taken some walks:

> *Boss asked me if there was much scrub on Mount Cook. I asked him why. 'If there is anything like what there is on the hills about here we have a nice job before us. Kaufmann and I have tried to get through some near here, and we would not do a mile in a week.' As I had Dr. Haast's book at my fingers' ends I explained to them as well as I could the style of country we should have to travel through, and set their minds at rest on this point.*[1]

Green's response to Boss's question is wonderfully optimistic and may have come back to haunt him during the difficult weeks ahead. The exchange between the two men also sounds familiar; it probably rings bells with many of today's mountaineers, especially those who have been led astray by friends in the name of adventure.

Adventure is one of the key ingredients of mountaineering. As a recreational activity, mountaineering exists on the continuum from alpine tramping through to advanced technical ice-climbing. Defining it can be tricky because of the fluid nature of the sum of its parts: according to century, year, season, weather, snow conditions and available equipment, or the age of the climber, their experience and technical skill. As a young kid I was roped up and climbed on Mt Temple in Arthurs Pass, but for my older brother and parents it was just a walk. Years later, during a winter ascent, my then-partner cut steps for me on the Otira Face of Rolleston while the other member of our group recited Roger McGough's 'Let me die a youngman's death'. I was so gripped I don't think I blinked for two hours straight, but it never occurred to either of my companions to take out or offer me the rope: in their opinion the climb was far too mundane to warrant its use.

For the purpose of this book, mountaineering is broadly defined as requiring the use of hands, either in direct contact with the terrain (scrambling, rock-climbing, plunged into snow) or with the addition of tools such as ropes, ice axes and belays. Such an open approach to the topic ensures that a wide range of voices and experiences will be located within this anthology. This book is not a Who's Who of New Zealand's greatest alpinists, nor a Top-100 unforgettable climbs. Rather, it is a selection of mountain writing that crisscrosses time, place, gender, age and genre.

'Mountaineering' in its broadest terms also allows a particular New Zealand identity to creep into the collection. In the introduction to *Two Against the Alps*, Graeme Dingle notes that a 'top mountaineer' must possess the 'abilities of an alpine climber', and,

> *... must also have a deep feeling for the mountains. He should be a good skier, be able to carry a heavy pack over difficult ground, and be able to coax wet alpine scrub into a life-giving fire – he must be a mountain jack of all trades.*[2]

The importance of being a 'mountain jack of all trades' was quickly recognised by Boss, Kaufmann and Green. Mountaineering in New Zealand in the 1880s was very different from the European experience with its infrastructure of transport, accommodation, maps, equipment and guides. A recurring theme in many pioneering New Zealand mountain narratives is that of exploration and discovery. Travelling through the unmapped wilderness was hard work; at times, locating the mountain itself was part of the challenge.

Bernard Head with guides Jack Clarke and Alex Graham made the first ascent of Mt Aspiring in November 1909. Initially they travelled up the east branch of the Matukituki, but it wasn't until they attained a height of 4000ft on a hill above camp that they were able to see they 'were on the wrong side to climb, as the route would mean bivouac on the snow and then a very long climb through snow before we could get to the actual mountain ...'[3] Altogether it took 13 days to reach a position to make a successful push for the summit, which they achieved on a 'very windy and cold' morning, staying only minutes before turning around and heading back down the mountain to the valley.

Despite the difficulty of locating routes up their respective peaks, both Green and Head took satisfaction and pleasure from being in the mountains, as did many of their mountaineering contemporaries:

George Mannering, Malcolm Ross, E.A. Fitzgerald, Samuel Turner and Freda du Faur, for example. The general tone of their writing is buoyant: mountaineering is a worthwhile adventure, a challenging recreational activity or sport that builds good character. Notes on travel, exploration, natural history, scientific observation or mountaineering technique add colour to the mountaineering narrative but do not define it; anecdotes enliven the stories, adding shifts in dramatic tension as the climbs unfold. Essentially, these early texts – like many mountaineering articles of today – aim to report and record attempts and ascents, and offer details of topography, weather, routes and climbing conditions.

Books on New Zealand mountaineering from the late nineteenth century to the mid-twentieth century tended to be published in Britain and, while important in propagating British mountaineering culture worldwide, they also introduced and promoted New Zealand mountaineering to overseas readers and provided valuable route information for local mountaineers. The establishment of the New Zealand Alpine Club in 1891 and publication of the biannual *New Zealand Alpine Journal* opened the way for even greater dissemination of local mountaineering knowledge.

The written word, as it relates to New Zealand mountaineering literature, rested mainly in the pen of the educated middle class. In nineteenth- and early twentieth-century full-length publications, descriptions of mountain scenery draw heavily on Romantic imagery with its fashion for dramatic adjectives and metaphors, as this extract from Freda du Faur's account of Mt Sefton illustrates:

> *We just walked on to the actual summit and off again – it was too bitterly exposed for human beings. Mists were driving round us, being blown apart now and again, and disclosing great banks of white cloud racing before the gale over the low passes, and hurling themselves against the defying walls of the high peaks. The cloud-level was at about 8000 feet, and out of it towered the summit of Mount Cook like a giant rising from a sea of foam.*[4]

From the 1920s a more low-key, somewhat laconic style gained favour in mountaineering accounts. The poetics of conquest and mountain majesty made room for the notion of mountaineering as the culmination of an honest, hard day's work, as can be seen in W. Scott Gilkison's chapter 'In Defence of Swagging' (1940), or Forrestina Ross's variation on the theme, 'Housekeeping on a Glacier' (1934). Sir Edmund Hillary reached the summit of Mt Everest on 29 May 1953. In a letter sent from Everest Base

Camp on 2 June 1953 to his future father-in-law, New Zealand Alpine Club president Jim Rose, he draws on this language of labour in his account of the historic ascent:

> *Well all the flurry and bustle is over, all the hard work is finished and at long last we've climbed the jolly mountain. Now Himalayan climbing can settle down into a more normal routine and the 'Everest' sense of values can be put aside. However I must admit that the whole of this expedition has been jolly good fun despite the very real dangers of the icefall and we've had a party that welded into a particularly useful and pleasant team. I think the great feature of this party is how practically every man went high and certainly all did a very useful job.*[5]

During the exploratory and pioneering days of New Zealand mountaineering, however, the real labour was often left to the guides. While clients spent the afternoons resting in camp, sketching, or filling the pages of their trip diaries, their guides took advantage of the soft snow conditions to cut steps further up the mountain. It is not surprising, then, to find few examples of work published by guides during the period in which they worked. Jack Clarke, employed as chief guide at the government-run Hermitage hotel at Mount Cook at the start of the twentieth century, was obliged to submit annual reports to the Department of Tourist and Health Resorts. In 1904 he wrote an account of the first crossing of Pioneer Pass, made in the company of West Coast doctor Ebenezer Teichelmann and guide Peter Graham. As might be expected in a 'report', the language is simple, focusing on descriptions of the location, route and conditions. There is little attempt to add imaginative or atmospheric flourishes to the account, but what stands out is the way Clarke downplays his literary ability and, by extension, his claim to a personal response. The tone of his writing is humble and self-effacing, and it is clear that Clarke is ambivalent about his role as author:

> *The whole trip from Haast Ridge was, I think, the most interesting I have ever made in the course of a varied mountain life. It would need the pen of the writing climber and not that of a climbing writer to do it anything like justice.*[6]

In a letter to Jim Glasgow dated 26 October 1954, retired mountain guide Peter Graham responds in a similar way to a request to write his mountaineering memoir:

> *For myself I have I fear a very low opinion of my own qualities and ability in being able to express in writing what I really feel about our mountains and what they have meant to me.*
>
> *In any case most of my major climbs have been written up by Miss du Faur and Mr. Turner, which books the club will have in its library, and will no doubt be available to all its members.*[7]

Peter Graham did eventually agree to write his autobiography (although he died before it was finished), but it is apparent that both Clarke and Graham found it difficult to articulate their emotional response to the mountain world in writing. It is as if their experiences through years and years of climbing and guiding rested too deeply within them to find an easy outlet on the page.

Few working-class guides were published in newspapers or journals, except in exceptional circumstances, such as when Tom Fyfe, George Graham and Jack Clarke made the first ascent of Aoraki/Mt Cook in 1894. As a result, first-person accounts of working-class mountaineers only enter the mountaineering canon after the 1950s and 60s, when more guides began to pen their memoirs or were the subject of biographies. Fyfe, Clarke, Frank Alack, Mick Bowie and Harry Ayres, among others, now have books written by or about them.

In general, guides' experiences appear in the margins of the writing of their clients, and this is particularly true of Māori guides. During the 1911–12 climbing season George Bannister guided Samuel Turner on ascents of Elie de Beaumont, Mts Sealy, Green, Walter and Sefton, and a complete traverse of the Nuns Veil. The highlight was their ascent of Aoraki/Mt Cook on 27 February 1912, when Bannister, who was 18 at the time of the climb, became the first Māori to reach the summit. His response, sadly, is unrecorded. Bannister's cousin, the guide Joe Fleurty, appears in Ida Corry's 1933 account of the mountain rescue of Mark Lysons from Mt Goldsmith but, again, his version of events is unrecorded. It has largely been left to alpine historians such as Philip Temple, Bob McKerrow, Graham Langton, Shaun Barnett and Lee Davidson to fill the gaps in our knowledge of Māori mountaineering history.

In more recent years the increase in the number of books, journals, bulletins and blogs has allowed a wider range of mountaineering responses and stories to surface. These often have their roots in the oral storytelling tradition of mountaineering, and have been instrumental in

shaping mountaineering culture, identity and particularly personalities: the team-member, the laconic outsider, the masculine jack of all trades, the emancipated and empowered feminist, or the introspective 'spiritual' mountaineer, to name a few types. Written accounts of adventure, misadventure, death and survival echo the nature of storytelling in the way they create atmosphere, build up tension and present a dramatic climax, before steering the reader towards a conclusion with humour, reflection, contemplation and, sometimes, emotional closure.

The degree to which mountaineers examine and reflect on their mountaineering experience, and the self-awareness and honesty they bring to the page, create an emotional depth that resonates for mountaineers and non-mountaineers alike. Pat Deavoll opens herself up to the subject of failure in her memoir *Wind from a Distant Summit*:

> *I find failing on a mountain hard to cope with and usually dread going home afterwards, building up the criticism I feel I'm bound to receive to almost unbearable levels.*[8]

Such self-doubt and vulnerability in the face of a critical audience is not new. Freda du Faur writes of feeling a similar pressure from a judgmental public when climbing from the Hermitage in the 1910s. But equally, women mountaineers record feelings of freedom, wellbeing and escape from society's restraint in their letters, diaries and books. Both Dorothy Theomin and Dora de Beer were able to commit themselves to considerable time in the mountains: Theomin in New Zealand, de Beer both here and abroad. As a member of the first New Zealand overseas expedition, to Mt Satseto in Yunnan in 1938, de Beer immersed herself in the adventure, admitting that while the goal of the expedition was to claim the highest peak, 'for me any objective would have done equally well.'[9] Her description of the preparation and the 42-day, 400-mile approach to the mountain from Burma to China provides insight to her frame of mind:

> *Aeroplanes and motor cars undoubtedly save time but one learns far more about a country if one goes on foot or on horseback, and what a mule caravan lacks in comfort, it makes up in interest.*[10]

Learning about the environment and, by extension, about one's place in the mountains, comes to the forefront in the writing of Aat Vervoorn. *Beyond the Snowline* (1981) and *Mountain Solitudes: Solo journeys in the Southern Alps of New Zealand* (2000) combine elements of mountaineering

and exploration with self-discovery, the mountaineer eschewing the persona of 'conqueror' to reposition himself as the student of the mountain, allowing himself to be guided by everything from weather and snow conditions to mountain thar:

> *I had been shown the best route into the Landsborough by a big bull thar in February 1964, although I did not understand it at the time. With a companion I was traversing the snow slopes below Scissors, making for the lowpoint on the Main Divide on the way out to Mt Spence. There we saw him. He was peering down from the ridge, with the early morning sun lighting up the blond ruff that framed his dark face ...*[11]

Such transcendental moments have the potential to lead to freedom from ego and the gaining of wisdom, but are often hard to come by and require an open mind to begin with.

As New Zealand mountaineers gained skills and experiences and pushed themselves towards greater challenges, they often headed offshore where the peaks are higher, the faces more challenging, the dangers greater. While this collection celebrates many successes, from Norman Hardie's ascent of Kangchenjunga (1955) through to Karen McNeill's ascent of the Cassin Ridge on Denali (2004), inevitably there is space devoted to death and loss. Some of the most powerful and moving pieces in this anthology are written by mountaineers paying tribute to companions lost in the mountains; some of the most painful works are those by friends and family whose links to the mountains are less well established, and who cannot easily make sense of what has happened. Jonathan Scott writes of the 'absence' of his father Harry Scott, killed on Aoraki/Mt Cook in 1960. Aged just two at the time of his father's death, Scott writes,

> *I was not aware of missing someone I did not remember having known. His absence, on the other hand, became immediately a powerful and pivotal family personality.*[12]

Poet Fleur Adcock in 'Flight, with mountains' sees her dead friend, David Herron, 'daily' on the faces of strangers as she walks down the road. She can conjure up images of him in her memory, can picture him animated, arguing or smoking, but in the end he is dead: 'Gone is gone forever.' I suspect that almost all of the authors in this collection have at some time been affected by the death of an acquaintance, friend, team member or family member in the mountains.

Poetry taps into the peaks and troughs of life and is frequently shared in times of celebration and loss, but it's interesting how being in the mountains brings out the poet in the mountaineer (and vice versa). The 'climbing writer' and 'writing climber' has a long tradition in this country: William Pember Reeves (b. 1857), Arnold Wall (b. 1869), Blanche Baughan (b. 1870), and J.C. Beaglehole (b. 1901) all penned works based on mountains and mountaineers. But whereas their poems have largely faded from public view, the mountain-themed poems of the next generation of poets – Charles Brasch, James K. Baxter and Denis Glover, for example – have remained more deeply embedded in our mountain-literature psyche. In large part, the loss of the earlier work may be put down to style, language and imagery. Beaglehole's 'The climber', its opening reminiscent of Tennyson's work, conjures a sentiment that feels out of place in today's world:

Striving, breast to the wind, on the desolate hill,
This, do I think, is the end and the summit of life –
Ever to strive with the fateful implacable will
Of the Invisible: strive, nor lose heart in the strife.[13]

The elaborate, heroic language and dense grammar become even more pronounced when compared to the first lines of Brian Turner's understated verse in 'High hopes', with its steady rhythm of rising and falling footsteps:

Climbed the mountain
with the sun in my eyes[14]

At times the lives of explorers and mountaineers have captured the imagination of poets and fiction writers. Thom Conroy imagines the 1839 ascent of Mt Egmont/Taranaki by Ernst Dieffenbach in his 2014 novel *The Naturalist*; Philip Temple's *The Explorer* draws on the life of West Coast explorer Charlie Douglas; and Rhian Gallagher's suite of poems from the collection *Freda du Faur* examines the life and mountaineering relationship between Freda du Faur and her guides Peter and Alex Graham.

Fantasy, romance and suspense have played their role in mountaineering literature, too. In 1893 a serialised mountain adventure titled 'The Pirates' Treasure Cave' appeared in the weekly *Otago Witness*. Penned by 'AJOR' (real name John Petrie), the story recounts a mysterious episode in the life of protagonist Arthur Rainey. Drugged by a shadowy French man, Rainey is led through wild countryside to a lake high up

on the slopes of Aorangi. Finding a boat, the men enter the side of the mountain via a tunnel, wherein they discover 'a sort of amphitheatre of ice arena, snow terraces, and steepled glaciers'.[15] Within this amphitheatre stands a troupe of frozen dancers, exiles from the French Revolution, and a pirate chief. As the dancers start to defrost, events take an even more bizarre turn. In style, 'The Pirates' Treasure Cave' imitates a true-life narrative and has its literary origins in such works as Coleridge's *The Rime of the Ancient Mariner* (1798), Edgar Allen Poe's *The Narrative of Arthur Gordon Pym of Nantucket* (1838) or Samuel Butler's *Erewhon* (1872) – tales that used real but largely unknown locations as backdrops for speculative fiction.

Today the mystery novel is more likely to be steeped in reality, as Trish McCormack's 'Philippa Barnes' series illustrates. *Glacier Murder* (2013), set in small-town Franz Josef, follows glacier guide Barnes as she tries to solve the murder of Vivien Revell, whose body is discovered in a crevasse. In Gina Cole's short story 'Black Ice' from the 2016 collection *Black Ice Matter*, a Nepalese Sherpa employed by a Fox Glacier guiding company deals with everyday racism and violence; while in Eleanor Catton's short story, 'Descent from Avalanche', the mountain provides the backdrop to the emotional retreat of couple Richard and Harriet. Both McCormack and Cole take advantage of the remoteness and isolation of their communities in constructing their stories, a feature that harks back to Edith Searle Grossman's *The Heart of the Bush* (1910) or John Mulgan's *Man Alone* (1939), in which the protagonists find themselves at the edge of civilisation, confronted by nature.

But despite all this literary activity taking place in the hills, it is – as Rangi Faith in 'Castle Hill, 2003' and Hone Tuwhare in 'Man in the landscape' remind us – the profound and great 'silence' of the mountains that seems to speak to us and affect us most deeply. It is in the mountains, beyond the reach of the human, that the real mystery takes place:

The sea beckons
again and again
to the mountains. Unmoved
the austere mountains ponder
a silence as profound as stars.[16]

Endnotes

1 W.S. Green, *The High Alps of New Zealand, or, A trip to the glaciers of the Antipodes with an ascent of Mount Cook* (London: Macmillan, 1883), 99–100.

2 Graeme Dingle, *Two Against the Alps* (Christchurch: Whitcombe and Tombs, 1972), 15.

3 Bernard Head, typescript account of expeditions up the Matukituki River, 1909 and 1911 (n.d.), in Robert Pinney, Papers in ARC-0587, MS-3184/002, Hocken Collections – Uare Taoka o Hākena, University of Otago.

4 Freda du Faur, *The Conquest of Mount Cook and other climbs: An account of four seasons' mountaineering on the Southern Alps of New Zealand* (London: George Allen & Unwin, 1915), 231.

5 Edmund Hillary, copies of letters to Jim Rose, New Zealand Alpine Club Archives, MS-1164-2/66/3, Hocken Collections – Uare Taoka o Hākena, University of Otago.

6 Tourist and Health Resorts Report, *Appendices to the Journals of the House of Representatives*, 1904 Session I, H-02, 13–14.

7 Peter Graham, letter to Jim Glasgow, 26 October 1954, Brooke Bequest and the Graham Memoir 1948–58, New Zealand Alpine Club Archives, MS-1164-1/6/21, Hocken Collections – Uare Taoka o Hākena, University of Otago.

8 Pat Deavoll, *Wind from a Distant Summit: The story of New Zealand's leading woman mountaineer* (Nelson: Craig Potton Publishing, 2011), 240.

9 Dora de Beer, *Yunnan 1938: Account of a journey in south-west China* (Oxford: Dora de Beer, 1971), 1.

10 De Beer, *Yunnan 1938*, 2.

11 Aat Vervoorn, *Mountain Solitudes: Solo journeys in the Southern Alps of New Zealand* (Nelson: Craig Potton Publishing, 2000), 28.

12 Jonathan Scott, *Harry's Absence: Looking for my father on the mountain* (Wellington: Victoria University Press, 1997), 13.

13 J.C. Beaglehole, 'The climber', in *Kowhai Gold: An anthology of contemporary New Zealand verse*, ed. Quentin Pope (Letchworth: J.M. Dent & Sons, 1930), 54.

14 Brian Turner, 'High hopes', *Inside Outside* (Wellington: Victoria University Press, 2011), 133.

15 AJOR, 'The Pirates' Treasure Cave', *Otago Witness*, no. 1851, 29 June 1893.

16 Hone Tuwhare, 'Man in the landscape', *No Ordinary Sun* (Dunedin: John McIndoe, 1977), 224.

PAUL HERSEY

Mountains with Words

A worthy and memorable adventure rarely just occurs. While there are times when adventure may be thrust upon us through luck or ill timing, generally it takes planning and preparation. Months of training. The accumulation of knowledge. The right equipment. A handful of days of clear weather. The wanting to exhaust oneself. The desire for a certain amount of suffering and, perhaps, a few moments of feeling scared. Of course, there is also the potential of it being 'fun'.

For me, preparing for a mountain climb is the time when my anticipation and psyche grows. When self-belief evolves. Maybe it's about the ownership of an idea, accepting a goal in my mind and figuring out what I need to do to achieve it. Perhaps the mountain or a feature on that mountain has chosen me as much as I have chosen it.

In 'Incantation' Richard Thomson writes of the different kinds of climbs that inspire him:

> *[There are] routes you've walked under or looked across at and thought, Yes, I have to climb that ... Then there are the last great problems. Talked up between bursts of winter effort on a plywood wall. Speculated about after untying from a summer's evening at the crag ... Next, there are the walls you've never seen. But you look at the topographic blur of Google Earth and think, There's something there ... Finally, there are the walls you never knew existed: panning across a mighty gash of grass-infested cliff, the eye of the imagination takes a higher sweep of red-streaked iron-hard rock. Its rumpled facets look as if they were shaped with a giant club hammer.*[1]

I have always been drawn to the aesthetics of high places and the potential of climbing routes upon them. The particular angles of a rock face. The way light strikes a ridge-line in the snow. The translucence of some types of ice and the opaqueness of others. The land and the elements have combined in such a unique, special way that I come to believe in them. And in myself.

While I train I imagine being on various aspects of what I have seen or imagined seeing. Places on the mountain where there may be difficulty. Terrain that my mind tells me I won't be able to surmount. My palms might

begin to sweat, my breath quickening at the thought. The prospect becomes something I can focus on. I swear to myself that I will train harder.

But there is also a place in my mind that refuses to decide on what is possible and what is not. Like any decent assessor of risk, it likes to hedge its bets for as long as it can.

* * *

There comes a time to commit to approaching the route, either to attempt to climb it, or to turn away. A climber, by nature, has to love the essence of challenge. The unknown elements. For without some level of doubt there can be no challenge. The same could be said of adventure.

Approaching a climb, as well as the physical travelling from the lowlands to high, also involves walking through a kaleidoscope of emotions. An internal dialogue that can't make up its mind. Anticipation. Excitement. Belief. Imagination. Doubt. Fear.

And sometimes, just as a blister might appear on my heel, one develops in my thoughts. The weight of the pack across my shoulders becomes the burden of self-doubt. Any excuse in my mind that can turn itself into a good enough reason to bail is seized upon.

Despite the doubt, for some obscure, stubborn reason, I find myself continuing to walk forward. I keep reminding myself, 'It'll be enjoyable – well, mostly.' Certainly there is a part of me that believes this, an anticipation of the unknown. Slowly, I draw closer to the mountain. And, in doing so, it can be as Rangi Faith writes:

your unease grows,
& points of reference
begin to change

as this curious land
unfolds from the earth
into the space we occupy[2]

Standing at the base of a climb is the time when I doubt myself the most. I have lost all perspective of what lies ahead – above. I am dwarfed by the sheer size of the mountain and by all of my insecurities. To cope, I focus on small things: re-tying my boots; adjusting my harness; unfurling the rope; taking a small sip of water; more small-talk with my climbing partner; gripping my ice axes – and then finally commit to take that first measured movement. Upwards.

* * *

First light lifts over hard country, a land falling away to nothing. Mountains of granite and schist reveal the morning's mood and the imperfections on their skin. Their quartz veins. Their freckled micas and feldspars.

Corners and ledges of blackened argillite fold into greywacke as furrows through the earth. Stunted trees might still cling to this shattered bedrock, flag-forming mountain beech perched a short distance from gatherings of sprightly alpine grasses who whisper to each other in the morning breeze.

Above these and the low valley fog, the snowfields glisten, poorly remnants of the monstrous glaciers that once covered all of this land. Now they are pitted with rock fall, sunken in their arches and cracked to their core from the increasing heat of the sun.

The air is dry. Cold. It grasps my lungs during each, laboured breath. My insides are warmed from the steepness of the ascent but my fingers and toes remain numbed. There is the sound of my breathing. Boots clomping over broken rock. The jangling of karabiners and ice screws clipped to my harness. A few words of care between good friends. Perhaps the raucous yet eerie cry from a kea flying overhead or echoing across the void from another mountain. (How long will these endangered mountain parrots remain our alpine companions?)

To become immersed in the mountains – the act of climbing – is to lose oneself to a landscape that rises so steeply, and to the vagaries of weather swirling from the horizon. These highlands that fill our minds and tax our bodies have been reshaped by our plans and goals, or have reshaped us because of what they might offer. The fundamentals of movement are so absorbing, so elemental, and can be so much fun.

If only this is where it ends.

'How could we have foreseen that such a magnificent day would end in death?' writes Aat Vervoorn in *Beyond the Snowline*:

> *A blue day under the crystalline sun of mid-winter, on which the mountains were carved precisely by the frost out of light and shadow and the air did not become mild until midday. The ice of Mount Sefton soared above us, leaping forward through the transparent atmosphere as the car rounded the last bend in the road: pure whiteness, the upper slopes blazing light, momentarily framed between the black cliffs of Sebastopol and the bulk of Mount Wakefield.*[3]

Later, while searching for a fellow climber who is late returning, Vervoorn comes across his broken body at the base of a climb:

> *It was Bruce. He was lying on his back down the slope, his left arm curved as if to guard his head against a fall, right arm out-stretched, its fist clenched in pain. He had been wearing his orange singlet to catch some afternoon sun. On the rocks above, just out from the cliff, lay his watch, its glass broken: it had stopped at twenty to three.*[4]

Vervoorn is writing about the death of one of his best friends, talented mountaineer and fellow guide Bruce Jenkinson. Climb in the mountains for long enough and you will likely lose a friend, a partner, a loved one. The inevitability of it is something we as climbers push from our minds, especially while we are in the mountains. But that doesn't change the fact.

I have lost two of my closest mates to climbing, as well as a handful of others from my wider friendship circle. I have watched best friends come oh-so-close to perishing, and my wife Shelley and I have both come within a hair's breath on more than one occasion. Good luck and bad, along with decisions that we should or shouldn't have made all played their part. Call it whatever you want.

I don't write these words flippantly or easily. I can't think about certain situations or bring back fondest memories without feeling emotional. Fragile. Exposed. Yes, it affects the way I climb and how I think about the mountains. Could it stop me from climbing? Not yet, but …

* * *

Afterwards, it is natural to reflect on a successful or unsuccessful climb, to try to put the experience into perspective. And so naturally does this relection enter the kingdom of the written word. For me, sense is gained through considering how to phrase something in a certain way, how to write about the ephemeral. The words may seem inadequate at first, but they are a start. As both a climber and a writer (and even after all these years I'm still unsure which holds the more significance), I gain some small satisfaction when I can merge the two.

Reading the musings of others who have also unearthed this relationship leaves me at ease with myself. It allows perspective. It reminds me of all the good reasons why I go climbing. It makes me want to climb again. The most profound climbing writing might be so because of its simplicity or its vulnerability. Ideas which – well, to me at least – become all the more

significant when framed within the lows and highs of a mountain climb. And when reflected against the vagaries of life and the certainty of death. Sometimes climbers have described feeling most alive when they are in the mountains. To me this is a continuing paradox, if not ironic and perhaps a little sad as a reflection of our wider lives.

So, in an effort to sidestep further explanation of this conundrum, I will defer to another whose life experiences clearly hold special the connection between climbing, writing and love. The final words are from Christopher Johnson, in an extract from a letter he writes to his wife while serving in Nigeria in 1942 during World War II:

> *All that survives of such a climb is seldom more than this sediment of small interest. From the constant companionship of the scenery and from the continuity of the action, the human interests stood out a little at the time and they endure as the clearer impressions because they were incongruous. In our less exalted valley humour we find them less in our glass of memory, and stir them diluted into a tale; but our vivid and day-long consciousness of the mountain, of each other, and of the drama which we and the mountain played out and at length together, cannot be reproduced faithfully. It has escaped all but our general recollection. The mountaineer returns to the hills because he remembers always that he has forgotten so much. Of one thing alone he is certain, that he will pass one more such irreproducible day somewhere among the mountain source of unspoiled pleasure.*[5]

Endnotes

1 Richard Thomson, 'Incantation', *Alpinist* 46, 2014.

2 Rangi Faith, 'Castle Hill, 2003', *Conversation with a Moahunter* (Wellington: Steele Roberts, 2005), 50.

3 Aat Vervoorn, *Beyond the Snowline*, Dunedin: A.H & A.W. Reed, 1981, 3.

4 Ibid., 4.

5 Christopher Johnson, Letter from Nigeria, 1942, *OSONZAC Yodellings*, no. 13, 30 October 1942, New Zealand Alpine Club Archives, MS-1164-2/009/11, Hocken Collections – Uare Taoka o Hākena, University of Otago.

EDITORS' NOTE

Extracts in this collection have been copied verbatim from various sources. Spelling and grammar in some archival material is idiosyncratic and has been retained where it did not detract from the clarity of the story. Imperial measurements and the original names of mountains and people have also been retained. At the request of some living authors, alterations have been made to recent publications where climbers' names were spelt incorrectly, or where articles were published in US journals using American spellings. Mount Cook frequently refers to the area surrounding Aoraki/Mt Cook taking in the Hermitage, Tasman Glacier, Hooker Glacier and the West Coast section of the national park, but it can also refer to the individual mountain. Mt Cook, Aorangi and the more recent Aoraki/Mt Cook refer to the mountain itself.

APPROACH

RANGI FAITH

Castle Hill, 2003

As you approach
Kura Tawhiti –
this landscape of stone
across the valley
from the mountain of the kakapo –

your unease grows,
& points of reference
begin to change

as this curious land
unfolds from the earth
into the space we occupy;

therefore
give this place a simple greeting:
tena koe, tena korua, tena koutou –
and respect –

place an open hand
on the first rock

& walk softly
through the great silence
of many years
where each stone
will surround you
with legend

as it did
those past travellers
who asked for shelter
& lay in the dark
listening to their ancestors' talk
dissolving in the rain.

REBECCA SMITH

Young, Short and Loving It!

3.35 The bell rings and I bolt out of the maths room. A quick wave through the window at my form teacher means freedom, 'til next week anyway. Bags packed in anticipation I excuse myself from the excited planning of the weekend's social outings and locate my Ferrari (being the deluded soul that I am this is my pet name for my 1985 Honda City – but it is red!). I successfully get the car started, no mean feat when the petrol arrow has been sitting on the big E for a few days, and proceed home.

4.00 Home at last, but no rest for the wicked – a quick hello to the family and the race is on, one hour till departure …

First things first, one must dress appropriately. For me this is my favourite jeans, a size too big with rips and holes appearing daily, some old T-shirt and my well-worn black polar fleece.

School uniform thrown on the bed brings me back to reality … HOMEWORK … teachers have no leniency for young climbers. I pull the masses of text books from my bag, a sure sign of a year 13 student, then separate the workload into two piles – one that will get me a life full of detentions if I don't complete, and one that I can hand in late if I merely flash my smile and puppy-dog eyes. I sit down and race through as much of the critical work as possible, the rest I shove in my backpack with a pen, hoping for some light on either the car trip there or back.

4.45 A quick glance at my checklist and I can finally tick off the crampons and ice axe that I'm borrowing from a cousin. These I picked up at lunch time today, the crampons slightly too big for my size six boots and the ice axe a tad too tall for my five-foot-five frame, but hey I'm a poor student thus my middle name is 'beg, steal or borrow'. Pack closed and thrown in the car I wait for Dad to finish the article he's reading in the paper, drink his coffee, find his cell-phone, find his keys, check three times when and where we're meeting and when I'm going to be home on Sunday night before he's ready to leave. A quick hug and kiss for Mum and her insistent voice calls, 'Be safe!' as I pull the front door shut.

In the car waits my little brother. 'Are you going to the *big, big, big, big* mountains Becks?' his three-year-old's voice pipes up. 'Are you taking

your Leki hole?' (One day we'll tell him that it's really a *Leki pole*!) 'Can you bring me some white snow, it's very cold isn't it Becks?' He's very into asking questions and using *lots* of adjectives – sometimes repetitively for added emphasis and annoyance.

5.05 We pull into the carpark a little late, but no one minds. A small group of similarly dressed people has assembled in a group with packs at their feet. Dad checks the details with me for one last time and then without warning I am enveloped in one of his infamous bear hugs. I feel blood rush to my cheeks. He, however, seems not to care and with a departing wave drives off with Riley grinning cheekily in the back seat.

5.15 Once we're in the car I'm equal. It no longer matters that I've been at school all day while the rest have been at work or uni. It doesn't matter that half my gear is hired or borrowed because my minimum wage job doesn't dent the climbing gear prices. I'll climb just as far, work just as hard (if not harder with my short legs!) and have just as much fun as the rest because I'm doing what I love.

Being a young, short climber is hard, we get a lot of crap, and also find it a lot harder to find people to climb with. Weighing in at 50kg, any climbing partner of mine would have to be pretty confident they wouldn't fall off while on belay as I wouldn't hold much. We also have to walk twice as fast to keep up with the long-legged members of our species. (Ross Cullen I know you're out there!)

So all you young shorties out there, you *will* have to walk three times as fast, and plug all your own steps because the ones done by others will be like crevasses at your feet – but it's worth it! Plus the photos provide great teacher distractions when you get back to class which will make you all the more popular with your classmates!

ELEANOR ADAMS

Child Explorer on the Milford Track (1889)

It was only a short while after my Father had returned from the Sounds where he had surveyed the Sutherland Falls – finding them to be only 1904 ft. high instead of about 4000 much to the disappointment of the discoverers – that he and I left the Bluff in one of the Union Co's boats to return to Milford early in 1889.

We had a very rough trip, and my Father being a very bad sailor was very glad to get into the perfectly calm waters of the Sound in the late afternoon. There were a number of English tourists on board and they were delighted that the ship had to call at Milford to land my Father and myself there giving them a chance to see Milford Sound, but the Captain was not at all pleased as it delayed his arrival in Melbourne. We had expected to find two survey parties awaiting us at Milford but there was no sign of them. However the Captain put us ashore in one of the ship's boats as soon as we reached the head of the Sound, and as soon as possible put to sea again. The tourists were distressed at leaving us there by ourselves – my father looked frail after the rough sea trip and I was only eleven – and they persuaded the Captain to let us have some food to take ashore with us. Sutherland was away and I never met him at all – but he had left his hut open for us to use.

My father and I watched the steamer until out of sight. It was terribly lonely with not another soul there and surrounded by such huge mountains and thick bush to the water's edge. Luckily I did not know how anxious my Father was at the non-arrival of the survey parties. They had planned to be at Milford days before we arrived – but bad weather and numerous avalanches near the Pass had delayed them.

We went to bed early – at least I did – and in the early hours of the morning my Father heard a coo-ee from across the water and knew that at least some of the party had arrived safely. Soon after daylight a tiny little canvas boat came over, and I think we started off the same day.

That little canvas boat was the only boat we had and it held only 2 or 3 at a time and it took some time getting the party over the river or lakes. Someone had to squat down in the bow and watch for any snags – Lake

Ada was full of them – that might hole the canvas. We had a very rough walk from the Sound to the Ball (now called Quentin) huts and it took a long time getting us up Lake Ada in the canvas boat – I think some of the party scrambled around the lake. It was lucky there were the two huts near the Sutherland Falls for we had to stay many days there on account of the bad weather. The huts were very primitive affairs but they, as well as Sutherland's hut, all had some very pretty curtains and I wondered where the material came from. One of the surveyors told me that it had been torn from a French Countess's dress, when she had tried to walk up from Milford to see the Falls, she had returned to the Tourist ship with only the lining of her dress left and no shoes.

One day while we were at the Ball huts we had a frightening thunder storm – in the flashes of lightening the mountains seemed to tower over us.

At the Ball huts the bush rats were dreadful but luckily I was not afraid of mice and rats, but all the same did not like their running all over me as soon as the lights were out. I begged a yard of the white calico – used for the survey pegs – from my father and cut a good many holes in it so that I could breathe, and put it right over my head. I felt quite happy that way. During this bad weather my Father was quite anxious and wondered when we could get over the Pass.

One day we saw the Sutherland Falls – we were about quarter of a mile away I think, but we were covered with spray. I lost all sense of distance among those huge mountains and thought I could throw a stone into the pool at the foot of the Falls.

At last a good day came and the party for Te Anau and ourselves started off over the Pass. It was hard work pulling ourselves up through the heavy bush but above the bush line the way looked very dangerous, especially skirting Mt. Balloon where the rocky ground was all slimy with moss and water. Quintin Mackinnon roped me to himself and my Father and we all got safely to the top of the Pass. The little tarn on top was called after me – Lake Ella. Looking down the thousands of feet into the valley we had left was awe–inspiring. The only way I could look was to lie down flat and pull myself to the edge of the cliff and get my Father to hold my ankles!

We camped somewhere near the foot of the Pass and all night long were kept awake with avalanches falling. Just over the Pass above the heavy bush we went through acres of the large flowered houhere or ribbonwood – it was like a cherry orchard in Spring.

Going down the Clinton Valley was the easiest part of the journey and very lovely. When we came to the Clinton River it was a raging torrent with huge boulders, and the younger of the Quill brothers carried me across. We could see the river coming out from a huge ice cave at the head of the valley, and also saw an avalanche falling near.

The track to Te Anau was fairly level and we caught lovely glimpses of the Clinton River with its clear greenish waters. The native birds were so tame, and the little robins would come and perch on our toes and hats while we had our meals, ready for any crumbs. And nearly always while my Father was surveying a robin would perch on his hat or theodolite. Wood hens were plentiful in the Clinton Valley and would run off with anything bright they could find in your tent. If you imitated their call they would come right up to you.

Above the bush line at the Pass there were many native flowers – unfortunately I did not know the names of many of them. I saw one big white mountain daisy and mountain lily and at the Sound the rata was ablaze.

The bush was magnificent – huge trees with their trunks covered with lovely mosses and ferns and long trails of moss hanging from their boughs. Wherever you put a foot down you had to tread on lovely kidney and other ferns and mosses and masses of tiny native plants. And waterfalls and lovely mountain streams were everywhere. I think it took us three weeks to reach Lake Te Anau, and then we had three days in Mackinnon's boat on a perfectly calm lake rowing all the way and camping two nights on lovely little beaches – once on the West side and once on the East.

Mackinnon shot some duck and cooked our dinners over a fire in a kerosene tin in the boat. One day we stopped under a huge bluff for our dinner and when we dropped our duck bones over the side of the boat we could see them sinking down and down for ages – the water was so wonderfully clear.

We stayed at a sheep station on the East side of the Lake for the night and next day we rode on horse back to Lumsden station where we got a train to Dunedin.

REVEREND RICHARD TAYLOR

from *Journals of Rev. Richard Taylor, 1833–1873*

28–31 January 1853
We reached the Tomokanga by six and there we encamped for the night.

We rose by 3½ and began our daily march by six. We walked about 20 miles before noon and then halted by a stream which gushes out of the side of the mountain where we dined and reached the Kowhiaroa to sleep. Here we left the path and encamped about 2 miles nearer the snowy mount which caused some of the boys to murmur. Another immediately said Oh, you are just like the children of Israel in the wilderness who were always grumbling. Our boys soon erected themselves very comfortable huts for the Sabbath.

I held services with the natives. We then took a walk up a part of the Parataitonga or Ruapehu as it is commonly called. We ascended to a lofty precipice which stopped our further progress, a perpendicular chasm of full 1000 feet down which the Wangaehu flows direct from the snowy plains. The features of the mountain are very grand, all being igneous rock and plains of ashes. We ascended above the snow line. The chief plants I noticed were a beautiful everlasting, the harebell, 2 kinds of gentian, a pretty speedwell, an epacris and several other pretty flowers, a wild carrot also abounded. We returned and had evening service in English and native. Walked near 20 miles. Near our encampment there were dwarf totara, rimu, and kahikatia trees which produced very large sweet berries in great abundance. We reached Waihohonu to dinner and thence walked 2 miles where we encamped, the Govr. wishing to ascend Tongariro which much alarmed our natives as the body of Te Heuheu being placed there rendered it very sacred and they feared Iwikau in his anger would kill them. The Governor, however, thought I was too weak to attempt the ascent and it was fortunate he did for we had no sooner got our tent erected than the rain came down in torrents and continued to do so all night. It also thundered and lightened; hail likewise fell. We felt thankful to have pitched our tent in time. The volcano also roared.

W. SCOTT GILKISON

from *Peaks, Packs, and Mountain Tracks*

In Defence of Swagging

Swagging – or, if you prefer it, back-packing – is more or less an essential part of every climbing trip. Grim and lurid are words used by some parties in describing their swagging efforts, and it is usually reckoned that swagging is, at best, a necessary evil, to be suppressed and minimised in every possible way. Various cunning schemes have been evolved for doing away with pack-carrying. Sometimes the alternative is successful, but often is less so (as, for example, our aeroplane experiment). In one form or another the problem is to be found, and dealt with, in every alpine district.

In most of our mountain districts the usual technique consists of the establishment of a comfortable base camp at the limit of assisted transport – which usually means, at the end of the bridle trail – beyond which one or more high bivouacs must be swagged in by members of the party until the peak is within range. Mr. H.E.L. Porter speaks of the 'hardy young mountaineers of New Zealand who, carrying 60 or 70 pounds on their backs, march for days on end in any weather to their final bivouac and then are not only fit for, but can also enjoy the alpine work, which is the reward and crown of all their preliminary toil'.

But these self-same New Zealander mountaineers have a word or two to say on the subject themselves. For example:

> *Carrying a swag of 50 to 60 pounds is exceedingly hard work, and those unaccustomed to it do not always appreciate their limitations.*
> – G.M. Moir

> *We farewelled our friends, on the pack-horses, and proceeded to load our packs on shoulders already beginning to stoop at the thought of the strenuous work which lay ahead.* – G.L. Edwards

> *Pack carrying is entirely unspectacular, but it tests the mettle of a man sometimes to a higher degree than a high ascent.* – J.A. Sim

> *Carrying heavy swags is merely a means to an end, not a pleasure in itself.* – J.D. Pascoe

> *Many times have we vowed never to do this heavy swagging again, but to go to some more accessible district or sunbathe at the seaside … In retrospect the torturing swags are always forgotten, and scarcely are we home again before suggestions are being made to enter some even more outlandish place.* – J.D. Knowles

> *The snow was a little on the soft side, and the packs made it a most dreary grind. I must confess that at times I wondered how anyone could, with his eyes open, undertake such hard work in the name of pleasure.*
> – J.A. Sim

> While from Greenland: *One cannot enjoy pack-carrying, but there are many worse forms of hard work than slow slogging with a reasonably heavy load. For instance, rowing and cross-country running, to name but two.* – Martin Lindsay

And a very genuine and human attitude is that adopted by Mr. G.E. Mannering: 'Ah! Good reader, have you ever carried a swag – a real swag, not a Swiss Knapsack, but a real torturing colonial swag? When you take it up and sling it on your back in the orthodox fashion you remark, 'Yes, I think it *does* weigh 50 pounds.' In ten minutes your estimate of its weight has doubled. In an hour you begin to wonder why Nature has been so foolish as to make men who will carry swags … But patience and rest gradually bring you round, and soon you regain strength and spirits in feeling that at last you have conquered a day's difficulties and have brought your board and lodging so far with you. Ah, think of it, you knapsack mountaineers, you feather-bed Swiss mountaineers, with your tracks, your hotels, your guides, your porters and your huts. No: this New Zealand work is not like yours. But then, you see, we are enjoying what you cannot get. Exploring and opening out virgin fields, learning to be our guides and porters from that best of masters – hard experience.' Even in New Zealand, things have changed a little, and in some parts porters are available; and in some districts it is possible to climb from a hut, without the necessity of taking your bed and breakfast with you. But these are not the districts which attract me.

On the whole I must confess I enjoy swagging. True, I find little pleasure in grinding along a dusty road with a heavy swag, or even in toiling up a track where we know that a pack-horse could do the same journey so much more easily. In my 'varsity days, I dragged my old

'omnibus' over many a trail where, had I been more financial, I would surely have saved myself much trouble and toil by employing motor car or pack-horse. But, once to the limit of the bridle track, I can really enjoy a few days' solid swagging. The exact reaction to the physical labour or carrying a swag is difficult to assess, just as it is at all times almost impossible to say whether there is, or is not, any pleasure in the actual performing of any heavy physical toil. And for myself I find that the actual work of pack-carrying is so closely bound up with the pleasure and delights associated with it, that I cannot define in any way the point where tribulation ends and enjoyment begins. As a patent food advertisement says: 'Forget that it is good for you: enjoy it for yourself.' And even if I take no count of the value to me of hard work done in the hills, I can still look back on my swagging holidays as being my best and most satisfying. Only by carrying your own swag can you get really off the beaten track, and in that must remain a very full justification of swagging.

The most joyous days in my mountain memory are those spent in pioneering new routes, in the exploration of unvisited valleys, in the working out and placing of unmapped physical features. It is in the unravelling of the unknown that the prettiest problems and the most generous rewards are to be found. As long as mechanical devices do not bring every part of the hinterland within easy range, the swagging mountaineer will never be without the richest reward. But when that day comes – when climbers with their goods and chattels can be landed at any desired point in the mountains, there to remain until the day when they wish to be called for again – when the pioneer will have his mid-day spell interrupted by a picnic party who have dropped in, by autogiro – then, assuredly, swagging will have lost much of its point and purpose, and I for one will be very sorry. To-day I am willing to accept the assistance of train, car, and pack-horse as far as I can, knowing that there is still any amount of good swagging work ahead, but I can honestly say that a trip without its share of real swagging would have lost its most valuable part for me. For in those days at the beginning of the journey, I am sure the foundations of future physical fitness are laid: fitness which will not only prove itself when the party is ready to tackle the climbing programme, but will also be of lasting value when the members are back at home. For a man fresh from sedentary occupation in the city, there can be no better re-introduction to the mountain ways than a day or two of good swagging. He will be

hardened physically for the strenuous days ahead, and will obtain again the feel of the hills. And there is more than a little truth in the jesting maxim: 'A heavy swag is a grand thing: it makes you forget all your other worries.' It does a man good to have all his usual cares and troubles banished by the immediate physical necessities of a hard day's swagging.

One of my most strenuous bouts of swagging was in the course of a three weeks' expedition from Lake Ohau into the Landsborough, and so by devious routes to the Hermitage. During the first few days swags were particularly heavy – due partly to a miscalculation of calories which left us a fortnight later with far too much food in hand, partly to our own lack of fitness for such work, and partly, no doubt, to their own innate cussedness. A climbing day and the day of rain that followed gave us a little respite from the swags. And from time to time we thought of another party who, heavily burdened, had filled in an off day playing cards, 'and as the stakes were high, the game was keenly contested. The first prize was two pounds, avoirdupois, in the shape of a tin of bread, and the second prize was a one pound tin of jam. This did not mean that the fortunate winner was entitled to consume his weight in provisions as an extra to his ordinary ration. The full value of the prize lay in the fact that he was entitled to have his tin opened first, and thus had so much less weight to carry on the next day's march.'

But in due course we arrived at the head of the Hopkins Valley ready to attempt the crossing to the Landsborough. The first day was another scheduled 'climbing' day, and we set out at daybreak for what proved to be nothing but a fogbound scramble on the glacier moraines. That evening the clouds lifted again, and we took the opportunity to push two loads of gear up the hillside, along the route of the morrow. And so early the next morning we were on the job. A hearty breakfast in readiness for the hard work ahead; a long delay at daybreak while we argued about the weather; then we broke camp, dismantled and packed the tent, and were away. The river alongside was easily crossed on old avalanche snow, the lower terrace traversed, and then we started to make height. In due course, and already feeling a little concerned about the weather, we reached last night's cache and burdened ourselves still further. Patience and a little hard work made good progress though, and in surprisingly good time we saw the pass just ahead.

'Have a spell here?'

'Oh, no;' I told them, 'we'll be on top in ten minutes.' So we headed up that final slope. Imperceptibly it steepened. A little rocky bluff held up the leader who promptly, and very wisely, called for the rope. Progress became slower, and as the slope steepened we moved more cautiously and presently onc at a time. In the rear, I found this progress excessively trying. I could appreciate the work of those in the lead, but I believe I would sooner have been doing my share with them than tailing along behind and hardly moving. And all the time I was dreadfully conscious of that dead burden which was my swag. But nowhere was there a chance to rest myself, or to relieve the weight on my back. And so the slow progress went on. Fog closed over us and we were toiling away in a little world of our own. Two hours later I felt I was going to faint. Hard work and anxiety had played their part, and this miserable progress and long delay did the rest. So I drove my axe in to the hilt and secured it firmly to my own rope, and warned the man ahead to take the strain if need be. A few anxious minutes, and then the weakness passed away; and so slow were the leaders moving I had not delayed the party at all. A little later we staggered over the crest and huddled together for warmth. And presently remembered that we had forgotten to remove our packs when we came to the level ground on top – we had become so completely used to them. We waited another minute for a bite of chocolate, then set out blithely over the easy western slopes towards the Landsborough.

The swagger has been compared with the curious fellow whose hobby was to hit his head with a hammer 'because it was so nice when he stopped'. In the opinion of many, the only good part of a day's swagging is the period of 'Spell-oh'. And these periods of relaxation are certainly very pleasant; for what in life is more delightful, and more wholly satisfying than hard-earned leisure?

'Jimmy was in the lead. He was carrying his possessions in a splendid steel-framed Bergan pack which he claimed made his load feel ten pounds lighter. Every 20 minutes or so the rest of us would plead for a spell and sink exhausted amongst the roots and moss. Three minutes of delightful relaxation and our indefatigable lead man would order us up and at it again. After two such rude awakenings, B. and I felt that the situation must be dealt with, and at the third spell, when the allotted period was almost up, an argument was started on some topic or other. Our number one could not refrain from taking part, and so the minutes slipped by,

unnoticed, from ten to fifteen. After that the strenuous periods were passed pleasantly in thinking up a subject for discussion at the next stop.'

Another way of enjoying the spell periods was tried out by a party toiling up a trackless bush-clad ridge. 'We weakly indulged this day in the foolish pastime of height guessing. During one of the frequent spells, someone would venture a query as to our height. "About 2,500 feet," says the optimist. "Eighteen hundred," ventures the deputy-optimist, satisfied that it is at least 2,000, but wishing to be cautious as becomes a mere deputy. "Fifteen hundred," grunts the pessimist. Then out comes the aneroid and discloses a miserable 1,200 feet. Then follows a moment or two of gloomy silence. "Let's push on," says someone, and the crashing progress begins again.'

To those who deplore the swag at any time, and confess themselves quite unable to see any pleasure in it, I can only repeat that I still enjoy swagging – both for its own sake, and as a means to an end. And it will give me great pleasure when I take off my swag at the end of a long day, to think of them and to remember that if they want to go where I have gone, and see the sights I have seen, then they, too, must carry a swag and come along. But when the circumstances are right, I can also enjoy an off day – a climbing day without a swag. The perfect expedition is that in which both swagging days, and climbing days, and real lazy days, are all featured, and a proper combination of all these spells a very delightful holiday.

PHILIP TEMPLE

from *The Explorer*

Betsy had not liked it at all, tied up while Duncan set off through the bush. But now, after three days, he had the chance to get high, to overlook the upper valley and a steep, boulder mountain creek was no place for a dog. He had started early, with the first flush of sun, but there were thousands of feet to climb and no time to be wasted hauling Betsy up slabs and boulders. She had yelped and whined as he made off under the trees, where it was still half-dark, and though the camp was soon lost to sight he could tell where it was from her noise.

He followed the bank beside a trickling bush creek, slashing away the lawyer and supplejack where he was forced, and blazed trees enough to show him the way back. Regularly he turned and studied the shape and contour of the bush behind him to impress it on his memory for the return in late afternoon.

The noise of the river quickly faded and there was a period of quietness in the trees broken only by the crash of the billhook which he swung with economy and rhythm. Sometimes a weka screamed among the ferns and he was startled as a pigeon flapped loudly above his head and flew low through the trees, wingbeats like the regular whoosh of a whip. And there were the liquid tones of the bellbird which he considered the king of the chorus singers. He had not heard them this time but when there were hundreds singing on the hills and in the valleys the effect was magnificent.

Duncan did not go for long without the sound of water. Soon the bush opened out and the ground dropped away in a crumbling bank to the big creek he had noticed from the riverbank on the day before. The bottom part looked rough and he had fears of a waterfall not far up. But if his eye told him right there would be a basin near the bushline and it would be an easy matter to climb a rocky point for the view. He could not credit the weather. There were broken layers of white cloud, low over the valley trees, but the sun from the clear sky above would burn them away. But there was no sun in the steep creek and it would be chill, damp and shadowy until he reached the tops.

The first difficulty lay in reaching the creek's bed, for the bank was high and unstable; so Duncan prospected the edge and found an easier rib of

clay. He let the swag down with his rope, then passed this double through the root he had tested with his weight and for twenty feet, nearly to the bottom, he could use it for support while he kicked narrow steps in the clay with the edge of his boot.

Good going for a while. There was not much water in the creek and Duncan climbed boulders like an uneven staircase, keeping his boots dry by careful choice of footholds. He climbed slowly and deliberately but never paused, taking short considered steps, trusting only the boulders that were free of slime and securely placed. His pace and care ensured no strain, no shortness of breath and there was time to look ahead and judge the way or glance at the gully scooped away beneath his feet.

The creek curved away to the left but he heard the hiss and splatter of the waterfall before he saw it. It swept down in a tall, narrow amphitheatre of dank rock, the air filled with spray which showed in colours high up where it curled into the sunlight. Duncan looked uneasily at the black, slippery rock and craned his neck to see above the waterfall. He could see nothing but rock and the beginning of tough scrub at the sides. Maybe he was wrong. Maybe this was not the creek to take him to the tops. He scratched at the angle of his jaw and debated. He had been going two hours and gained a lot of height. It was as good a time as any for a smoke.

Duncan ate a biscuit first and washed his mouth with water. Then he found a dry spot and sat down. He took the pleasure of looking down first. The sides of the gully blinkered his view but already he could judge the nature of the hills on the other side of the valley. The lines and shelves where ancient ice had fashioned the valley were distinct where they had not been worn and cut by water. They tallied with the shapes and forms he had seen at close quarters on his own hillside, and by looking at the nature of the opposite higher slopes he could judge what lay above him.

It seemed that once he passed the waterfall and climbed a little higher in the creek bed he would be able to move out to scrub then tussock as he chose. Yet his only chance lay in the jumbled slide of rock beside the waterfall and he studied this reluctantly. Rough country no longer made him anxious or afraid. He was confident in his skill; but skill did not help a twisted ankle much, or a cracked head. Only a mate. No future in risks on his own.

But now that he had come this high, a little more effort would gain him what he wanted. And where the sky had been clear there were thin plumed clouds moving from the west. The clouds always caught you unaware. Too

busy looking at the ground ahead, he supposed. You never looked much above the level of your eyes. The sky was clear and then it wasn't. The clouds were moving quicker than he liked and urgency was added to his need. From a good vantage point higher up he could tell about the weather as much as the land and he must get there before the cloud filled up the valley head.

Care could not be sacrificed for speed on the rock slide and he tested every hold for his feet and hands. As he climbed higher, the consequences of a slip became more severe. The slope became steeper and fragments of broken scree slid more easily against the wet bedrock. With patience and calm he edged towards the lip of the waterfall where a ledge opened up, wide enough for his boot. He did not look down. The billhook was a nuisance now and he wavered for a moment with indecision. Then slowly, without moving his feet, he slid the handle between the swag and his back. A few more minutes and he stood beside the clear rushing stream that disappeared suddenly over the smooth edge of the rock.

Duncan plodded steadily up the creek bed and pulled himself through the big boulders where the rapids were. Hundreds of feet higher the creek forked and after a short, sweaty struggle with the scrub that grew on the spur between, he finally grasped the first coarse snow grass and pulled himself clear. His energy was beginning to flag. But he felt a release of spirit, rising clear of the tangling growth and the insistent pounding of water on fallen rock. He could feel the wind now and his eyes watered from the unaccustomed cold; but there was freedom in the soaring lines of waving tussock, an impulse to go with the wind. He pushed on, half from the cold; half from eagerness to see, now that he had come this far.

Damn this blasted knee. And he rammed the billhook handle into the earth for support as his foot slipped on the shiny tussock. A pipit burst from its nest and swooped away, its call of alarm rising and falling in the wind. He grabbed at the strong leaves of a Spaniard in his haste and snatched his hand away in pain as the needle pierced his hand.

At this he stopped, back to the wind, and bent to ease his panting lungs. He should know better. He dropped his swag and pulled out his jacket. He felt more comfortable with that. Duncan wiped his eyes and looked up and saw that another hundred feet would take him to the crest of the ridge. Calmer, he carried on, placing his feet firmly on the back of the tussocks, climbing in gently angled zigzags.

The view from a new ridge was never what you expected. It was always more and less. More from this ridge because he had not expected to see the big tributary on the other side, running for miles to a wide valley which could only be the Humbert. No doubt this was that fool Courtney's short cut to the Awarora. Duncan felt a glow of triumph at this proof that he had known better. And to the west he could look clear out to the sea, what there was of it through the cloud. For it surged thick and grey over the coast, fingered the valleys, and had begun to rise swiftly with the wind up the hillsides.

The view was less to the east. The ridge curved higher into fine scree, then smooth rock slabs that rose from its crest. He could see a tongue of old snow at the top. But the slabs cut off his view of the upper valley.

How many times had the weather beaten him? How many times had he slaved through the bush to an open knob and at last been beaten by the fog? Duncan stood and wondered if he should make the effort again. His knees ached and the small of his back was sore from the chafing swag. The batwing down there seemed the focus of comfort as the wind began to gust with force, lifting the brim of his hat and parting his beard. The cloud was spreading and rising; but maybe there was time yet. He looked at the slabs. Half an hour. Duncan turned up his collar and pushed his hands into his pockets. There was no question. He must try it. He must go on. If not, he was weakening on the job. Worse, he would be failing himself.

At the foot of the slabs he left the billhook and then his boots when the nails scratched and slid over the smooth rock. He had never tried such smooth and steep rock before and knew nothing of alpine climbing. But stockinged feet seemed to be the answer. At least his feet did not slip and he could feel the wrinkles of the rock under his toes.

At first Duncan was slow and shy of the danger but he found something easy in rock that didn't shift under his foot, a piece of ground that didn't stab him in the hand or trip him over. He forgot his aches and tiredness in the rhythm of the climb.

Halfway, he stopped to look behind and down. The cloud was smothering all the ridge to the scree and he could only see the creek and bush in patches. The summits of the hills towards the coast stood out like black islands and all the air seemed thick with vapour. He would not be beaten now. With a determination that brooked no physical reluctance, Duncan spied out the best line on the remaining slabs and climbed on, quickly and with strength.

At the top it seemed as if he would be finally beaten. The mist lapped at his heels and his climb turned into a crawl where the slabs broke into shattered rock which pressed and cut at his feet. With a curse of frustration he went down on his knees and pulled himself over the last crest.

It was all there. A big peak with its head in the cloud and a blue, riven glacier in frozen cascade. High cliffs were streaked with waterfalls; thin, black gullies stained by falling rock. Snow filled the basins beneath the uneven summits of the range and beyond were the space and shadows of valleys he could not yet understand. The valley head was scree and boulders, raised banks of moraine and the river was a braided white ribbon between them. Duncan saw that the way to the top of the valley meant a gorge, not a mile above camp, then generous yellow flats which delighted his eye; a neck of forest then a second flat which ran into scrub and in winter would be covered by snow.

Duncan felt the moist chill of the rising cloud as it blocked the last, thin sunlight and shadowed his face. The pass. Was there a pass? To see better, Duncan stood up and moved forward. The valley head was still in broken sunlight, but, as if he had breathed hard on his spectacles, his vision faded with the cloud. He raised his arm and shook his fist in anger. As if he had cast a stone in water, the cloud ripped and broke and for a few seconds there was a ragged window.

There was no answer. Beside the big peak lay a high broad saddle, red and streaked with snow. And at the very source the scrub persisted with the scree and drew a dark line into grey basins finally disguised by overlapping buttresses of rock. There might be and there might not be. He did not see enough to make him turn and call it off. He did not see enough to make him sure of going on. For the pass. But pass or not he had seen too much to stop now.

It had been a wicked scramble back. Nothing to buoy him up, the only goal to get down and the thick cloud that turned to fine rain, dripping off his hat brim, down his neck, trousers soaked from the wet scrub and his knees stabbed with pain going down steeply, jarring, there was an ache in his gut from hunger and the strain of keeping control when his muscles wanted to relax and let him slide, hands crabbed from the wet cold, jacket brown and tacky from slipping on the clay.

But he had never lost the way. He was at the camp, nearly dark, and the batwing had collapsed at one corner because Betsy had caught her rope

around the peg and she looked at him, guilty, half covered by the canvas where it angled down and spilled a steady rivulet of the rain on the foot of his blanket. The billy, stuck with morning porridge, lay rolled in the wet, black ashes of the fire. His dishes, mug and spoon were scattered under the trees and the tin of treacle, half-spilt and sticky, showed where the wekas had finished their mischief.

Duncan said nothing, to himself, the bush or the dog. Words would not help. But he drove the blade of the billhook into a stump with unusual force and kicked the billy aside. He untied Betsy and her nose went to the ground as she wandered round the camp, scenting for the birds.

Duncan fixed up the batwing and when he had picked up the utensils and scraped back the treacle – bits of leaf and dirt did no harm – he crouched over the fire and cleared away the ashes until he came to the white, dry bed, still warm from the morning. He pulled a dry log from under the fly, split it into four, then carved off slivers with his knife. He piled these in a pyramid, lit a nob of candle underneath and as the trickle of smoke thickened and the flames grew he added more pieces of wood, exactly and expertly.

Duncan hung the blanket to steam before the increasing blaze, fetched water from the river. When the billy bubbled, he tossed in a handful of tea, and Betsy came back. She put a brown, speckled weka at his feet and looked up, waiting, her muzzle splattered with mud. Duncan sat down heavily on the bracken beneath the fly and pulled Betsy roughly to his side, scruffing her ears. He laughed. 'We mek a fine pair lass. A fine pair.'

FORRESTINA ROSS

from *Mixed Grill*

Housekeeping on a Glacier (1890)

Before I was a proprietor of a mansion of my own, I started housekeeping on a glacier, for our honeymoon trip was spent in the Alps, and was my first experience of ice in bulk. In New Zealand, beyond the golden tussock plains, and the blue foothills, there lies a very wonderland of beauty – the New Zealand Alps. There great frozen rivers curve and creep between huge mountains draped with gleaming ice and purple precipices. There the air is an elixir of life, and the aged and world weary, breathing it, become youthful and care-free.

It was necessary to carry our provisions with us, as no tradesman had been pushing enough to start business on the great Tasman Glacier. Nowadays a paternal Government has provided comfortable huts stocked with food and blankets. We were pioneers however, and had to carry tents, blankets, and a change of clothing, as well as the provisions. It did not matter how aristocratic one's back was, it had to bear the burden.

I was the second woman to go so far up the glacier in those early days, and by reason of my sex, I was constituted housekeeper and chief cook in our gipsy camp under the shoulder of Aorangi. Our two tents stood on a grassy plateau. Near by a little stream chattered down from the lily-covered slopes, to be silenced presently by the icy touch of the glacier. Here we got water and our dessert – a little red berry that grows on an alpine pine. It took a great many to make a mouthful, but fortunately we had plenty of time. We cooked outside on a fire-place made of stones, and when the meal was ready we beat two tin plates together to summon the party, who sat around on more stones and ate largely. Never had we seen such appetites as the glacier produced. Cliques go for naught when an alpine hunger is to be assuaged, and people who would not call on one another in the far-off world fraternise affectionately as they eat sardines with their fingers and fish for bits of bacon out of a frizzling frying-pan. Wisdom in the shape of a ponderous German professor, and wealth and frivolity incorporated in the person of a pretty heiress to many thousands, drink tea together out of one battered, red-hot mug, and gather the scanty firewood with merry laughter.

I still recall with gusto the memory of a stew of keas or Mount Cook parrots kept in a crevasse instead of an ice-chest. It was made with many onions and much pepper, with a dash of Liebig to render it less pallid and more tasty – I have dined well many times since, but would give all the chef d'œuvres of a *cordon bleu* for a replica of that meal eaten on the glorious heights of the Tasman Glacier.

Our utensils were few, two billies and a frying pan, and it required a master mind to grapple with the difficulties of making tea, stewing chops, and heating water to wash up with, all at the same time and on the same gipsy fireplace. The firewood, too, was of the scantiest. In one place a twig the size of a pencil was swooped upon in triumph, and water had to be carried up a mountain path 300 feet high. We did without frequent ablutions in that particular camp!

Experience teaches you what provisions to take a-camping, and while you are learning you will probably suffer. We did. On one expedition a Glasgow man was to make his debut on the Tasman Glacier, and he resolved the commissariat should be most récherché. We ordered all sorts of luxuries in tins, delicious things with French names, and as we stumbled over the rough moraine and riddled our ankles with the spear-grass, the thought of the savoury contents of those tins, so heavy to carry, kept us up. Life is a vale of tears. One after one those tins were opened. At first the party used to collect around and lick its lips in prospective delight. The perfidious tin might be labelled *pâté de foie gras* or devilled chicken, but it always contained stewed kidneys. At first they were eaten, but gloomily. But stewed kidneys are apt to pall if you have them six days running, and when from the seventh tin, called 'beefsteak pie,' the well-known odour floated out, a tremendous swear word broke the silence, and the wretched thing was hurled far out of sight on the glacier. Even our mountaineering appetites could not manage a menu consisting solely of stewed kidneys. When our party returned to civilisation a wrathful deputation waited on the tradesman who had deceived us. We laid our case before him. 'The tins *do* get labelled wrongly sometimes,' he said calmly. 'But stewed kidneys! That's strange! Why we haven't had tinned kidneys for years! You must have got very old stock!' We came to the conclusion that the only way to make sure was to sit by while the tins were filled and to carry them away directly after. There is a biscuit, a kind of sandwich of sultanas, that campers-out much affect. Six pounds of these were lugged up sixteen miles of glacier,

in addition to tremendous 'swags' of blankets and other provisions. It must be understood that our glaciers are crossed by great embankments of sliding slippery stones, and gashed by crevasses, the largest of which must be traversed till a bridge is found, while the smallest can be jumped over. One becomes so proficient at this leaping method of progression that one is afraid of developing a permanent walk à la Kangaroo.

JACK COX

Guiding Memories at the Hermitage and Franz Josef 1929–1938

When I arrived at the Hermitage early in 1929 I spent the first fortnight washing and drying dishes until about 9.30 p.m each night. I had innocently imagined that the duties of a porter to assist the guides was to help the guides, not the kitchen maids. At the end of this period I was promoted to the kitchen for a while, where I learnt to peel potatoes and wash more pots and pans. Then with a turn in the bake-house I had completed the first part of my apprenticeship. Then came the day I was told to accompany Betsy Blunden to the Mueller Hut with a tin of kerosene and I knew I was making my start as a porter. Betsy was very fit and kept me moving. To relieve my extreme tiredness when I took my first load off, I took off my boots and felt as if I was floating away in space. I had a six weeks' spell with the pack horses taking stores to Ball Hut. In those days there was no road to the hut and tourists also were taken on horseback or by the cage across the Hooker River and along the pack track of which a few traces can still be seen on the hillside. About this time the road bridge was re-built to avoid the troubles of the ford. Most of the time until April I was kept packing the stores to all the huts. I was really thrilled when I made my first trip up the Haast ridge and gazed in awe at Mounts Cook and Tasman. The Hermitage in those days was controlled by the Mt. Cook Motor Company with Rodolph Wigley at the head. The Hermitage manager when I went there was Dave Clark and was followed by Charlie Elms. The Chief Guide was Vic Williams and on the guiding staff were Alf Brustad, Arne Larsen, Mentz Engelstadt, Erling Aagard and Jack Crombie. Mick Bowie arrived later that year about the time I left for the Franz.

It would be the 13th April 1929 when Duncan Darroch looking at the high clouds prophesised early snow. According to the old hands there was usually a fall in the middle of April, then by May the heavier falls would start and continue through winter. However, snow started falling that evening and continued until the morning of the 17th. Of course, this gave the guides plenty of extra work. Two of us were given the job of controlling the levers of the snow plough. Swinging on those levers to three or four

miles past Glentanner Station and back to the Hermitage gave me an insight to what hard work meant. The trip had its bright moment, for Mr. Elms arrived twice and gave us a good toddy of whisky and hot milk. It was 10.30 p.m. when we arrived back and to me the pile of snow on either side of the road about seven feet high was awe inspiring. There was very little thaw and with the ensuing falls, by the August school holidays there were very few bushes showing around the Hermitage. There were over 300 people at the Hermitage so it was decided that the first winter sports carnival at the Hermitage would be held.

A Mr. J. McLean of Hawkes Bay was the convenor and with the guides, Betsy Blunden, and a contingent from Timaru comprising Lud Mahan, Lin Murray and Fred Chapman the sports meeting got under way. There were two slalom courses, one on the big scree going towards Kea Point, and the ladies' came below the bridge just past the garage. To us the course was very difficult with about seven flags and apart from the Norwegian guides and Vic Williams no one mastered the course. There was a toboggan race but after the third run and a broken leg this was called off. The first day of competition finished off with a rugby match in the snow, Timaru versus the Rest. Timaru won the Test.

The big cross country race was reserved for the next day, plus the jumping events. The cross country was a handicap event and there being no past performances and a large number of entries, it was nearly 11 a.m. before the committee had everything sorted out. The big event was scheduled for 2.30 p.m. to give everyone a chance to look at the course and get their skis waxed. I think it was Vic Williams, Alf Brustad and Arne Larsen who took off on their skis and placed the flags marking the course, which began under the bridge at the Hermitage, made a direct line towards the Hooker road bridge, then up the Hooker River bank, across the flat towards the big scree, up the scree across behind Sealy Cottage and down Stony Creek to the finish line under the bridge. The limit markers went away and as the minutes sped by the other contestants left the mark. The scratch men Vic Williams, Vic Clark, Mentz Engelstadt and myself strapped on our skis to be ready for our start on the count of 20 minutes. We took our places, grabbed our ski sticks and were just taking off when the winner who was on the limit flashed past the finishing line, followed by Mrs. Vic Williams in second place. Nevertheless we took off and spent the next hour or so helping out contestants who had fallen in the bushes when

the snow gave way. For the first handicap ski race the drinks were on the handicappers.

The jumping session was scheduled to begin about 9 p.m. when the moon was well up. The jump was constructed opposite the dining room windows with the take off at the road and landing on the slope above the tennis courts. Snow had been packed and beaten down to a hard surface for a swift take off. The contestants queued up on the flat above the jump ready for their turn. Mentz Engelstadt was to jump first to show us how it was done. He moved to the top of the jump, turned around quickly and took off. Down he flashed, but alas, from this bit of tuition we learnt only that it hurt if you fell. Erling Aagard was next and suffered the same fate. This dampened the spirits of most of the contestants who slunk away to get a better view on the road below. Alf Brustad, Vic Clark and myself seemed to be the only ones left. Alf took off and landed safely making the first successful jump. Vic was next and did all right too. It was then my turn, so off I went, landing properly and making the best jump of 63 feet. Alf was enthusiastic over this and induced me to go straight back and try again. Now, he said, lean forward as you go down the jump and as you near the take off try to lean forward further. I did as instructed but must have leaned too far for I took two somersaults in the air and that was the last I remembered about the first sports meeting at the Hermitage as I did not come to until 10 a.m. next morning.

Alf Brustad had a party of people, mostly nurses, at Ball Hut and as food was getting short he sent a guide to the Hermitage for more supplies. The manager sorted me out and told me there were some stores to go to the Ball Hut and to leave immediately. He also told me to stay at the hut until the next party arrived. As there was snow all the way it was a ski job. With my rucksack full of meat, butter and bread and with a crate of eggs strapped on top I set off, late in the afternoon. I reached Husky Camp in the dark just as an old man blizzard set in. There was an old rock hut beside the moraine (part of it is still there) so I decided to spend the night in what shelter it gave. I wrapped myself in an old tent but I just could not stand the cold so I decided to go on to Ball Hut. I put on my skis, took the loaded pack and set off. I had to put on my goggles, though it was pitch dark, as protection against the driving snow. I knew that if I kept in the gut between the lateral moraine and the mountainside I would have no trouble. I plugged on and finally came to the rise leading to the hut. As long as I kept

climbing I knew I would be all right. Most of the hut which was smaller than it is now was covered with snow so I started prodding with my ski sticks and with a bang I hit the iron on the roof. Talk about relief!! I took off my skis and crawled along the side of the building until I saw a light, and started digging with my hands to find the door handle. This took some time but eventually I succeeded, opened the door and more or less fell into the room. There were people, mostly girls, sitting on the table and stools, some screaming and some white as sheets and at least one had fainted. Alf had been telling a ghost story and just as it was ending they heard the bang on the roof and the scrabbling on the door which became more vigorous, and when the door suddenly opened and I fell inside covered in snow, it must have been a terrifying sight in the circumstances. Alf at last got over the shock and then proceeded to tell me off for not knocking. But I defy anyone to stop and knock at 10.30 p.m. with a blizzard howling around one's ears. After a few cups of Norwegian hot cocoa and when I had shed my load of snow, I felt like and was received as a normal human being.

MICHAEL GILL

from *Mountain Midsummer: Climbing in four continents*

The Darrans: An unknown array

Falling in love with the mountains is like any other love. You may, before, have been stirred by a voice or an alluring shape seen in a crowd, but there comes a moment when you are suddenly aware of someone uniquely and bewitchingly different. So it is with mountains – when I first saw the peaks of the Darrans I was smitten hopelessly. And though there was no sign of acceptance on their part, no sly wink from Madeline, no gesture from the old warrior Te Wera, I felt that I would see more of them.

I was on the summit of Mitre Peak in December 1955. With a friend I had set out early that morning from a camp near Milford Hotel and in a canoe we had crossed the Sound, its walls rising like the battlements of a fortress from a moat. Dominating the scene was the rock wedge of Mitre, sheer from the sea on its northern side but with a bush-covered ridge dropping more gently to the east. At its foot, in a small cove, we pulled the canoe ashore and set off. The ridge was long, much longer than we had thought, and in the bush we were held back by the vines, the fallen trees and the fern, which lay in a tangle over the cliffs and tumbled boulders of the mountain. It was 3 o'clock before we reached the bush-line and above us still was a steep rock ridge. From there I went on alone.

At 5 o'clock I stood on the summit. Below were the black waters of the Sound and the hotel, dwarfed by the surrounding precipices; westwards the Tasman Sea gleamed pale bronze in the later afternoon sun, and to the south was a host of lesser peaks.

But my attention was held by the mountains to the north-east, the Darrans, an unknown array of ridges and ice-falls and grey rock faces. At 5,000 feet I was on a level with tussock ledges and expansive snow fields, above the gloom and oppression of the valleys. Two of Captain Cook's officers had climbed such a peak: they reported that 'inland nothing was to be seen but barren mountains with huge craggy precipices frightful to behold … ' That was nearly two hundred years ago. They were men who had been sailing in unknown seas for months on end and they longed, no doubt,

for green fields and open forests, not that inhospitable tract of Fiordland which lay before them, spreading to the horizon. But in the mid-twentieth century when there is hardly a corner of our overcrowded earth that has not been thrown open, it is only in these last, remote, areas that the urge to explore the unknown can be satisfied. To me those mountains were not barren or frightful to behold, for in there, I knew, were the places I dreamed of, the unclimbed ridges, the lakes, the pockets of land where no one had been.

The descent to the Sound that evening was long and it was near midnight when we were paddling home. The sea lay sleek and black in the moonlight. And then, bringing that perfect day to a close, above the silence we heard a soft splashing sound as a school of porpoises glided out of the darkness, sliding effortlessly around the canoe as if to escort us back.

Next day I found a map to identify the peaks I had seen. The Darrans are at the northern apex of Fiordland. Their north-eastern boundary is the Hollyford Valley; Milford Sound and the road leading to it lie south, and to the west is the Tasman Sea. The highest peak is Tutoko (9,042 feet) with Madeline beside it, and south of these is a less accessible group, the Central Darrans, with Te Wera amongst them. Fiordland itself occupies the whole south-western corner of the South Island. The configuration of the valleys is different from those farther north, for the rock is uniquely hard, and where the glaciers of a past ice-age have ground down into it they have left U-shaped valleys with vertical walls and level floors. It is a land on which one can shower superlatives: the greatest precipices are there, the heaviest rainfall, the thickest bush; the rock is harder than that of other regions and the rock-climbing better; there are more sandflies and fewer people.

On his second voyage in 1773 Cook made his landfall in Fiordland at Dusky Sound where he spent a month. His impressions have been echoed by all those who have come after him. Of the rain and the sandflies he wrote: 'The most mischievous animal is the small black sandfly which are exceedingly numerous and are so troublesome that they exceed everything of the kind I ever met with. Wherever they light they cause a swelling and such an intolerable itching that it is not possible to refrain from scratching and at last end in ulcers like Small Pox. The almost continual rain may be reckoned, another ilconveniency attending this Bay … ' And of the topography: 'The Country is exceedingly mountainous, not only about Dusky Bay but all the southern parts of this eastern coast and exhibits to our view nothing but woods and barren craggy precipices, no meadows or

havens are to be seen nor plains, flat land of any extent; the land near the Sea, and the shores of the Bay and all the Islands are thickly covered with wood of various sorts …'

From 1956 to 1961 I studied medicine in Dunedin, an aging city two hundred miles east of the Darrans. Though I knew I wanted to climb in Fiordland, it seemed I had no one to go with nor any easy way of getting there. But then I met Phil Houghton. At the time I hardly realised what a stroke of good fortune this was. For one thing Phil had a car. Friendships have been founded on less but there was more to our association than that. Our attitude towards life in Dunedin was the same. We preferred climbing to football, and bivvy rocks to ski huts; we believed that climbing took precedence over other activities and so had a cavalier attitude towards the medical course – and if an anticyclone formed over the Tasman Sea on a Thursday we were there to meet it in the Darrans on the Friday. Each of us had an independent streak and together we resisted such limitations as early marriage or the more cautious precepts of mountaineering.

We met at the hostel where we both stayed. On the door of the room next to mine was the name P. Houghton, and when the door lay open – as often as not, a pile of books, clothes, sleeping bags, records and old boots (many of them his own) made it impossible to shut – I saw on the wall a map of the mountain area around Mt Cook. Occasionally we passed in the corridor. He was of medium height, strongly built, with a tanned face and steady blue eyes, and he had an air of mature self possession which gave the impression of someone older than eighteen. For three weeks we barely glanced at each other – his nickname 'Rock' seemed unusually apt. And then one day I saw a new ice-axe being delivered to his room. I could contain my curiosity no longer. Cautiously poking my head round the door I nodded at the map.

'See you do a bit of climbing,' I said. 'I do a bit myself.'

Briefly we exchanged notes on where we'd been.

'We may as well go off together one of these weekends,' suggested Phil.

'Good idea,' I replied – and the matter was settled.

So began a climbing partnership which took us through the Darrans from end to end. Two is not the ideal number in terms of safety, but then safety is not the only consideration. We found we worked well together and in the course of weekend excursions we learned something of the art of climbing and of living in the hills. By the end of the year we had reached a few minor summits and felt ready for something bigger.

SARA KNOX

Climbing

(for my father, who wanted to be forever young)

We walked miles that day – my sister and I.
It was summer; we were not
ourselves –
were what we could be
at our best; free
and with different names

in the mountains, tramping
over gravel track and swingbridge,
past forty Japanese tourists wearing white,
cameras swinging at their necks
like baby monkeys

walked nine kilometres
to the base of the mountains,
there stopped by the fear
that any further
would be called
'climbing':

a thing we could not do,
at least not without
crampons pitons
swiss climbing packs
two hundred feet of rope
two pairs of socks in well-worn boots
strong legs
confidence
no fear of heights
(in other words – whole other lives)

so we two girls
stopped and had our picnic

while a party of young Aussie men
swum in the nearby Hooker
yelling, white-lipped, at one another:

'It's not *that* fucking cold!'
and our father's ghost
ran swiftly past us
with a crate of beer (taken on a bet)
for urgent delivery
to the admiring ghosts
of other
strong,
young,
forgetful
men,
high in the mountains overhead.

LYDIA BRADEY

from *Going Up Is Easy*

I Could Be a Climber

Arthur's Pass village in the 1970s could be a gloomy place. It was shaded by the surrounding mountains, and featured railway buildings, baches, shops, a chapel, a visitor centre and the outdoor recreation centre. A single-storey wooden building that somehow managed to look institutional, the centre was separated from the main road by an often boggy, but immaculately mown, lawn.

I was with a group that arrived on the train from Christchurch and there was something pretty haphazard about our appearance: some of the kids had big Mountain Mule packs borrowed from older relatives while others lugged suitcases or hauled oddly bulging duffel bags. Poorly rolled sleeping bags were attached to the outside of bags. Boots or 'practical' outdoor shoes swung by the laces from their owners' fists. Most kids, in preparation for being in the mountains, wore woolly hats and black Japara parkas. Underneath were layers of woollen vests and jerseys, though some might have bush shirts. This was the age before polypropylene, polar fleece and cheap down jackets.

I had never been in the mountains before so I was nervous. The instructor, a guy called Paddy Freaney, came out and welcomed the group and introduced the week ahead, telling us that our first big outing would be a walk up to Temple Basin, a club ski field located near the Main Divide.

The route to Temple Basin followed a bulldozer track that zigzagged up the face of the mountain before levelling out towards the scree basin. In the absence of a road, the track provided the main access for visitors to the ski field and took anywhere from a little over an hour to two hours to complete. The area contained a mixture of tussock and golden Spaniard and in late spring and summer the mountainside was festooned with Mount Cook buttercups and daisies. It was quiet except for the sound of the wind and distant traffic but the tussock was alive with grasshoppers, blowflies and moths. Nearby waterfalls cascaded over rugged bluffs, and the water glittered and splashed in the sunlight.

It was a very hot walk. There was no shade and the glare from the surrounding scree and snow slopes was dazzling. We'd pause to drink from the small streams that cross the track. The water in these streams was crystal clear, icy and had an almost metallic taste and feel against the tongue. It was also gritty from the fine gravel-sand carried down the mountains.

This was my first experience of walking in the mountains and I was amazed at the magical world I found myself in. As I made my way up, I felt huge drops of water falling onto my cheeks. At first I thought the drips were falling from the flax bushes but as I climbed higher, above the bushes, the droplets continued to fall. I didn't know where they were coming from but decided it must be related to the high altitude or the alpine clouds because I had never encountered such a strange phenomenon before. It only slowly dawned on me that the drops were my own sweat.

Within a short time I began to enjoy myself and I became engrossed in the act of walking itself. I liked the way my body felt as I encountered and negotiated the stony track and the rough terrain. I concentrated on my breathing, inhaling and exhaling in rhythm with my steps. There was a strange, unfamiliar tightness in my muscles and, little by little, I started to feel something akin to excitement and joy. Finally, in walking, I had found an activity I had the potential to do well and enjoy.

Near the end of the trip, Paddy Freaney congratulated the class. He said something like, 'One day some of you may become trampers. But one or two of you might even become *a climber*.' At the sound of the word climber, I looked up. I had almost no idea what a climber was but the tone of Freaney's voice, and arguably his Irish accent, made the word sound mysterious and exciting. Could I be a climber? From that point on, the idea quickly became fixed in my mind and I decided that that was what I wanted to be.

Even then I believed that by becoming a climber it would be possible to distinguish myself from all the other people I knew – the kids at school. And I also thought that being a climber was something that would make my mother proud. However, I had no real idea of what a climber did.

I guess the first hint of what mountaineering entailed came when I joined the Peninsula Tramping Club in Christchurch. Two members had a huge impact on my life during those early days: Jim and Margaret Clark. They took care of me and both of them were real storytellers. They had

such energy and the evenings in their company were entertaining and happy. One trip stands out in my mind as being particularly important in terms of my future. It was a winter trip, over Queen's Birthday, to Cannibal Gorge in the Lewis Pass. At one camp our group met with another from the faster and stronger Christchurch Tramping Club and Jim and I ended up being invited to join a three-day trip along the tops. A tops trip is something of a Kiwi tramper's rite of passage. As the name suggests, trampers stay high above the valleys, traversing the ridges and peaks. On this trip I got to use crampons and I was buzzing with excitement. It was such beautiful landscape. There was snow not only on the ranges but on the beech forest below and the contrasts between the dark bush-covered hillsides, the snowy beech, the open tussock and scree areas were superb. On that trip, I realised that I loved being up high, and that my future happiness would be tied to the mountaintops.

I started going to the Christchurch Tramping Club meetings once a month and I also joined the tramping club at Hagley High School, which meant I began to go to Arthur's Pass on a more regular basis. One day I did a trip up Avalanche Peak from the Crow side in a good, fast time and a couple of boys I'd met kept saying, 'You gotta go climbing. You gotta go climbing!' They kept encouraging me and in the end I said, 'Okay, I'll join your club then'– the Canterbury Mountaineering Club – and they replied, 'You can't. It's for men only.' When I heard that my immediate reaction was, 'How stupid.'

All the other tramping and mountaineering clubs, like the New Zealand Alpine Club, permitted women, but the Canterbury Mountaineering Club seemed to have this weird notion that women shouldn't, or couldn't, mountaineer. Fortunately for me, there was already pressure from women like Margaret Clark to see the club enter the twentieth century and as a result women were admitted around 1980. So I became a member but I recall that a few of the older men weren't pleased and some of them may have resigned. However, I was stoked to be in a climbing club and became one of its most active members, making tips up Mount Rolleston in Arthur's Pass, Mount Edward above the Dart Glacier and, when I was 17, up Mount Aspiring in Westland National Park.

Margaret Clark took me up Aspiring, my first, serious 3000-metre peak. The night before the climb I had this vivid dream that there were all these angels flying up out of the valley below, singing 'Hallelujah!', and then this

big, friendly monster walked up and when he got close he unzipped his skin and stepped out of it. So it was pretty full on and I was super-excited. Margaret took care of me, belaying me all the way, and once I reached the top I got a huge kick from standing on the summit of a big mountain.

By this time, I'd left school and home. I'd gone through a bit of a stressful period trying to figure out what to do with my life, what I'd do when I left school. The trouble was that I found too many things interesting and, perhaps for that reason, the school guidance counsellor hadn't been that helpful in suggesting career or higher education options. I remember wandering around town one day, worrying, 'What shall I do?', when I had this sensation of someone tapping me on the shoulder and this voice said, 'Hey, just go climbing.' It was a real epiphany and I was like, 'Whoa, that's a great idea!' And that's what I ended up doing basically. I found work at Bowron's tannery in Woolston, where I'd been working during the school holidays, and later on I did gardening for the Heathcote council before eventually landing a job at Aoraki/Mount Cook.

Royce was very sweet when I left home. I was surprised by her kindness because I always knew she wanted me to be independent and I also guessed she would welcome the additional space in the house with me gone. But she must have felt slightly sensitive about me moving out as she offered to help with things like laundry. We were still close, though, and continued to share stories about characters and books and suchlike. When I'd started getting serious about mountaineering she began reading classic mountaineering books like *The White Spider*, Heinrich Harrer's account of climbing the Eiger, or English rock climber Joe Brown's *The Hard Years*. She had some idea about what I was getting into but she didn't have first-hand experience of mountaineering so may not have appreciated some of the risks I was taking. One of my early trips had almost ended in disaster when I'd slipped on a slick, muddy slope on Mount Edward and gone for a long slide, almost toppling over a 500-metre drop. The great thing about Royce was that she encouraged me and was proud of what I was achieving. She didn't want to live her life through me, but she thought it was important that I have lots of interesting experiences and lead a full life. She would have been very disappointed if I'd wasted my time or turned down opportunities that came my way.

I'd met a real mountaineer named Jon Visser through the Christchurch Tramping Club and I knew that he was 'famous'. So I was already asking

questions about mountaineering, pestering him with questions like 'How long are your days?' Jon is Dutch, more than 20 years older than me and a very, *very* funny guy. He'd reply, 'Christ'– always pronounced as two syllables with a rolling 'r'– 'Christ. Twenty-four hours, of course!' He has a very particular way of talking because he learned English from the deer cullers he worked with when he first came to New Zealand but, on top of that, he has a love for ornate language and fancy words. When he tells a story your find yourself focusing on the language – you know it's going to make you laugh.

Like Jim and Margaret Clark, Jon Visser became a mentor for me. We both loved stories and, being driven and competitive, we were both up for adventures. Looking back, one of the things that stands out from this early period is that I was almost always tramping and climbing with older, more experienced and skilled people. I was conscious that boys of my age, 18-year-olds, were able to go off with friends and learn through experience. They might make mistakes but they learned from them, and they were definitely going with mates rather than being taken. I missed the companionship of women of my own age. I wanted a girlfriend to do things with but it was virtually impossible to find anyone as motivated as me.

On the other hand, the people I was going out with were all decent and extremely generous. People like the Clarks, Barbara Chinn and Jennifer and Sandy Sandblom would lend me equipment, and give me advice and instruction. But more than that, they valued adventures. They were kind of old school and they believed in giving back and helping people like me.

I had turned 18 when I climbed Aoraki/Mount Cook with Jon Visser. It was the summer of 1979–80, and we flew in to the Grand Plateau (2200 metres), intending to make the ascent via Zurbriggen Ridge, a route that had first been climbed in 1895 by the Swiss guide, Matthias Zurbriggen. Jon had already done some big climbs but I was still new. We arrived in the morning and Jon, who loves the sun and heat, spent the entire day sunbathing on the rocks, outside the hut. I didn't know any better so did the same. We started climbing at midnight and by the time we reached the bottom of Zurbriggen I was in bad shape: totally sunburnt and dehydrated and I couldn't stop vomiting.

The climb became something of an endurance test, the situation lightened only by the fact that Jon was so funny. He was dressed in a kind of nylon, turtle-neck skivvy, with white zinc on his nose and lips, and he

had a head torch that wasn't functioning properly. By today's standards it was old-fashioned – the batteries were carried in a separate unit, and the two components were connected by a wire. Anyway, the torch was malfunctioning and Jon was getting increasingly angry. I could hear him ranting, 'Fucking Christ, God in heaven …' and eventually, as the sun was rising, he tore it from his head and threw it away. It was like a cartoon. The torch went bounce, bounce, bounce, down the mountain and as it disappeared into a crevasse the light flickered on.

I was slow, finding it hard to front-point, and Jon had to belay me up the mountain. The views from the summit were epic – you could see the West Coast and across the plains to the east – but I was still very sick so the descent down the Linda Glacier was extremely slow. My torch ran out of batteries and as the descent tracks made by other climbers had been wiped out by an avalanche we ended up having to bivvy on the glacier. I learned how to keep myself warm by banging my arms against my body. There was a strong, katabatic wind but it began to ease at dawn. As it turned out we were only about an hour from Plateau Hut but we hadn't been able to see it. Once the sky lightened we set off and we reached the hut around six in the morning. I was incredibly stoked by what I had achieved, but I vowed never to get that sick again.

AAT VERVOORN

from *Mountain Solitudes: Solo journeys in the Southern Alps of New Zealand*

April 1987. I wanted to go further down the Landsborough River, cross the Solution Range and climb Mt Hooker, then follow the Otoko River down to the West Coast. So there I was, in Barron Saddle Hut again, waiting for the wind to die down, contemplating the pile of food and equipment I would have to carry. After a fierce snowstorm, the surrounding mountains were coated in ice. It looked like the beginning of winter.

Wind has to be taken seriously at Barron Saddle. It lies near the heads of three big valleys – the Mueller and Dobson on the eastern side of the Main Divide, the Landsborough to the west – and the wind blows from all directions, rising suddenly and gusting violently. Among steep rocks and snowdrifts below the saddle, on its Dobson Valley face, lie the remains of the original mountaineering hut here: sheets of corrugated iron, broken timbers, flooring. In February 1977 the entire hut was blown off the saddle with four climbers inside it. On the saddle itself, just back from the edge of the drop, the snapped ends of its anchor cables nod forlornly on the wind.

There is no easy route into the Landsborough, particularly for those with heavy loads. The route I had followed out of the valley three years earlier, Hardies Gut, presents no problems when there is enough snow to cover its smooth rock slabs, but now those slabs were likely to be coated in ice. Moreover, in the interests of comfort I was wearing soft, bendable hiking boots rather than stiff mountaineering boots, which made the idea of encountering steep ice particularly unpleasant. The original route into the Landsborough from Barron Saddle and the head of the Mueller Glacier was Fyfe Pass, first used by Tom Fyfe and George Graham in 1894. A recent guidebook comments that nowadays this route is rarely used. The descent on the Landsborough side of the pass is down another one of the nasty slabby gullies so common to the area; this one, however has an additional little surprise in store for those who venture down it. Over the years, the retreat of the ice of the Spence Glacier has exposed overhanging rock where once the gully led out onto easy snow and ice. The fact that the route is 'no longer so popular' probably has something to do with this. Another

guidebook advises that the best way into the Landsborough is probably over the top of Mt Spence. Well, Mt Spence is a pleasant climb, but it leads nowhere, and no one in their right mind would consider it as an access route unless a guidebook told them so.

I had been shown the best route into the Landsborough by a big bull thar in February 1964, although I did not understand it at the time. With a companion I was traversing the snow slopes below Scissors, making for the lowpoint on the Main Divide on the way out to Mt Spence. There we saw him. He was peering down from the ridge, with the early morning sun lighting up the blond ruff that framed his dark face, his horns as sharp as the rocks around him, and his long hair quivering on the cold wind that blew out of the shadows of Westland. He stood motionless, broad and muscular against the sky, with a vaguely contemptuous expression on his face as he watched our progress: Amateurs! Then he turned, flashed his rump, and vanished on the Landsborough side of the ridge. When we reached the ridge a few minutes later, we found we could proceed in the direction the thar had taken only by hooking our fingers over the actual crest of the Divide and scuttling along crabwise. It really was most humbling. If ever the expression 'running rings around someone' meant anything, that was the occasion.

Thar are more reliable than guidebooks. They have only lived in the central New Zealand Alps for one hundred years, but they have studied the landscape well. I have learned not to question their judgement. They do not take unnecessary risks, and while sometimes their objectives differ from those of humans, much of the time they are the same. Their skill at route-finding is such that when my decisions coincide with thar mountain sense I feel proud and pleased with myself. Once I was caught by a snowstorm on the valley wall above the head of the Karangarua River. Being unsure of the way down, I decided that caution was the best policy and retreated the way I had come, over Mt Gladiator. With remnants of the storm blowing around me and night closing in, traversing the exposed ridge was nerve-wracking until I noticed thar tracks leading from one rock outcrop to another. All I had to do was follow them. Through whiteout and encroaching night they led down unerringly, taking me along the safest and easiest route all the way to Douglas Pass.

Between Scissors and Mt Spence, where I was given my lesson in mountain movement by that bull thar, there are frequently thar tracks too,

climbing straight out of the Dobson Valley to the lowpoint on the ridge. There is no doubt that this is one of their routes across the Main Divide to the Landsborough. So I had a good idea of where to go, at least to that point on the ridge. However, standing on Barron Saddle at midday, bracing myself against buffeting winds, getting there did not look easy. The peaks were plastered with ice and fresh powder snow swirled over the rocks; and with a heavy pack on my back and lightweight boots on my feet the snow slope leading towards the low point looked uncomfortably steep. To avoid it, I climbed directly up the ridge in the direction of Scissors, seeking shelter from the wind on its Mueller side, until wide snowy ledges led left to where the thar cross the range. Then below me lay the Landsborough Valley.

JOHN PASCOE

The Reconnaissance of Mt. Evans

There is one minute unit of the exploring mountaineer's equipment that is so obviously indispensable that it never receives credit for the major part it plays in the reconnaissance of new alpine territory. I refer to the camera lens. A quiet release of the shutter may be more productive of future developments than volumes of fine and accurate writing. If there is one photograph to bear this out, it is to be found opposite page 17 of the Mikonui Geological Report, reproducing the Wilkinson setting of Mt. Evans, 8612ft.

Little did the late James Park, of Hokitika, think that the work of the fraction of a second would be the unfailing incentive of a future climbing generation. Through the medium of this photograph in the Geological Report, the massive beauty of Mt. Evans has become historic.

During their graduation from the low foothills of Canterbury to the more salient vantage domes of Waimakariri and Mathias Peaks, our Canterbury Mountaineering Club had become fascinated by the increasingly familiar summit of the distant Westland mountain – Evans – knowing it for the crest of the massif pored over from time to time in reference library illustration.

A hurried ascent of Louper Peak in April, 1931, gave a closer acquaintance with the redoubtable Westland virgin. The acquaintance was to ripen. But, naturally, the more immediate 'eastern icicle precipice' of Mt. Whitcombe, and its culminating rock peak of 8658ft., took just precedence in our panorama from Louper Peak. So that is was not until the primary objective of our Rakaia visit in December, 1931 (namely, Mt. Whitcombe), fell to half the party, that an attempt was made at the solution of the inaccessible problem 'over the road' in Westland.

Our attempt at Mt. Evans was unsuccessful. Laboriously we climbed to 8200 odd feet on a route that at last resolved itself into certain impossibility. From their inherent completeness, records of successful climbs do not dwell upon the capricious element of the interesting unknown. This, then, will serve as an excuse for the following narrative of a failure: –

The geographical position of Mt. Evans was never in our doubt. The

geological surveyors had done their splendid work too well for that. We knew that a mile north of the Main Divide lay the 8612ft. peak, a giantesque escarpment rising from the Westland glacial system which feeds the Big Wanganui and Whitcombe Rivers. Seven miles south of the Main Divide lay our (Canterbury) Jim's Knob Base Camp, about 3500ft., near the terminal moraine of the great Ramsay Glacier. At 5 a.m. on the 30th December last the 'daughter of Dawn stretched forth her roseate fingers' over the rugged outlines of the ranges down river. Chester, Wyn. Barnett and I left the base and, travelling light at a fast pace, made good progress up the Ramsay Glacier to the Erewhon Col. Unfortunately, Basil Honour had to be confined to the base camp with a sprained ankle. Before 10 a.m., a mist-permitting view of the Evans massif had given us our necessary bearings. A short descent from the Erewhon Col led us to the elevated Westland snow plateau, the Bracken Snowfield. Traversing with rope taut took us to the 'Full Moon' Saddle.

Named by Westland surveyors, the Full Moon Saddle is worth a digression. If the rivers Big Wanganui and Whitcombe, which enter the South Pacific Ocean some 40 miles apart, were to upset the scientific proprieties by flowing uphill to their sources in the perpetual snows, their initial watershed ice would merge into the curve of the Full Moon Saddle of the Bracken Snowfield.

Prosaically, therefore, the 'Full Moon' is a saddle of the utmost geographical importance. Far from being a mere alpine ornament, the saddle is a col of extreme beauty. There is quality – the quality of symmetry sweeping to fall on either side to the Evans and Wilkinson icefalls. There is quantity – the quantity of seraced ice curving into the chaotic crevasses. Should the poetical seek description, the following lines by Housman do justice:

West and away the wheels of darkness roll,
Day's dreary banner up the east is borne.
Spectres and fears, the nightmare and her foal
Drown in the golden deluge of the morn.

At noon the highest ice of the Bracken Snowfield had been notched with hurried steps. Then, was the unknown … an eastern ridge promising the only access to the desired. The promise was unfulfilled. From the sou'-east, the Evans massif is comparable to a turret, with the eastern ridge a tentative 'creeper' up an elsewhere unbroken wall.

The initial buttress of this ridge looked bad. Appearances are ever deceptive, and a hillman can't tell what his rock is like till it wriggles under him. In fact, the ridge was worse than it looked. In the unusual strata, two Bergans were tied to a niche with an optimistic bootlace, and left there till our 'Mavoureen' return. Apologies for belays were loose on the tricky outward slab work. Beyond the buttress lay a slender cornice-crest. No 'golden road to Samarkand' that day. One man moved at a time. The rope was paid in, and monotonously out, around the axe-belay. The ridge narrowed to a knife of narrow hissing snow outcropped with many gendarmes. With no upper cohesion, the gendarmes are of loose foundation, and each is characterised by a definite overhang into the Wilkinson Icefall. Naturally, no gendarmes could be turned. Only route was up, and over. The Evans and Wilkinson tributary hanging glaciers, flanking either side of the ridge, were mist-hidden in the eerie below, but incessant avalanches boomed of their material existence. I thought of the 'Brewery Baths at Pont Nieppe' that occurred to E. Miller in the Bledisloe Gorge of the Matukituki.

Poised aloft, the party could not (like Flecker's 'Hassan') gnaw the nail of hurry. Some three hours passed. It became increasingly evident that Evans was built to ignore traffic from the Bracken Snowfield. It was no question of the eastern ridge alone, though that was difficult enough – but the ridge ended not in Samarkand – if, indeed, an eastern city can be compared with a Westland alpine summit. The golden road ended in a bluff, above which rose further complications. A sheer sustained face of loose rock was set under a high ice wall.

A situation recurrent to the nightmare of imagination – rarely found in the route of reality. Absent was the rock ridge necessary to back up the efforts of the would-be wizard who would set out to fashion his staircase of ice hand-holds. Above, overhung a crowning delight. A large cornice – the crest of peak 8580ft. The high peak of 8612ft. lay yet further back.

An unexpected turn to the ramparts of an already impregnable fortress. Our 'creeper' had faded away into misty air. Further sou'-east access on 'Evans' is refused with as incisive a mien as on other Southern Alpine unclimbed ridges of history. We had climbed to some 8200 odd feet, some 400ft. below our goal – little enough on a map read with armchair optimism. It is relevant to point out that the weather was settled, general conditions were good, and the party was fit and keen. Time was no object –

if the ultimate problem had been climbable, it would have been tried, even to the extent of continuing operations into the nocturnal hours.

Photography at this point was difficult – a matter of hurried snapping, with unshaded lens, into the sun. The tilted camera failed to record reality, yet the results have an element of difficulty, flattering the original.

The return of the 'traffic down the road' was a matter of cautious reverse belay. At 5 p.m. – the realm of golden sunlight. Mist sank to the Westland valleys.

The Big Wanganui River, which in the morning had been revealed, from its source in the Evans moraine, past the Vane Cleft, to the Lambert–Adams junction, now became enveloped in the all-enshrouding strata of fog. Revealed above was the great wall of Mt. Whitcombe and the satellite 'Snow Dome'. Distant was the archipelago of Mts. D'Archiac, Cook and Tasman.

The packs at the foot of the initial buttress were reached with relief, and not without a certain element of surprise. Descent to the Full Moon Saddle was varied by glances back to the ridge above. Cut out of the ragged dip of serrated strike, grinned an unkempt gargoyle – whiskers all smeared with snow. He was one of the gens d'armes traversed – a smile on the face of that tiger.

Prominent from the Full Moon Saddle was the fine unclimbed 'Red Lion' Peak. The 'Red Lion' was named by the Geological Survey, to corelate with Mt. Evans.

For some years we had wondered whose name was perpetuated on peak 8612ft. We knew that the Polar Evanses would not be implicated, because Mt. Evans appears on very early maps. It was with very great interest that I met Mr. D.J. Evans, of Hokitika, and learnt from him that 8612ft. was named after his father, who had done pioneer work in the Waitaha River, and had later taken up a run in the Big Wanganui. Mr. Evans, senr., was the builder of the Red Lion Hotel of Hokitika, evidently an oasis which was not forgotten by the surveyors as they toiled in the Evans moraine.

Return over the Main Divide was unhurried, late as it was, till the evening chill on the Ramsay Glacier gave fresh vigour. A literal run over the crevasses and moraine brought us to the base at 9 p.m. A very satisfying day out on the hills.

We had learnt that the best map route was one against which future traffic should be warned. From our east ridge we had looked at the north

ridge, also infeasible. Nor could the cirque between the Red Lion Peak and Mt. Evans (a very 'Col de Lion Rouge') be gained from the Bracken Snowfield, because of the southern wall rising sheer from the Evans Glacier.

It is our belief that the McKenzie Col, of the Wilkinson Valley, will give the surest route to the desired summit. This route has its inaccessible moments, like southern Tutoko, but it will be visited at every opportunity by some. Mt. Evans is, in fact, a hill to which you cannot but say 'Au 'voir' … 'let hillmen desire their hills … '

STEVE HART

Alpine Reflections: A values-based approach to climbing

Nearly twenty years ago I left Wellington for my big OE. How time passes between climbing trips, work, and family commitments. My infrequent trips back to the homeland brought occasional treasures such as the summits of Mounts Dixon and Tasman in the Cook region, Talbot in the Darrans and a lovely romp up the Dazler Pinnacles with that mountain man of Milford – Stan Mulvany. Trips to the Himalaya, Alaska and life in general brought their own prizes and a broader philosophy about time in the hills.

Recent events have encouraged me to put pen to paper to muse on our magnificent wild places. Alone, and with others, I have been reminded just how open the mountain environment is here. Being completely alone in the Whakapapa Hut after an energetic solo scramble in summer along the loose west ridge between Paratetaitonga and Tahurangi. Spending a few days with six others in a full McCoy Hut while attempting to get in to the Garden of Eden. The essence of life in the New Zealand outdoors is different from many other more populous areas of the world. I have loved my time climbing in the European Alps and with a more stable climate it is fairly easy to get a lot of climbs in while still being, at times, very close to civilisation. But the mountains of this country have a magic all of their own.

So why talk about values? The old 'because it is there' line thrown to a harrying reporter by Mallory in the 1920s is not enough and never has been. I suggest that we all need to look at our own values when talking about and being in the mountains. We enter the environment with all those values in ourselves, and sometimes they surface for others to see, both for good and bad. I am going to state my own, which may just ring bells to some readers. I do this not for self publicity but because I believe that not standing up for one's values is tantamount to appeasement of other less open attitudes.

As mountain courses will often tell you, avalanches happen whether people are there or not. In these times of risk aversion and attempted regulation of the mountain environment, it is our values that determine what will be done in those environments. An example of different

interpretations of outdoor values is the recent televised climb of Aoraki/Mount Cook by Mark Inglis. The personal challenge to Mark was in conflict with other people's wish for an inviolate space in which they might pursue their own goals. The filming required helicopters to fly close to the mountain itself. All parties were of course taking risks and the sound of aircraft sometimes annoys me in the hills. However I do wonder how many walk in and walk out of Plateau or prefer the speed of access available with the use of the plane and the helicopter taxi service. I guess that the parties who, along with Mark, summited that day, as with many others who attempt Cook, still gained a great deal of pleasure from the climb.

The thing is, I respect both parties' values of wilderness and challenge. The fact is that there will always be conflicts of values in the hills. Ours is not a highly regulated activity, as with traditional sporting activities. The more regulated our environment becomes, the more personal risk and adventure will disappear. Differing views and styles of climbing will always create controversy, and sometimes entertainment.

I will wear my own values on my 'paper' arm. I value people. They are important. For even the reactionary, bigoted ones serve as a reminder that we are all different, that we all need to have our values met in order to be who we are. Over the years and decades those values may change to reflect our age or circumstance, or the wider societal values.

Mountaineers, trampers, hunters, skiers, mountain bikers, parapenters and the many other hill users, are all part of the outdoor society. To disregard other users of that outdoor environment, and indeed other parts of society, is arrogance and self absorption. Respecting other people's map of the world as it is to them may not be easy but it will bring about a better outdoor world and a healthier personal outlook. Care and consideration of the environment is another of my core values. The freedom, which we have to utilise the outdoors in all our chosen activities, can sometimes come at a high cost. The release of deer into the hills in previous years created a great arena for hunters. It also brought about considerable erosion problems. Skiing is a very satisfying sport but brings with it mechanisation and, at times, over-population in the hills that many of us seek to protect. Climbing Aoraki/Mount Cook is a fantastic thing to do, however the overcrowding in Plateau Hut and on the mountain also creates its own pressure. Again it is the respect for others which will enable us to manage ourselves in the use of the outdoors. The environment is not an everlasting

gift to us. We must take personal responsibility in what we do. The only way to preserve and conserve is to totally ban human usage, a draconian option and unpleasant thought.

I also believe that in order to live in, and sometimes survive the outdoors, valuing oneself is essential, not in an egotistical way but, as many other climbers do, in putting themselves at risk in order to develop themselves. Sometimes that is hidden in the search for success or greater technical prowess but if you look you will often also find a better person. Sometimes it comes from going to the Himalaya and Andes as I did in search of bigger hills to climb. That, at least in my case, can lead to a wonderful opening of the mind to the way other people and cultures live. The connection of the intellect, the physical body and the soul is one of the great treasures in climbing, a feeling hard won and all too easily lost in the great maelstrom of modern life.

The aging of the self has led me to re-evaluate my acceptable risk level. Too many near misses, a wife and two children have also helped. But then the introduction of those two young minds into the outdoors has also been a marvellous thing to do, in watching them grow as confident and hopefully more respectful individuals. I have no wish to box them in, either as the children of outdoor enthusiasts, or as people stuck solely in the more traditional Kiwi style of living. In time they will choose. I can only hope we give them the right tools to work with.

So on to my core value: freedom. Freedom to be me. By that I do not mean lack of responsibility. Quite the reverse, as I believe personal freedom brings with it a great deal of personal responsibility. But freedom from constricting attitudes, self-defeating doubts and fears. Some would say oneness. Some of you will know that feeling, when on top of some hill, whether got there by a struggle or not. The really great thing is to bring that feeling into everyday life. So that the mountains and our modern complicated ways of juggling work, relationships and other calls on our time become all part of the same complete person that we are, or can be.

As Eric Shipton once wrote, 'There are few treasures of more lasting worth than the experience of a way of life that is in itself wholly satisfying. Such, after all, are the only possessions of which not fate, no cosmic catastrophe can deprive us; nothing can alter the fact if for one moment in eternity we have really lived.'

Or as Peter Pan put it, 'Ah to live, that is the real adventure!'

ROB KETTELS

Tokens of the Spirit: Exploring objectivity, emotions and fate in the Southern Alps

At the beginning of the year I experimented with my thought processes on a couple of alpine ascents. I tried to remove all emotion to see if there was any benefit to focusing on pure objectivity when climbing. At the same time I examined my beliefs about fate.

Let me explain why I have become interested in exploring objectivity, emotion and fate. Seven years ago, on an ice climbing course in Glen Coe, Scotland, I experienced my first proper avalanche. It had been raining for 12 hours straight and we were climbing a gully route on Buachaille Etive Mòr. For some reason we got out of the gully – I think to untangle the rope – when a fairly large avalanche slid down the gully, hissing like a snake. I dived horizontally, rugby touchdown-style and slammed my ice axes into some ice to avoid getting taken out. I was quite happy with my performance and so, when the instructor growled at me, 'Next time run out of the way – do *not* dive,' I was pretty annoyed. The instructor was an Old Timer and he was totally nuts. He had us doing really bold stuff like squirming up a tiny hole he had dug through the roof of a 20-foot cornice. Later, we met some hardcore climbers in the Clachaig Inn who were talking about some 'crazy guys' they had seen digging a manhole through a 20-foot cornice. 'Yeah,' we said, 'that was us, and this is a beginners' ice climbing course!' I have forgotten the Old Timer's name now but he was famous in the hills of Scotland, and after decades of ice climbing I guess he knew a thing or two about staying alive. Anyway the cornice collapsed the next day, in the same rain that caused the avalanche.

So now let's jump forward in time … two years ago while travelling on a bus to Aoraki Mount Cook I sat next to an old Asian gentleman who was maybe 75 years old. He was a T'ai Chi Master and he laughed as he spoke. But when I told him about my intention to climb Mount Cook, his face went pale – as if he'd seen a ghost. He confessed he had a premonition that something bad was going to happen up on Mount Cook. Two nights earlier, I had dreamed about a massive avalanche. But I decided not to tell my climbing partner about either of these occurrences because I thought I was just being superstitious.

While we were making our final preparations to leave for the climb, I felt something wasn't right; here was a feeling vibrating in the air. I have never felt that before or since. Anyway, I climbed with extra care, not rushing anything. We made the summit and started the descent. The weather was perfect and all was going well, until we were 150 metres below the Gunbarrels ice cliff. Without warning a major section failed catastrophically and thousands of tonnes of ice collapsed, taking all the seracs with it. Instantly, I went through my options: dive … No, *run*. It was déjà vu. I did what I had done in my dream only a few nights before and ran to the side, screaming at everyone to run and they followed me. Ice chunks exploded around us as we ran but the main thrust of the avalanche continued down the Linda Glacier. If we had stayed where we were, we would have been killed. The avalanche had covered the tracks we had made as we ran out.

The impact of the event shook me up for a while; I started thinking about my T'ai Chi friend's prediction and my avalanche dream. My rational side says mountains are indifferent objective geological formations; they have no concept of right or wrong. Had the avalanche experience in Scotland and the memory of the Old Timer's growl saved my life? What would happen then, I wondered, if I distanced myself from my ego, if I removed myself from all human forms of attachment and trained myself to think like a mountain – cold and emotionless?

This is the process that brought me to my first experiment: to climb the South West Ridge of Mount Aspiring, objectively, without emotion, and solo.

The climb started well. French Ridge was a breeze, but the Quarterdeck was a little sliced up and I put a foot down a crevasse. 'Crevasses are just cracks in the ice,' I told myself. 'Do not attribute emotion to these icy mouths that swallow people whole, never to be seen again.' I cursed myself for allowing my pulse to race. At the top of the Quarterdeck I could see the wonderful arching South West Ridge sweeping up to the summit. 'Don't worry,' I thought, 'it's only an uplift on the surface of the earth and I am just meat and bones.'

I crossed the Bonar Glacier to the base of the South West Ridge and scaled its side until I reached the narrow ridge that gets exponentially steeper as it meets the summit. Up I went. The first rays of dawn lit up the South Face and my heart sang with joy – my experiment was quickly going to pot. Eventually I got to the base of the famous couloir and stared up at an overhanging ice bulge about fifteen metres up a near vertical ice gully. I

tried to weigh up the challenges of this terrain objectively; I had to go right into the gully, stem out to the left, and then reach over the overhang. If I fell here, I would slide 350 metres down the South West Face, to my death – pure objectivity! Inside, my emotions exploded, impossible to contain, and my heart raced as I climbed on. My focus narrowed until I was oblivious to the world outside of the square metre in front of me. After climbing above the worst section, I was awash with endorphins, smashing my experiment to pieces. I cruised up the rest of the couloir to the summit where I punched the air with delight. I spent the rest of the day getting down the North West Ridge and back to French Ridge Hut.

My plan to climb without emotion had been unsuccessful, but I was not quite ready to give up on my experiment. I had another test I wanted to carry out; what would happen if I blended a purely objective approach to climbing with my normal, highly superstitious nature, I wondered. This trial would take place on Mount Tasman via the Silberhorn, solo – a much tougher climb than the South West Ridge of Mount Aspiring. So I drove on towards Aoraki Mount Cook National Park. I must admit I was quite apprehensive about visiting Mount Cook again. I turned off the highway and drove along the shores of Lake Pukaki. At the far end of the lake, piercing the sky, was Mount Cook, its flanks bathed in late afternoon sun. I pulled over into an empty tourist lookout to take photos and noticed another car pulling in. The driver, a woman, waved me over, so I went across to see what she wanted. She was a beautiful Indian woman with shoulder length hair, around 30 years old. When she stepped out of the car, I saw she was wearing a sari! I couldn't believe my eyes. In a lovely Indian accent she asked about accommodation in Mount Cook Village. I explained the very limited accommodation options at Mount Cook Village and offered her a spot in my two-person tent. That was probably the wrong thing to say to an elegant Indian woman who was travelling alone. But to my surprise she agreed to come with me as far as the campground. As we drove in convoy into the village, it dawned on me that this woman was actually my Guardian Angel, sent to protect me on Mount Tasman. My Guardian Angel and I had dinner together on a picnic table and we talked into the night about the atmosphere and ocean currents and the Himalayas and stuff like that. She told me she was a marine biologist but I knew she was really from heaven. I hesitated in telling her I knew who she was, in case she vanished into thin air, but eventually I told her anyway, 'If I die on Mount Tasman and go to

heaven then I hope all the other angels will be wearing saris too'. That night I slept serenely in my tent while my angel slept in her car. In the morning my Guardian Angel gave me a good luck note. I knew that if I took it up Mount Tasman with me, nothing bad would happen, so I carefully put it into my climbing bag with my other lucky charms – a key ring with a rubber baby on it, and some multi-coloured ribbon.

Later that morning I arranged a cheap flight up to the Grand Plateau Glacier and arrived at the hut. A dozen other climbers were there too because of the forecasted weather window. Everyone was there to climb Mount Cook except me. A quick look in the hut logbook revealed that no one had climbed Mount Tasman via Silberhorn for 18 months. The reason for this was a wide crevasse that cut across the ridge just below the Silberhorn – but, looking at the crevasse through a pair of binoculars, I saw a possible way past, by down-climbing the East Face or the unknown southern side.

After a few hours' sleep, it was time to set off. I tried to read the air for premonitions … nothing. I took this as a good sign.

In the pitch black of a moonless night I crossed the Grand Plateau Glacier and then moved up to underneath the East Face. Freezing temperatures had locked up the snow pack, aiding my progress through the tangle of crevasses. Stepping onto frozen snow bridges that spanned dark voids below, I felt confident.

Thwack went my ice axe. Up and over the steep crevasses I went with ease, but I knew I was on borrowed time. The forecast was for freezing levels to go above 3500 metres, meaning that this snow would be slush by the time I returned, on my way back down – increasing the danger that I could fall into one of these icy mouths. Before long I was ascending the side of the Silberhorn Ridge – an ice arête with one horrible section of rock. I climbed a narrow gully of ice to get above the rock band, then continued up until I reached the major crevasse that cuts the ridge horizontally. Faced with the crevasse, my only option was to down-climb one of the sides of the ridge and pass below the gaping slot. In the end I opted to descend the East Face side until I could traverse past the crevasse. I looked down between my feet at an unimaginable abyss that is the East Face. The moment marked a turning point in the climb and my attitude experiment.

If I considered the risks associated with crossing the crevasse again in a strictly objective way, the risk to cross was unacceptable. However, the

emotional part of my mind desperately wanted to cross. I realised that, unlike mountains, people are driven by emotions, this is what makes us 'human'. Mountains have their set of universal laws and we have ours. It was then that I understood that climbing mountains has more to do with the human spirit than it does about the mountains themselves.

So I committed to the final moves above the abyss, a sequence of awkward steps that is extremely exposed. After making it across, I was filled with relief. Then I climbed back up a horrible section of the East Face that had stones frozen into water ice and was covered by a layer of loose snow. I soon reached the summit of Silberhorn and looked back towards Mount Cook to the spot where the avalanche had swept past me and my climbing partner two years ago. I thanked the Scottish Old Timer, the T'ai Chi Master and Aoraki. Then I turned my back on Mount Cook and faced the serrated knife-edge ridge that spans the Silberhorn and Mount Tasman. It looked elegant and horrendous in equal measure. I inched my way up the ridge until I finally reached the summit. There I stood looking out towards the West Coast and across the Southern Alps. I didn't know what I felt but then something welled up inside and I screamed, 'Fuucckkiinngg yeeaahh.' The words – the feelings – came from the past, the future and the here and now.

Then I started the long down-climb. It was a battle against high winds and soft rotten snow. The major crevasse was only marginally better on the southern side. The lower I got, the softer the snow became until I was crossing crevasses on my stomach, stretching out as much as I could to distribute my load. But I could not cross the final crevasse that way, and I realised I would need to find a new way. Luckily I had taken a photo of all the crevasses on my digital camera the day before, so I could now use the digital image on the back of my camera to find an alternate route out of the maze and down to the Grand Plateau.

Back at the hut, I discovered that a climber had left dinner on the table for me, with a note saying 'Please help yourself.' In some strange way it felt like a final sign; not a premonition but a simple gesture of humanity. I may never know if fate plays a hand in mountain climbing but I no longer care. For me, climbing has become less about reaching a summit or ticking off a new route. Now, it's about feeling alive and connecting with the human spirit.

BRIAN TURNER

Ancestors

(for Phil Temple)

I came this way to shed some care.
Every stone I stumbled on, every

root that snagged my foot was
bastard discontent. By the time

I'd reached the hut I was too tired
to complain anymore. Shucking my pack

I lay in the grass that shimmered
in the breeze. The blue sky

preened itself. Wheels of sunlight
bowled along the valley. I dozed off

until evening crept over forest
and mountain. I knew they would

find me sometime. My speechless ancestors
played like mice among my dreams.

It grew cold. And colder. I woke
to the river running over my bed

of stone. I have come to know
that where a river sings a river

always sang. I listen.
This much I have learned.

PHILIP TEMPLE

Fire and Ice

(for Brian)

the night air strikes my forehead
cold-branding memory

shoulders hunched
a thin scarf licking your chin
you pick at pieces of kindling
the way you picked once at ice
on a mountain too big for both of us

not certain of the height or time
the swing of your axe questioned
will this step hold
will this fire burn
will the rock fall
will the heat comfort
will we ever come out of this alive

the room flickers with our talk
familiar as coals and ashes
there is warmth after all
though since we came late off the mountain
we have descended into the shadows
of valleys that never seem to end

CLIMB

JAMES COWAN

from *Hero Stories of New Zealand*

First over the Alps: The epic of Raureka and the greenstone

Cold and hunger, daily risk of death were the lot of the first explorers and gold-prospectors who penetrated the ravines and climbed the rocky ranges and forded the mad torrents of the Southern Alps and the mountain world where travellers now speed in smooth comfort from Canterbury to Westland by a wonderfully engineered railroad.

But long before the golden days of the Sixties, long before ever a *pakeha* foot pressed New Zealand soil, brown adventurers, clad in flax mats and shod with sandals, pressed up through these gale-swept mountain solitudes and descended on the West Coast in search of the most precious thing of their era, the *pounamu* or greenstone. And even before their day a Maori woman made the first crossing of the Southern Alps; she travelled east, from the Greenstone Coast to the plains that are now Canterbury.

This woman was Raureka ('Sweet Leaf'). She was a chieftainess of the Ngati-Wairangi tribe. This clan was kin to the Ngai-Tahu of the eastern parts of the South Island, but it had been isolated so long on the coast of Westland, near where the town of Hokitika stands to-day, that the eastern tribes scarcely knew of its existence. Raureka it was who first made known to the dwellers on the Canterbury Plains the treasure-country of the far West. I have heard the story related with true Maori wealth of detail by the old people of the Tainui and Meihana families at Arahura, and also by the last of the learned old men of Tuahiwi, in Canterbury.

In the heart of the Southern Alps, close to Mount Cook, there is an ice-peak which the map-makers have named Mount Raureka to memorise this long-gone explorer. It is on the dividing range, looking down upon the Hooker Glacier. It would have been more fitting, however, had they given the name to one of the mountains above Browning's Pass, far to the north of the Hooker, for it was there that Raureka made the crossing. Unlike the white pioneers, it was from the west that Raureka came, and it was in a curious way that the first Alpine trail-maker made known to the tribes of the plains the existence of the wild and mysterious land of Poutini, as the Maoris called the West Coast.

About two hundred and fifty years ago Raureka, as her descendants relate, left her village at Arahura, as the result of a quarrel with the people of her tribe, and with one companion, a slave named Kapakeha, wandered far up into the mountains at the head of Lake Kanieri. Quite accidentally the fugitives discovered a pass between the Alps that overlooked the head waters of the Arahura, and toiling on, high into the snow-powdered heights, shod with *paraerae*, or sandals of flax leaves, they crossed the divide. It was midsummer. They descended the valley of the Rakaia, and emerged on the Canterbury Plains. They trudged across the gently sloping prairie, a great lone land of tussock and cabbage trees, until they came to a place near where the town of Geraldine now stands. Here, exhausted and starving, they were found by a party of Ngai-Tahu men, who were out on the warpath. The wanderers were in sore straits for food. 'Te Kopa a Raureka' – 'the tiny food basket of Raureka' – is to this day a proverbial expression among the South Island Maoris, and is used when reference is made to the necessity for husbanding supplies lest starvation come with the winter.

Raureka's few handfuls of food were quite exhausted when the Ngai-Tahu discovered her. The starving couple were fed and given warm garments to replace their tattered mats, and at the camp fire Sweet-Leaf told her new friends about her home and the people on the forest land beyond the snowy heights. She told of the greenstone – Te Ika-a-Poutini, or 'The Fish of Poutini,' as it was called in native folk lore – which was to be had in plenty at Arahura, and she exhibited a small axe of *pounamu* which she had carried across the mountains. And she softly chanted a rhythmic song to herself as she chipped away with the little axe at a piece of *kauru*, the saccharine root of the *ti*-palm which she was scraping preparatory to cooking it. This is a translation I have made of the chant she crooned, a *karakia* or charm used by her people when felling forest trees and supposed to give additional efficacy to the woodman's axe and more strength to his brawny arms: –

I lay my sharp axe to the foot of the tree.
How it bites, O my sons,
How it sounds through the woods!
How keenly I long
For this tall child of Tane!
For Tane the Tree-God,
Towering so high –

Tane felled, prostrate, at my feet.
See how the chips fly from my axe!
Bared to the light of outer day
Are Tane's children,
Once pillared lofty in the forest shades,
Now stripped and prone,
*On Tane's sacred day.**

While Raureka was telling her story, one Puhou, a warrior of the Ngai-Tahu, lay quietly listening but pretending to be asleep. He heard of the wonderful *pounamu* treasure, and he determined to steal secretly away and exploit this rich new land for himself.

In the morning the expedition continued to march northward across the tussock plain to Taumutu and Kaiapoi. The artful warrior contrived to secure charge of Raureka, and as he had to all appearances been asleep when the woman displayed her axe of *pounamu* no one suspected him when he announced that he and several of his companions intended to make a scouting detour and rejoin the main body further north. Out of sight, Puhou and his men travelled inland and ascended the valley of the Rakaia. He induced Raureka to pilot him across to Westland by the pass she had discovered. She gave him her little axe and taught him the magic 'chopping song,' and, moreover, became his wife.

The scouts made *paraerae*, sandals of flax leaves, for the rough passage over the trackless range of rocks and snow, and by devious and perilous days, by mountain, flood and forest, they reached Raureka's home at Arahura. There they made friends with the Ngati-Wairangi and became possessed of much *pounamu* in the rough, and also in the form of weapons and ornaments. It was a treasure house of the Maoris, that camp on the bank of the Arahura.

Puhou explored the country as far north as the forestgirt lake named Te Kotuku-whakaoka ('The Darting Heron'), now known as Lake Brunner. Then he returned to Arahura, and he and his companions loaded themselves with all the greenstone they could carry, and set [off] back over the range to the East Coast, skirting Lake Kanieri and crossing the mountains by Raureka's Pass.

---

* For the original Maori of this chant see the Maori Poetry section of J. Cowan, *Legends of the Maori* (Harry H. Tombs, publisher). The name Tane (in full Tane-Mahuta) is pronounced Tah-nay.

They had been absent from the East Coast several months and it was summer when they emerged from the Rakaia Valley and kindled a great fire on a hill overlooking the homes of their tribe.

The Ngai-Tahu at once realised the truth. '*Aue!*' they said, 'the cunning of that sleeper! He has outwitted us all. He has found the Fish-of-Poutini.'

And wearily but triumphantly Puhou and his greenstone-bearers marched into the village square, set down their heavy burdens, and exhibited their spoils of *pounamu*.

This was the beginning of annual expeditions across the mountains to Arahura, the wonderful Greenstone River, the Ngai-Tahu carrying loads of preserved food delicacies packed in *totara*-bark and sea kelp baskets to barter for the treasure-stone. It was the beginning of grievous trouble for the Ngati-Wairangi. Raureka was indirectly the means of her clan's ruin. Soon the Ngai-Tahu, being numerous and fierce, ceased to carry barter goods over the pass, but obtained greenstone by the process of killing the owners, whom they also ate.

After several generations of fighting, peace was at last made between the East and West Coast people, cemented by the giving of a Ngati-Wairangi girl in marriage to Te Whatarangi, a chief of Kaiapoi. The peace was not a permanent one, for the *pounamu*-greed was on the outer tribes again, and in the early years of last century Tuhuru and other Kaiapoi chiefs ravaged the Poutini coast with Ngai-Tahu war parties. They all but exterminated the unfortunate Ngati-Wairangi and carried off their stores of the Maori jewel-stone; and it was Ngai-Tahu who sold the West Coast to the *pakeha* Government agents in 1864.

There are three passes at the head of the Rakaia waters – Browning's Pass (4,800 feet) above the source of the Wilberforce, a tributary of the Rakaia; Mathias Pass, and Whitcombe's Pass. These give access to the West Coast, but it is Browning's Pass, although the highest of the three, that Raureka discovered, as it is the most readily reached from the Arahura, by way of Lake Kanieri, and it was used for generations by the trans-Alpine Maori pilgrims and warriors.

BILL WHELEN

The Climb of the Ancient Mariners

In April 1998 a group of 13 climbers re-enacted the first mountaineering trip undertaken by Europeans in New Zealand: the ascent of Mt Sparrman, a little-known peak in Fiordland, 225 years ago.

The first European ascent of a New Zealand mountain started in the early hours of April 23, 1773 – St George's Day – from Pickersgill Harbour in Dusky Sound, at the start of Captain Cook's second visit to the country. Cook had set sail from the Cape of Good Hope four months earlier, and Dusky Sound was his first port of call after a voyage which had taken him within the Antarctic Circle – further south than any explorer had ever ventured.

The climbing party comprised the Swedish botanist Anders Sparrman, *Resolution*'s third lieutenant Richard Pickersgill, the ship's master Joseph Gilbert, and one other, who could have been an able seaman acting as a porter.

The naturalists George and Johann Forster were to have accompanied the group, 'but a violent flux attended with gripes' confined them on board – a misfortune attributed to the carelessness of their cook, who, according to Johann Forster, had 'dressed our victuals in a pan which was full of verdigrees'.

Sparrman himself was a ring-in.* He happened to be in the Cape of Good Hope undertaking a botanical survey for the Swedish government when *Resolution* put in to take on fresh provisions. Sparrman met the Forsters, who invited him to join the expedition.

The father-and-son team seem to have felt under pressure to live up to the precedent established by Banks and Solander on Cook's first voyage. They evidently hoped the addition of Sparrman as an assistant naturalist would help their cause.

---

* The son of a clergyman, Anders Sparrman (1748–1820) had been a precocious youth – enrolled at Uppsala University at the age of nine and beginning medical studies as a lad of 14. He was later one of the leading students of Sweden's great naturalist Carl Linnaeus, the man who gave the world the binomial system of classification of plants and animals, and eventually became a professor of natural history and pharmacology in Stockholm.

Sparrman, at that time an 'adventurous and exuberant' 25-year-old, appears to have relished the opportunity. His enthusiasm is evidenced by an incident during the voyage. According to his biographer: 'When the *Resolution* reached 71 degrees 10 min south and was forced north by the ice, Sparrman placed himself as far to the south on the boats as he could, and was later able to boast that he had sailed farther south than anyone else.' We cannot be sure, but perhaps the climb in Fiordland was his idea, too.

The party's clothing and footwear, though designed for a sea voyage, would have proved adequate for mountaineering. The officers had 'an everyday uniform of frock jacket with breeches and stockings ... while the seamen wore blue frock jackets, checked shirts, red waistcoats and canvas trousers'. They may also have worn their 'Fearnaught jacket and trowsers', issued by the Admiralty for voyaging in Antarctic waters.

A prelude to the climb was a four-kilometre row to the foot of the mountain in one of the ship's small boats. The weather was described as 'Pretty fine ... considering the Place but mostly Cloudy with now and then a shower.'

The route led up 'beside a large magnificent waterfall'. This had been visited several times previously by various crew members, and from the climbers' vivid descriptions and the celebrated painting by official artist William Hodges, *Cascade Cove, Dusky Bay*, we can assume the scene held some significance for them.

Beyond the waterfall, Sparrman records, 'I managed to clamber to a high mountain ridge, though with much difficulty ... After a few hours' effort we found ourselves at two o'clock on the peak of the mountain; here owing to its greater height, it was free of forest ... To mark our successful climb we set fire to the extremely dry grass there before descending.'

It would be natural to describe the ascent as a simple act of exploration within a long voyage of discovery. But the time the *Resolution* spent in Dusky Sound seems to have been regarded by Cook as a time for rest and recuperation, with exploration a secondary consideration.

A day spent in the mountains might easily have been considered recreation. On St George's Day, in particular, the routines of shipboard life might have been eased to allow for relaxation. After all, a decision to leave the area to rendezvous with *Resolution*'s sister ship, *Adventure*, at Queen Charlotte Sound had been made, and the ship's company was simply

waiting for favourable winds to negotiate what is now known as Acheron Passage and make open sea.

Cook's own records describe the party's aim as no more than 'to clime one of the Mountains', while Sparrman's enthusiastic account of having made a 'successful climb' indicates that reaching the summit was at least one purpose of the expedition. April in Fiordland affords only 10 hours of daylight, which would certainly have left little time for botanising on such an ambitious trip.

As it happened, Sparrman did return with some plant specimens, including the common South Island Forstera (*Forstera sedifolia*), while others – the leaves of a 'Cabbage-Palm-Tree' – were lost during the descent, but their collection appears to have been incidental to the main aim of reaching the top of the mountain.

From all accounts, an informal atmosphere pervaded during the time in Dusky Sound. Historians tell us the crew was 'able to enjoy five weeks of rest, fresh food and recreation,' and that they 'entertained themselves with hunting expeditions'. Captain Cook even 'relaxed a little … [and went on] an aesthetic excursion'. It was in this climate that Mt Sparrman was climbed – or 'mounted', to use Johann Forster's quaint expression – and the endeavour consummated with a fire on the summit, so all might witness the birth of New Zealand climbing.

Our ascent, to celebrate the 225th anniversary of this long-forgotten historic climb, started from the relative comfort of the M.V. *Tutoko*, moored in Cascade Cove. Here we could listen to the latest weather forecast while breakfast was prepared, and study the most recently published contour maps of the area. Our flight into Cascade Cove the day before had given us a fleeting view of what lay ahead, while our clothing, packs and footwear came with all the advantages of the last two-and-a-quarter centuries of technological advancement. We were ready – but it was raining.

Determined to make the ascent on the same date as the original climb, we motored to the foot of the mountain under low cloud, hoping the weather would improve during the day. Moving up past the waterfall, we recognised Hodges' painting and Sparrman's description: there could be no mistake that this was the route taken in 1773. Beyond the waterfall we continued in steady rain and poor visibility, entering a hanging valley after avoiding some bluffs. From here we found our way to an exposed ridge, presumably the one described by Sparrman, by way of an ill-defined

spur. From this vantage point, brief glimpses through swirling mist hinted at a spectacular view to the west beyond the coastline and north across Resolution Island. We continued along the ridge, passing through subalpine vegetation and, eventually, over open rocky ground, arriving at the summit at 1 p.m. after a five-hour climb.

Unfortunately, visibility was limited, and the weather was deteriorating rapidly. We made a quick search of the summit area with a metal detector, in case anything of interest remained, but obtained no positive readings. After the obligatory group photograph, a bite to eat and a cursory inspection to ensure we were indeed on the summit and not merely a bump on the ridge, we beat a hasty retreat down to the protection of the trees. From there we were reminded of Sparrman's account: 'The descent of the mountain was much quicker but much more dangerous; sometimes we were stopped by numerous climbing plants, sometimes perilous ravines barred our way.'

Towards the bottom of the descent we lingered at the waterfall, described by several on the *Resolution* who kept journals. Hodges had been employed 'to give a more perfect Idea than can be formed by written description', and his painting certainly did more than document the scene before us. According to art historian Bernard Smith, Hodges 'could put his hand to anything. Navigational views, plants and animals, portraits, landscapes and something rather new, a sequence of drawings depicting historical events on the voyage … He sought to combine the documentary art of the scientific voyages with the classical art of the academies.'

In an exhibition catalogue Hodges stated his aim was to give 'dignity to the landscape', and the mood he imparts to this particular scene is strongly romantic. He first sketched the waterfall on April 11, and finished the painting in London two years later.

We can now confirm that the summit of Mt Sparrman is indeed the peak depicted on the skyline of the painting, even though it cannot be seen from the base of the waterfall as Hodges has shown it. In addition, the Maori family posing beside the waterfall was not seen there, but elsewhere in Cascade Cove. Hodges used the sublime setting of the waterfall to display recent incidents, such as the ascent of the mountain and the meeting of a Maori family. Sir Joshua Reynolds, in dictating the artistic taste of the day, allowed that 'paintings could be contrived from diverse elements, provided they were harmonised by the controlling imagination'.

Sketches for other paintings featuring Mt Sparrman were made from the *Resolution* as she entered and exited Dusky Sound. These coastal views were recorded for the benefit of future mariners so they would be able to recognise the area from the sea. Richard Pickersgill and Joseph Gilbert drew or copied them, and when they are compared with Hodges' faithful representation, a vertical height exaggeration is evident, as is the omission of some background detail to accentuate the ridge we climbed. This technique is not unlike the cropping and tilting of photographs practised by some mountaineers in more recent years.

Artistic licence of another kind is thought to have stemmed from this first visit by Europeans to Mt Sparrman. Some literary scholars perceive in Samuel Taylor Coleridge's epic poem *The Rime of the Ancient Mariner* an allusion to the waterfall painted by Hodges and described in poetic detail by William Wales, Cook's astronomer and meteorologist.

In his journal, Wales described the waterfall as 'One of Nature's most romantic Scenes', and was moved to quote the poet James Thomson:

In one impetuous torrent,
down the Steep
It thundering shot, and
shook the country round

(The selfsame Thomson also gave us the stirring words to 'Rule Britannia'.)

After the voyage, Wales taught mathematics, Coleridge being among his students. The two were in contact for at least 13 years, making it quite likely that Coleridge would have absorbed both Wales' verbal and written accounts and seen Hodges' painting. Perhaps it was thus that the great poet, who had a passion for climbing and invested mountaintops with a mystical significance, was inspired to pen the lines:

Like waters shot from some high crag
The lightening fell with never a jag
A river steep and wide

It was still raining as we left the waterfall and made our way down through the forest to be picked up on the shore. Our party of 13 had taken over nine hours to compete the round trip.

The sense of history was palpable. No receding glaciers had changed the landscape since the day Sparrman and his party had trodden the same route. Apart from the browsing of introduced animals, isolation and

seclusion had preserved the integrity of that first ascent. It was as if we had climbed through Hodges' canvas with a 1773 guidebook, and re-emerged tired, hungry and wet through – despite our modern mountaineering equipment.

Our day's amusement on some high crag was over, and we were in admiration of those who had led the way all those years earlier.

THOM CONROY

from *The Naturalist*

And so on the 19th of December, Te Kake, one of his slaves, Black Lee, Tangutu, Worser Heberley and Ernst began a second ascent of Egmont. On the first attempt, it had taken a week to reach the island in the Waiwakaio River, but in the full sun and with a fresh store of provisions, it took them only four days. Past the island, they lost the way once or twice, stumbling through the same thicket that confused Tangutu, but Te Kake's slave had been born on the mountain as well, and he righted them each time.

The men followed the Waiwakaio, ascending its left bank three miles further up the slope from the spot where Tangutu had turned off. From there, they climbed along a narrow ridge where the trees began to thin. Here Ernst halted the party for twenty minutes while he sketched a small, crooked pine and stuffed several of its cones into his pack.

'We passed a thousand trees today,' Worser Heberley said, coming beside the naturalist and dropping his pack onto the ground. 'Why this one?'

'It could pass for the *Taxus baccata*,' Ernst replied. When Worser groaned, Ernst explained. 'A European yew,' he said. 'A potent poison can be made from its leaves. I haven't seen this specimen in New Zealand before.'

From further up the ridge, Lee called down to the two men. 'Boys, if you're done gawking at trees, you'd best run along before you're left behind.'

The next morning was Christmas, and, after breakfast, Tangutu led the party in a short prayer service. After, they descended into the blue basaltic chasm of the Waiwakaio gorge once more, climbing down for several hours before scrambling back up the escarpment on the far side to the platform out of which the final cone of the mountain arose to barren and windswept heights.

They continued for two hours more, scaling loose rock and cinders, to the edge of the snowline. As they climbed, the wind increased until they had to shout to be heard over the constant roar. Small, dry flakes of snow were blowing down from the clouded slopes above, at the sight of which Black Lee stopped and removed his pack.

'Too cold to keep climbing,' he said, blowing out a cloud of breath. 'Never thought I'd come up this way again, and I've gone as far as I need to go.'

Te Kake and Tangutu sank to their knees in a small patch of moss, bowed their heads, and began to pray in unison. Te Kake came to his feet and informed Ernst that he and Tangutu would also travel no further.

'I have surplus clothing in my pack,' Ernst offered. 'You might wrap your feet with it.'

Worser Heberley drew Ernst aside. 'It ain't the cold, Doc,' he said, speaking as quietly as he could in the lashing wind. 'They're afraid. The atua does not permit them to continue.'

In single file, Ernst and Worser Heberley began the final ascent of the volcanic cone. They climbed a narrow ridgeline, bordered on each side by a sheer escarpment and blocked in places by shards of rock spewed forth from the mountain in ages past. When they stopped to rest in the shelter of an outcropping, Ernst felt his head growing light. Below them, the surface of the mountain swayed as mists of snow scattered down the slope. Here and there, spots of distant green or blue appeared and almost as quickly vanished again. The susurrus of the wind brought to Ernst's mind the murmuring song of the Waiwakaio.

It required little effort of imagination to transform the drifting shapes of the mountainside into all manner of phantoms and beasts, and Ernst understood how easily the native mind had peopled the alpine heights with the most fantastic creatures. It was this same sense of imagination driven by fear which gave rise to all the world's superstitions. And yet in the whispering and incessant motion of the wind there was a kind of presence, the same nameless consciousness Ernst had experienced at Zerig's farm outside Strasbourg. The voice of Nature Herself, he thought. But was there hardly any difference between the voice of Nature and the song of the mountain?

Ernst felt Worser Heberley's gloved hand on his shoulder. 'You ready to get moving? Everything all right?'

Ernst's knees were nearly locked with stiffness, and he came to his feet with considerable effort. Now a gust of wind battered them with snow, and they both hid their faces. When it passed, Ernst assured Worser he was fine.

The two men had to hack each step into the snow during the final portion of the climb, and Ernst found his legs growing weaker as he pressed on. In Zurich, he and Franz had made several ascents past the limit of

perpetual snow, but Worser Heberley was obviously the better climber, and it soon became apparent that he would be the first to reach the peak. Ernst thought of his conversation with Charles. *Egmont: 1839 Dieffenbach.* Now this honour would go to another. Another door, it seemed, was closed.

Twenty minutes behind Worser, Ernst reached the peak of Mount Egmont. To the north the coast formed the edge to a country of undulating and unbroken green. The expanse of sea shimmered in the west like a desert of fine blue sand, while the peaks of Ruapehu, Tongariro, and Ngāuruhoe stood sharply white against the grey of the sky to north and east. South the coast curved inland, following the base of the mountain on which they stood. The Ruahine and Tararua ranges were a snow-capped spine down the island's centre, and Kapiti sparkled, a green nail that seemed to fix it all in place.

'Merry Christmas,' said Worser Heberley, fanning his arm across the view before them. 'You're on the map, Doc.' Ernst turned to Worser with a puzzled expression. 'Look,' Worser said, shouting to be heard over the wind. 'I don't give a jot for being the first one here. Go ahead and claim it.'

Ernst's head was still dizzy from the exertion of the climb, and his chest heaved with the emotion the panorama inspired. He had been given such a gift merely to stand here.

The shore whaler came and put his arm around Ernst's shoulders. 'I'm giving it to *you*, Doc,' he said. 'This ascent is yours – hope it gets you home.'

Ernst remained quiet. He took in the vista before them, but he only felt his emotions surging all the more. The uncertainty he had felt regarding the future of this land dropped away. On the peak of Mount Egmont, the menace of colonisation struck him with sudden clarity.

'These forests … ' Ernst said, turning to his companion, 'in a generation, the view will be farmland, cities, roads, cotton mills.'

A wall of fog was enclosing them, and the view was vanishing. 'Better head down,' Worser Heberley said. 'Weather's turning fast.'

The cloud closed around them, and the country in front disappeared. Ernst drew in a long breath and composed himself. For a few minutes, the only sound was the roaring of the wind. At last, Ernst took off his pack and set it down among the rocks where they stood. Speaking to no one in particular, he said, 'I must boil water.'

'Begging your pardon,' Worser replied, 'but we could find a better spot for a cup of tea.'

'To determine the elevation,' Ernst said. He knelt to unpack a pannikin, a thermometer, and the kindling they had brought with them. Once the water was boiling, Ernst measured its temperature at 197 degrees. He estimated 55 degrees as the mean temperature of the mountain, and from these figures calculated the elevation at the summit to be 8839 feet.

By the time he had packed up the equipment again, Ernst's grip had gone clumsy and slack from the cold, and he knew they must descend rather than wait any longer for the cloud to clear. He had brought journals, ink and a store of the *Tory*'s pens, but had inadvertently left these with Lee and Te Kake below, and so, in lieu of a note, Worser suggested they leave a charge of shot and his gun flint in an empty bottle. It was hardly the testament Ernst would have preferred to mark his life's most notable achievement, but it would have to do.

JOSEPH O'LEARY

Letter to W.J.P Hodgkins describing an ascent of Mt Earnslaw, 1894

Cardrona March 17/3/1894
To Mr. W.J.P. Hodgkins
Dear Sir

Your Favor of the 13th came to hand in due time. I am much pleased with the views considering the weather that they were taken in.

It is with pleasure I give you an account of the ascent of Mount Earnslaw by the Party from Alpine Club Hotel.

I joined the party on the 7th March in the Rees Valley who were respectively Mrs. Price a lady from 'England' Miss May Daniel Mr. F.H. Daniel and a Master Gordon Daniel of The Alpine Club, having left their Buggie at the Rees Gorge. We all rode joyfully along through the bush untill we reached the open valley. After crossing the Rees River at the Bend we were cantering along at our ease when suddenly the horse Mr. Daniel was riding fell under him and broke his leg. Mr. Daniel escaped with a severe shaking. This accident causing about a quarter of an hour's delay. And by double banking we reached Lynx Falls about 2 o'clock in the afternoon having had some lunch, we made up our swags, while the ladies tied up their dresses and prepared for the rough bush climb. The day was hot and our swags heavy. It being now about 3 o'clock and Mr. Daniel having not quite forgot the effects of his tumble we made a start for the climb to the top of the bush line or level. I must mention here that the ladies were not quite prepared for such an undertaking, Mrs. Price having a beautiful black dress and Miss Daniel dressed in white.

Still we climbed on Master Gordon in the lead I having being slightly handicaped with my swag and Mr. Daniel in the rear 'the seat of his trousers having got torn' winding our way through some burrnt logs sometimes falling amongst Bidybid and over Burrnt Timber Miss May was the first to change appearance.

As we endeavoured to wipe away the sweat from off our forhead we left a black mark instead and could not look in each others face with out

laughing. Who was the blackest now it would be hard to say, but Miss May's white dress I can't well describe. Mrs. Price's black dress by this time well covered with Bidybids began to look in poor condition having lost several pieces of braid and an occasional rip in it. But however in spite of all difficultys we reached the rock shelter above the bush line shortly after 5 oclock not much the worse for our climb.

Having had a drink of tea I engaged my self erecting a tent for the ladies in a small clump of bush above the rock shelter while the others amused themselves in a walk round the Earnslaw basin directly below the great glacier. Having erected the tent and made a good bed of leaves I collected some logs and made a real log fire before the rock shelter. Having a good sharp axe it did not take long. We soon made a hearty meal. After we satisfied our hunger, I amused our Company by the way I roasted a leg of mutton before the log fire on a long pole. We retired to rest at an early hour.

Having had breakfast at between 5 and 6 oclock on Thursday 8th and we made a start on our upward journey carrying with us sufficient provisions for the day extra clothing and also small flask of Whisky. It was a beautiful morning the sun shone bright and the sky was clear we made good progress. As far as the Birley Glacier Passing between Birley Glacier and another small sheet of ice 'Mr. Daniel called the Daniel Glacier' on our upward way gained sunny or Western side of the leading range overlooking Hunter's Creek. The travelling now became more difficult being shingle and broken rock. We gained the top of the 'peak' called O'Learys peak directly over the Birley Glacier about 12 oclock. As our route now lay in front there is a drop of about 500 feet down on to the saddle between the two peaks, we came to a stop. I explained to the ladies the time it takes at fast walking to reach the Main Top of the highest peak of Mount Earnslaw. I asure I spoke in serious tones. I never expected they the ladys would venture to proceed any further.

But soon came the answer from both ladies 'We will make a hard try for it.' So on we went and soon after Miss May wore the soles clean out of her boots which she soon replaced by another pair of shoes. So we called it 'Mays Saddle' her old shoes will still remain to be seen by the next ladies that will attempt the undertaking.

Having had some lunch and pure ice-water on the saddle we made for the Monster or Joint. in earnest when helf way up Mr. Daniel proposed to

have some whiskey and by the aid of some matches we were able to melt some snow for to have in the whiskey which gave fresh vigor to us. By this time the wind began to whisper and was like a 'Stepmothers Breath' which they say is very cold. The ladies having no gloves on began to feel it. But by a word of cheer from Mr. Daniel occasionally and a little assistance to the ladies when required we reached the top at last. I having had the pleasure of shaking hands with the first lady's that has ever been on top of Earnslaw.

What we seen from the top far away to the N. East we seen Mount Cook looming up in the distance with its white cap of eternal snow. Quite close to us we seen Mount Aspiring. By the aid of a sleeping bag I think I could scale it. To the South West lay Mt. Christina but as far as the eye could reach was a field glaciers West and N. West lay the Blue Pacific Ocean. 'But we could not see breakers on the shore looking over the Coast range brough our eyes too far out to sea.' The day was beautiful and clear and save where the mist and the mighty ocean met the blue line of mountains far away in the McKensie Country were to be seen and towards Omaru we had a splendid view. The Remarkables hid from our view a large track of country. Lake Wakatipu looked lovely and calm yet the wind still whispered around us. The sight looking down on the great glaciers on the slopes of Earnslaw was magnificient and will never be forgotten by those who seen them from abouve. Lake Kenneth looked grand but lonesome and also lake Alice.

But after all I will take a much more abler pen to describe the wonderful sight then mine.

We could not stay long. The piercing wind and cold made us think of returning so leaving their cards in match box I left my Miner's right for my card, we collected the former momentos left by Ross and party of my last visit and left the top at ¼ past 3 oclock. I gave my pocket hankerchief to Mrs. Price to tie round her hand and to prevent the rock and shingle from cutting it her hand as she sometimes fell. It got dark on us before we got below the Birley Glacier. So the party were obliged to rest at times while I looked for passes to come down from the morane. At times the stars shone on small lagoons and the ladies thought that some one were coming to look for them with a lamp. By this time the ladies were getting about tired out. I herd Mrs. Price once say she would give 10/- shillings for on cup of tea. Mr. Daniel was tired out also and proposed laying down till morning but I knowing the what effects of a nights frost on an elevation of

about 8000 feet would mean. I done all I could to keep them moving never resting more than 10 minutes we reached the camp at 11 eleven oclock at night and the longed for drink of tea was soon in readiness and retired to rest about 12 oclock.

I rose at 7 oclock on Friday morning 9th got the breakfast under way and dryed the ladies stockings and shoes. We all breakfasted between 8 and 9. Mr. Daniel went out and collected some mountain plants and meanwhile I rooled up the swags and we left the Bush line for the Flat and Lynx Falls and arrived there 12 oclock. The next thing was to collect our horses which did not take long and half an hour later we were walking quitely along the valley. We reached the buggie about 3 oclock where I left the Alpine Party and made for Earnslaw Farm where I was employed.

I must mention here that I never came across a lady with the same courage and coolness of head as Mrs. Price considering she done no climbing and lately out from England. Of course Miss May Daniel deserves the same credit but I expected more from her than the other lady being brought up in the locality and being young and active I would like to have had a 'photo' taken of the Company when they reached there home. Their faces were dreadfully sun burrnt. Miss May was minis her skirt it having got torn on the rocks Mrs. Price wore the sides out of her boots. Mr. Daniels the seat out of his pants. Great praise is due to Mr. Daniel for the way he encouraged and kept up a pleasant conversation during the roughest of the journey. Young Gordon was as fresh as I was and a little wonder for his age being a mere boy of 11 or 12. I should think I was not in a pleasant moode thinking we would have to spend the night amongst the Glaciers which might mean freezing to death. It is great honor for ladies to have reached the sumit of Mount Earnslaw.

But it was a trying trip although we had lovely weather for it. It is a feat that many ladys may attempt but I think few will accomplish.

We had a pair of glasses with us. They made objects show up a little plainer in the Valley below, but when put up to a distance were of no use. This is the second time I have been on the sumit of Mount Earnslaw and each time with out a glasses.

I may say I never seen the Mountain in better condition than this time we passed over very little snow on the ascent but passed great masses of iciles hanging on the projecting rocks.

I could get there (to the top) by three different routes with out crossing the Birley Glacier.

Yours respectfully
Joseph O'Leary

I think I could scale Mount Aspiring providing I had a proper sleeping bag and the necessary appliances connected with Ice work and sutch as a good heavy Ice Axe with me. If I got any encouragement, I would go there season up till end of April.

P.S. Mr. Hodgkins you must excuse this account and if you publish it I hope you will review it and put it in proper form and if you happen to see accounts wrote by Mrs. Price to Home Journals you might be kind enough to send me them when you are finished reading them.

I will remit postage to you of any news papers you should care to send to me. I am mining on Cardrona just now and will be here during the winter. I am very sorry you were not with us this last time when you come up next year bring with you a telescope or good glass and let me know a week before hand when you come.

(Aside) This will be a blow to Mrs. Ross. She is suposed to be the best Alpine Lady Climber in New Zealand.

I remain yours respectfully
Joseph O'Leary
Miner
Cardrona Lake County

BERNARD HEAD

Account of Expeditions up the Matukituki River, 1909 and 1911

In November 1909 I found myself at the Hermitage, Mount Cook, with two guides, Jack Clarke and Alex Graham. Being too early to climb in the Mount Cook district, decided to go and have a look at Mount Aspiring which was unclimbed and very little known.

Left the Hermitage on November 6th arriving at Pembroke on the 7th. Spent two days getting stores together and trying to get information about huts that were supposed to exist up the Matukituki River. Although the spot where the River divides into the East and West branch is only 30 miles from Pembroke the inhabitants could give us no information.

We left Pembroke on November 11th with three weeks' stores and got up safely to the spot where the rivers fork; but could get no further owing to a bluff and the river being full, so camped.

We also had to spend the 11th waiting for the river to go down. A man named McPhearson, who owns the Aspiring run, finally turned up on the 12th and took us across the river by a ford he knew and helped us to take our tent and food up the East branch of the river to a spot three hours from the junction, where we camped as we could get no further.

Opposite our camp was a good sized stream, running due West to East, and bringing down a lot of glacier deposit.

November 13th was a very dull and foggy day and we could see nothing so spent the day putting camp straight and just walking round.

The next day was also dull with rain. We crossed over the main stream and also the side one, and walked up an old track on the right bank. About two miles up it opened into a flat about two miles long with high cliffs at the end. We could see very little owing to fog so returned to camp.

November 15th – Lovely day. Climbed up hill East of camp and at about 4,000 feet got a fine view of Aspiring. We at once decided that we were on the wrong side to climb, as the route would mean bivouac on the snow and then a very long climb through snow before we could get to the actual mountain, so we decided to move round to the West branch of the river.

It took us altogether five days to get to the head of the West branch

having put in on the way up a base camp as far as we could get the horses and having to swag the last four hours.

Spent November 21st exploring the actual head of the valley.

The divide was easy from the East side, but the descent on to the West would be impossible owing to rotten rock.

On the 22nd bivouaced at 5,600 to 5,700 feet. Guides went forward to kick steps in the snow on the ridge that led on to Aspiring. Most glorious view from bivouac, numerous peaks, and part of the Dart Valley with Earnslaw in the distance.

November 23rd. – Left camp 2.40 a.m. and reached a spot 7,500 ft at 3.55. This is the actual divide of the Matukituki and snowfield of the Bonar glacier which comes in between this unnamed ridge and Mount Aspiring. Had to wait an hour and a half owing to fog and then dropped off the ridge about 500 ft on to the lowest point before we really began to ascend the mountain. Reached the top about 9.25, very windy and cold, but could not stop any time as also there was not much room.

Came straight back down to bivouac as quick as we could as a North-westerly fog was coming up. Could not rely on any readings from Aneroid as being accurate, as readings taken at the same point with five hours difference show a difference of 600 ft. Packed up our bivouac and camped at the head of the river for the night. Went down to our base camp next day and then on to Pembroke. Could not wait up the valley to do more exploring as was due back at Hermitage, and also weather was looking very bad. The fact of this dash to Aspiring was that I wanted to re-visit it so as to be able to explore to the head of the East branch of the Matukituki and then explore the plateau from which Aspiring rises.

I revisited it in November 1911 and luckily got Jack Clarke as head guide, and also another excellent guide Jim Murphy.

We started again from Pembroke. Here I was joined by two students from the Otago University, K.E. Tapper, Medical Student from Botany, and R.A.W. Southerland, a Geographical student.

We left Pembroke on November 23rd camping at the junction of the East and West Branches of the river for a night.

Next day, the 24th, we crossed the river and camped at our previous camp up the East branch which was known as Disappointment Camp, putting a comfortable camp as we intended to stop some considerable time. Next day, the 25th, we crossed the river and the stream opposite camp and

worked up the right bank. Luckily it was finer than when we last visited it. We found the valley ended in a very steep cliff which runs up practically to a peak called the Pope's Nose. Coming into the stream from the North is another valley and stream. We went up this valley some distance and found it practically choked with avalanche snow, the water running out of this causes the whiteness.

Unfortunately it came on to rain, so I was unable to get any good photographs of this valley.

Next day we left camp and worked up the left bank of the Matukituki east. About half a mile above camp the river is gorged so we had to strike into the bush and cut our way up to about 2,000 ft. We finally got to a spot at 4,250 ft and got a magnificent view of Aspiring and numerous other peaks, and also saw right up the East Matukituki, which was much longer than I expected it to be, and it is shown on the maps. We decided, two guides and myself, to start next day and get up to the head of the river.

November 27th. – Rain. Too wet to start.

November 28th. – Wet.

November 29th. – Started at 1.30 and tried to get across the river and try to get up the right bank but found the gorge cut us off, so had to return and work up the track we had previously cut. Camped at a spot 2,800 ft for the night.

Thursday, 30th November. – Thick weather. After talking things over decided that the guides should go forward with a few stores and cut a track down to the river again, as we were now clear of the bluff again and the bush was very bad, so I returned to camp.

Friday, 1st December. – Started out again with more stores. Quite an easy track up to our camping spot and then had to work another 400 ft higher up and found where the guides had cut their track. Found the bush even with track very bad going. Much interested to see the tracks of Kakapo or ground Parrot, very marked worn by them and chewed Tussok and Celemesia. After very rough journey got down to the river at about 2,100. Pretty rough going for some distance over boulders and bush and finally came out into a river flat. Started to rain and bitterly cold so we camped about 4.30 near a tributary stream running West and East.

December 2nd. – Rained hard all night, with sleet. Left camp at about 11.00 a.m., and worked up to the head of the river. Very fine glacier cirque and many water-falls, but no glacier. A couple of good [gap in text here].

Photographed in bad light the head of the valley. Would much like to have been able to climb up on to two saddles we saw but it was absolutely impossible owing to the fresh snow which covered everything above about 4,000 ft. Returned to camp and studied a peak due West of camp which we took for Glacier Dome.

December 3rd. – Intended to go up towards Glacier Dome so breakfast at 3.30 a.m. Much too foggy and cold to do anything. Go back to bed. Had another look at it at about 9 a.m.: still bad, and owing to a sore heel I did not turn out. The two guides went up and got on to the snow after pretty rough scramble.

Going due West up the stream we believe there is a saddle which leads into the valley we discovered before on the other side, and also a valley to the North which should lead into one of the West coast rivers. Started to snow at night and very cold.

4th December. – Snowed all night. Minimum temperature minus 1 centigrade. Packed up and left camp at 10 and reached Disappointment Camp 6.55 in the evening. The trip was successful up to a point, but was greatly spoilt by the badness of the weather.

Note. – The following birds were either seen or heard: Cuckoo (long tailed), Morepork, Ruru, Kakapo, Paradise and Grey Ducks, Seagull, Wren, Sparrow, Bull-finch, Thrush.

J.R. DENNISTOUN

First to the Summit: Mitre Peak, Milford Sound

In November 1909 I was lucky enough to visit the West Coast Sounds in HMS *Pioneer* as a guest of the ward room. As soon as I saw the wonderful Mitre Peak in Milford Sound I determined sooner or later to make a big try to get to the top. My brother and I intended to make the ascent, but the weather broke and we were unable to make the attempt.

In March 1910 I went with a party over to Milford Sound, via Lake Te Anau and the Government track over McKinnon's Pass. It is a most wonderful walk, and everything is made easy and comfortable. I meant to have a try at Mitre Peak this time, and made enquiries at Glade House about a porter. One's party must be at least two in number on these occasions, although I fear I am inclined to disregard this precaution at times. The Chief Guide was not at all hopeful. However he said that if I wished to try I could have one or two of the track porters. He could tell me nothing as to the most likely route, etc. I talked the matter over with the porters, but they could not help much either. Of course, it is out of their beat, and they knew no more about Mitre Peak than I did. They do not get any climbing either, all their work being on the track. I decided, under the circumstances, that one was enough, and as one of them had read Whymper's *Scrambles* that helped me in my choice.

Mitre Peak is 5560 feet high. It falls sheer down on one side into Milford Sound, and on the other into Sinbad's Gully. Great smooth slabs of granite are to be seen, with only patches here and there where ferns or scrub can get a hold on the perpendicular walls. Running up towards the head of the Sound is a long, narrow spur connecting with the peak. This spur is bush-covered, and ends where Sinbad's Gully joins the Sound. You see this spur end on from Sutherland's. I believe nobody had previously tried to climb Mitre Peak. This is no doubt because it is so out of the way, and not because of its difficulty, although many believed it to be unclimbable – a very big word nowadays.

I had hoped to go down to the Sound the day before making an attempt, and study that side of the peak. I thought it would be shorter and easier to go some way down and then strike straight up through the

bush, joining the ridge at the last big declivity in it before the bush ends. Unfortunately Sutherland was mending his launch, so I was unable to do this. My porter had great stories to tell of Sinbad's Gully, and wanted me to go up the Gully and then strike up onto the ridge. This I decided against at once. Sutherland strongly advised me to climb the big bushy knob facing Sutherland's and follow the ridge all the way along. This I decided to do, but was far from sanguine, as the ridge was very long, and I expected the bush to be very bad. I felt we ought to manage to get out above the bush and see what the final peak was really like – from Sutherland's through a telescope it looked very smooth and slabby, and not at all hopeful – then I would know more about it next time. I was sure there would have to be a next time.

On Monday, March 13th, 1910, Joe and I left Sutherland's at 6.30, and rowed about two miles across the end down the Sound to where the creek from Sinbad's Gully enters the Sound. Here we tied up the boat, and started climbing at 7.30 – about an hour and a half later than I had planned, but the clock had failed us. We took plenty of tucker, camera, telescope, 20 fathoms of good, light, but strong rope that Sutherland had lent us, and I had a pair of indiarubber sandshoes, which I thought might be useful if I ever got as far as the final slabby rocks. It was still a dull morning, not very promising looking. We made great progress up the big bushy knob, keeping on the ridge as much as possible, and finding the bush very open and good for West Coast bush. This was a great surprise, and we just romped up, having two five minutes' spells, and getting up to the top at 8.45. Then the long ridge began – never very steep, generally a very easy slope. The ridge is very narrow, and there was no trouble in keeping our direction; also, the bush was very open; it is always best on a ridge.

I had apprehended there were many ups and downs on the ridge, but they proved very slight ones, and we travelled very fast. At 10.15 we came to the big dip in the ridge – 500 feet, I should say, and very steep. The bush was getting thicker, too. It was annoying, but down we went, getting to the bottom at 10.30. Then the bush became much worse, with scrubby, stunted stuff, and it was very steep. However at 11.10 we got out above the bush, about 3500 feet above sea level. Then a little steep snowgrass brought us to a fairly wide part of the ridge, sloping gently upwards; but it soon got very steep again, and the ridge became narrower and narrower as we went on. However, there was a lot of big snowgrass, and if the foothold was not too

good, the handhold was. At a height of about 4200 feet, and about 100 feet below where the ridge levelled off again before rising in the final peak, Joe sang out for help. His arms, unused to such violent exercise, had begun to cave in, and he was losing his grip of the snowgrass. I soon got him into a snug place, where he could sit and rest. Apparently he was quite unable to go further, and wanted me to put on the rope and take him down to the level place, 200 to 300 feet below. This I refused to do, telling him he was safe where he was. I had now a possibility of making the ascent, which I would not have if I wasted energy and time in taking him down to a safer place. We had some very much-needed grub, and a spell of fifteen minutes. Then at 12 o'clock I started off with my sandshoes in my pocket, and nothing else, telling Joe to sit still and not to move. As soon as I got up to the level piece of ridge 100 feet above, I saw the final part of the peak, and felt I would succeed. I shouted to Joe that I was going on, and would be away two hours. I wanted to get him up to where I was, so that he could watch me, as I knew in theory it was all wrong to go on alone, still it was too tempting, and I couldn't resist. Joe said he would sooner not come any higher.

The ridge is nearly level, and the narrowest I have ever seen. It literally falls 4000 odd feet sheer down on both sides. It is all rough, big blocks of granite, much broken, but the blocks are big and firm for the most part. At the far end of this ridge are two big gaps of 100 feet or so, cutting it off from the face of the final peak, which rises about another 1200 feet. I reached the end of the ridge at 12.25, it having given no trouble, and I got past the two gaps a good deal easier than I had expected. Luckily there was no wind. It would not be a nice place to be in if there was, or if one's head was not good.

Here I took off my boots and left them. The sandshoes gave a splendid hold on the rough granite. Some of the slabs were big, and very smooth, and I don't think it would be possible to have got over them without the sandshoes. Here, being on a face, one does not quite feel the same as regards the wonderful steepness that I felt along the narrow rocky ridge. The rock was all very solid and good, very different to the mountains round the Hermitage – due, I suppose, to the slight amount of frost to which they are exposed. I reached the summit at 1.15, and built a small cairn, putting a white linen handkerchief in it. I had nothing more lasting that I could spare.

It was so dull that the view was not very good. Tutoko was in a cloud. The view towards Te Anau was shut out, and Pembroke Peak was rather cloudy. I noticed a pretty little lake up the river coming into Harrison's Cove. It is, I believe, unexplored, and must come from the west of Mount Tutoko. The lake was not known before. I got a good view up the Cleddau River to the S.E. The sound looked splendid, and the walls of the hills into it are extraordinary, especially those of The Lion just opposite. The Bowen Falls looked very tiny, and Sutherland's launch was just getting home after taking visitors round the Sound. I could see the grampus jumping round the launch. Outside one could see a long way up and down the coast.

I left the top at 1.30, getting back to my boots at 2.5, and reaching Joe at 2.30, having been away two hours and a half. Joe was quite safe and sound. We picked up our gear, and I put on the rope and had him down on the broad grassy place in a quarter of an hour. Then we had a long spell and much food, and I for one wanted both badly. At 3.45 we set off again, and reached the bottom of the big dip in the bush at 4.15. I then made a great mistake. To avoid the 500 foot climb and then the long ridge, we turned to our right, and dropped straight down into Sinbad's Gully. It was only a distance of about 2500 feet (supposing the creek bed to be 500 feet where we struck it), and though very steep, imagined we would be down in no time. We got there, but not till 6.45, and often I thought we would never manage to get down at all. If we had only stuck to the way we knew we would have just about reached the boat at this time. Four or five times we had to lower each other over bluffs of rock. We took a turn round a tree, and then when we were both down pulled the rope after us. It was a slow, tedious, uncomfortable job, and once or twice the rope was only just long enough. We were wet through by the time we got down, as it had been raining steadily for the last two hours.

We thought our troubles were over when we safely reached the creek, but they were only just beginning. We were nearly three miles from the Sound following the creek, and it very soon got dark. We kept in the creek bed as much as possible, as it was lighter there; but we tumbled about a great deal, and often were forced into the bush by big pools or cascades. In the bush we couldn't see a yard ahead of us, and literally had to feel our way along. We were frequently separated, and then I would have to shout and shout and shout till Joe caught up on me. We stumbled or fell every few yards, and had a great doing altogether. Once we caved in, and decided to

wait till morning, but things were too wet and dark to get a fire going, and in a few minutes we were cold, and anything was better than waiting, so on we went. The noise of the creek when we were in the bush gave us our direction. At 9.45 we reached the Sound, and soon found the boat. Luckily there was no wind, and we arrived at Sutherland's at 10.30.

The rest of the party were rather anxious about us, and were trying to get Sutherland to go out and look for us, which he refused to do, and certainly he could have done nothing till daylight if he had gone.

I feel sure that the way we went, though long, is far the best and the easiest. It would be impossible to get up from Sinbad's Gully, and I don't advise anyone to come down that way! I am also inclined to think it would be impossible to get up from some way down the Sound, as I had thought of trying, as I now imagine there must be bluffs of rock in the bush on that side, as the side into the Sound is steeper if anything.

I don't know if it will be long before others make the ascent, but when they do they ought to start much earlier, take sandshoes, and go and come by the way we went up. It is a wonderful climb, and one has rather the feeling of being on top of a steeple 5560 feet high!

On a clear, bright day the view must be glorious, as the colours of the sound and bush and distant peaks from such a height must indeed be splendid.

BOB McKERROW

Maori Mountaineers of South Westland

They lived in a remote corner of South Westland in small settlements of Heretaniwha (Bruce Bay), Hunts Beach, Mahitahi and Jacobs River and together made a huge contribution to New Zealand mountain exploration. Most are descendants of Te Koeti Turanga.

Colonial historians and explorers undervalued the contribution of Maori guides and companions and writers such as Charlie Douglas, Edward Fitzgerald, Arthur P. Harper and John Pascoe, clearly denigrated the Maori role in mountain exploration and later, mountain guiding. Gerhard Mueller and Thomas Brunner were notable exceptions. Mueller[1] writes with brotherly love about his companions Kere Tutuko and Werita Tainui, and valued their skills and friendship. 'To Ekehu I owe my life – he is a faithful and attached servant,' wrote the ever humble Brunner.[2]

So many early writers missed out key information which would have proved so clearly that the Maori were experienced mountain people. Take Gerhard Mueller's friend Kere Tutoko.[3] In 1835, as a 12-year-old, he travelled up the Grey River, on to Kotuku and up the Taramakau River to Harpers Pass, down the North Branch of the Hurunui, past Lake Sumner, until it reached the Waitohi tributary and so on to Kaiapohia (Kaiapoi). Yet writers like Arthur P. Harper, in his book *Memories of Mountains and Men*, write of the first crossing of the Southern Alps in 1857, when the Maori had been crossing the main divide for centuries. This is typical of many reports of colonial exploration where Europeans were not discovering, rather retracing existing Maori routes.

The outdoor skills of the South Westland Maori were not confined to the bush and mountains; they also travelled regularly along the coastline by canoe. Kere Tutuko, his brother-in-law Te Koeti Turanga and his grandfather Tuarohe, were highly skilled canoe builders. Records show that they made regular sea voyages from Bruce Bay to Te Horo and Anita Bay in Milford Sound.[3]

The inquisitive exploratory spirit of the early Maori took them to all the remote corners of the South Island, and they quickly gained first-hand knowledge of snow and ice.[4] The mana and beauty of the Pounamu was an

added attraction to cross the divide again and again, all the while gathering further alpine experience. Their pre-European glossary of snow and ice, whilst not as comprehensive as the Inuit (Eskimo), certainly proved that they had rubbed their paraerae (sandals) on the high mountain passes. *Whenuahuka* described the permanent snow on the high peaks and *hukapapa* was the name for the huge snowfields. The snow slides from the high peaks were *hukamania*, and as they grew and took on avalanche proportions, they became *hukahoro*. The glaciers that drained the snowfields were called *hukapo*, the glacial sediment *waiparahoaka* and the snow-fed water, *waihuka*. *Kipakanui*, or ice, was seen in the shady valleys in winter, and the thick ice which never saw the sun was named *waiuka*, meaning solid water.[5]

One of the first Europeans to record contact with Chief Te Koeti Turanga, who married Ripeka Patiere, daughter of Tutoko, was Gerhard Mueller, in October 1865, when he stayed at Bruce Bay.[1] The first contact modern mountaineers had with the Te Koeti family was in 1895 when the British mountaineer Edward Fitzgerald, with his Swiss guide Mattius Zurbriggen, met Dan Te Koeti, one of four brothers, at the Scott's homestead in the Karangarua River valley. Fitzgerald was impressed from the outset: 'Certainly if his physique is a typical instance of that of the Maori race, a fine race of Alpine guides might be cultivated from them.'[6] This was a prophetic statement from the astute Fitzgerald as Dan and his two brothers Mark and Butler (Buck) Te Koeti, all became guides and mountain men in every sense.

Dan Te Koeti accompanied Fitzgerald, Zurbriggen and Arthur P. Harper for the next leg of their journey which took them down the Karangarua River to the sea, along the coast to Gillespies Beach and up the Fox Glacier to Chancellor Ridge. Fitzgerald, not known for his favourable comment about New Zealand mountaineers, comments of Dan's ability, 'I was surprised to see how well he walked on the ice where he seemed to be quite at home, though I understood that this was the first time he had ever attempted in his life' ... and later, 'He was an immensely powerful lad; indeed I was told by Scott that he had carried iron pipes, weighing 140 lb., up a steep hill in the neighbourhood of the homestead.[6]

What Fitzgerald didn't realise was that Dan had spent a lot of his time as a shepherd for Andrew Scott grazing sheep in alpine vegetation in areas up to 5000 ft. He discovered much new land, some of it snow covered,

so he wasn't a stranger to snow. One feature he discovered as a shepherd was an alpine lake, situated at just over 4000 ft and feeding into the Makawhio (Jacobs) River. Arthur P. Harper named the lake after Dan, Lake Rototekoiti.[3] The misspelling of Te Koeti still appears on today's maps.

Two years later, in October 1894, Ruera Te Naihi, another relative of the Te Koeti brothers, also known as 'Bill the Maori', joined Charlie Douglas and Arthur P. Harper on their exploration of the Karangarua. Douglas, struck by ill health again, left Harper and Ruera Te Naihi to complete the exploration of the Karangarua and the Twain valleys and they returned to Scott's homestead the following year after 19 weeks in the hills.[7] Trish McCormack in her book *The Maori in Westland*,[8] 1982, writes:

'Ruera Te Naihi's assistance to Arthur P. Harper in packing loads and procuring food has largely been forgotten' … and later … 'From Harper's account of this expedition some of the sterling characteristics of his Maori companion emerge. Unfortunately Harper showed a somewhat condescending attitude to Bill, in view of the fact that he was not a highly skilled mountaineer like himself.'

Ruera Te Naihi later became a ferryman at the Waiatoto River, but was tragically drowned some years later.

The next to make his mark in mountaineering was Butler Te Koeti, brother of Dan, Mark and George. In 1905, fellow South Westlander and close friend Guide Peter Graham invited Butler to work with him as a guide at the Hermitage. The Maori families of Bruce Bay, Hunt's Beach, Mahitahi and Jackson Bay had, over the years, become close friends of the Graham family. This relationship started in the mid 1860s when David Miller Graham, father of guides Peter and Alec Graham, was shipwrecked at Jackson Bay after rowing and sailing round the South Island in an open whaler. Both Peter and Alec Graham acknowledge this in their respective books.[9,10] A quote from Alec's book shows their respect:

'Fortunately for them there were a few Maoris at the Bay and to their kindness they owed their lives. The Maoris helped them make a Mai-Mai and provided them with food. My father never forgot their kindness and ever after had the greatest respect and kindness for the Maoris.'

In 1905, Butler Te Koeti and Peter Graham guided Annie Lindon onto Glacier Dome and also took her on the 3rd crossing of Barron Saddle. One of the legendary feats he left was his crossing of Copland Pass from the Hermitage to Jacobs River in 15 hours when there was no formed Copland

track. After spending a night with friends and family he returned to the Hermitage the next day again via the Copland Pass.[8] Unfortunately a number of Butler Te Koeti's mountaineering achievements went either unrecorded, or need to be unravelled from being recorded incorrectly. In the publication *Jubilee History of South Canterbury*, by Anderson, his name is recorded as B. Kosti,[8] and to future generations it would be easy to surmise that Kosti was an Italian guide.

Butler Te Koeti enjoyed his mountain guiding and later brought his young nephew George Bannister, who was just 17 at the time, to work at the Hermitage. George quickly teamed up with fellow South Westlander and guide Darby Thomson of Ross, who knew the Te Koeti and Bannister families well. George Bannister quickly learnt the trade of mountain guiding with the first traverse of Nun's Veil, the 4th ascent of Elie de Beaumont, 7th ascent of Footstool, the 3rd ascent of Walter and Green,[8] but his great moment was yet to come.

In February 1912, Samuel Turner returned to the Hermitage to attempt his second ascent of Mount Cook, this time by the Linda Glacier route. He chose, for his guides, Darby Thomson, who climbed Mt Cook five times before his untimely death on Mt Cook in 1914, and 18-year-old George Bannister. In the early afternoon of February 27, 1912, George Bannister stepped onto the summit of Mount Cook, and looked towards his birth place. It was a special moment – he was the first Maori to climb Aoraki. It was a perfect day and it is quite likely he would have seen Mt Tutoko in the distance, named after his great-grandfather. His client, Samuel Turner, describes the moment:

'It was a glorious day and a more glorious view. It pleased Bannister so much that he could not attempt a description. It was the first time a Maori had reached the summit of Aorangi, Cloud Piercer, or the long white cloud, as his forefathers called it, and afterwards called Mount Cook; but although most of New Zealand is now owned by white men, some of whom do not know the consideration due to the native race, nevertheless the mountains were never bought from the Maoris, and must belong to that race still.'[11]

George Bannister must have mourned the loss of his friend and fellow guide Darby Thomson when he was killed by an avalanche on the Linda Glacier, while descending Mt Cook in 1914. It was also the year George walked from Bruce Bay to Hokitika to enlist for the First World War, only

to be told by the Doctor he had flat feet and would never be able to do long route marches. George promptly waked back home, completing the 400 km walk in about a week.[12]

However, nine others of his extended family were accepted to fight for their country. Two of them became famous when Butler Te Koeti and Dave Bannister competed in an unofficial world wood chopping championship in Niepe Forest in France on April 9, 1916. The reigning world champion axeman, serving in the Canadian Army, challenged the best axeman in the British Empire. He wasn't to know that two New Zealand Maori from South Westland had been wood chopping all their lives. The crowd was stunned when the brash Canadian lumberjack was beaten. Butler was placed first and Dave second.[3]

George Bannister was later recorded as doing the first ascent of the high peak Mt Lyttle with Tom Sheeran in 1931 while he was building the Douglas Rock Hut in the Copland Valley. Guide Mick Bowie tells of the way the hut was constructed:

'They selected suitable Totara trees, felled them, and somehow took them to a large rock about quarter of a mile from the hut site. Here they arranged a sawing pit, cut them with a pit saw into lengths and thicknesses needed, and without waiting for the timber to dry carried the boards back to the site, and built the hut. The roofing iron was taken up the valley by packhorse.'

Mick Bowie also recounts the story of George Bannister carrying a 100 pound roll of malthoid on his back and treating it like a feather. Mick, carrying only a small pack himself, had trouble keeping up with George on the journey from Welcome Flat to Douglas Rock.[8]

Perhaps the last comments on George Bannister are best left to an outstanding female climber of that era, Dora De Beer of Dunedin, who wrote the following in the 1954 *Alpine Club Journal* about Lyttle Peak, Navigator Range.

'George was a gentle, attractive giant, partly Maori. He had been a guide, and was at the time working on the new hut erected to replace the old bivouac at Douglas Rock. He helped cut the track up the Ruera, and once at least, George visited our camp (1931) there bringing mail and stores, also a delicious soda loaf he had baked in a camp oven. He died a short time afterward, and the rock in Ruera (Bannister's Rock) was named after him.'[13]

George Bannister is buried in the Whataroa cemetery, alongside members of the other great West Coast guiding family, the Grahams. And, on a fine day the high peaks they spent so much of their time near, watch over the graveyard.

Jim and Bill Bannister, both brothers of George, contributed to the mountain scene. Jim was on the 3rd ascent of Mt Sefton with Darby Thomson and Samuel Turner and Bill worked on the first Hooker bridge.

Bill Bannister's trade as a bridge builder had taken him all over the country, and his work on the Hooker bridge was one he recalled fondly. In 1914, while his brother George was guiding at the Hermitage, Bill built the first wooden bridge over the Hooker. The bridge was carried away in an ice-flooded river in 1927. Bill's son, Jack Bannister, still living at Mahitahi in South Westland, clearly remembers working with members of his own family and Dan, Mark and Butler Te Koeti, cutting tracks up the Copland Valley. 'The tracks were so wide you could have driven a jeep up them,' he said.[12]

For a number of South Westland Maori families it could be said that the Copland valley was their second home for many years. They cut the early tracks, built the first Douglas Rock hut and were involved with subsequent hut building at Welcome Flat, track upgrading, rescues and recreational hunting. But when the occasion was right, family climbing had its place.

Bob Wilson,* formerly of Hunts Beach and now living at Haast, recounts a story of a double crossing of the Copland Pass, when he was 12 years old, with Butler Te Koeti.

'We were in at Douglas Rock hut and the conditions must have been right. Butler suggested we go over the Copland. We left very early in the morning, crossed the pass and went down to the Hooker valley, recrossed the pass back to Douglas Rock and down to Welcome Flat late in the evening where our horses were waiting. We rode back in the dark to Bruce Bay, arriving about 2am.'[17] In under 24 hours a 12-year-old boy had crossed the Copland Pass twice. The family history is full of amazing endurance feats – remembered by the old people, Mick Te Koeti, Bob and Kelly Wilson and Jack Bannister – but few have been written down.

Perhaps the most readily recalled name in Maori mountaineering is Joe Fluerty. In 1926, some entries began to appear in the Glacier Hotel visitor's book under this name; the comment 'Packing Stores'. Thus starts

* Bob died in late October 1991, shortly after proofreading and approving this article.

the illustrious guiding career of George Bannister's cousin, a larger-than-life character with a quick wit who soon became a master of step-cutting, learning much from Alec and Peter Graham. Surviving movie film footage shows the sheer brilliance of Joe's step cutting in one sequence as he cuts up a vertical ice wall. The other outstanding mountain guide of the 1930s, Jack Cox, pays tribute to Joe's skills, 'I learned the art of step cutting on the daily glacier trips, with much help from Joe Fluerty who was a master of all climbing skills.'[14]

People liked Joe Fluerty. His trips were fun, safe and comments in hut books written by his clients, record great enjoyment and fun on his trips. There is a wealth of information available on Joe Fluerty, who in his 18-year guiding career, touched the lives of so many people.

Joe started off his career by packing tins of kerosene and food to huts, glacier guiding and guided ascents of peaks like Moltke, Roon, Drummond and St Mildred, before graduating to the high peaks.

Horo Koau, later named Mt Tasman by European settlers, is a mountain of special significance to the Maori people of South Westland. It stands supreme over all the others, including Aoraki (Mt Cook) and is clearly visible from most parts of South Westland on a fine day. As a boy and young man, the view of Horo Koau became a part of Joe Fluerty's daily vista. Unlike Aoraki, which he considered tapu and once turned back close to the summit,[14] Horo Koau was a mountain he wanted to climb.

On March 10, 1932, Joe Fluerty, together with fellow guides Jack Cox and Jack Pope, did the first ascent of Mt Tasman from the West Coast side of the divide. The Christchurch *Press* of March 12, describes the climb:

'The party left the Glacier Hotel on March 8, for the Almer Hut, next day crossing over Newton Pass to the bivouac on the Pioneer ridge at the head of the Fox Glacier. On Thursday morning the party set out at 3am, crossing the Fox Glacier neve, and ascending the steep couloir between Mt Tasman and Mt Lendenfeld, and reaching the divide at Engineer's Col. From here, except when negotiating an awkward schrund below the shelter of Mt Tasman, where the party was forced out on the east face, the main north-east arete was followed for its entire length, the ridge between the shoulder and the summit being exceedingly narrow. On the descent the party deviated from its route at Engineers Col and made the complete traverse of Mt Lendenfeld to the bivouac … The whole climb occupied 11 hours 20 minutes.'[8]

Next year Joe played a key role in the rescue of Mark Lysons, who broke his leg on Mt Goldsmith.[14] In the one day, Joe helped carry Mark Lysons back to Almer Hut from near Teichelmann's Corner, splinted his leg in the Hut, went to Franz Josef township to get a doctor and rescue party and returned to Almer Hut the same day. The next day he helped carry Mark out to the road.

In January 1935, Joe, together with Mark Lysons, guided Molly Williams on the first traverse of Mt Haidinger, a long 21½–hour climb.[16] The following year Joe guided a Dr Bradshaw on an ascent of Lendenfeld.[8]

Apart from the numerous guided ascents achieved by Joe Fluerty, the one quality that fellow guides commented on was his uncanny navigation skills. Gar Graham, who still resides at Okarito, recalls a crossing of West Hoe Pass in 1936, with Joe and two clients: 'Joe led us over West Hoe Pass in complete white-out conditions and with an unerringly accurate sense of direction, led us to Chancellor Hut,' said Gar Graham.[15]

Gar also recounted the dark night that two tourists failed to turn up for dinner at the hotel, and Joe led Gar out to find them. 'Around midnight Joe discovered the cold couple sitting under a bush, off the track up near the Callery River. He had found them without using a torch and to lead the couple back he picked up a handful of glow worms, put them on his shoulder and told them to follow the lights back.

As a teenage climber I remember older mountaineers who knew Joe Fluerty, saying that he was able to smell his way to Fox or Franz out of the high mountains. Dorothy Fletcher recalls her father, Alec Graham, saying that Joe knew whether people were in the hut or not, when he was some distance away. He would tell Alec that he could smell them.[16] Jack Cox also talked of Joe's keen sense of smell and superb navigational skills.

Hundreds of quotes on Joe's humour abound, and a typical one comes from a former client of his, the Rev. Bower-Black:

'At my request, the Maori guide Joe Fluerty was assigned to us, and to say that we all liked him is a mild way of putting it. He is one of the senior guides, and has the Maori unfailing patience and good humour. He is capable and reliable, and his sturdy figure striding on ahead gave us all a feeling of confidence and security. Joe was full of mischief, and as ready as an Irishman with his tongue. "Why do you wear those pieces of cloth round your ankles," asked a rather gushing lady at one of the huts. "To keep the dust out of my eyes," retorted Joe. Whereat the boys gurgled gleefully and the lady took it in good part.'[8]

The Second World War disrupted the proud West Coast guiding tradition. Joe Fluerty enlisted, together with Mark Lysons. Joe never returned to Franz and his fellow guide Mark Lysons, with whom he shared so many memorable climbs, was killed at Monte Cassino.[16]

Meanwhile, some fifty years later after they started their apprenticeship with the mountains, Mark and Butler Te Koeti, in their early sixties at the end of the war, continued to do a lot of track work up the Copland, with Jack Bannister and Bob Wilson, both of whom still live in South Westland.[12] Arthur Graham describes a meeting with Mark Te Koeti in the Copland Valley:

'In 1948, my cousin Stephen and I had crossed the Copland Pass and were slogging our way down the Karangarua Valley towards the main south highway. Some miles from the highway we came across old Mark Te Koeti who had, at that time, a contract to upgrade the track.

Neither of us were quite sure which of the old Te Koeti brothers we were talking to and it was obvious that Mark was equally puzzled as to who we were since we had not been in the district for many years. Imagine the light in his eyes when we told him we were the sons of Peter and Alec. "You'll be wanting some tucker, lads," said Mark. "Take my horse and get down to the camp – there's some cold mutton, bread and cheese – make yourselves at home and get a brew going. I'll be along later."

Sure we were hungry and there was no denying the warm sincerity of this fine old Maori but to leave him to walk home was unthinkable.

"You'll promise to get a feed at my camp then," said Mark. We promised, and so, with handshakes all round we were on our way. The more we thought about the offer the more we disliked the idea of breaking into his hut. It was a tough decision and having finally arrived at the hut, we sat down to discuss the situation again. Yes, we must go on in otherwise Mark will be greatly offended … Mark turns up in the nick of time and we follow him into the hut. The billy is soon boiling and Steve and I do our best with the tucker and huge enamel mug of hot tea. There followed a friendly conversation, enquiries as to the health of our parents and reminiscences … '[8]

Today Jack Bannister, Bob and Kelly Wilson and Mick Te Koeti, all in their late sixties or seventies, continue to pass on the valuable knowledge of the land, mountains, rivers and sea.

A small article in the *West Coast Times*, dated September 3, 1991, shows that the Runanga Te Koeti O Turanga is still strong:

'Four generations of Wilsons, a well known Westland Maori family gathered at Jacobs River last weekend for a double christening ceremony in the old church there. There was standing room only in the old church where 64 people gathered to witness the christening …'

Ka pu te ruha, ka hao te rangatahi

A new generation takes the place of the old.

Sources

1 Gerhard Mueller, *My Dear Bannie.*
2 Philip Temple, *New Zealand Explorers.*
3 A.A. Pullar, *Wilderness Days in Bruce Bay.*
4 Keri Hulme of Okarito, personal conversation.
5 Barry Brailsford, *Greenstone Trails.*
6 E.A. Fitzgerald, *Climbs in the New Zealand Alps.*
7 John Pascoe, *Mr Explorer Douglas.*
8 Trish McCormack, *Maori in Westland.*
9 Alec Graham & Jim Wilson, *Uncle Alec and the Grahams of Franz Josef.*
10 Peter Graham, *Mountain Guide.*
11 Jim Wilson, *Aorangi.*
12 Jack Bannister, personal conversation.
13 *NZAC Journal.*
14 Jack Cox, personal conversation.
15 Gar Graham, personal conversation.
16 Dorothy Fletcher, personal conversation.
17 Bob Wilson, personal conversation.

RHIAN GALLAGHER

from *Freda du Faur: Southern Alps 1909–1913*

Guides

They were your interpreters of path
in that high terrain – you slept with them
as ice clawed on the canvas of the bivouac,
men-pillows – they had your back covered.

Peter, Alex, Darby – you could afford
the best guides in the country;
on the great divide of class and sex
immersed in the adversity

till so far out of range of society
that transaction changed
– they roped their lives to yours
and yours to theirs.

△ △ △

Peter's steady lead
climb by climb
pushing out your reach

not to waste the summit
on a race – mere fame
of being first

but versed
by each new challenge
take Aoraki's measure

when you're ready
fully fledged, the prize
is the ascent – the tough,
the wings of pleasure.

△ △ △

… wielding axes to ice in a marathon
the arête to the summit
razored, the flight of their steps
you followed, a strength
to your steadfast – you matched them!

The Frozen Dark

You lie awake, rehearse the route,
ghost yourself into the scene
fired up yet suspended

whatever you anticipate
by 2am at 7000ft
it's like the world has ended

△ △ △

crawling from the bivouac:
solid frozen snow, the dark
no map could show

Peter holds a candle to it
the flame staggers; if I could see you
as the far stars see you

a fragile halo, the coursing cold
dragging limb by limb,
a heavy undertow and nothing

to generate against it
except yourself –
by candlelight you go

within this gravity
'keep
        moving
just   keep
    moving.'

Ridge

You leave behind
miles of tedious moraine,
melt water streams
become an echo

the grassy meadow
where your senses swam,
that last night's repose
rugged up to watch the evening glow.

Beyond a day-walk's distance
open and exposed,
in reach of upper atmosphere
the valley far below

fleeting fame you leave
either side is air
it's barely earth, a sill
upon the brink

you leave behind a self
become more of yourself
by vanishing
in a concentrated
narrowing

the heart
of the climb begins.

Summit

Whatever lay in wait –
doubt, fear, haunt of failure
– you'd risk yourself to answer it

pushing through the dark;
the limits placed on you – a cage,
a sort of corset of the mind

broke

you went up like a bird
dazzled and amazed
was this the summit? Look

the gods themselves
were lighting up the peaks, the morning
leapt with panoramic reach.

No woman could, it had been said,
you did! North, south, east, west
'this wide world was limitless'.

FREDA DU FAUR

from *The Conquest of Mount Cook and Other Climbs: An account of four seasons' mountaineering on the Southern Alps of New Zealand*

First Traverse of Mount Sefton (1913)

We just walked on to the actual summit and off again – it was too bitterly exposed for human beings. Mists were driving round us, being blown apart now and again, and disclosing great banks of white cloud racing before the gale over the low passes, and hurling themselves against the defying walls of the high peaks. The cloud level was at about 8,000 feet, and out of it towered the summit of Mount Cook like a giant rising from a sea of foam. We managed to take four photographs, and then hastily descended. It caused us a great regret not to follow the ridge from the saddle to the lower peak, which is still virgin; but the weather was so bad we dared not spare the time, knowing the long descent ahead of us. As things turned out we were wise; if we had persisted and been an hour later, we would probably never have returned. From the saddle we followed our footsteps back for half an hour, then turned sharply to the left, and descended a steep snow slope to the brink of the large crevasse that cuts across the western face. The mists rose and fell, giving us an opportunity of discovering a route. Thomson led, as he had been up this face of the peak the previous year. Graham had never been on it before. The crevasse was broad, and we had great difficulty in finding a crossing-place, but at last managed to jump it, and followed the lower lip for some distance. It was a wonderful sight. The crevasse shelved backward, forming an overhanging cave. From its roof hung great icicles of every conceivable size and form. Some joined the floor and formed beautiful pillars, which, catching stray gleams of sunshine through the fog, sparkled like diamonds and flashed with rainbow tints.

We paused in the shelter of the cave to drink tea and eat wine biscuits, at the same time anxiously scanning our surroundings through the shifting fog. The slopes were terribly broken with crevasses, and did not present an alluring prospect for the descent. We wished to reach the western rock arête which overhangs the Copland Valley, and follow the ridge along until we came to a pass leading down into a large snow basin. This snow

basin leads to a rock ridge and steep grass slopes, by which it is possible to descend into the valley. Everywhere else are precipitous cliffs down which it is impossible to climb. We could see one very bad break in the ridge. Fearing it might be impossible to negotiate, the guides decided to skirt away to the left and try to join the ridge beyond the break. We set off and spent an exciting hour circumventing crevasses and broken ice. The weather was getting worse, and the gaps in the fog less frequent. We turned to the right and sought a way on to the ridge. We could only see a few yards ahead; in vain we waited for the fog to lift and give us a chance of finding out where we were. It settled down like a blanket, obscuring everything. We toiled on and on till suddenly a peak reared itself up in front of us. It loomed dimly through the fog, and seemed to pierce the heavens, its ridge uninvitingly sharp and narrow. We paused for a consultation. Thomson was hopelessly puzzled, saying there was no peak like this on the ridge. Should we climb it or retrace our steps? They decided we must climb it, as we could not be far enough on the ridge for the pass we were seeking. We climbed up it; the ridge was so narrow we walked with a foot on either side. Fortunately the snow was good and soft. Never have I known anything so eerie as that phantom peak looming above us, and below us nothing but a void of shifting mists. Quite suddenly we came to the summit; its height had been deceiving owing to the fog. We descended to a flat bit of ridge, then up again gradually, the ridge vanishing ahead of us in the fog. With every yard the guides grew more and more puzzled, less certain where we could be, or what to do. Suddenly another peak loomed up in front of us worse-looking than the first. We stopped and decided to descend to the left and follow round it. The mist turned to snow, falling in big flakes. Desperately we wandered on till we were brought up short on the edge of an uncrossable crevasse. We all looked at one another helplessly and sat down on the snow to think it over. I suggested tea and food, and we all ate a little.

The men's faces were grave, and I could see they were beginning to be greatly disturbed. It was 4.30 p.m., and we had been wandering about not knowing where we were for the last two hours. Unless we could shortly find the pass we must make up or minds to a night out in the snow. We were wet through, and there was not a protecting rock or ice cave anywhere. Under such conditions our chances of surviving the night were small, and even if we survived one night there was no reason to believe the following day

would be fine; and if it were not we were worse off than ever. We retraced our steps to the flat bit of the ridge near the first peak. It sloped away gradually into the mists on the Copland side. They were sure it was not the pass, but it seemed our best hope; so we descended there, keeping always to the left in the hope of finding the right pass. The descent was easy. It led us under the rocks of the arête and followed along beside them. Suddenly we heard far away beyond us the roaring of a torrent. We paused to listen, and the guides declared it must be Scott's Creek. If so, we were not so very far out of our way. Broken ice loomed up ahead of us. There was no way of getting round it, so into it we went. It had been a day of adventures and surprises, and this broken ice was the finishing touch. We really performed some strange feats in our passage through it. The snow turned to rain as we began to get lower, and at last through the drizzle we distinguished a big snow-field to the left of us. Thomson let out a shout of joy on recognizing it as the one we were looking for, and, immensely relieved, we hurried towards it. Crossing it we kept along the ridge, almost running in our excitement and relief. Another shout announced the site of last year's bivouac. We were safe as far as knowing where we were, but it was 6 p.m. on a wet evening, and we had thousands of feet to descend to the valley through very rough country. This was no easy task in daylight, and in the dark we might easily come to grief. On we raced along the ridge, but when we came to the steep grass slopes, soaked and slippery with snow and rain, we had to slow down and descend them with the utmost care. More than once the rope saved one of us from a nasty fall; it took us an hour to descend them. Then Thomson made a traverse into some scrub, through which we had a desperate battle; the bushes closed over our heads, and creepers and roots tripped up our feet. We emerged into a steep stony creek-bed scratched and breathless. We followed the creek-bed down, climbing over wet rocks and slipping into pools and waterfalls; we were soon soaked through, and plastered with mud. The last 100 feet of the creek were very bad, and we congratulated ourselves that we got down them in the last gleams of daylight. Darkness overtook us at the junction of our creek and another that flowed on to the Copland River. It was 8 p.m., and we paused to light our lanterns. We stood beside a raging mountain torrent, swollen with rain and melting snow, flashing white in fierce rapids over great boulders, or green in deep pools.

I think the next two hours were the most extraordinary in our eventful day. We followed that creek by the fitful light of two candle-lanterns,

sometimes jumping from one slippery boulder to another, sometimes wading waist-deep in the icy water. When the rapids were too strong, or the water too deep, we struggled along the bank, pushing our way through the dense scrub. We slid down rocks into unknown depths of bushes, falling over decayed trunks and creepers, and crawling through dense undergrowth. Now and again the swish of a wet bush would put out our lights, and we would grope in the dark for ten minutes before we could re-light them. I found if I did not get my weight on the bent shrub before the leader removed his, they sprang back in my face and the leader and lantern were lost to view. It was a weird and wonderful progress. I was worked up to such a pitch I did not feel tired or know the meaning of fear. I seemed to be standing aside and calmly watching someone else do extraordinary things as a matter of course. Once when we took to what we thought was the bank to avoid a rapid, the lantern went out at a critical moment; when I was re-lighted we found ourselves standing on the tough out-growing branches of a tree overhanging the river, with nothing but space between us and the rapids we were so anxious to avoid. We took it quite calmly, and scrambled back on to the bank. We were all past surprise, and concluded Fate would see us through unharmed. At last we came to the junction of the creek with the Copland River, and groped about in the bush until we found the track. In ten minutes we were at the road men's camp.

DOROTHY THEOMIN

Letter describing a five-day camping trip from Fox Glacier to Franz Josef Glacier, 1926

My dear Family

Since I sent my wire saying we were going camping to the Fox, I've had one of the most wonderful and delightful experiences of my life. Alex and young Dave Graham, his nephew, took me for a five day trip, starting from here to Weheka by motor, in itself a sufficiently thrilling experience and ending up by going to the Head of the Fox and crossing a Pass to the Franz Josef. We left here last Thursday and camped 1½ miles up the Fox. The men carried a tent and fly, three blankets, and masses of food. To give you an indication of how much, the bread supply was 3½ whole loaves! 18 eggs, 2lbs prunes – tea unlimited, and sugar, which towards the end got rather scarce. Our first camp was on the moraine of the Glacier as nowhere else would have been safe if it had rained. A roaring fire just below the camp kept us out of 'bed' until ten o'clock on a beautiful moonlight night. Next day we went on to a high camp at about 4,500 ft on Chancellor Ridge, a divine place well worth the struggle up steep creek bed and scrub. The view of the huge mountains and also bush, river-bed and ocean is gloriously beautiful and of course one is right on top of an enormous glacier, larger than the Franz Josef. Have just had an interval for afternoon tea with the Alex and as there is peace in the room, will proceed with my narrative as Kipling says. Next day was not a very strenuous one, as the following day's journey had to be long. We went to the top of Chancellor Ridge and sat there for hours taking in the glorious view. One seems to be quite close to Tasman and Cook and all the main peaks there, as well as many a beautiful one which lie entirely in Westland. Our last actual camp in the tent was only about 3 or 400 ft lower than the top of the Ridge, to enable us to get away before daylight next morning. It was glorious – high up in the world with a wonderful misty sunset showing over the sea and brilliant moonlight as soon as the sun went down. We struck camp and left by candlelight about 5.30 next morning and saw the magnificent sunrise from the top of the Ridge. If my many photos turn out well, you will understand all my ecstasies much more clearly. From the Ridge we dropped down

over a few rocks into the Fox névé and from then on travelled on various sorts of snow, hard, soft and middling (!) until we came under Newton's Pass over and through which we crossed to the Franz Josef snowfields. Followed the latter for hours in gorgeous weather and scenery until finally we joined up with the Graham Saddle route and so in an hour or so to the Almer Bivouac. The latter felt quite like home though rather a poor substitute for Olveston! Two cups of cocoa were very cheering – though really I was very little tired, so little that when Alex asked what I'd like to do the next day – I voted for staying up and climbing something at the head of the Glacier. We didn't really do that as we left the Bivvy too late in the morning – went instead right onto the head of the Spencer Glacier under Elie de Beaumont and then climbed a tiny snow peak which gave me the shivers it was so steep! The day was even more wonderful than the previous ones and we sat for hours in the sun, going back to the Almer by a different route – Ten hours out that day, only about six of which were energetic, and 11½ hours the day before, mostly fairly solid going – what Alex calls the longest snow-walk in N.Z. On Tuesday we came through from the Almer. One cannot come through the Glacier to Defiance, as it is too broken up, so instead take the same steep grass and rock slope as Peter took us up two years ago, landing out on the North bank of the Glacier opposite Defiance. We went across to the latter, all in pouring rain, had some good hot tea and bread and jam and then through the Ice-fall to Waiho thus ending one of my greatest experiences. The whole thing was so lovely and new to me – I've never before had a camping trip of the kind, Alex hadn't been that way for many years and then only once before through from the Fox to the Franz Josef, and to Davy and me the whole thing was new. One never really knows the Grahams properly till one is out with them on long trips and it was a great joy having Alex out again, as he has not done anything for some years, and was just like a baby with a new toy! Yesterday it just teemed and the telephone wire was down between here and Ross, so my wire didn't get away until today.

Ever your loving
Dorothy

DOREEN PICKENS

Karangarua–Landsborough

South Westland – blue bush, blue cliffs, ragged ridges, and rushing torrents; a land of sharply interlocking spurs, deep gorges, and, above all, a land of shadows; tree shadows, mountain shadows, and the ever-present shadows of clouds.

We went up the Regina Creek, and the going was as rough as we had been told it would be. Large boulders and always the entangling bush. But ahead was Mt. Glorious, with glaciers to lift our eyes to as we emerged from tunnels of greenness. Of evenings the sunsets were deep with haze, and at night the stars were held away by mist nets looped to the ridges.

After two days we stood where we could look back and ahead. Back down the deep valleys and ahead to vast neves and new mountains. Mountains as strangely shaped as the precipices which support fairy-tale castles, unreal with pinnacle and leaping sharply. Mountains fluted and fragile with ice. Mountains friendly with long ridges and snowfields.

Swinging files of torpedo clouds nudged us to the valley. A night of stillness and a morning of great heat beside the Horace Walker; then the joy of swinging freely across river flats and the monotony of moraine.

How truly A.P. Harper has written of the wonders of the Douglas! As we lay under Harper Rock we thought of him seeing, framed by the stone and tussock, the same view of cliff, ice wall and peak. The avalanches would vibrate as loudly and the stream outside move as noisily.

We tried to race the clouds over Fyfe Pass. The clouds won, and we used wind and sleet to enforce our retreat from the slabs where we balanced above 7,000 feet. Back to the desolation of the Spence with frozen ropes and suddenly heavy packs.

Then the Landsborough. One night we camped on a tussock flat where wineberry trees showed pale against the beech. Above the shingle and the swirling waters, green spurs went up to plateaus white and sweeping as seagulls' wings. During our three days in the river we saw many scenes of equal beauty. The weariness of long packing days is soon forgotten, for, as Renoir has said, 'Pain passes – beauty remains.'

LAURENCE FEARNLEY

from *The Hut Builder*

It was dark when we left the camp next morning. Light from our torches created a fragmented path that we followed, one behind the other. Hillary put Harry at the front, with me in the middle between the two of them. I was groggy from lack of sleep. As I stepped carefully into the shallow prints left by Harry's boots I dipped in and out of the conversation that was playing between my two companions, the words bouncing back and forth above my head. I almost had the impression that they had forgotten about me entirely. I heard Harry mumble something about the perfect conditions. It was the second or third time he had mentioned the weather and the snow. The first time had been shortly after our alarm went off and he slipped out of the cave to look. Part of me had hoped the report would not be good, and that I would be allowed to slip back into sleep. I was just stretching out my legs, enjoying the warmth of my sleeping bag, when Harry returned to deliver his verdict in dry tones: 'Wind's from the east; three days at least.'

The rhyme stayed with me as I laced my boots, struggled with a pair of crampons and shouldered my pack, and now, as I walked behind Harry the words created a restful background sound, helping me along one steady step at a time. *Wind's from the east. Three days at least.* The words still in my head, I took in enough of the climbers' conversation to realise that Harry had climbed Cook less than a month before, that this was his second trip up the mountain that year and that he expected the climb to be straightforward. His authority gave me a confidence and I began to believe that I really was in the company of the 'greatest climber or our age', as I had heard Wim refer to Harry the day before. I began to relax, enjoying the waltz-like three-step – my ice-axe, right foot, left foot – as we sidled across the snow slope.

I had only once walked in crampons before and I was impressed by the difference they made on the ice. Although I occasionally miscalculated the increased length of my boot and tripped over my toes, each step felt solid by comparison to the step-slip of boots alone. The sound of the sharp points slicing through the frozen surface was pleasing, bringing to mind

the sensation of biting into a new season's apple. Even the snow itself, its texture and colour, became apple-like in my mind and I spent a happy twenty minutes or so imagining myself as some tiny creature, an ant maybe, traversing up a peeled Granny Smith, arriving at the summit to find a single tree-like stem under which to sit and rest.

In this dreamy state it took me a while to notice that Hillary was asking Harry about an accident that had taken place on Cook the day of Harry's most recent ascent. I had not been paying enough attention to catch the names of the men involved but it was clear that three of them had met their death somewhere on the mountain. From what I could gather, Harry had been resting on the summit when he had heard voices calling back and forth, sometimes loud, sometimes muffled, far below him. It was not until he returned to the hut and made radio contact with the Hermitage later that evening that he learned about the accident and realised that the voices belonged to members of the search party. I was surprised by how easily the words 'met his death' edged into my thoughts, knocking my homely apple image from its branch. Firmly lodged in my head, the phrase now began to niggle away at me. In my mind I saw myself slip and imagined the speed I would travel, first sliding and then tumbling over the snow, bouncing like a tyre rolling down a slope before hitting a rock and soaring up into the sky, then falling again, landing with a thud, bleeding and broken at the bottom. *Met his death, Granny Smith, Three days at least, Wind's from the east*. Words jumbled in my brain, keeping pace with me as I fixed my eyes on Harry's boots, snatching up each of his snowprints the moment they became free.

We had not yet gone far and I decided I could suggest turning back if I spoke up soon. It would be easy to feign illness – a stomach bug – and retreat to safety. I was certain my climbing companions would not miss me; they would most likely be happy to be rid of the burden. I was on the verge of opening my mouth, when, from behind me, I heard Hillary ask, 'How's it going there? Enjoying yourself?' It was the perfect opportunity to mention my upset stomach, my sore shoulder or whatever other aliment was available to me. Instead, I answered, 'I'm fine. It's not as hard as I thought.'

I heard Hillary respond that things would 'liven up a little' once we got further up and I heard myself reply with a confident, 'Fine. Good.'

With the ice shelf above us the terrain steepened and Harry began to cut steps into the snow using the adze of his ice-axe. At times the axe dislodged sizeable blocks of snow, creating a complete step with one blow, but more

often than not the surface splintered, sending fragments of ice flying into the sky, showering us in frozen dust. As I stood still, waiting to step forward, I kept my eyes on the shadowy bulk of Harry's back, its darkness creating the impression of a deep hole, while around it, halo like, shards of ice glistened in the torchlight and sparkled, diamond gold.

As Harry worked I began to feel the cold of inactivity. It was shivery, standing still while he cut his steps or placed an anchor for a belay, and I bounced gently on my feet trying to get the circulation going. The straps from my crampons were pulled tight across my feet and I could feel my toes beginning to grow numb – not enough to warrant loosening the straps but enough to make me try hard to wiggle my toes, scrunching them up inside my heavy wool socks. Meanwhile Harry grumbled about being too hot. Steam formed around his neck like a collar and he appeared somewhat ghost-like, a match for Coleridge's Ancient Mariner. Every now and then Hillary would urge Harry on, jokingly instructing him to make a good show of it, to which Harry would retort with some remark about his pay not being high enough to warrant so much work. The good-natured banter took my mind off the steepness of the slope we were standing on. I imagined Walter back at work on the hut, fixing the last of the cables to the shelter, ensuring that it would not blow away in the first major storm. Around us the air was still, and I noticed that even though I had been working quite comfortably at 8000 feet over the past few weeks I was now short of breath and panting.

'It will start getting a bit lighter soon.' As he spoke Harry paused and gestured with his axe towards the sky which, though an inky blue and starlit, was seeped through with a paler greenish tinge towards the east. For a moment I simply took pleasure in looking at the sky, measuring out the stars and recalling something my father had said about the night skies above Egypt during the war. He had occasionally talked about the beauty of the desert night. Despite the cold, the sky had wrapped itself around the men and made them feel enclosed, protected. The stars, he said, were the brightest he had ever seen and had filled him with a sense of wonder. But it was not until he was returning home and had looked up one night to see the Southern Cross high above the ocean that he had felt at peace. 'That was my homecoming,' he told me. 'The sight of the Southern Cross.'

The climbing was steeper now, and as we climbed higher the snow became harder, broken up by large areas of hard ice. My crampons, which

up to this point had cut into the surface, began to skitter every now and then in an alarming manner, forcing me to concentrate more fully on how I placed my feet. Once my foot slipped from under me and I fell to my knees, my hands gripping my ice-axe in fear as I tried to regain my footing. The fact that I was tied on to a rope did little to alleviate my anxiety. Harry was unimpressed. 'You don't go on your knees unless you're praying,' he scolded. 'And there's no point praying – that won't help you.' He was half joking but I made a concerted effort to be even more careful. Part of my worry stemmed from the knowledge that if I slipped I might knock Hillary off his feet too. For the most part he was not directly below me but I could imagine the headlines. 'Bumbling Butcher Sends Himalayan Hero Hurtling.' That – and the shame I would cause my father – was enough to scare me half to death. I don't know about going down on my knees but I do have a vague memory of praying.

It was only when Harry drew my attention to the sunrise that I was able to put an end to the headlines that circulated through my brain. We had reached Porter's Col and were shortly to begin following an icy ridge towards the Middle Peak of Cook. We had been travelling for over four hours and, at Hillary's suggestion, we stopped for a short break.

Sitting in a scoop in the lee of the ridge we sipped from our bottles, quietly taking in the view. Straight across the valley La Perouse rose up in front of us, a flattened dome like an old-fashioned beehive. In the clear morning air, scale and distance were distorted, and the features of the mountain appeared simultaneously monumental and detailed, as if magnified under a lens. At times I wasn't sure if I was looking at a real mountain or simply a table-top-sized model of one. Hillary and Harry began to talk quietly and I became aware of the faint smell of tobacco as smoke from Harry's cigarette puffed over my head.

The first rays of sun touched the peaks and ridges and the sky was suddenly drenched in salmon pink. As far as the eye could see, the tops were bathed in warm skin tones whereas on the snow slopes and cliff faces beneath us everything was slate-black. It was as if two separate worlds existed: our world of light and at our feet a world of shadow and mystery. How can I explain the effect of climbing up out of darkness and into the light? It filled me with the joy of life. I was glad I was not alone. My companions, although speaking little and giving no outward sign of being moved by their surroundings, must nevertheless have had a similar

reaction. I couldn't believe that anyone – not even a man who had climbed the highest mountain in the world – could ever grow blasé about being, simply, in the mountains.

Given my excitement, I was restless to be off and stood up before the others, willing them to hurry, but my childish attempt came to nothing. Harry sat peacefully, ignoring my shuffling as he drew on his cigarette, inhaling deeply and then blowing out a steady stream of blue smoke. Hillary picked raisins from a small bag of scroggin, pushing to one side any monkey-nuts and remarking absentmindedly that he wished he could get a cup of tea.

Eventually, Harry's cigarette stub flicked to one side, we recommenced our journey, following the ridgeline which, in places, was steep and icy. As I trailed behind Harry, grateful for the rope between us, I thought of nothing apart from putting one foot in front of the other, climbing one step at a time. I was aware of the cool breeze against my face, the glare of the ice, the sound of my breath, but my mind was remarkably calm, clear of thought. If anything, I was in a kind of trance, and when Harry paused to rearrange the straps of his pack I practically bumped into him. I was vaguely startled when I looked up. The act of climbing had disconnected me so completely from my surroundings that I could barely believe how high we had come. The sensation of height was intensified when I glanced over my shoulder and was amazed to see the Low Peak of Cook beneath us. Mount Sefton, the massive, heavy-set sentinel I had sat looking up at from my seat on Foliage Hill, now appeared at eye level, but no less of a mountain for that.

As we continued up towards the Middle Peak I began to experience problems with my crampons. The fault was not in my crampons as such, but rather in my lack of skill in using them. The ridge was increasingly steep and icy in places and on several occasions I had to kick my boot into the ice, taking my full weight on the front points of my crampons. This development unnerved me. It was one thing to have one's feet planted squarely on the ground, but to be clawing one's way up a steep mountain was terrifying. I became so tense that the peacefulness of the previous few hours left me and I found myself talking aloud, telling myself to focus, to remain calm, to pay attention. Although belayed on a real rope by Harry, the words I intoned to myself became the safety rope onto which I clung, hoping not to fall.

And then, suddenly, we were standing on the Middle Peak.

I heard Harry joke, 'You can look now,' and it was true, I could. But there was so much to see. There was just so much to see. I did a complete turn, trying to take in everything at once, and then I was shaking hands with Harry and Hillary, pumping their arms up and down, burbling my thanks as they surveyed me in bemused silence. 'Look at it!' I gushed, making a sweeping motion with my outstretched hand. 'Who would have thought? You can see for miles!' I turned around in a full circle. 'You can see the entire country.' Although far from true, I did not feel that my last remark was an exaggeration. It truly seemed as if the whole country was laid out below me, as if I had risen above the land and was hovering in a place that might as well have been called 'Above and Beyond'.

Afraid of missing something – some important landmark – I scanned the valleys, settling on the glaciers of the Tasman and the Hooker and following them down, marking each transition – from green-white ice, to moraine, to blue-grey river. In time even the river became a shimmering lake and then, far away, beyond the yellow-brown plains, my eyes searched out a paler blue haze – the east coast and the sea itself. The Pacific Ocean. I turned away, lowered my eyes to the snow at my feet and then faced southwest, and there, close by, below the dark, bush-clad hills was the Tasman Sea, a long ribbon of surf defining the coast.

Despite – or perhaps because of – my great elevation, I was conscious of standing on a ribbon of land defined either side by a vast, limitless ocean. I was so small by comparison – a speck poised on this marginal strip of land. And, apart from my fellow climbers and a few companions back at the hut, no one in the world knew where I was. The fact that I could see so much – and could even make out roughly where my house should be – while being invisible to anyone looking my way, was both thrilling and frightening. Except in the minds of a few people, I really didn't exist.

A pale puff of smoke floated past me and I breathed deeply, filling my lungs with tobacco, a smell I found reassuringly human. I could hear Harry and Hillary talking quietly behind me but I didn't join in. I stood with my arms folded across my chest and soon I was barely conscious of thinking at all. An immense calm enveloped me. Everything that had happened in my life, everything that might be important in the future ceased to matter. I looked down at the hut far below and I thought I could make out the figures of my companions, black dots against the white snow. For several minutes I watched them and then raised my eyes to the high, sun-sparkling

peaks, and deep within my heart I felt a great surge of gratitude. To be standing on this mountain, on this narrow strip of land, was my good fortune. And if I couldn't preserve this day, I could at least honour it. Quietly, I gave thanks.

RANGI FAITH

Cushioning the Blow

Ask any tramper,
or read the explorer's diary
where he says

for a good night's sleep
you'll need to find the place

where your hip
fits into the earth

at a comfortable angle
that will take time –

like positioning & repositioning
a piece in a jigsaw –

if it fits, it fits,

don't make it –

the earth doesn't give up
that easily.

DORA DE BEER

from *Yunnan 1938: Account of a journey in south-west China*

In 1938 travelling abroad on an extensive scale was still possible for the unprivileged private individual. He was not fenced about with endless restrictions, he could transfer money from one country to another without first obtaining the consent of the Bank of England, visas for foreign countries were readily granted, and he could book a passage on an ocean liner nearly as easily as he could buy a railway ticket from London to Glasgow.

It was then that I had the good fortune to be one of a party of six mountaineers who went from Burma into China. For five months we travelled and camped in Yunnan, our objective to discover a route up the highest peak of the Yulung Shan, or Satseto, the Snowy Mountain of Li-kiang. That was the ostensible reason, but for me any objective would have done equally well.

We began the journey at Myitkyina, the railhead in Burma, with a mule caravan. Sometimes we were on the Burma Road, at that time unfinished and rather mysterious, and sometimes on the centuries-old mule tracks. Our route crossed some of the greatest rivers of Asia, the Irrawaddy, the Salween, the Mekong, and passed through the towns of Teng-yueh, Hsia-kwan, Tali-fu, until it brought us to Li-kiang, a city of little rushing streams situated in the great loop the Yangtze makes when it leaves Tibet. Our objective, the mountain massif of the Yulung Shan, also called Satseto, rises about ten miles' distance from the city. Davies mapped but did not measure it. He estimated the height to be about 20,000 feet, for various reasons we thought this too low.

We did nothing especially remarkable, we had neither thrilling adventures nor hairbreadth escapes; for the greater part of the way we followed the old track, used by trading caravans in the time of Marco Polo, and not new then. Provided we did not stray far afield, it would have been difficult to lose ourselves, there are neither puzzling cross-roads nor wheeled traffic to confuse the traveller on these lonely narrow paths.

We took forty-two days, of which, however, only twenty-nine were travelling days, from Myitkyina to Li-kiang, and covered over 400 miles.

It is because such journeys now perhaps belong to a nostalgic past, that I think ours may be worth recording, for who knows when, if ever, they will again be possible?

Aeroplanes and motor cars undoubtedly save time but one learns far more about a country if one goes on foot or on horseback, and what a mule caravan lacks in comfort, it makes up in interest. None of our party knew the East, and we suffered in many ways from our ignorance. However, in spite of all the difficulties and discomforts – which were at times considerable – it was an enjoyable journey.

(Sometimes I would wander along, gazing around, and thinking exultantly 'I am actually here, in China. That is the Salween, or the Mekong, or the Yangtze.' The very names were enough to stir the imagination.)

Five of our party of six met in Rangoon on 2 August 1938. Kurt Suter, the remaining member, had arrived a fortnight earlier and gone on to Myitkyina to engage an interpreter, a cook, and two other servants. Our leader was Miss Marie Byles, a lawyer from Sydney, and a very enterprising traveller. Some years earlier she had heard of a mountain – an unclimbed mountain – on the marches of Yunnan and Tibet, and had been filled with desire to attempt the ascent. She began planning and working to collect information, and slowly her plans took shape.

Miss Marjorie Edgar Jones was from the South Island of New Zealand. She had a fine climbing record and though small and slight possessed remarkable endurance, also a useful knowledge of animals and plants. She spent many hours collecting and drying seeds and her enthusiasm inspired me to follow suit.

Mick Bowie and Kurt Suter were professional guides. Mick Bowie was a New Zealander and for many years after the war head guide at the Hermitage, Mt. Cook. Kurt Suter was a Swiss, who had worked as a guide at the Hermitage for some years. He and Mick were old friends and made a grand pair. They were not only skilled mountaineers, they were also capable and experienced campers.

Fraser Radcliff was a young Australian. He had done little climbing but was keen and eager to see and do as much as possible.

I was 47, the oldest of the party, and had climbed in both Europe and New Zealand, my home until 1931. I first met Marie Byles under the Douglas Rock, the old bivouac on the west side of the Copland Pass (Mt. Cook) now replaced by a hut of the same name. She was camped there

with her two guides, Alf Brustaad and Arne Larsen – Norwegians who had originally come to New Zealand as ski-instructors. They were resting after an unsuccessful attempt to climb Sefton, an attempt which Marie describes in her book *By Cargo Boat and Mountain*.

On this occasion I was far from fit, I had arrived too recently from Europe, and one day at the Hermitage after four weeks at sea was not sufficient to get me into training. It was a hot nor'west day, tiring at any time, doubly so to me. We were a large party all crossing to the West Coast. We had followed the usual programme, leaving the Hermitage one day and sleeping at the Hooker Hut, close beneath the steep climb to the Copland Pass. We left the hut early and were over the Pass in fairly good time. Just below the steep rocks on the west side we halted at the Luncheon Rock and made tea. Cups are kept there but we were such a large party that there were not enough to go round, and I think no one had a thirst-quenching amount to drink. I disgraced myself by sampling every watercourse, even so I arrived at the Douglas Rock thirsty and almost exhausted, crawled under the overhanging rock into welcome shade, and gradually revived as kind Alf gave me cup after cup of tea.

I met Marie several years later in Sydney. She was already making plans for her Chinese expedition and told me enough about it to make me very interested. Then in 1937 she wrote inviting me to join her party. My home was now in London and when I accepted she asked me to look after a good deal of the equipment. I found it a difficult business and doubt if I could have done it without the help of experienced Himalayan climbers, such as Eric Shipton, and alpine specialists, in particular Robert Lawrie. However, when two outfits for porters were wanted we were all at sea. No one had any idea of the size; the result was two under-sized men in two outsize windproof suits, with boots so much too long it was a wonder they could walk in them, much less climb, but they loved them. I also bought a number of extra pairs of thick woollen socks which we gave to any of our men who were going high. One day a Tibetan who worked for us was given a pair, which he was about to pull on at once, until stopped by an outcry from the others, who surprised us by protesting that his feet were too dirty he must wash them first.

I am going too fast, I must return to Rangoon, which we found hot and tiring. This was hardly strange, as we did an enormous amount in the 3½ days we were there. Serious riots in which Burmese had attacked

Indians had taken place just before we landed and Rangoon was in a queer unpleasantly tense state, with armed police patrolling the streets and many shops and businesses closed for fear of further disturbances. This meant we had to buy some of our equipment at the more expensive European shops (and Rangoon was not cheap) instead of in the Indian bazaar, for though I had bought tents, boots, ice-axes, alpine rope, pitons, Bovril pemmican, a pressure cooker, etc., in London there were still a number of things we needed, including camp-beds, lanterns, mosquito-nets, to mention only a few. There was some discussion about camp-beds, I was firm that I intended to have one, Marie thought it an unnecessary luxury, until I pointed out that it saved one not so much from lying on the hard ground as from lying on a dirty floor, a very different matter. We did not take any folding chairs, rather a pity, as the extra comfort would have been worth the cost of another mule load. There is nothing gained by courting hardships that can be avoided; in fact they can lessen one's powers of resistance to cold and fatigue. Also we had not a good lamp, only stable lanterns, which are handy but do not give sufficiently good light for reading or sewing. However, one learns by experience, and after all, these were not essentials.

As well as shopping we had to arrange about money. This involved several lengthy visits both to the private house of a Chinese merchant and then to the business office of his firm. Marie had been advised that the best plan was to buy drafts from Rangoon merchants which their partners in Teng-yueh and Hsia-kwan would cash for us. We did this but in China we found that cheques on the Hong Kong and Shanghai Banking Corporation were readily accepted. Early travellers write of the inconvenience of carrying heavy silver currency; we never used silver or copper, always paper, and used to conceal large packets of banknotes in our luggage. The favoured notes varied, sometimes those issued by one bank were more popular than those issued by another. It was all puzzling and complicated, and counting large bundles of grimy notes – often of infinitesimal value – was tiresome, one so rarely got the same total twice!

Marie, Marjorie, Mick, and Fraser landed on Tuesday, 2 August, and somehow in the 3½ days between then and Friday, the 5th, we managed to complete all the necessary shopping and visit both the Chinese Consul and Mr. Lawson, the Commissioner of Police. He and his wife made time, in spite of the unsettled state of Rangoon, to look after us in many ways.

They gave us much wise counsel, including advice on the treatment of bites by snakes and scorpions, of malaria, of dysentery. The instructions for the correct treatment of malaria were alarming, how could we follow them if we were on the march? Fortunately no one contracted it, if one of us had, I don't like to think of the consequences. It was the rainy season, and they impressed upon us that we must take every precaution against being bitten by mosquitoes.

Friday afternoon was a hectic scramble until we climbed into the train at 4 o'clock. After rushing about in the damp heat it was a great relief to be able to sit quietly and relax. Saturday morning early the train halted for an hour at Mandalay and we motored round sight-seeing in the clear morning light. The wide moat was attractive, also the flights upon flights of steps with pagoda-like roofs that climbed the steep hillside to the temples. We had all that day and another night in the train and arrived at Myitkyina at 5.30 on Sunday morning. Kurt met us at the railway station; he had a youthful interpreter with him. Soon we and our fairly considerable baggage were settled at the comfortable Circuit Bungalow.

Then followed an exhausting day spent in making arrangements with a portly Chinese mule-contractor and his elegant silk-clad Burmese lawyer, who also acted as interpreter, engaging a cook and two other servants, previously interviewed by Kurt; and ordering some rough wooden cases to be made, that could be lashed on to the pack saddles. Endless talk seemed the inevitable accompaniment to all these transactions and took up valuable time when we were longing to do some necessary repacking.

It is the preliminaries that are so irksome, once away, no matter what difficulties arise, one is free from the fuss and bother of deciding what to take and how much.

Mr. Hill, the Police Officer, to whom Mr. Lawson had given us an introduction, was away. No doubt we should have felt his absence more if Mr. Dudrow, an American Baptist missionary, had not come to our assistance with much practical advice. He and his wife were kindness itself.

By the evening most of our repacking was finished, and some of our party went to the Club to meet the local residents, but I had worked without a pause all day and was too tired. Expense was one reason for hurry. Staying at the Circuit Bungalow was fairly expensive, or we might have had a second day there. As it was we left the bungalow at 7 a.m. on Monday, thus avoiding the charge for another day. The Dudrows gave us

a delightful farewell breakfast at their friendly home. I was seated next to their young son, and we had a happy time reciting nursery rhymes to each other. Mick had unselfishly gone ahead with the baggage and was waiting on the far bank of the Irrawaddy, overseeing the loading of the mules.

We had the choice of crossing the river either in the Government launch or in a dug-out canoe. Economy made us choose the latter, and in pouring rain we paddled four miles down the wide river to Waingmaw. The canoe was a large hollowed-out tree trunk, with bamboos lashed on top of the sides. We sat on these, holding our open umbrellas. From Waingmaw we were able to drive about ten miles as far as Waa-hsawng. We went in a narrow Ford car, our last vehicular travel for months, and the first stage of the journey to Teng-yueh and Li-kiang.

EDMUND HILLARY

Letter to Jim Rose from Everest Base Camp, 2 June 1953

Dear Jim,

Well all the flurry and bustle is over, all the hard work is finished and at long last we've climbed the jolly mountain. Now Himalayan climbing can settle down into a more normal routine and the 'Everest' sense of values can be put aside. However I must admit that the whole of this expedition has been jolly good fun despite the very real dangers of the icefall and we've had a party that welded into a particularly useful and pleasant team. I think the great feature of this party is how practically every man went high and certainly all did a very useful job. It was far from the case as in previous expeditions, including the Swiss, where a couple of men did all the work.

I must admit that I haven't quite got used to the idea of climbing Everest although I had a couple of wonderful days high on the mountain. After all it is only a couple of years ago that four very ignorant New Zealanders went to Garhwal. We're all back at Base Camp now after some hair raising incidents in our final descent of the icefall and we're very thin and lacking in energy at present as we organise things to start off on our long trek to Kathmandu tomorrow. We expect to arrive at the British Embassy by June 20th. John Hunt wants me and Tenzing to fly to England with him and meet our patron the Duke of Edinburgh and attend all the official functions. As they will be paying my fare I was only too willing to agree. I expect to be back in Auckland by the middle of September.

Regarding the climb, I'll give you a brief account of the incidents leading up to it and the climb itself.

By May 19th George Lowe, Mike Ward and la Tenzing were in Camp VII at 24,000′ but the Lhotse face attack seemed to have lost its punch and little or no progress was being made towards the traverse to the South Col. However on 20th the first lift of nine Sherpas under Wilf Noyce laden for the South Col went from Camp V to Camp VII and George and his party came down without having made much progress. On the 21st we watched eagerly but only two figures (Wilf Noyce and a Sherpa) left camp VII and made their way upwards to the South Col. At the same time

Charles Wylie and another bunch of Sherpas went from V to VII. This meant that fourteen Sherpas were at Camp VII and even though Wilf had made a route to the South Col it was absolutely essential that on the 22nd the whole bunch of Sherpas should go from VII to the South Col or food would run out and the whole attack break down. John decided therefore to reluctantly send Tenzing and me up to ensure that the lift went through according to schedule. Tenzing and I went from IV to VII in 4¼ hours on the 21st and on the next day the 22nd we had our great triumph – we set off with 15 Sherpas and three Sahibs and got 14 Sherpas and all the loads to the South Col. Tenzing and I had a strenuous day having to kick and cut a good route the whole way up. Tenzing and I then returned right back to IV. This day was the turning point in the expedition. We now had the South Col stocked.

On May 24th Tom Bourdillon and Charles Evans – the closed circuit team with their support party John Hunt, Da Namgyl and Balu went from Camp VII to the South Col in very slow time in bad conditions. The following day they had to rest on the Col while Tenzing and I the open circuit team with our support party George Lowe, Alf Gregory and Pember, Ang Nima and Angpember went up to Camp VII. We also had five other Sherpas who were carrying loads to the South Col and then descending.

On the 26th we all left Camp VII and set out for the South Col. We soon saw figures on the ridge to the South summit and had a great thrill watching their progress. Tenzing and I were in good form and went on ahead to reach the South Col in 2¾ hours from Camp VII. We were in time to receive an exhausted John Hunt and Da Namgyl who had packed a tent, oxygen, food and fuel to about 27,350 ft. Meanwhile Tom and Charles went on and finally reached the South summit at 1 p.m. This was a great triumph. We doctored John Hunt and watched eagerly for the others who finally arrived back at 3.30 completely exhausted. They both had terrible tales of the ridge from the South summit to the top and even expressed the opinion that it wasn't climbable. This night was a terrible one with very strong wind and great cold. On the 27th there was no hope of us moving upwards and the best we could do was escort a very weak and exhausted party over the Col and down to the long traverse. Both Balu and Angpember had become sick and also went down. Another ghastly windy night followed but the 28th was rather improved. However we had another blow – Pember was sick leaving us only one Sherpa Ang Nima for the carry

up the ridge. We had no alternative but to carry the stuff ourselves. George Lowe, Greg and Ang Nima left at 8.45 a.m. carrying about 40lbs apiece and working on oxygen at 4 litres. Tenzing and I carrying nearly 50lbs left at 10 a.m. and followed in their tracks. George was going very well indeed and led nearly all the way up to the main ridge and the old Swiss Camp at 27,200′. This involved a good deal of step cutting in firm very steep snow. We caught up to the others on the ridge and we continued up another 150′ to 27,350′ where John had dumped his gear. We still considered this too low for a camp so decided to increase our loads and push on. I added a tent to make my load well over 60 lbs and the others had mostly about 50 lbs. The ridge was steep but the upward sloping rock strata made the climbing reasonably easy. We pushed on and on and couldn't find a spot even the slightest bit flat. After a long pull we followed Tenzing's advice and did a traverse out onto the steep face on the left and finally found a possible spot under a rock bluff. We estimated it was about 27,900ft and decided to camp so the others dumped their loads and returned to the South Col, Tenzing and I spent from 2.30 to 5.30 making a camp site large enough to pitch the tent and even then it was on two levels – I spent the whole night sitting up. Our oxygen due to the reduced lift was very short and I worked out that if we worked on the reduced flow rate of 3 litres per minute we'd have sufficient endurance for an attempt but it would be pretty fine. We also had enough oxygen for four hours sleeping at 1 litre per minute.

At 6.30 a.m. on the 29th we left our tent and set off up the ridge. We were going well but slowly. It was a magnificent morning with astounding views everywhere. Taking turns we plugged up the ridge and then reached the enormous 300ft slope leading to the South summit. This was very steep deep snow with a light crust on top and made us both very unhappy. However we persisted and finally reached the South summit at 9 a.m. We were eager for our first view of the ghastly summit ridge and I was very relieved to see that although it looked impressive it didn't look by any means impossible. On the right overhanging the Kangshung great fingers of cornices and then a steep snow slope running down to the 8,000 ft rock bluffs dropping to the Western Cwm. I was worried about oxygen endurance so got to work. I cut a trail of steps just above the rocks and made good progress often dodging larger cornices by getting onto the rocks themselves. A vertical rock patch I got up by jamming between the rock and some vertical snow on the right. A forty foot struggle and I was on top

of it and I was astonished at the energy I had. I handed Tenzing up – he wasn't going quite as well but was a good safe and sound companion. I felt now that it would take a lot to stop me and cut steadily along until a final bump loomed up and I moved up on a tight rope and was standing on top of the world. It was quite a moment. Tenzing so far forgot himself as to embrace me and I banged off a number of photographs. I collected a few stones one of which I'm keeping for you if you want it.

I was very worried by our oxygen shortage so we wasted no time in hastening back to the South Summit, down to Camp IX and finally very tired indeed down to the South Col after a tremendous day. The next day we descended to Cwm and so to Base.

Well, this is the bare story Jim. I must apologise for the dry nature of the tale but we're all rather anxious and find it hard to concentrate. We'll have plenty of opportunity for discussing it in the future around your hospitable fire.

We've just heard by radio that the Queen and Winston Churchill have sent messages of congratulations to us at Kathmandu so we are understandably excited. Also old Sid Holland has said some kind words. What a business!

Well, Jim, I must close and send this letter off tonight with the runner. I would greatly appreciate it if you could give some of these details to my Mother and to Rex if it's not asking too much. I've written short notes to them but no climbing details. Our main interest now is to reach Kathmandu and hear what's occurring.

Regards to Mrs. Rose and yourself
a somewhat confused
Ed.

DEREK CHINN

The First Clyde Ascent of Mount Everest

When I was fourteen years old I went to a talk given by Doug Scott in Christchurch about the first ascent of the South West Face of Everest. I was spellbound. Projected onto the screen was Dougal Haston silhouetted against the setting sun on the summit. I couldn't imagine really being there.

A friend was staying in my house twenty four years after that slide show, he suggested that if I really wanted to climb Everest all I needed to do was call Russell Brice. Under the influence of quite a lot of beer I called Russell, and for the first time in my life I became a participant on a commercial expedition. At the same time I added an additional couple of years to our mortgage. After two decades of expeditions around the world, being a participant on a commercial expedition was a difficult concept for my ego to swallow – but hell, it was my best chance. Russell's organisation and setup are second to none and way better than any expedition to Everest that I could put together.

Everest is no wilderness now. If you want unclimbed routes and remoteness go elsewhere. I arrived in the Rongbuk Base Camp along with 20-odd other members of our expedition and around 150 other hopeful summiteers from other expeditions. Everest attracts all sorts of people, from the outright incompetent to the spectacularly experienced. They are all there. There is not much opportunity for mere mortals to do 'firsts' from here now – but people are still trying. Now 'first' needs qualification: the first ascent by an amputee etc. One Australian member who kept bees thought it would be great to be the 'first Australian beekeeper to the summit' the opportunity for the first New Zealand beekeeper being already taken. As far as I was aware no one else from Hazlett Street in Clyde had yet been to the summit – or at least my poll of the neighbours hadn't detected any. Here was my chance for my very own 'first'.

The Northern (Tibetan) side of the mountain is cheaper to visit than the southern side as you can transport the expedition to Base Camp in trucks. It has less objective danger because you do not have to negotiate the Khumbu Icefall. There are generally fewer people on the North Ridge than the South Ridge from Nepal, although this may change with the political instability

currently in Nepal. The North Ridge has a reputation for wind and cold and the high camp is at an extremely unpleasant altitude of 8,400 meters. The route from there to the summit is more technically difficult than the south side and more difficult to lose height from should the weather go to custard.

Acclimatisation is the single most important thing that you can do on a trip to very high altitude. Acclimatisation is a term that can be used to describe a wide variety of activities from reading thrillers to gentle walks and heavy drinking. I had enough of a headache to forsake the heavy drinking. Rongbuk Base Camp is not the most salubrious location, it is cold and dusty. Certainly the facilities provided as part of the expedition were the very best possible but it wasn't too dissimilar to camping in the Treble Cone skifield car park for two months.

We made an initial slow foray up to our Advanced Base Camp at 6,300 meters and an even slower trip to Camp One at the North Col at 7,000 meters. I had teamed up with a Dutch climber, Kiek Stam, who had been within 300 meters of the summit on the south side but had turned around with a defective oxygen system and the effects of extreme cold. He was damned if he was going to miss out again. We made a somewhat snail pace trip most of the way to Camp Two at 7,500 meters before being driven back all the way to Base Camp by high winds and snow. Advanced Base Camp is just a little too high to remain at for an indefinite time.

The weather was terrible for the best part of three weeks. Would it never improve? Had I spent all the money I had (and a fair proportion of my parents' available cash too – you'd think when your offspring reach their late 30s they will stop asking for money!) for nothing other than the world's coldest camping holiday? But eventually the long-range weather map (delivered by satellite phone and laptop computer) indicated a clearing in about a week's time. The remaining team divided into two groups travelling a day apart. There had been some attrition as four members became sick or failed to acclimatise sufficiently and went home early.

We plodded up to ABC again and then on to Camp One. The weather was not perfect. It snowed and blew sufficiently that we had to have two nights in Camp Two at 7,500 metres. The trip to Camp Three at 8,000 metres was unpleasant. It was cold and windy and there was a distinct lack of oxygen in each breath.

At Camp Three everyone adopted bottled oxygen for walking and

sleeping. Bottled oxygen helps warmth, digestion, sleeping and walking. From Camp Three the route to Camp Four climbs a broken rocky ridge (like the route to Haast Hut only a little colder and has less air) and then the route traverses out onto the North Face to Camp Four. Camp Four is not a desirable piece of real estate: it's cold, windy, there is no air and the parking is shocking.

The weather improved slowly; the clouds dropped away and the wind decreased. Kiek and I got to work with melting snow, filling our water bottles, re-hydrating and getting our gear together. There was no hope of sleep and just after midnight we were up and outside the tent. It was pretty chilly outside. With a surprising lack of messing about we were all off into the night. We were a team of about 15 members and Sherpas. We were the only group heading for the summit that morning. A few days before a group of Bulgarian and Korean climbers had been caught in poor weather and five people had died. So it was with a bit of trepidation that we headed into the dark.

We climbed in the dark and cold up through the fractured limestone of the Yellow Band to the summit ridge. A short traverse brought us to the first step. I was paused on the step in the dark (paused is a euphemism for head down and gasping) and I glanced up in time to catch a flying crampon from above. Fortunately it didn't have a boot or foot attached. Some very muffled shouting through oxygen masks followed and I clawed my way up to Mark, who was hopping around on one foot.

We arrived at Mushroom Rock at dawn. Mushroom Rock is an unlikely looking feature and – you guessed it – is shaped like a mushroom. We changed oxygen bottles here, stashing the mostly spent first bottle and changed to our second bottles. The route traverses along the 'scary traverse' to the base of the Second Step. The traverse consists of sloping shale ledges perched above the North Face. This is a popular spot to fall off if you are feeling a little shagged. The sun lifted above the horizon and the resulting view was indescribable. The 8,000-metre peaks around caught the first rays and the summits glowed orange. To the East Kangchenjunga, Makalu and Lhotse, above Everest and to the west Cho Oyu catching the rising sun.

The recently dead bodies of two Koreans were snuggled up together at the base of the second step. We tried to ignore them and scrambled up the step to the 1974 crevasse ladder fixed at the top of the step and a brand new ladder placed earlier by our expedition. It was beginning to look like

a painting contract with the ladders! At the top of the second step was another body, that of a recently departed Bulgarian climber.

The Third Step was easy scrambling. I plodded slowly up the snow slope above and then over the broken rock of the Dihedral, a corner that avoids the spectacular cornices overhanging the Kangshung Face on the ridge proper. There was the summit, about 100 metres away along an easy section of ridge.

I was on the summit at 9.40am. The first Clyde ascent was achieved! It is supposed to be a monumental occasion, the top of the world, the pinnacle of your dreams. Instead I was just tired and I wanted to go down. The summit was a bit untidy with offerings, prayer flags and some old oxygen bottles poking out of the snow. It didn't look like my expectations. Where was Tenzing with the flag?

I took the world's most appallingly poorly photographed panorama and whipped out a banner from a sponsor, Works Infrastructure. After a couple of photos the banner was whipped over a cornice by the wind and disappeared down the Kangshung Face.

The descent to Camp Four was unremarkable except that I was pretty tired. I called my olds from the satellite phone at the camp, forgetting in my oxygen deprived state that it was about 1.30am in New Zealand: 'We are back at Camp Four from the summit, pretty tired but well, we will descend to ABC tomorrow.' There was a pause on the line then my Dad answered in a very sleepy voice, 'Who's speaking?'

The descent to ABC is a long way and we staggered in mid afternoon. In a couple of weeks I was in Clyde, about 12kg lighter than when I left. Two weeks after getting home I met Doug Scott in Hawea, 'Can I see your pictures lad?' he asked.

NORMAN HARDIE

Five Feet from the Gods: Kanchenjunga, 1955

Before the conclusion of the 1954 New Zealand Alpine Club Himalayan Expedition, a cable from Sir John Hunt was received in Kathmandu, inviting Sir Edmund Hillary or R.C Evans to lead a 1955 Kanchenjunga Reconnaissance Expedition. The former declined the invitation, and the latter accepted on condition that he had enough of the appropriate manpower and equipment to make a summit attempt should the reconnaissance reveal a feasible route – if there would be time for both in one brief season.

Evans, unlike many other leaders, had complete freedom in his choice of party. Of the nine members of the team, six had been to the Himalayas on previous occasions, and from them came experience gained and tales to tell of Tirich Mir, Rakaposhi, K2, Garhwal, Annapurna, Cho Oyu, Everest, the Barun, the 1954 'Snowman' and many small typically Evans explorations. We were R.C. Evans (leader), T.A. Mackinnon, A.R. Streather, G.C. Band, J. Jackson, J.N. Mather, J. Brown, J.H. Clegg, and myself (deputy leader). All were given departments to administer, and most of the initial organisation was done by the Expedition members. Fortune smiled early, the crises passed, and we were all ready to sail together from Liverpool, always expecting something would delay one of us, and necessitate flying alone to India.

From Bombay the main group went by fast trains to Calcutta and Darjeeling, but Mackinnon and I, accompanying the baggage, had to follow by slow train. Streather, in charge of transport, flew to Darjeeling to recruit coolies and purchase Sherpa food. Tony Streather had been transport officer on Tirich Mir (25,300ft) and as the lift to the top camp partly failed, he had carried a load, on this, his first mountain. Undaunted, unroped, without an ice axe, and wearing a golf jacket, he had followed the main party on to the summit. Evans flew to Delhi and Gangtok to discuss the question of summit permission. We were to operate on the Nepalese side, with full permission, but the actual summit is on the frontier of Sikkim, and for some years the Sikkimese have permitted no one to approach Kanchenjunga from their side, for alleged religious reasons. Although we

were climbing from Nepal, we were asked not to stand on the summit, and the Sikkimese wished to impose on us a much lower limit than the one finally adopted. Assuming the Great Shelf at 23,500ft could be reached, we were of the opinion that the crux of the climb would then be the bluff, fifty feet below the summit on the Nepalese side, and to turn back below it would not have proved the mountain to be climbable.

On March 14th 1955, the first party, two hundred and twenty in number, left Darjeeling, followed a day later by Streather with one hundred more. The journey to the Yalung glacier was interesting but uneventful. For a time we followed the Singalila ridge but after two days descended to the warmer and more sheltered valleys in Nepal. We were pleased with the progress of the two groups, for to have lost a day would have involved a loss in wages alone of one hundred pounds. Travelling in two parties meant that when the main group had coolie desertions the loads would be dumped in a village and the local headman, with a day's notice, could usually raise enough labour to send the loads on with Streather the next day. Streather would be warned by walkie-talkie of all coolie troubles. On March 24th, at a camp beside the terminal of the Yalung glacier, the coolies were paid off. Sixteen Sherpas were retained for high altitude work and twelve for middle altitudes. In addition another twelve were kept as wood carriers, mail runners, and cook's boys, etc.

After a rest the first acclimatisation period began and most of us had some experience at the 17,000ft level. It included a food seeking visit over the high passes to Ghunsa, a reconnaissance up the main glacier, and a surveying trip for me to fix the heights of the main features on the south face of our objective. These and the first transport up the glacier were carried out successfully, but some damage was done to tents owing to the still wintry winds.

The second acclimatisation was concentrated mainly on the push up the glacier with only one major diversion when Jackson Brown and I, with three Sherpas, departed for eight days to climb peaks east of the Yalung. For five nights we slept above the 19,000ft level, fed well, and returned having climbed two new ice peaks of a little over 20,000ft, but having failed on Koktang through cold and a reluctance to press too hard so early in the Expedition.

Apart from an unsuccessful attempt on Talung Peak all activities were now concentrated on Kanchenjunga and its approaches, and by April 15th

we were all camped scarcely two hours from where the climb would begin. Hours were spent in examining the face. From the col west of the high summit a snow slope (the Gangway) descends steeply to the Great Shelf at 23,500 feet. Most of the Shelf avalanches over an impossible precipice, but a portion of it flows west down an icefall (Upper) to a smaller shelf at 20,200 feet. From here the Lower Icefall tumbles to the main glacier, just beside our proposed Base.

The Yalung had several early visitors, but the party of Dr Jacot-Guillarmod in 1905 was the only one to climb any of the ice slopes above the main glacier. They concentrated on the area west of the Lower Icefall, but unfortunately their attempt was abandoned after Lt. Pache and three Sherpas were killed when a soft snow avalanche swept them into a crevasse. One of the party had advised them not to go out that day, and when he heard the cries of the injured he did not go to their assistance. A few days later, in his article to the *Pioneer*, he described the incident and commented 'not that I was over anxious under the circumstances to render help'.

The activities of the other early visitors are summarised in Smythe's *Kanchenjunga Adventure*. Before Dyrenfurth's 1930 Kanchenjunga Expedition left Darjeeling to attempt the north west face Smythe looked at the Yalung (south) face through a telescope and wrote, 'But a minute's examination was needed to assure us that it was futile to seek a way from the Yalung glacier. Though only the upper part of the route was visible, the long sloping icy shelf the climber would have to ascend is exposed to avalanches of ice and stones, while the icefall up which the party would have to reach the shelf looked unassailable.'

A major contribution came in 1953 when a small party led by John Kempe saw, from the slopes of Talung Peak, the possibilities of the Upper Icefall. Kempe returned with a larger party in 1954, but after trying several routes he was not able to get more than two-thirds of the way up the Lower Icefall. The same point was reached by climbing rock buttresses east of the Icefall. They attempted to reach the Great Shelf from the direction of the Talung Gap, but the party retreated from below the Gap after two men had been injured in a fall of ice.

While our transport to Base was continuing, Band and I, from that Camp, followed Kempe's buttress and established Camp I at the highest point reached in 1954. On the buttress we used 30 pitons and carabiners and 400 feet of rope. For two days we pushed into the icefall which Band

described as far worse than anything seen on Everest. It was evident we could eventually get through it, on a route impossible for Sherpas. While we worked I saw an alternative which might be feasible by using the Pache's grave approach. We reported by radio to Evans, and he joined us with Jackson. For two more days we pushed hard on the Icefall, virtually reaching the first Shelf, but Evans agreed with us – it was no place for Sherpas.

Band and I descended to Base Camp, crossed to Pache's grave, and began an upward route from there. The others retrieved old Camp I, and they decided to move Base onto the solid ground away from the groaning glacier, more in line with the new approach. We established another Camp I, and were successful in our new route, crossing a col, and descending for three hundred feet the only narrow gap in an otherwise impossible wall. Thus we had gained the shelf between the two icefalls, and found the site for Camp II. After escorting Evans and Brown to this site, Band and I were rested for a few days while the others were escorting Sherpa teams up to the new Base and then through to Camp II. This latter carry was very long, and in the early days was usually a battle with the new snow which fell every afternoon, and it always required a heavy escort of climbers.

Evans fixed the site for Camp III and then descended. Streather, Brown, Mackinnon and Mather all lived at II for a time for the pushes to III. Some fixed ropes were needed, and besides being a considerable lift in altitude it was again an ordeal in soft snow. Evans made plans for major concentrations of supplies at III and then I accompanied him to that Camp. With the assistance of closed circuit oxygen, and Annalu and Urkien (the two strongest and most technically capable Sherpas) we put in a tent, so establishing Camp IV, which was level with the Great Shelf. We knew we had qualified for a bottle of brandy on our return to Base. The bad breaks visible from below, in the vicinity of the edge of the Shelf, had given us some worries, but they all relented under pressure. The two Sherpas descended. Next day we advanced, still using oxygen, and after minor problems were on the Shelf with a clear line ahead for several thousand feet. We climbed and chose a platform for Camp V, returning to III on the same day. Ideas soared to the heights. Assault parties were chosen, and then, in conference with Streather at Camp III, we chose the Sherpas for the highest camp lifts.

Band and Brown were to be the first assault pair, and Streather and I the

second. My partner, although invited to descend for a rest, decided to begin stocking Camp IV, as his theory of acclimatisation permits no large losing of altitude. Meanwhile Evans and I returned to Base and prepared for the final lifts and assaults. The other major moves were that Mackinnon and Jackson were to take two lifts of eleven men to Camp V – perhaps the most critical part of the Expedition as the six best Sherpas were reserved for the Camp VI lift, and oxygen was available for Sherpas for that top lift only. Evans, Mather and Dawa Tensing would go to V and remain there as the assaults moved through, to provide escorts and reserves.

A mild excitement reigned at Base. In our letters we decided to keep silent regarding our future duties, wishing that if success came our way credit would come for the Expedition as a whole, not for the summit pair or pairs. Mackinnon and Jackson left for their climb to Camp V. Then the first assault and escort followed, and I accompanied them so that I could check their oxygen when it was collected at Camp III.

The long lift to V at 25,300 feet on May 19th was a great strain on the Sherpas, and the supplies they carried had to be dumped just short of their objective. It was on this carry that Pemba Dorji was completely exhausted and unfortunately he died of cerebral thrombosis at Base Camp seven days later. On May 20th the weather broke. An avalanche removed some of the loads near Camp V, and some of the oxygen and food was never recovered. First assault party in Camp IV, and second in III, kicked their heels as they watched their target dates go by.

Eventually the hoped for clearing came. By radio we learned that the monsoon was already in the Bay of Bengal and that the preliminary disturbances were even nearer. The two assaults moved up one camp each. It was at IV that Streather and I learned of the avalanche losses, and by radio we were informed that we would have to carry up our own stove, personal kit, Sherpa food and oxygen for climbing and sleeping. We had two Sherpas with us – luckily true tigers. The four of us carried over two hundred pounds to 25,300 feet, but as we toiled upwards we were cheered by the sight of first assault, escort, and four Sherpas advancing up the Gangway to complete the extraordinary lift to Camp VI at 26,900 feet.

I was surprised at the distance and difficulties between camps, for laden porters; but anyone who knows the Dawa Tensing Sherpa team and Evans, will understand. Charles treated them well and stretched them far. The Sherpas' determined and uncomplaining efforts, and their splendid

co-operation at every stage, were probably the biggest contributions to the eventual success of the Expedition.

Band and Brown were left in the top camp while the others descended on the same day to V. Their Sherpas were too exhausted to go through to IV as planned. Thus the supports, escorts and second assault were in one small camp for the night. And the second party's Sherpas spent the night without sleeping bags, as we had relied on their being able to use those left by the men who had intended to descend.

Next day, May 25th, the first pair (using open circuit oxygen) left their camp at 8.30, ascended the Gangway, lost an hour in turning off it too soon, and then made steady progress up a rock buttress. They climbed an arête to the west ridge and remained on its rocky crest until below the summit bluff. On this they located and climbed an almost vertical crack, and at 2.50 p.m. reached a point five feet below the summit and about six yards away from it.

Meanwhile Streather and I with Urkien and Aila (or Ela) Tensing ascended to Camp VI, perched on a tiny ledge cut out of the Gangway ice. As there was no sign of the first two climbers we sent our Sherpas down unescorted. Band and Brown were to have descended in time to continue to Camp V in the afternoon, thus leaving the two sleeping bags and the two-man tent for Streather and me. Time went rapidly. We prepared warm drinks and quoted Smythe's *Kanchenjunga Adventure* to one another. Still the others had not returned. Darkness increased our anxiety. At 7 p.m. they appeared; and they ended a great day by squeezing in with us. Their oxygen had given out at 3.30, so their descent had been slow and tiring. With the bedding shortage, the lack of space, and very little sleeping oxygen, it was a worse than miserable night, and our congratulations lacked warmth.

In the morning we drank much and ate little. Streather and I left at 8.30, and acting on the information of the first pair we were able to improve on their time to the top of the Gangway. Here the webbing which held my larger oxygen bottle stretched sufficiently to send the bottle bouncing down the mountain. Streather stoically gave me his bottle and took my small one, with the arrangement that I was to lead all the way using two litres per minute, while he followed on one or two. The buttress between the Gangway and the arête was crossed without removing crampons. Above the arête I chose an ice and snow route under the west ridge, below that taken by Band and Brown. Thus we avoided the rock ridge where the first

pair had lost time removing and replacing crampons. Progress around spurs and occasional flutings provided steep but quite reasonable ice work. The summit buttress loomed ahead, and there dangling down the critical pitch was a sling Band had considerately left for us, but as the ascent by rocks necessitated removing crampons I searched further east and found a snow ramp leading to the south ridge. At 12.15 we too were there.

Our oxygen was removed and for 55 minutes we remained on a shelf below the summit, ate some food, took photographs and admired a brilliant view on a lovely day. The Zemu spur, pressed so hard by the Bavarians, looked a long way below. Streather changed his small bottles but owing probably to annoxia a mistake was made, and I foolishly did not check the change. Consequently, after ten minutes of descent, he had no oxygen. He refused to take my set, saying that on two previous climbs he had been beyond 25,000 feet without oxygen, and he would be safe, although we were at an altitude only eight hundred feet below the summit of Mount Everest. He also said something about my greater technical experience and hence ability to hold a slip if I used oxygen and he did not. While I thought about that, Streather resumed the descent, but we too took a long time to get down, reaching Camp VI at 5 p.m.

On 27th and 28th the descent continued, and at the appropriate camps we were welcomed by the escorts and reserves, with their stocks of food, fuel, and good company. They were reminders that we were an Expedition which had been extremely happy and successful. As individuals we had all been participants and contributors to one victorious adventure.

KAREN McNEILL

A Ridge Too Far: The first female ascent of Denali's Cassin Ridge (2004)

The air had a tropical warmth and cloudless blue hung in every corner. There were rainbow striped toys everywhere.

Then I came to. I was with Sue Nott at 20,000 feet on Denali, swaddled in a whiteout that did nothing to protect me from the incessant wind, tugging at my clothing and boring -25 degree Celsius air into my bones. It was our third day without food and for three days I'd been bleeding into my powerstretch pants. I felt dirty and smelt unpleasant. When I tweaked my knee, my mind, fed up, went to a more friendly place.

Despite the fact that Cassin is considered one of North America's fifty classic climbs, it was never on my tick list. The route seemed foreboding and I thought it was too difficult for me. Since its first ascent in 1961 it has become a sought after climb. Numerous parties have attempted it. During most seasons one party usually succeeds and climbs the route, but some seasons go by without a single ascent. The Cassin Ridge is an aesthetically pure line that ends literally 300 feet below North America's highest summit: 9000 feet of steep granite, corniced ridge and ice need to be climbed to reach the top. The combination of the mountain's height of 20,320 feet, its high latitude and terrible weather make the environment unique to any mountain outside of Antarctica. Recently it had been noted that the climb had yet to see a team of women ascend it. This thought set the cogs in motion. I'd known three parties of women who had attempted the climb in the past few years. These women are talented and competent in the 'hills' and I have a lot of respect for them. Their lack of success seemed more reason for me to stay away.

On April 30th this year, Sue Nott and I flew into the Alaska Range. Our objectives: The South Face of Thunder Mountain and … the Cassin. Somehow I had changed my mind. If I were to attempt the route with anyone it would be with Sue. Both tenacious, we have a partnership that works. Most often Sue is out in front leading. But when it comes to the descents I take over. Sue is bolder, but with our different personalities we keep each other in check. I also have a better sense of direction. As we flew,

thoughts of the Cassin still haunted me. The mountain was big and not to be taken lightly. I wondered how I would do the climb.

Bumping over to the Kahiltna Glacier our weather luck was about to change. For the past seven days stable weather had enabled us to climb *Walk of the Schnitzelkings* on Thunder Mountain. On the Tokositna Glacier I had felt antsy. I wanted to be moving up Denali, ready to be on the Cassin when the weather was right. But this climb had also been good preparation for our next. As we flew, blue skies and stable weather were replaced by high winds and poor visibility. We had no idea that this system would hover around Denali for the next month.

Five days after setting out to acclimatise on Denali's West Buttress, Sue lay in the medical tent at 14,000 feet incapacitated. Connected to her nose were plastic tubes that ran to huge metal tanks. Oxygen flowed freely down the elongated plastic, into her depleted body. I'd never known Sue to be ill. I'd never known Sue to be affected by the altitude. But somehow this woman with an iron constitution had gotten HAPE. At 11,000 feet we'd had a heated argument as to whether to continue up or stay another day. In frustration, I threw a snow stake on the ground. We went on, both thinking Sue had a common cold. Normally cautious with altitude illnesses, the news was like someone slapping my frozen cheeks. In the medical tent I looked on, acting cool and calm. Back in the quiet of our tent I allowed myself to cry. Tears streamed down my face. After this brief outpouring I had to turn the faucet off, very tightly. Growing up, my family had frowned upon all displays of emotion – including the happy. Even now I still have difficulty expressing myself. But I was upset. Partly for missing the diagnosis, but mostly grieving for friends lost in the hills. My thoughts turned to Gary. I met Gary while on a trekking trip to Nepal – he was attempting Everest. The last time I saw him we were both off on adventures. I was heading to the south face of Douglas Peak in New Zealand. Gary was leaving for Nepal. Although I was due back before his departure, we never saw each other again. True to form a southerly rolled in off the Pacific Ocean, stranding me in Pioneer Hut. I had climbed my route. Gary returned to the store where my boss relayed my news. He left feeling proud. High on Dhaulagiri Gary died from altitude sickness. What a waste! Sue's situation was triggering a lot of memories for me.

Returning to 14,000 feet after some R & R, the season's second rescue was underway. The next day we were enlisted to help. Ironically Sue's medic, Steve, arrived at our belay station and was pleasantly surprised. Days ago

Sue was his patient – needing his expertise. Now, Sue the rescuer, attached herself to the litter with Steve, to help guide it down. The unstoppable Sue was back!

With the rescue winding down we began to notice the white board. Daily the rangers would write a brief weather synopsis on the board and place it outside the mess tent for all to view. Most climbers made their climbing decisions based upon the board. For two days in a row, Sue and I observed that the weather forecast had been wrong. The weather appeared to be more settled than predicted. Firm in my decision to leave I still talked over our plan with the Jackson boys who were working as rangers on the hill. I respected their experience and wisdom. They didn't try to dissuade us. It was time for the Cassin.

It was an inauspicious beginning. Two hours from camp quiet mists descended, hiding the crucial cut-off point to the West Rib, our descent. By descending this way, we avoided travelling up the death trap that is the North East Fork of the Kahiltna Glacier. We had to erect our tent. Hours later when all was clear, we tried again. This time we made it to 14,000 feet on the other side before the mist once again halted our progress. Descending below the cloud level, we got our first views of the route. Initially I felt intimidated; it looked steep and long. 31 hours after our initial departure we arrived at the base of the route. Each time I peeked at the route I felt better. The Japanese Couloir no longer looked out of my league. I was warming up to the climb. Unfortunately for us a team of Germans had arrived minutes before we did at the base. Their plan was to 'fix' the climb. Luckily Sue's charm worked wonders and we got pole position.

Our first couple of days on the route were uneventful. Following our topo we navigated our way through the first rock band and camped below the second. Being an older route, the nature of the climb was to follow the path of least resistance. Often this meant traversing. Continuing in this mode Sue and I traversed our way past the entry point to the second rock band. By the time we realised our error, Sue had discovered an alternative route. As Sue left our belay, the wind picked up, swirling spindrift around and often throwing it on our exposed skin. We felt cold to the core and needed to find a bivvy site. Earlier that morning, while attaching my crampons, I wasn't able to tighten the strap on my right crampon to its usual tension, but I thought it would be okay. As the rope came taut I got ready to climb. Stepping out from my stance I felt sickened as my right foot suddenly

felt lighter. My tardiness had been rewarded with a crampon AWOL. Feeling ill, I watched the very unnatural metal object rolling easily away from me. It was heading toward a drop-off. With each roll my mind raced with possible solutions to the predicament a lost crampon would place us in. Miraculously the crampon stopped at a point where another roll would have sent it flying into space.

The wind made communication virtually impossible. As I yelled up to Sue she imagined that I had been hit by falling rock. I carefully descended to the crampon. With nervous energy surging through my body I reattached the crampon and raced back to a teary-eyed Sue. After several more pitches we found a huge boulder perched just below the ridge. The perfect bivvy. Still feeling the affects of the adrenaline rush, I carved a tent platform and pushed Sue inside the tent. By that time it was after midnight, the clouds had lifted revealing incredible beauty. All I wanted was to fall inside the tent and sleep. Unfortunately the arduous task of melting water consumed many more hours before we were finally allowed to rest our weary bodies and sleep.

Minutes before the slab released we'd been howling with laughter. The base of the next big rock we had come across the following morning was littered with numerous old ropes. We were back on route again. Up until this point we had been belaying every pitch. Ironically, here we went without the security of an anchor. I stood beside a rock that had potentially perfect cam placements, my tools patiently waited in the snow beside me. Sue stepped onto the slope, commenting that the snow was bad. At the same moment I thought we should be weaving our way up through the rocks. The release was silent. As I watched Sue sliding past me I braced with my legs in an attempt to stop her. The act was futile and I too, was catapulted down into the moving mass of snow. I've heard that a lot of people in similar situations see their life before them. Not me! I like to chat to inanimate objects. On one hand I pleaded with the snow: 'please stop now, please now, please slow down, please slow down'. On another level I puzzled over the thought that this couldn't be happening. I was sure we were going to climb the route. The release was inches deep and carried us about fifty feet. When the momentum stopped we raced back up to the rock and set a solid anchor. Feeling nervous and shaky we continued up the ridge. The adrenaline we felt after the slab had left our bodies feeling empty, so we camped earlier than we usually did. That night my body decided

to do some of its own releasing. My period began early. Of course I was unprepared.

Adverse weather continued to impede our progress. Close to the top of the route we were forced to camp again. At a belay I beat the snow furiously, begging for a reprieve. We didn't deserve these conditions. The climb felt intense and the mountain wasn't about to let up because I threw a 'hissy fit'.

On June 2nd we awoke to silence. Dense pea soup-like mist had replaced the wind. Tentatively we crept along the ridge. Up ahead I noticed a snowy pyramid. When I stared for long enough I could make out a wand on its peak; this signified the top of our route, Kahiltna Horn – we'd made it! From the Horn a mere 300 feet of ridge travel would take us to the summit of Denali. I noticed more wands. Concentrating on discrepancies in the snow I made my way along the ridge from wand to wand. At the third, another wand much further down the slope distracted my attention. Caught off guard I look a large step and landed in a divot. My pack lurched forward, throwing me to the ground. As I fell, a sharp pain tore through my knee. I came to rest facing down the slope. My knee ached and I felt woozy. I quickly righted my body and rested my head on my knee, taking deep breathes. Then I passed out. Maybe it was Sue's squeaky voice that brought me back to reality. When she asked how my knee was, there was only one possible reply 'it's fine'. I wasn't going to allow my body to compromise our safety. We had to take care of ourselves up here.

The summit was lined with wands, decorated with different countries' flags. These wands were our only means of guessing we were on Denali's summit. Mist obscured all views. After the obligatory summit photograph that could have been taken anywhere, we discussed the descent. Both thought we should go the opposite way to the other. As we headed off into the murk, the winds picked up. The only realistic option was to yet again bivvy. Twenty feet below the summit we found the perfect flat spot. We fought with the wind while erecting the tent. Inside we pulled our frozen sleeping bags apart and brewed up. We even had enough fuel to make hot water bottles, a pure luxury! Outside the wind buffeted our tent, forcing opposite walls to meet.

During our time at the 14,000 foot camp, Sue and I had developed strong bonds with many of the Park Service workers. The unmistakable throbbing of the Llama's rotor nearing our tent got our attention. We had

taken longer than anticipated to climb the route and people were now concerned for our safety. Afterwards the rangers told us that they thought we had only taken four days worth of fuel. Had this been true, our situation would have been quite desperate. As Sue waved at the chopper I toiled over what it exactly meant. In our world we were fine but no-one else knew that. I felt bad for potentially putting other people, like the pilot, at risk. But in hindsight, I realised that if we had needed their help, I would have been cheering to see them. These guys do an amazing job and were only concerned for our well being.

As the chopper left us we got ready to descend. I realised my partner Brad had probably been notified. I cursed feeling bad for him. He doesn't climb. I prayed that he wasn't too worried. The air temperature was probably -35 degrees Celsius with wind chill. We couldn't stand still for long. Our brains felt taxed and our bodies were running on empty. On the Football Field not far from the summit, Sue discovered a square of chocolate. We shared it, telling our bodies we didn't need more. As we continued the descent, the air warmed and filled with oxygen. We began to encounter climbers heading up. Most knew who we were, incredulously asking: 'are you the girls who slept on the summit'? This time I felt like crying with tears of joy. Of course I didn't. We passed through 17,000 feet where two rangers, Rob and Dexter waited for us. We were fed, and made phone calls on the satellite phone, telling all we were safe. By the time we reached 14,000 feet it was getting late. John, Sue's concerned boyfriend came out to meet us. Our last few steps into camp were overwhelming. Many climbers came out of their tents cheering and clapping. We were down.

Flying out of the range felt strange. Alaska has come to be one of my favourite places. Years ago I read how it gets into your blood. I too now feel this way but I can't exactly explain why. Our descent to Base Camp had been quick and a whirlwind of activity. I was now leaving Sue and John behind to stay on and climb some more. As the Alaska Range disappeared from view I finally had time to ponder our climb. For a route that had initially intimidated me, I didn't feel scared on the climb. We'd been thrown a lot of challenges. One by one we dealt with them and slowly we climbed the route. Our experience guided us and lead us to the top. I felt very proud of what we had achieved.

BRIAN TURNER

High Hopes

Climbed the mountain
with the sun in my eyes

descended the mountain
temporarily purged of lies

came down from the mountain
under perfect skies

came down from the mountain
with tears in my eyes

MICHAEL GILL

from *Mountain Midsummer: Climbing in four continents*

The Ramsay Face of Whitcombe

> *Time was pressing us now. We were very tired and there was still no hint of an end. Looking down we could see Ian using his knees. Mike rebuked him, saying that even if he were bone-weary there was no excuse for such bad technique when climbing. Ian looked up with a mystified air. 'Climbing? Who's climbing?' he said. 'I'm praying.'*
>
> Phil Houghton, *NZ Alpine Journal*, 1962

I came back from the Himalayas in June, resolved at first to give up climbing altogether. But the grim memory of Makalu faded and summer grew near. I wrote to Phil, who replied that he had grown weary of working a hundred hours a week as a house surgeon and that a trip into the hills would be a good start to the year or two of beachcombing he planned. And Ian Cave and John Nicholls, they too were keen. Where should we climb? Nicholls was adamant. The Ramsay Face of Whitcombe had to be climbed. 'This year,' he wrote, 'it's the front pages or the back,' the front pages of the *Alpine Journal* being for the more spectacular climbs of the season, the back pages for the obituaries.

Mt Whitcombe is in the Rakaia country, the land of Samuel Butler's *Erewhon* and of John Pascoe's mountaineering classic *Unclimbed New Zealand*. The approaches to it are through the Canterbury foothills, a landscape as different from Fiordland and the Darrans, as Tibet is from Nepal. Just as the Himalayan Divide and the Nepalese foothills break the force of the monsoon, so do the West Coast and the Southern Alps bear the brunt of the recurring nor'-westers so that a few miles east of the Main Divide the winds are dry. There the hills and plains are carpeted by brown tussock and only the flooding of the great rivers draining east gives notice of the rain and snow beating on mountains enveloped in the gloom of a storm.

We had made an attempt on Whitcombe in the Easter of 1960, Ian Cave, John Nicholls and I. When we set off from the end of the road it was late on a fine autumn afternoon. The low sun moulded the soft contours of the

hills on either side of the Rakaia Valley, down which as Butler wrote 'the river ran in many winding channels, looking, when seen from above, like a tangled skein of ribbons, and glistening in the sun.' In the folds of the hills golden poplars flickered like flames, and across the horizon, etched in black and white, were the snow-covered peaks of the Divide, sharp against the luminous blue of the sky.

We walked till nearly midnight, and all next day we tramped steadily up-valley, feeling on our faces a soft breeze already nipped by the cold of approaching winter. Dust blew across the shingle flats, forcing us to shelter behind drift-wood when we lit a fire for a brew. At length we reached the source of the river where it emerged from a black cavern in the terminal ice-face of the Ramsay Glacier. We looked up-valley. It was a bleak and gloomy place, a corridor enclosed between the Divide on one side and a lesser range to the east; forming the floor of the corridor was the glacier covered by grey hummocks of loose moraine through which no white ice was visible, nor was there any vegetation. Beyond, an immense rock-face bulged out, cutting off our view of the upper névé. It was the Ramsay Face of Whitcombe.

In 1866 Sir Julius von Haast said of Whitcombe, 'It can scarcely be surpassed by any other mountain,' and in *Unclimbed New Zealand* Pascoe wrote when describing the view from a near-by peak: 'To the west Mt Whitcombe rose sheer from the Ramsay Glacier and so held our attention that we were unwilling to dwell on the view of the lesser mountains of the Lyell valley. With a last glance at the immense Whitcombe buttresses we began the descent …' It was from Pascoe's book we had the idea of climbing the face for the cover photo shows, on a jagged rock ridge, two climbers, one with ice-axe aloft, against the back-drop of the Ramsay Face. In an early guide book to the region he thought the face was 'likely to remain inviolate' but in a later edition he spoke of 'new challenges awaiting the coming generation.'

That was us. Sitting on our packs we looked more closely at the face. The most clear-cut routes and those which had caught our attention on Pascoe's photo, were two magnificent buttresses on the southerly part of the face below the Low Peak, each 4,000 feet high. Segments of the left-hand buttress had fallen away leaving big steps but that on the right rose steep and direct, complete except in the uppermost part where it ran into a vertical wall two or three hundred feet below the summit. Probably the

key to the climb lay in the forcing of those last few pitches. The lower part, where big scree fans lay against the face, looked easy.

We talked about the route as we hopped from boulder to boulder up the moraine. 'You know where this stuff comes from, don't you,' said John, kicking at a heap of shattered rubble. 'From the face. The whole lot of it.'

'It's too steep to be really rotten,' I replied, developing a theory of mine that the steeper the angle, the sounder the rock. Judged by this the Ramsay Face should be like diamond; but in the event the theory was proved conclusively wrong.

Late in the day we pitched camp near the foot of the buttress. There were signs of a nor'-wester in the offing and when we woke next morning, cloud was settling down over the tops. Before mist swallowed the face completely we climbed a thousand feet, enough to confirm that the lower part was easy. Then the winter set in. When we caught a glimpse of the face two days later through a break in the clouds, fresh snow was plastered everywhere and we knew that for that year the climbing season was over.

That was in 1960, so when we laid plans for our climb in 1962 we knew something of what lay ahead of us. We arranged to meet up the Rakaia in February. While hurrying down the North Island on a motor-bike to keep the appointment, I was involved in a collision with a larger vehicle, a miscalculation which knocked the back end off the bike, leaving me intact but two days behind schedule. Phil waited for me and together we tramped up the Ramsay hoping to find the other two comfortably dug into a snow-cave. But there had been no suitable snow and instead they had camped under a previously undiscovered bivvy rock, about a thousand feet up-valley from the foot of the buttress. They showed us two cramped sleeping-benches at the end of a narrow tunnel.

'Fairly snug under here,' they said, 'but not a lot of room for four people. You might like to have a look for something better. Plenty of rocks around here.'

There were indeed, and 200 feet farther up we found an overhanging boulder facing north-west, giving a good view of the storm that was rolling in from that direction. In thickening cloud we blocked in the entrance with a rock wall and watched the first of the rain blowing through cracks on to our sleeping-benches. When we went down to the other bivvy for the evening meal, Phil wisely took his sleeping-bag with him and stayed there. Very early next morning, wet if not soaked, I joined him, thinking

regretfully of easier times when there had been Sherpas and water-proof tents.

The nor'-wester was short-lived and that evening the wind swung south. When we woke at 6 a.m. the sky was clear. Within two hours we had eaten breakfast and crossed the glacier to the foot of the buttress where it rose out of the heaps of rubble cast off from the crumbling face.

The climb began up a scree fan followed by a succession of debris-strewn ledges which led to an alcove, a hole left in the side of the buttress by the subsidence of a pocket of loose rock. We were almost at the highest point of our abortive attempt two years earlier. This was where the real climbing started. We roped up, Phil and I sharing the lead on one rope, Ian and John on the other. A few runners and a camera around my neck, pitons clanking from a waist-loop and I led off.

The first pitch though steep and exposed was made easy by an abundance of good holds. It was a fair sample of the sort of rock we encountered on the whole of the first two-thirds of the climb. We zig-zagged up the line of the buttress following inter-connecting ledges which seldom made us think twice about where the easiest route lay. Falling rocks were mainly a problem for John and Ian who were having to dodge rocks being sent down by us, as well as those from the upper parts of the mountain. More of a problem was the cold. There was little sun on the face and last night's southerly had sprinkled the holds with crystals of sago snow, so that intermittently we were sucking at numb fingers to restore feeling.

At 12 noon we called a halt for lunch, just over half way up the face. 'Is that where you usually carry your camera?' someone said, pointing to my feet. Looking down I saw that the strap had broken, leaving the camera dangling from a buckle jammed in my waist loop. I had been too intent on the climbing to bother about photos anyway so I stuffed it away in a rucksack. We chewed biscuits and chocolate, shared a quart of orange-juice and looked uneasily at the weather. Streaks of high cloud showed overhead, and gathering around the summits farther south were ominous shreds of grey vapour. The Ramsay Face was no place to be caught in a storm.

When we set off again there was a feeling of urgency creeping into what had so far been an easy climb. The ledges, which had felt so secure, now vanished almost completely leaving us on smoother rock rising sharply upwards. Where before we could look down on comfortable shelves of rock, spread below like a net, now there was nowhere the eye could rest on. One's

gaze swam about in the dizzy void opening below. On either side were flanks of smooth grey wall, while above, the upper part of the face looked dark and menacing.

I began to use pitons, at first as anchors, then for protection between belays. We came to a point where the buttress was too steep for a frontal assault and followed a line of holds on to the open face on our right. Seldom have I felt so small and insecure as there, clinging to that vast, featureless face.

'I think this is going to be my last climb,' said Phil quietly as he came up to the belay position. 'This is getting too bloody dangerous.'

The other two were close on our heels but we were too preoccupied with the climb to carry on a conversation. There was the occasional warning cry of 'Rock!' as we knocked something down in their direction, and a few comments on the ones we sent down without warning. Mostly we climbed in silence. And then the light began to go. We had forgotten the weather, till suddenly, like a clammy hand, the mist enveloped us blotting out the sky, and then in grey twilight the sense of urgency became more acute. We were committed now, as surely as if in a small boat we had sailed out of sight of land and found ourselves in a gathering storm.

At 4 p.m. after clambering up a rotten gully to the left of the buttress, we anchored ourselves to a piton at the foot of the final wall. The top was close now, perhaps 300 feet. This was the crux of the climb. There was no problem about the choice of route. There was only one: a steeply rising slab slanting upwards with a narrow crack where it was welded to the black, vertical rock of the face. Snow filled the crack, and the small holds on the slab were greasy. I began climbing, jamming the finger-tips of one hand into the crack on one side, and gripping the outside of the slab with the other, while my feet slithered on uncertain holds. I ran out ten feet of rope, twenty feet, and still there was no big hold where I could stop and secure myself with a runner. I grew less and less happy, but forty feet up the slab came to an end as a sharp crest standing out from the wall. Closing both hands over it, I hauled myself up and swung a leg over the top to sit astride; secure at last, the tension gone for the moment, I put in a belay and called to Phil to come up.

Looking downwards I saw the other three crowded under the wall. Behind them the grey mist eddied back and forth, and through it I saw, two hundred feet away, the profile of the other of the twin Ramsay buttresses, a

chaos of loose rocks piled one on the other in a tottering heap. Neither the top of it nor the bottom were visible in the mist and I wondered uneasily whether the rest of our own buttress was like that. Phil and the other two followed up the slab so that all four of us were crammed against the wall, with a vertical drop below and an apparently vertical face above. I tried tackling the face direct but even in the first few feet felt too insecure.

There was an alternative: a rubble-covered ledge running out to the right at a lower level. Climbing down, I worked along it for twenty feet with the leaning face pushing me towards the edge. I hammered in a piton for a runner. Then the ledge came to an end. Precariously on balance I reached up, feeling for holds. A pile of rubble tottered off balance, tugging at the rope as it fell away past me. When I took weight on a hand-jam, half the face seemed to shift towards me and a few boulders spun off into the mist. I realised that any moment now the same thing might happen to me. I tried pitons but each time the rock fractured. The ring of steel on steel echoed across the face, a rising note then a sudden fall as the crack broke open. And then one of them seemed to bite. I felt desperate – we had to get up.

Reaching high, I took hold of the piton with one hand and the firmest piece of rock I could find with the other. What if that piton pulled out? For a moment panic rose within me as in imagination I fell backwards into the mist. Then I swung out and up, scrabbling for a foothold and frantically searching above as rock tumbled from around me. Then I was up and secure. Another runner and I moved back to the left on a higher ledge.

I climbed higher on the rotten face till there was so much friction on the rope dragging through the pitons and over sharp edges that I could no longer move upwards. Nevertheless I was close to the foot of a small gully with plenty of room in it. It might lead to the top. After anchoring to a rickety piton I belayed Phil up to a position above me. Only then did I realise that the others, crouching under the face for the last hour with a shower of rock pouring past them, had been having no easy time of it either. Phil untied and dropped the loose end to John who climbed the face direct. He was still amazingly cheerful. While Ian came up, I followed the small gully above, turning a corner out of sight of the others. Fearful of what we might find, I looked up – and then I felt my heart thumping with excitement and I let out a wild yodel. We were at the top.

It was 6 p.m. We were on the summit of the Low Peak. There was no

wind but light snow was falling and the High Peak was hidden in the mist. I hunted for a parka. No parka. Apparently I'd left it behind.

'How do we get off this mountain?' asked someone. We looked blankly at each other.

'Who's got the guide-book?' None of us had it. We all had a vague idea that there should have been a big flat snowfield running up to Whitcombe from the west; that we had only to amble south along this till we reached a low point on the Divide, cross it and drop down to the Ramsay moraine. The trouble was, there was no snowfield, nothing but a steep rock face dropping into the mist. Perhaps we could traverse south along the crest – but there were too many rock towers on the ridge for that to be an easy alternative. I peered down the Ramsay Face for the last time and for a moment felt fear prickling through me. There was only one thing certain – we weren't going back down there.

We began traversing south along the western face hoping that eventually the crest of the ridge above would become easier. Un-roped, we moved quickly in a slanting line down and across the face, kicking across narrow snow couloirs and swinging from hold to hold down the rock. There was no wind. Big snow-flakes fluttered silently out of the mist, settled on the rocks and melted; rocks clattered away from under our feet and for a long time we heard them bounding down the mountain-side till their noise was smothered. It was a strange silent dream-world, isolated and calm, with no sign of the storm we had feared. At times we ran up against big towers in the mist, or the steep wall of a couloir, and each time we lost more height and swung farther west. When at length we regained the crest of a ridge, though we were unaware of it at the time, we had left the Divide behind us and were on a side-spur running to the west.

Down the ridge we hurried expecting at any moment to catch sight of the Ramsay moraine on our left. But when the mist began to thin, it was not the Ramsay we saw but a wild mountain landscape which was completely unknown to us. Ahead and to the right, a great ice-fall loomed out of the mist, its terminal face tumbling over a ledge into a deep valley. Then, with a growing uneasiness, we saw on our left the upper reaches of a high unfamiliar névé. And when a few minutes later, as we dropped below the cloud ceiling, the whole of the landscape was revealed to us, we stopped short as if we were seeing a vision of another world. On either side névés and huge ice-falls unfolded, and ahead, in the distance, radiant in the

soft light of late evening, we saw a great valley, its walls steep and clothed in bush, snow on its upper slopes; through the clouds shone shafts of light, eery, lime-green, luminous; we had stumbled into Erewhon itself.

There was no sign of the Main Divide and for one wild moment I thought we might make a break for the West Coast by plunging down that valley. But when later the clouds lifted further, we saw far to the left across the névé, a gap in a rock ridge which might be the Divide. Sliding down a rotten rock-face we raced across the snow to the gap only to find beyond it yet another névé draining to the west, and at its head, showing briefly through the cloud, yet another rocky gap. We turned towards it, this time uphill, and in the gathering darkness scrambled up the final stretch of rock.

Without doubt we had reached the Divide at last and dimly below we saw the Ramsay. A black steep-sided cleft fell away at our feet and into it we hurried, spidering our way downwards, slipping and knocking rocks on to each other. When we were blocked off by a fifty-foot drop we rappelled off it to a tongue of ice, working as much by feel as by sight for it was now dark. And that was the end of the climb, for though there was still a long descent on crampons, a tortured stumbling traverse of the moraine and the final climb to the bivvy, we knew that we were safe. The anxiety and excitement that had kept us going at a fever pitch all through the day, faded, leaving only weariness. At midnight, under a sky clustered with stars, we staggered into the bivvy.

One day the Ramsay Face will be climbed again. More pitons will be left there, loose rock will be cleared from the holds and the new-comers will laugh at our difficulties. But they will not see those last pitches, unknown and swathed in mist, as we saw them, nor will they rejoice as we did as they step on to the summit; they will not walk home in a dream; for that sort of experience comes only once in a mountaineering lifetime.

ANONYMOUS

Ngauruhoe (1965)

The weather had by Sunday convinced itself that it was fine. So the party tackled the middle mountain. Ngauruhoe is a Geologist's paradise – all the rock you can carry and enough for the next billion geologists that come that way. What is more it is all loose. It took 2 hours to get to the north saddle from the hut. We then laboriously zig-zagged up the mountain. 50 minutes later we arrived at the top. This resembled a large hole with numerous people staring into it. There was practically no snow at the top, just lots of people. It took 10 minutes to get to the bottom although Philip did the descent in 7 as he had no ice-axe to break his fall. We then followed the track that leads to the Mangatepopo hut and Chateau Tongariro as far as the soda springs. Here we camped the night. The springs are 30 minutes walk from the Mangatepopo Hut where numerous Auckland Varsity types were ensconced.

AAT VERVOORN

Plateaunic Melodrama

Act I: *Cast: Eric Saxby, Aat Vervoorn and others. Scene: Linda Glacier – night*

Eight blobs of light appear from bottom stage right; plod to centre of stage and stop. Much muttering in English and Japanese: – 'Oaths and obscenities! I hate breakable crust! Etc.' Pink light diffuses from stage right, slowly lighting props and revealing backdrop depicting Graham and Silberhorn, looking very life-like; complete with ice-bulges and avalanche debris. All members of cast sit on ice axes meditating on line of shin deep tracks which follow line of action and stop at their feet. Silence … 'Better get going. See you later.'

Six of the cast (including Peter Meffin and Oriental section) head off in the general direction of Cook, leaving Eric and me to nip smartly off to one side, there to toil up steep slope under hanging glacier of Vancouver. Meanwhile, all lights have been turned on; making good imitation of bright sunlight. Alas revealing big seracs directly overhead. 'Let's not muck about here!'

Quick pace up to the right to safety of steep ridge. Deep breaths, then kick steps up wet powder snow, across a couple of 'schrunds and hey presto! scene has changed to Main Divide as seen from summit of Vancouver. In the distance is big cardboard replica of Dampier, painted brilliant white – no rock is visible. Over a period of three and a half hours it gradually becomes closer, until at 10.30 we are sitting underneath it, looking up and meditating. Three quarters of an hour's silence.

'Let's get in amongst it. Don't particularly want to go back the way we've come.'

The cardboard Dampier now looms large – no longer cardboard, horrors, but the real thing! Much agitation amongst cast. We've been had. The only possibility seems to be that ice chimney almost completely closed in by sastrugi.

Two and a half hours and 200 feet later two figures are seen emerging from the top of the gully, looking somewhat pale and drawn, muscles sagging and nerves twitching. Stagger on to summit to collapse in heap

(3 p.m.). It seems the actors are sadly in need of more rehearsals, judging by the poor performance.

Coffee break; then down ridge towards Greens Saddle.

'I'm euchred! let's abseil down the east face instead of climbing down this flaming ridge.'

Many rope lengths later: 'Good to be back in the Linda; even if the snow is thigh deep.'

Slumping cast then lurches drunkenly downhill and out of view.

Act II: (*much later*). *Cast: Dave Drake, Aat Vervoorn. Scene: Interior of hut, with new cast.*

'We won't try unless there's a good frost.'

(*Three stormy days later*):
'We'll have a bash if it's fine, whatever the snow's like.'

Scene changes to ice-fall under the Mad Mile. Once again – night. Two characters are following a line of thigh-deep footprints (?) which they've cunningly placed previously so that it seems to onlookers that they know where they're going.

'If the ridge isn't solid we'll go back.'

A quick dash across the Mad Mile (as quick as knee-deep snow permits) and up the flank of Symes Ridge. Here the snow is a much better consistency, so with great flourish crampons are produced by entire cast. Much happiness.

Dawn breaks, brilliant red over the top of dark cloud covering the Plateau and Tasman Valley. Up sharp ridge, beautiful in its symmetry, here crampons, there kicking steps in powder snow. Glorious knife-edge up onto north shoulder; there pause to look at a type of morning all too rare in the Southern Alps. Ahead, Tasman is a perfect column of ice, white on the east, merging into deep blue on the Westland side against an almost black morning sky.

The ridge rises steeply, and safe really exhilarating ice work leads on to where we can crampon to the summit.

Dave consults the officious looking sundial strapped to his wrist – 7.30 a.m. Drop down off the summit out of the cold wind, sit and meditate. Terrific! Feel bloody good.

Then down the ice towards Silberhorn. A big ice-wall across the ridge makes our bottom jaws sag for a while, but this is turned by going down

a very sneaky chimney on the east face. Once again straight down on crampons and on to the summit of Silberhorn, to sit and gaze in retrospect. Look at that mountain! Magnificent. Look at sundial again. 9.30. Decide that Graham and Teichelmann would be a definite anti-climax, so turn backs and descend to lesser levels via the Silberhorn ridge, tip-toeing cautiously down very treacherous ice and wet snow, and so into the world of men.

ROSS CULLEN

Economic Man

Could a man who lives and breathes frugality learn something from a professional economist? A tough challenge, but I had a crack: 'Bill, do you really need to heat water to make yourself hot milk to have with your rolled oats? You could make up the milk powder with cold water, and halve your monthly power account.'

Bill was taken aback by this brutal line of questioning at 5.20 in the morning.

'I quite like my hot milk. I will have to think about that.'

A guy like Bill could really benefit from a second-year course in microeconomics I thought to myself. Bill had already slashed the power account for his house to $30, and getting it even lower would undoubtedly require ever-greater sacrifices.

'Bill you do realise that substituting other inputs for electricity as you slide around the isoquant will become increasingly difficult for you?'

Bill was not that easily bullied.

'I think I will continue having hot milk on my rolled oats in the morning.'

Only when he is at home of course. In the mountains, Bill carries little unnecessary gear, has some very basic food. Rolled oats, and peanut butter sandwiches. Just like he has at home, but in the mountains the water is cold from a meltwater stream. Should I point out that inconsistent behaviour, I wonder? No, its best not to needle Bill too much, he might mention my inability to follow a compass bearing, or my occasional failure to remember some essential item of gear for a trip.

'Ah well, shall we get started on this adventure?'

The Barrier Range is a pleasant backwater, reserved appropriately it seems, for aging climbers. A short walk in to the base of the climbs, no more than 750m vertical of climbing on moderately angled rock, and uncomplicated descent to tussock-covered camp sites by babbling streams. Several untouched and unnamed buttresses, just the spot for Past Presidents and friends to extend their climbing careers. More opportunities for us to dream up witty route names that will appear in guidebooks. It is odd that so few people have been drawn to seek new climbs in this region.

Weta Prowl, a pleasant 12-pitch rock climb on a fine but breezy day. We had swapped leads on this climb, with its plentiful protection, excellent clean rock, romping up to the summit in four hours. The Scree Weta I had noted prowling down a block while I was belaying, had provided a pleasant diversion from our tightly focused climbing. The summit came soon after and we unroped and looked around us.

The view from the summit of Steeple Peak is great. To the south-east, Lake Ohau, a large icy pond draped around the flanks of Ben Ohau. Just 400 metres to the south the craggy North Face of Peak 2200m which I had climbed five years ago, believing in error that I was summiting on Steeple Peak. 'Got you now by seven metres matc.' A few kilometres to the south Mt Maitland, Elusive Peak, and Mt St Mary glow in the afternoon sun. Bill and I had climbed Mt Maitland and Elusive Peak just four weeks previously, when early snow had deterred us from Steeple Peak. And here we were, enjoying lunch, packing the rope away after another alpine rock ascent on a western buttress.

Bill finished his peanut butter sandwich and turned with a question: 'Do you know how to drain the hot water cylinder in your house?'

'I intend to drain my hot water cylinder and disconnect it from the electricity. I will heat hot water when I need it on the stove.'

It's a brilliant comeback. With a queasy feeling I admit to myself what is painfully obvious, a professional shopper will usually be a couple of steps ahead of an academic economist.

Maybe a change of tactic is needed. 'Do you have your boots today?'

Bill was not that easily thrown. True, he had decided not to take any leather boots with him on our earlier ascent of Bruce Peak, and had spent the night sitting on the col between Bruce and Steeple Peaks, while Geoff and I slept soundly in our lightweight bags back at the campsite. But he had always intended to sleep near the summit. Bivvys are a treasure to Bill, and he marks them on his maps. The lack of boots was an odd mistake, but the night was calm, and he had padded down the scree slope soon after daybreak to catch us still sleeping in our bags.

Butterfly Buttress, definitely a top day. We had walked down from Gunsight Pass, within touching distance of the impressive west flank of Bruce Peak, to reach the toe of the South West Buttress. A few minutes checking for the best starting point, then rock-boots and harness on, we were away, Bill whooping with excitement, leads off on his first climb for

two years. The second pitch is a cruise and Geoff and I race through and bring up Bill. Pro is not easy to find from here and Bill leads throughout, bringing Geoff and I up on separate ropes.

It is a glaringly hot, calm day. I drink plenty to ensure I do not falter from the heat or the exposure. Showy marguerites, anisotome and gentians soak up the sun's rays. Large black Butlers Ringlet butterflies flutter across the slope, harvesting the sugars available on this stunning February afternoon. Our day mirrors that of the butterflies. We float up the route, a jovial group thriving in the sunshine, climbing on warm rock, following Bill's great lead. His skill at gear placement is superb. We wait patiently as he eases occasional loose stones to security, smile and say 'I'm safe', casually standing on ledges at belay stances. In six hours we climb half the height of Yosemite.

Geoff, always efficient, unropes at the low summit, heads off and I follow him 400m across to the high point. The half antler I had placed on the summit thirteen years earlier has been blown fifty meters down the slope, and I wonder if I should collect it and place it back on top of the cairn I had built. It seems an unnecessary gesture. Bruce is honoured by the name of the peak and the route we have now created on the South West Buttress.

Seven pm. Time to head home. Geoff and I lace up our leather boots and head for the col, a couple of minutes behind Bill hobbling down in his Sportivas. We pass Bill, reach the col and continue down the scree towards the camp site. I glance back and gesture Geoff to look towards the col. Bill is soaking up the sun's radiant energy, a biblical figure glowing in white shirt and longjohns, ecstatic at the prospect of yet another mountain bivvy.

At our campsite I look down to the tarn in the South Temple valley and search for the spot I had reached three years earlier, on a reconnaissance to telephoto the buttress. I had gaped at the spire in 1981, en route to a winter ascent of Mt Huxley, unaware that Carol had died that morning in a fall on Mt Egmont Taranaki. Carol, Bruce. No wonder Bill had been troubled in Twizel by a dream of a tree falling on us during the climb. 'No tree this time' I assert to myself.

I drop Bill at his house and drive one kilometre to our house in Rata Road. The High School rowing group had recently departed and the hot water in the cylinder will soon be cooling. Anything less than twenty minutes in the shower would be a mistake. Chalk one up for rational economic man.

NICK CRADOCK

Oh Where Have You Been My Blue-eyed Sons?

Midday isn't really the best time to start a climb, especially when it's winter and the weather has that definite 'crapping-out' look about it. These thoughts, plus a few others about certain people's mentality, entered my head as we stood at the bottom of our chosen route on Walter. Being the least fit (keen?) and thus the last to reach the belay I was given the dubious honour of leading the first pitch. The sudden transition from wading through bottomless snow to precarious climbing on steep iced-up rock was a bit hard for the body to handle. Consequently after 45 feet I was balanced on a small ledge contemplating the alternatives of going up or down. Fortunately below me I had two indomitable spirits to give me encouragement: Nick laying back on his belay smoking, completely oblivious of my predicament and Bazza telling me how great I looked when I was gripped ('please stop shaking – it's making photos hard to take'). Anyway after much deliberation my ego dictated up, so after some desperate moves I'd still rather not think about and a lot of swearing I was over the crux and able to cut out a belay stance. Nick led the next pitch following an ill-defined ramp, still mostly mixed climbing but, all the same, really enjoyable. After the first couple of pitches our system of moving with three people started to work efficiently: Nick and I leading while Bazza self-belayed himself on the trail rope, took photos and rolled the odd cigarette. A few more pitches and the ramp ended. Nick led across a difficult traverse into the top of the large obvious gully on the face. Once Bazza and I had seconded him into the gully we realised we wouldn't reach the top before dark. Instead of the straight-forward front pointing we had envisaged from the neve, the climbing was just exhausting 'swimming' up deep powder over rock. Gradually darkness descended on us and we were forced to put on our headlamps.

Finally after an eternity we reached the summit. Nick immediately took off his harness and had his much needed crap (apparently the best he had ever had), Bazza rolled some smokes and issued them out and I delved into our non-existent food – 'Have half a biscuit Bazza?'

After gazing at the clouds hanging around us for half an hour or so,

and deciding it really wasn't the best place to be at 9.00 p.m., we decided to descend. After two or three pitches down the ridge Bazza decided to frighten us a bit more by announcing that we were on wind-slab. Going up again was too much effort and going down too risky, so we just dug a hole, pulled on our duvets and tried to squeeze into a two-man bivi sack. After a season's climbing with Bazza I was used to unplanned bivis, but this one really took the bloody prize – intimate would be the best way to describe it.

The night was long: Nick discussed the pros and cons of women, Bazza tried to roll smokes only to find he only had two papers left and I tried (unsuccessfully) to find a position further away from Bazza's crutch. Light eventually entered our little home and on poking our heads out the opening cunningly devised to let in snow (well done, South Col), discovered a white world. Anyway to cut a long story short, we finally got down to the neve again and apart from a little incident with helicopters, the whole descent was rather dull – the boredom broken every once and a while when I came out of my bindings for the hundredth time and flew into fits of rage beating the snow with my poles.

Party was Nick Cradock, Nick Kagan and Barry Jury. First ascent and first winter ascent of the East Face of Mt Walter. Cruxes involved on steep mixed group near the base of the climb before reaching the central couloir. June 1977.

EPIC

WILLIAM SPOTSWOOD GREEN

from *The High Alps of New Zealand* (1882)

Ascent of Mount Cook

On leaving the head of the Linda Glacier we ascended a steep slope, and crossed a ridge to the foot of a couloir leading upwards between two rocky ribs, nearly parallel with the main northern ridge. On this slope the steps had to be cut very deep, and the greatest caution had to be observed, as it ended below us on the brink of a profound abyss.

Kaufmann paused a moment to ask me which couloir I preferred to take – the one near us, or that next the main ridge. As there was nothing to be seen of the upper portion of either, owing to the mists which were now driving over the ridge from the north-west, I said, the nearer one; and as some blocks of ice came down while we were speaking, we cut our way as quickly as possible up to the shelter of the rocks. The rocks being quite inaccessible, we continued our way up the ice slope, keeping close to the rocks, and when a report from above the mists told us that an avalanche was coming, we clung in to the crags as the ice-blocks splintered themselves on the sides of the gully. Some blocks whizzed over our heads with a scream like a shot from a 35-ton gun. The ice in the lower part of this couloir lay at an angle of about 45°, getting steeper near the top where we left it for the rocks on the right. But in a few yards we came to their upper termination, and found ourselves enveloped in dense driving mists. Just before entering the clouds we got our first and last view of the western sea over the Mount Tasman arête, which we were then high enough to overlook.

Matters now took a serious turn. It was past 3 p.m. The rocky ridge we were on extended no farther; but an ice-slope stretched from where we stood to the blue wall of a great bergschrund, which we could see looming through the clouds and extending round the mountain to the right. To cross this couloir seemed too dangerous; we preferred to attempt the ice-rampart above. We cut steps up to its base, and shoving Kaufmann up, followed him with the help of the rope, but found ourselves over what was only an outwork of the great ice-cliff, built of loose séracs from which the avalanches came, and which was perfectly insurmountable. Cautiously we

retraced our steps to the rocks and held a short council of war.

The rocks on the opposite side of the couloir extended upwards, and might 'go.' Should we risk the couloir?

My men asked me, did I see the danger? I said, of course I did, and feared we must turn back. This would have been a sore disappointment to me, and, as I saw by their faces, an equally great one to them, I asked them were the ready to chance it? They replied that on leaving home they expected to meet some danger; here it was, and they were ready, but I must give the word.

'We will top the peak if we go on,' said Boss; 'to turn now is to give it up altogether.'

The 24,000 miles of travelling also rose in our minds as a strong argument against retreat; and as the sun had gone in, which lessened our risk, and no avalanche had gone down for some time, I said 'Forwards.'

A large avalanche block had stuck just mid-way in the couloir, and afforded us shelter when half-way across; so with anxious glances upwards, Kaufmann cut away with all his might. No time was lost; and reaching the rocks in safety we once more breathed freely.

Unfortunately, however, the rocks proved inaccessible; the most we could do was to scramble through a notch, and after the nastiest bit of climbing in the whole ascent, we reached the ice-slope beyond.

A partial break in the clouds revealed to us that there was still heavy work before us; and the anxious question was once more discussed whether we should proceed or return. Hitherto we had calculated on being able to get back to our provisions, and possibly to reach the great plateau, before dark. Now however if we advanced there was no hope of this. To go on meant to spend the night on the peak without food; to go back meant a delay of a week or probably much longer before we could again reach the point where we stood – for our supplies were so nearly at an end that we would be obliged to descend to the lower camp, obtain a sheep from Birch Hill, 'swag' it up the glacier again, and all this possibly in broken weather.

These thoughts flashed rapidly through our minds. There was no mistaking the aspect of the weather; a bad night was brewing. It was 4 p.m., we were about 11,000 feet above the sea. A partial clear showed us the top of the slope before us rounding off to the summit; and as the last rock of the main northern arête, which we recognised easily a short distance above us on the left, gave us exact knowledge of our whereabouts, I asked

Kaufmann how long he thought he would take to cut up the slope. He said an hour at least. They asked me was I ready to spend the night on the peak? I said I was; so at it we went, Kaufmann sending the ice flying about our ears at every blow of his axe. A rapid thaw had now set in, and as we broke through the thin crust of frozen snow which lay on the ice, water spurted out, filling the steps and soaking our clothes, as we could not avoid resting our knees or arms occasionally against the slope.

While coming up the lower couloir we had noticed showers of hail sweeping down the slope; and we had now to face a continual stream of this disintegrated ice, some pieces being so large as to hurt our hands through the mittens. To avoid this annoyance as much as possible, as also to make use of any grips which might be available, we cut our steps close in to the rocks on our right. On any portion of this slope we might, if advisable, have made a traverse and gained the main arête, but there was no object in doing so until the highest rock, and the bergschrund proceeding from it, were passed.

At 5.30 we reached the highest rocks, from which an easy slope led up to an icicled bergschrund, which, starting from the cornice of the arête, ran round the cap of the summit from left to right, and Boss remarked, 'If we had taken to the Mount Tasman arête that would have cut us off.' The wind now for the first time struck us with full fury; we had to shout in order to make each other hear. And though we had ocular demonstration that it was not actually freezing, the blast seemed bitterly cold.

We bore away to the left to avoid the highest part of the bergschrund above us, and surmounting the cornice without any difficulty, at 6 p.m. stepped on to the top-most crest of Ao-Rangi.

Our first glance was, of course, down the great precipice beneath us towards the Tasman Glacier – the precipice up which we had gazed so often – but the dark grey masses of vapour swirling round the ice-crags shut out all distant view.

A look backwards, down into the dark, cloud-filled abyss out of which we had climbed, was enough to make us shudder, it looked fathomless; and this white icy ridge on which we stood, with torn mists driving over it before the fierce nor'-wester, seemed the only solid thing in the midst of chaos.

Mount Cook was now practically conquered. We advanced rapidly along the cornice, which rose at an angle of about 20° towards what was

mathematically the highest point, now and then cutting a step for greater security, but in most cases trusting to the grip gained by the nails in our boots.

Sometimes a blast would come upon us with such force as to compel us to crouch low and drive in our axes firmly, to guard against our being blown off into space. Fierce squalls would shatter the icicles of the cornice and send them down the slopes up which we had climbed. Descending with a swishing sound, they soon pounded themselves to pieces, and so accounted for the showers of coarse hail which had proved so disagreeable on the final ice-slope. Now the mists would vanish, giving us a clear view of the summit. Again the inky black clouds would come on, almost obliterating Kaufmann from my sight, though he was only eight yards distant. From the moment we had gained the arête, anxiety about beginning the descent had filled our minds – as should darkness overtake us on the summit of the mountain, our chances of ever returning to the haunts of men would be but slight. The weather was settling in for a thoroughly bad night. The storm at present blowing was sufficiently unpleasant; if it came on to blow any harder we would not be able to hold our grip. There was no chance of a view. We were hundreds of feet above any rocks, so that we could build no cairn, or leave any record of our ascent. We were all agreed that we were fairly on the summit of the peak, and that we ought to commence the descent. Ten minutes more and the last bit of snow would be under the sole of my boot, when there came a sudden gap in the cornice. A bergschrund broke through it. There was no open crevasse, but a step down off the cornice of five or six feet, a flat, and then a step up of eight feet.

To go round it to where Kaufmann pointed with his axe would have been easy enough, as the summit of the mountain was now comparatively flat. But when little more of an hour of daylight remained, we dared not risk the loss of twenty precious minutes, for what seemed a mere matter of detail. So, pulling out my aneroid, I took down the reading of 19·05 in my note-book, scribbled a sketch of the ridge, and, shouting the word of retreat, we commenced the descent. Owing to an unfortunate accident having happened to my thermometer I was unable to take the exact temperature; that it was above freezing-point was however evident, as the ice was wet, and our clothes, which had been soaked coming up the last slope, were still soft. In similar situations in Switzerland I have often

had my clothes and beard frozen hard; but now, though our fingers were benumbed and painful, I believe the temperature was not lower than 35°, and it may have been as high as 40°.

The slope beyond the gap where we turned, was about thirty feet higher, and this would make my measurement, when compared with the simultaneous observation at sea-level, coincide almost exactly with the trigonometrical height of Mount Cook –12,349 ft.

The great problem we had hitherto longed to solve was: Could we get up Mount Cook? That question was now settled. A more anxious problem yet awaited solution: Could we get down?

KIM LOGAN

Hongi's Track

First winter ascent of South Face of Sabre. Possibly one of the most serious alpine routes yet completed in New Zealand.

Party: Kim Logan, Bill Denz.

'Kim, will you join me to climb Jannu, direct North Face?' (Not a bright reply). 'If I can't climb Sabre, I can't climb Jannu direct!' 'Well, when do we go?' (referring to Sabre).

The day previous to the climb, Bill and I were hunting in the Routeburn. Hunting had proved to be bad. We decided to throw the hunting in and climb the South Face of Sabre – now! A cold southerly was blowing at 5 knots. The chances were good that the weather will hold for another 2 days and hopefully the snow would have consolidated enough. We went back to Flats Hut, and with Sharon and Vivian, headed out to the car. By 2 p.m. in Queenstown. 5 p.m. on the way to the Darrans. Arrived at the start of the Marian Track 9 p.m. and slept in the Van. No comforts of Homer Hut.

Day 1. Up 7 a.m., gear sorted out, packs weighing about 40 lbs. Gone by 8.15 a.m. Weather perfect, snow on the Hollyford Road. 2½ hours bush walk with knee deep snow. Made fast time over Lake Marian. 100mm of ice on the surface which saved half an hour walking around the lake. About this time we decided to call the climb 'Hongi's Track'. Knee and thigh-deep snow to the base of Marian Cirque which we reached about 3.30 p.m. We knew we had Sabre climbed, without touching it yet. The only thing said from Bill was usually 'we're grinding the f---er down'. 5.30 p.m. and the Upper Rock Bivvy. Over 9 hours, which normally takes 6! Before dark high cloud was coming over – a bad sign. By supper time the temperature was down to -5°C. Nothing much was said. I cooked macaroni cheese with bacon and some soups, plus filled the water bottles for the next day. Five minutes conversation in 3 hours. You can lie down in the bivvy and look directly up at the South Face. It's the most evil face I have seen, able to crush your mind before you set foot on it. From my previous trips in this valley in winter, I've learnt it's important not to look too long. I look away, tea finished and concentrate on other things – sleep by 8.30.

Day 2. Alarm at 4.00 a.m. Still not much said. Bill cooks breakfast, bacon and a litre of tea each. I'm ready to go by 4.30. There's a lot of plugging to do and as I know the way I leave Bill to the mess. 6.30 at the base of the Wall. Bill caught me up in the last 50 metres or so.

It takes us about ¾ hour dressing up – full wind-suits, the lot. I am very nervous, my stomach's making a mess of my toilet habits. We climb on 2 ropes, 1 9mm and 1 8.8mm.

Pitch 1 and 2, Bill leads. I follow, both moving together while Bill places runners. The ice is excellent, coming down in waves at 60°–70°. We cover 90 metres in about 30 minutes. It's light now, about 8 a.m. We're on target – perfect timing. Bill places a belay, I come up. I am thinking of the next pitch – and freaking out! I stay cool and take the rack off Bill. Got to get away from Bill fast, so he won't know my inner turmoil. 15 meters up I place a screw, 20m and come to a dead end. 90° thin ice on smooth rock, practically touches my nose (mine's flat!) What goes through my mind, 'well, well, f--k f--k f--k, Jesus, Jesus, Jesus' … I look between my feet – Bill's looking up. Our eyes meet for a second, then he looks away – nothing said. I can remember closing my eyes, concentrating on my breathing. I look again at the ice, 16 minutes pass, blank, then it comes. 1 metre to my right. There is a stalactite ending up about ½m from the wall just below my feet. I chip a notch out in the stalactite about hip high. I place my 'big bird' in my right hand; I put my right crampon front points delicately in the notch. No more negative thoughts going through my head, it's 100% concentration and commitment. It's now or never! I pull on my right hand and lift on my right foot and swing out around and up in one motion. Once on the hanging ice, my left hand tool goes in fast, a reprieve. I work fast, trying to make my 12½ stone weigh 2. After 7m and 80° ice, it lays back to 70°–65°. I place a runner. I scream like hell. 'This is war!' Bill comes up and just says 'f--k' (which is the first time I have heard him swear unintentionally). Takes the rack, and off.

Pitch 4 – Bill's climbing good ice, but steep, and goes around another steep ice and rock corner and out of sight. It's now getting quite cloudy and a few flakes fall; my mind wanders off. I look down, 10m left. I scream out '10m – 5 – 1 – cut!' I don't know what's going on, Bill's pulling like frantic. I know he can hear me, but I can't hear him. I wait 5 minutes. Bill's still pulling – I quickly take out my belay and climb like mad to the first runner 12m up – a solid screw and work like hell to tie off and place another. The

rope is feeding out again and stops with 3m left. Bill's belay is on. I climb up. At about 30m I see where Bill had the trouble – a nasty little corner, blank wall with shitty snow. I pull out about 5 bits of protection, the combined protection of which would be sufficient to hold a 2m fall, enough to get him over the wall to safe ice. Bill's belay is in a main ice gut leading through the second rock buttress, except it's mainly powder snow on ice holes. I climb up and take the rack. Pitch 5 – is vertical, I can't climb the tricky conditions and decide to climb the rock to the right of the gut.

Bill wants me to take the gut, I want the rock. My lead. I take the rock. 10m up and it's weird climbing – 55° smooth granite with 5mm of water ice on top. I come up to a good-looking crack; put in two Friends. Another 10m to an over-hanging roof, but good protection. I am sidling to the right, place a Friend and lower myself off 3m into a good ice gully then climb another 10m. My rope's jammed under the roof. I place my belay. Bill can't hear what's going on. He waits ½ hour, then comes up on one rope – he's guessed what's happened. Bill takes over – leads a straight vertical piece of good ice, an 'ice cool' piece of climbing – 30m of 70°–80°.

Pitch 7–14. Is standard South Face Hicks Central Gullys stuff. Good ice and to save time we were both running out 100m each until we ran out of gear. Place a belay, the second would come up and run another 100m. The 7 pitches took up roughly 3 hours. Reaching the top just before 5 p.m. about 12m to the left of summit. I'll always remember Bill's grin – I guess mine was pretty big too!!!

The Descent. On the summit, we are looking over the top of a solid black wall of cloud coming in from the coast and a purple sky with thin streaks. It's been snowing lightly for 2 hours now. The easy way off Sabre is towards Sabre–Adelaide Col and that's no easy matter, a good grade 5 winter climb from the Marian. Bill knew the way, just as well as there's no way I could have found it in these weather conditions. With 50ft between us, I lead the way, down climbing 100m of 50°–55° good ice to a point where abseiling is necessary. 1 rope length to the Gendarme, the only safe way down. It's 5.45 p.m.; the storm has hit us.

I feel tired, cold and my wind suit feels like hard armour made of ice. My thinking is slow. Karabiner gates are all jammed with ice. Bill is still down climbing. I take off my ropes once I found the anchor. It's getting dark, my face feels like it's getting sand-blasted. There's a deafening roar in my ears – I feel like sleeping. Bill reaches me and yells something about speed.

The ropes are now sliding through my figure 8; it's vertical abseiling; for Christ's sake – there's a knot in the rope! – ½ hour later I am 3 metres short on the abseil. I swing around and let go landing on the Gendarme – it's a near vertical drop on both sides. Bill was at my side 25 minutes later. He had lost his hammer. We both knew things were going wrong. I would like to carry on abseiling. Bill says it's too dangerous and very unlikely we can reach the col alive. He suggests a snow cave within the Gendarme. We're both working hard taking turns. 1½ hours of hard work later, we have created a reasonable home roughly 7ft x 5ft x 4ft.

We climb in, cut out a few blocks for a ledge behind our heads, re-using them to seal the entrance. Light a candle, strip, put on dry under-garments and replace the wetter ones on the outside. I put my sleeping bag cover inside Bill's Gortex bivvy sac, and we both crawl into the bag cover. Put the cooker on the ledge and light it. Out comes the food – refresh, salami, chocolate, etc. Half an hour later it's like a 5 star hotel. I laugh – the fear that was with me before the climb has returned. We have a temporary reprieve. Bill's face is glowing, he has to laugh too. We talk nonstop for two hours, then drift off to sleep.

Day 3. 6 a.m., candles back on, breakfast – 1 litre each of hot refresh and fried salami on crackers. We place a bet on what the weather would be like outside. Bill's guess – snowing lightly. Mine is – radiantly clear and calm. However we put on storm clothes and batten down any exposed skin. At approximately 8 a.m. I push out the door with my feet. Spindrift is pouring off the rock walls – I lose! The cave entrance is on the lee side of the wind, but the weather is still fairly lousy. I go first, with the rack. Bill follows. We climb over the Gendarme heading into the full blast of the storm. We down climb together placing runners. An hour later we start the first of two abseils and by 12 noon we are on Sabre–Adelaide Col.

From the Col I climb a full rope length. I set off a large wet snow avalanche. This is good as it's made a reasonably safe path for us. We reduce the rope back to 10m between us and down climb, reaching the Upper Marian Bivvy at 2 p.m. Into warm sleeping bags and sleep. During the night approximately 30cm of snow fell. The rock bivvy is not fully sheltered and we were fairly well covered in snow ourselves.

Day 4. We approached Marian Cirque 30 minutes after leaving the bivvy, avalanches all around. It's getting very serious. After down climbing 70m Bill rap's off, places a belay and I down climb. While climbing down 5m of 65°

ice, I hear an avalanche above me. I brace myself. It bounces and rides over my head. The rope goes very tight with the strain of the snow, then it hits Bill and takes him down. Fortunately for us both, Bill is tied into a solid 'dead man'. The avalanche passes. I down climb like a rocket thinking 'gotta get outa here'. 10 minutes later we are out of the avalanche run.

We stop and take off the ropes – we're safe. Ropes packed away, pack back on my back and half a second warning and then another avalanche hits us. I feel tremendous pressure as it's trying to drag me down. It feels like minutes before it passes. I look up. Bill's smiling at me and says 'it's good to see you'; we head off. Half an hour later we reached the bottom of the Cirque and safety.

4 p.m. and we reach the car in pouring rain. We reach Queenstown about 10 p.m. after a victory drink at the Te Anau pub. No lights, no wipers and only enough spark, we arrive back home.

I would like to make two points. One on Sabre itself, the other for those who wish to winter climb in the Darrans. Bill and I both agreed that Sabre was not as hard as we thought. Having about 4 hard pitches (extreme) instead of the imagined 8 or so. However, it had the hardest pitch I have ever climbed (3rd pitch) unaided to date.

The Darrans ice is tough climbing to the limit. I do not know the fancy words to express to you New Comers – 'you blow it just once, and you're dead!!'

There is only a small group who climb D.I.C.E.* Country. I have a great respect for them all, it's ballsy stuff. No one watches you to admire or clap your grade 6+ pitch. There's no comforts of a cosy bed on the nights out in storms, there are only a few people who can appreciate the extreme demands of Cul De Sac, Heart of Gold, Gomer, etc., and credit goes to those few climbers, that no one has lost his life climbing this level.

What is there left to be done?

Well, there's about 20 Balfour faces and dozens of cirques yet to be visited for the first time in winter.

Bill is dead now – there will never be another Bill Denz – however, let our climbing skills go forward and push towards new challenges.

* D.I.C.E. – Darrans Ice Climbers Express – words from Lord Perry of Darran Land, VC, DSO, SIS and Hon. Doc. to the institute of Cirque Creek.

JILL TREMAIN

Letter to Mavis Davidson, 1971

Christchurch
24-9-71

Dear Mavis

Graeme and I have more or less been pressured into coming to Christchurch from Arthurs Pass, for radio, lectures etc., so I thought it a good opportunity to write and let you know that we have used some of the food you had left at Murchison hut. We left Mt Cook allowing 12 days' food to get to the Rakaia valley, but unfortunately it took us 24 days to reach Manuka Point, and 12 of those were spent at Murchison! About the 6th day we were scratching around in every nook and corner hunting hopefully for a grain of rice or 2, and eventually came across your tin. There had been no other food at all in the hut, so we were really grateful for our find and hoped you wouldn't mind if we used some of it …? I think there were prunes or apricots in it, and they took the strange colour of mould so we threw them out, the raisins were slightly alcoholic (hic) and probably just eaten in time. The service biscuits were all broken and soft, which we remedied by 'frying' so it was a big event in our day! We had the occasional clearing which we made use of and had several good runs from the hill above the hut.

We did get food dropped into us just before we left but we still lived sparsely. One day for entertainment I ruled a horizontal line around the walls, the NE side (corner) is 7½″ lower than the NW. The portion jacked up is level virtually … Pen's just run out on me! … please excuse the biro. We eventually left Murchison in a howling gale, but the saddle remained 'clear'. Cloud poured over the divide, seemingly in a vicious temper, the glacier took on aspects of the Sahara, I could hardly see Graeme in front of me, for the driving snow was deep, almost to our waists. We skinned up to the saddle still uncertain to the day's outcome, however the wind surrended a part of its tempo and we gained the Classen side of the pass. D'Archiac stood dark and distant in the turning skies, we looked down a steep gully and sidestepped most of it, wondering if we could get through the hanging

ice. Shortly our worries ceased a smooth passage was made to the Joie de Vivre. The skiing was on powder and most enjoyable, some time later, 5.30 we reached Godley, at last on our way.

I have found this trip so far, beyond expectations, it has been truly magnificent, as you will probably imagine, knowing so much of the mountains and the way of life they dictate. I hope you don't mind your food loss too much Mavis, we will be happy to have some more food flown in if you wish. I hope Wellington and Spring are giving you some reasonable weather, sunny days and not the equinoxial gales of Oct.

It will be good to see the old city again!, & our friends.

Best wishes and Kindest Regards
From Graeme and Jill

ALLAN UREN

White as a Sheet

I don't know why I decided to solo White as a Sheet, a 300-metre ice route on the slopes of Mt. Crosscut in the Darran Mountains. It was possibly the stupidest thing I've ever done. The idea came to me in a flash, probably for the usual blunt reasons: ego, naivete, a feeling of wild comfort in the mountains, the need to prove myself, the desire to do something no one else had done before, the yearning to experience total commitment, and the fact of simply being a young man.

Back then, I was generally a shy, mild-mannered person who apologised all the time – not the most technically adept climber – but when the ice got hard another identity, one I refer to as 'the alien,' emerged. It was something so far from my normal demeanour that it frightened me. The alien first appeared during a squash match when I was eighteen. I yelled and threw myself across the court. I might have just been overly competitive that day, but it felt like the eruption of an uncontrollable violence. Afterward, I stopped playing squash. The mountains were a better place to express that much passion – vast enough to soak it all up.

And White as a Sheet was the perfect arena. Seen in profile, the climb looked like the tongue of some great mythical ice dragon, a white line slobbering down a granite slab, surrounded by a semicircle of black stone buttresses. Like other Darrans cirques, this one is steep and U-shaped, with no safe zone free from avalanches – you feel as though you're in a dead-end alleyway on a dark night, pursued by a fast-walking stranger. Up close, the climb drapes at an average eighty degrees, seemingly without ledges. I didn't know it then, but it has the added hazard of never fully forming – the ice on the upper pitches will just barely support body weight.

When Dave Vass and Richard Thomson made its first ascent in 1989, they named it for the pallor of Richard's face after he fell off a three-metre vertical icicle. Richard later told me that finishing that pitch was a 'small point of pride. But I was fried after that – psychologically and also physically.' Since then, the climb has only had six or so ascents.

In August 1992, Phil Penney, Clinton Beavan and I had just climbed Cul de Sac, a 1500-meter ice route on the buttress of Crosscut. After Phil

and Clinton went home, I remained alone at the Homer Hut. Before I knew it, I'd stepped off the Milford road and crossed the Hollyford River, lurching from boulder to boulder in my bare feet, on my way to White as a Sheet. The waters were so clear that they seemed invisible; I only knew they were there by the rushing sound they made and by the agony of my cold skin. On the other side, boulders covered in brilliant orange lichen poked out of the snow. Soon the only colour came from the moss, frozen in great green-brown carpets and blobs. An earthy smell rose from a small patch of bush – a last vestige of softness. Beyond it, avalanches had gouged deep, unstable ruts in the rocky ground, covered with dry powder. Crampons didn't help. I kept moving.

Once below the route, I didn't feel any fear. The slides had formed grey, easy-looking smears that led to the upper section where the 'Sheet' proper intersected with thicker, chandeliered ice. But mountain routes always appear shorter and less steep than they really are. Even now, after thirty years of mountaineering, I still get it wrong. Maybe my highschool teacher was right when he wrote on my term report, 'Allan has trouble grasping new concepts.'

I started climbing on the right-hand side where the snow-ice was thickest. The angle was only seventy degrees, and I didn't encounter any of those typical Darrans 'seemingly good' axe placements that end up piercing a thin crust into depth hoar. I paused beside an aluminium conduit rappel anchor and felt smug. *I'm not going down*, I thought. Soon I realised I couldn't descend: fifty more metres and rotten ice patches began to break with my passage, leaving large, toothless gaps of smooth black slab that make it impossible even to traverse off. One hundred and fifty metres up, I finally reached a ledge.

To my right, the Sheet looked like steep bitumen covered in a skiff of new snow. In places, you could see a change in texture and colour that indicated ice, but it was difficult to know if it was consistent. Once I stepped off the ledge, I felt as if I were walking out across a barely frozen lake, afraid that at any moment I could plunge into the depths. Some fifty metres wide the Sheet had a spooky, spacey sense of omnidirectional exposure – up, down and sideways. Dinky toy cars inched along the Milford road far below. No one could have made me out in that vast expanse of mountain. If I waited for help, an avalanche would most likely have hit me before anyone reported me missing.

Without a crease or ripple to ease the strain, my calves began to burn. Oddly enough, I was enjoying myself. Untethered from the world, I had a powerful sense of freedom. I tapped on the thin ice lightly, like a mayfly alighting on a river, to keep it from shattering. I was still going up.

Richard's icicle drew closer. Now it appeared steeper and twice as large as it had from the ground. I finally grasped the concept that what I was doing could kill me. At the juncture of the Sheet and the chandelier ice, I clung to my tools and kicked my points in to try to create a comfortable stance. Water dripped onto my helmet as I rested my head against the ice. The plastic amplified the noise, augmenting my panic. *The fucking thing is rotten,* I thought. *Melting*. 'No, no, no!' I moaned. I could already feel the moment of weightlessness that would envelop me as I plummeted. Nausea welled up, and I began to sob. I didn't want to die. On the squash court, the alien had been a raging, unfocused mutation. But now it had matured into something else, something that could focus intense energy and manage fear and self-doubt to the point that it could easily lead to my demise.

It wasn't a conscious choice to move – my decision-making powers had been reduced to their most basic. I made the first placement in the icicle and sank, as the soloist must, into a place of absolute calm and confidence where the fear of falling is no longer considered. My tools felt buoyant. *Thunk, thunk, thunk. Kick, kick, kick.* I was still going up.

The next small patch of ice was the only thing that mattered.

I floated up the final 100 metres oblivious to the shower of ice from the snowfield above. The beginnings of a small avalanche? Who cared? All that mattered was that I was still going up. Unconsolidated snow in the standard exit gully forced me out onto steep blobs of ice. I talked to myself: 'Come on, Allan, you can do it, that's a good placement, drop your heels. Keep doing that, you'll be fine.'

I topped out. Pinned on the snow by disbelief, 300 meters up a mountain, I faced a descent nearly as dangerous as the ascent had been. Why had I left my harness and rope behind? Did I really think I was that good, that in tune with the mountains?

Maybe.

For months after I climbed down those steep, avalanche-prone slopes, ever aware of the menace that remained above me, terrified that a bluff would trap me in the dark, I had flashbacks and nightmares. I don't remember even looking back up at the route when I finally walked, once

more, beneath it. Down at the road, I hitched a ride with a Korean family who'd been sightseeing at Milford Sound. I sat in the back of their camper van with their two little boys. They stared at me with that directness that children have, wondering what this wild-eyed man had been up to and why his face was as white as a sheet.

CAROL DIAMOND CHRISTIE
and DAVID BAGULEY

Ruapehu, 23 September 1995, 5.08pm

Glancing towards the summit of Ruapehu I see it silently explode above me. White trails cut through the ash and mark the path of hot boulders.

My startled scream penetrates the windswept silence and alerts Paul Bamforth and Peter Jemmett. A huge rock whistles past and lands ten metres below as I run for my life towards the top of Te Heu Heu ridge.

Soon exhausted, I slow to a fast walk, one step, two steps, a glance behind. Boulders are bouncing down the Gut. I am worried about lahar. A cloud above Ngauruhoe gives it the appearance that it is erupting too! On top of the ridge I kneel in the snow, ring my parents and rasp that Ruapehu is erupting. Bopping up and down I try to keep the signal clear. I let them know that this may be IT, that I love them and that there are two parties on the mountain.

I turn around with a fearful exclamation from Amanda. A cloud of steam shoots up from the crater. It has been steaming all day but this is more fierce. White steam quickly covers half the sky and a second later I watch in disbelief as black objects fly out of the steam and high into the air. Black rocks, dust trails flaring behind, rise higher and higher.

I'm craning my neck still higher when I'm numbed by a sudden realisation: the rocks are coming down on us.

'Run!' I scream to the others.

I see the three others move but I watch transfixed for a second more. The sun is gone, the sky now black. There are too many rocks above us and not enough spaces between. In the shadow of death I run, the image of falling rocks fills my mind.

We hear them first before they land: the incredible sound of jagged rocks falling from over a kilometre up in the sky. In fear we run. We hear a constant battering as rocks begin to land all around us. I think of putting my pack above my head as a protective measure but a rock the size of a small car lands three metres ahead of me burning a deep hole into snow. I stagger feeling utterly helpless. There is black everywhere. Nowhere to hide. Nothing to be done. I hunch my shoulders up as I run, a futile protective measure against the terror.

My partner David Baguley and three others were at the top of Te Heu Heu ridge, about 1500 metres from the crater lake. I'm aware that they're probably now dead. Boulders are raining down the Gut towards the skierless rope tow. Clouds of smoke and ash blow east. Paul and Peter have run to Restless Ridge and between us lies a potential lahar path. I am all alone.

After running 30 metres we are pelted by a rain of sulphurous muddy water and ash. I look up and rejoice. The rocks have stopped falling. Amazingly none of us have been hit.

Amanda is blinded by the acidic rain and trips over. Thinking of lahars I scream to keep running and pull the rope that links us to guide her. After another 20 more metres we pause. Rocks are still rolling down the hill, down the gully towards where my girlfriend and her two companions are. We can't see them.

I look above. A mushroom cloud the size of a mountain is forming. The snow is black around us and the holes from the larger craters steam green smoke.

The action eventually subsides and Paul and Peter spend a long time retrieving the $500 avalanche transceiver I had been tracking down. The steam clears and I am stunned to see the others appear at the top of Te Heu Heu ridge, but cannot tell if there are three or four.

We wait and wait. I try to phone to see how they are – engaged signals mean David must be alive! Paul digs into the snow on the lee side of the ridge. We hope this might provide at least psychological shelter during the next eruption. I'm sure she's going to blow again.

I ring 111 so that they can locate our bodies. The police make me repeat everything twice. Curiously I am told to stay where I am and to ring back in five minutes to let them know our situation.

With the ash settled the sun returns, but looking over towards the summit of Ruapehu I freeze. A moving black finger of death slowly extends down the mountain. From two kilometres away I watch the black mass flow down towards the far west T-bar and gain speed. The lahar covers most of the valley. If anyone is down there …

The ski fields are closed aren't they? I look for confirmation at the stationary T-bars. What about the park staff? I rush to my pack. Where is my phone? We haven't heard the lahar warning system.

I find the phone and dial. I pause when I have the choice of services: 'Fire, police or ambulance, Sir?'

'Police,' I say after she asks again.

Someone answers.

'… a lahar is racing down the far western T-bar,' I say.

I am told to 'stay where you are,' and I'm put through to the Turangi police. Frantically I tell my story again: 'Can you please contact the ski patrol staff.' They can't do so immediately. I think again of my girlfriend and look down. I can see all three of them. Two are on one side of a valley, another higher up on a ridge. Is that Carol? She is motionless.

The four above are not moving. We are very nervous and expect the mountain to blast her sides towards us. Two lahars in nearby valleys reinforce the magnitude of the eruption.

After a discussion Peter begins to walk up the ridge. We hope the four will see him and start descending from their precarious spot. We can't leave them there.

David soon descends the ridge and is running towards me. I am afraid to touch him, he stinks of sulphur and is covered in mud. He is alive.

I don't know how to react to him, my emotions are all mixed up. I feel angry, relieved, scared and amazed all at once.

I move down with dread in my heart but soon with relief: all are moving. Carol is talking on her phone, her face covered. I walk towards her. She looks into my eyes unbelievingly.

We meet the ski patrollers and are given a ride down. As we reach the bottom people cheer and take photos of us ash clad but alive human beings.

ANDREW LINDBLADE

From *Expeditions*

Jannu

It was a different sound. Without talking, we both felt violence was approaching rapidly. It felt hard. Not snow. Not another spindrift avalanche. Immediately, I felt a sickness in my empty stomach. I was just about to exit our portaledge, having got my full clothing, boots and helmet on, when we were hit.

Total helplessness overwhelmed us as rocks and ice tore through the 'ledge's storm-fly and exited the other side, near the floor. There was nothing we could do. We hunched into ourselves as the onslaught continued, an incredible vortex of spinning snow, rocks and ice, blue and hard. Black and grey rocks streaked through like a shark's shadow underwater. It was impossible to see anything, to visually decipher what was happening.

Within a few seconds we began to expect that anything could happen. We weren't tied in independently from the 'ledge to another anchor. If the 'ledge's anchor rope was cut it was all over. Curtains. I had a vision of my anchor rope lying under this latest avalanche mess outside, waiting for my frantic, numb hands to burrow in, grasping for the safety it promised.

I found myself staring in disbelief at Athol's helmet, only inches from my face. It seemed to take forever for my mind to realise *it wasn't on his head.* The overpowering noise made it very difficult to think. What was coming next? Perhaps all this was merely a warm-up for the big rocks teetering on their edges a few hundred metres up the mountain. The terror came from a sub-conscious recognition of what the noise meant, of how very close we were to being killed by the rockfall.

My mind fumbled, imagining rocks hitting Ath's head. I saw his eyes searching for *something* to put over his head. Then nano-seconds later I thought, 'What if he's already been hit?' I tried to unclip his helmet but my fingers moved too fast, uncoordinated. To my relief, I saw Ath's hands reach out and grab the pot from the hanging stove, and place that on his head. Soon he had the helmet.

The careful and tedious effort of keeping our sleeping bags, brew gear, food and other personal kit organised had now been rendered a white,

frozen waste. As the thunder of rock and ice abated, we found ourselves staring at the inside of the 'ledge, and at each other. 'Are you OK?' It sounded so glib, like we had just tripped over a gutter, or stubbed a toe. We were both trying to comprehend what had occurred, as if we disbelieved it. Light shot in through the shredded storm-fly in rods, and in the side of the 'ledge behind Athol. He turned back to me after inspecting the damage, his face ashen.

He picked up a rock from the debris, and it reinforced our amazement that we had not been hit. I literally felt sick as I looked around, exasperation nearly bringing tears to the surface. 'I've got to get out,' I said, and cautiously began unzipping the door. I knocked the heavy snow build-up away as I struggled to slide the frozen zips down. The snow was packed like concrete, pressing in the shredded fly like a yacht's spinnaker under full sail.

With the remains of snow from the avalanche on my face melting and running down my neck, I reached out and into the snow, scraping it away, pawing like a pathetic mouse. I was trying to get one of the anchor ropes. After a few minutes I had it, clipped a jumar in, and awkwardly clambered out. I still didn't have my crampons on, but was able to stand on the heavily packed snow while I snapped them on, my hands turned very cold and numb from the metal; fingers sticking like a tongue to ice. I thrust them into my armpits for a few minutes, and waited for the slow return of warmth. I told myself that I had always enjoyed that painful re-warming process, the feeling of rushing, then creeping blood struggling to make its way to the extremities as the fingers hung limp and useless.

Stepping into the clear light was an enormous relief, the massive space and height offering an escape from our near-tomb. The sky was a pale blue over the northern horizon, already washed of the richer dawn colours. I stood carefully on a small, sloping stance, just big enough. I reached into my pockets and threw out old chocolate wrappers, watching them fall down the steep, hard ice. They were lifted by the soft breeze, and fell again. Like watching butterflies. The claustrophobic confines of the 'ledge kept returning to my mind despite the calm morning. It felt all the more shocking when outside, starting to receive the first warmth from the sunlight. Such a large space – the mountain, the Himalaya – but we had nowhere to run, even move. It had become so quiet during the minutes after the avalanche, like nothing had ever happened.

Athol was sorting out the destruction inside the 'ledge, or better said,

on the 'ledge. I could hear his solemn voice, 'This is fucking outrageous in here, I can't believe it.' I turned and watched the shredded fly gently flapping as small amounts of spindrift slid over the cliff above and dropped in. We both became absorbed in our own thoughts about what we were going to do. I climbed down a few metres to untangle a rope as Ath began making repairs with some tape. For an hour we both worked away under the lukewarm sunshine. There wasn't any wind, just small, short breezes that ceased as soon as we felt them. I never made any progress on the rope. I needed to pull one end right through, but kept looking for shortcuts. My bare hands melted the snow and thin ice stuck to the rope. Pulling the endless loops and knots through one another was exhausting work. I could hear Ath working quietly away, the sharp sound of his teeth ripping tape penetrating the awesome mountain silence.

I stared out to the horizon and down onto the Jannu glacier where we had carried our loads across from base camp so many times during the last month. Base camp was out of view, hidden by the thousand-metre rock buttress we had climbed to get from the glacier to camp two. Dark clouds were already churning with anger and lifting higher towards us. We knew we didn't have a lot of time before it would be snowing and we'd be tortured by the spindrift avalanches again.

We talked about what options we had. It was very stressful. We both felt exhausted and slightly shattered by what had happened. The upper part of the mountain was already clouding over, taking the sun away to leave us with a sullen sky, the temperature rapidly dropping. Snowfall was imminent. Ath said we could try shifting the 'ledge higher, to a more protected site. I admired his optimism but was very doubtful about this, knowing the 'ledge was finished, and also sceptical about getting a better site. We talked the idea through. Tiny, isolated flecks of snow began to drift around us. I felt stunned that after so much effort we were faced with making a decision in such difficult circumstances. My head was buried deep in my hood as tears fell over my face. I fought very hard to keep them away. I watched the snowflakes passing my eyes. I looked at Ath – his eyes were watery and red and he looked back at me. Right then I felt like we were little boys, brothers, who had run outside, confused and shocked by the sights and sounds of our parents fighting. We searched for words that would offer our impending retreat some dignity. The shock of nearly being killed an hour ago was coming to the surface, to the edge.

But the thought of descending brought on most of the anguish. It was not about the 'summit at all costs,' or other associated clichés. We were absorbed deeply in the mountain, in the route. It was taking shape. We were moving, the only living things on Jannu. We had 14 days worth of food and fuel, and a large rack of gear to deal with the massive headwall of the route. I recognised the hurdles: the feeling of wanting to crawl under a rock or bed when faced with the seemingly insurmountable, then turning about and walking headlong into it all, grinning.

It was very quiet. There was a faint rush of wind across the headwall, like a wind across the other side of a wide lake, pushing the trees. It looked deathly, black streaking clouds like scars across the sky. Our effort had hit silence. It took some time for both of us to finally say to ourselves and to each other, 'Fuck it, that's it, it's over.' We began moving gear, slowly but certainly.

Our decision was probably inevitable, as I write here with the benefit of hindsight. The 'ledge couldn't have sustained any bad weather, and as we found out, it would have received loads.

We both dearly wanted to climb the mountain. We were trying a new, direct route up the north face, but with this attempt rendered a failure, instinctively we decided to climb the Wall of Shadows, a route up the left-hand icefields and rock barriers of the north face.

The snowfall became denser, we knew the spindrift avalanches would soon be upon us. Ath passed our sleeping bags out of the 'ledge along with shards of blue ice and clumps of snow from the avalanche. It was incredibly depressing. I stuffed the bags into our packs and warmed my hands up with exhaled air. Soon I would have to put my gloves on, but I tried to do as much as possible without them as it was faster, less cumbersome. We quickly packed everything, some of it into the packs and the rest into the haul bag. All the gear was frozen and sticky with cold, like rigor mortis.

All of a sudden I hated the 'ledge; that which had protected us so much, had made life possible on the route. We pulled it apart: it felt like a skeleton, clacking and folding like dry bones might. It made an awkward bundle. We rammed it into its long black bag, clumps of ice sticking to its side. I neatly tied the top of the bag and clipped it to the underside of the haul bag. We were ready to go. Small rivers of snow from above broke over our legs, below the knees. I had put my goggles on but tore them off in frustration when they became coated with snow and ice. I stuffed them inside my

down suit, and struggled to get the zips back up to my neck as more and more spindrift hurtled down.

We started abseiling. I went first. Athol disappeared from sight within a few metres, so heavy was the snowfall and cascading spindrift. I heard him yell: 'Watch out!' I glanced upward and met a rapidly expanding cloud of avalanching spindrift with my eyes. Like a downward-exploding atomic cloud, grey and violent. It passed after ten seconds, leaving the rope vibrating like a plucked violin string. It left me spitting melted snow from my lips, white like a snow-covered pine tree.

The entire descent occurred as if in slow motion. It was a series of abseils, repeating the same process: I would abseil first as Athol simultaneously lowered the haul bag alongside me. I pushed (or often just kicked) it free when it became stuck on some ice or rock. Sometimes it was like trying to move a dead animal. It was incredible what the haul bag became stuck on (a small loop of webbing would catch on a little spike of insignificant granite in a near-vertical section, for example). It was always surprising how quickly the haul bag took off once I'd dislodged it. At the end of my rope, I'd make an anchor (one ice screw), clip myself and the haul bag into it. I would then disconnect myself from the abseil rope. 'OK!' I would yell, projecting my voice upward, hoping Athol could hear me. Our voices always seemed to be absorbed by the immensity of the mountain, to evaporate. Ath would then abseil and once he had arrived at the new anchor, we'd pull the abseil ropes down and begin again.

Soon the avalanches started again, pushing against me like a swelling wave. I turned my head into the snow and muttered 'Fuck off.' It probably sounded like there was actually someone there to talk to. As the avalanches fell lower, they spread out, like a sheet falling, wave-like, over a bed. Cold air rushing aimlessly, pushing against our faces, trying to get into our suits.

From the other side, the north-west, the clouds had grown and were closing in on us. We could feel the air growing colder and colder. Almost snap-freezing. My feet were getting cold. *They're not freezing, so just ignore it.* We laboriously kept abseiling. The lower we went, the more features or rock and fins of ice we recognised. By late afternoon we were on the névé, the flat. Safe. We trudged a couple of hundred metres out and away from the wall as the bad weather simultaneously lifted. 'That'd be right,' said Athol softly. We were oblivious to the time that had passed. Early sunset colours reached through the pulsing clouds. We pulled the ropes

into where we stood. Our shoulders drooped. I sat down on my pack after letting it fall carelessly from my shoulders. We sat there, too tired to say much. I wanted to go to sleep. The previous 36 hours, culminating with the rock avalanche and getting off the face, seemed to have caught up. Light snowfall drifted past. We stood and began to walk back to camp two, keen for food and sleep.

Athol took some photos as we made our way back. I stopped every 20 steps and leant over on my knees to rest. I couldn't understand why I felt so tired. I was even too shattered to take my pack off, let alone get my camera out like Ath had. I realised I was probably severely dehydrated. The muscles in my legs were burning, twitching with thirst. My throat was unbelievably dry, catching on words. At the point on the névé where we did a sharp turn down to camp two, the soft light radiated all around and I felt a lot warmer. Ath asked me to pause so he could get a shot and I looked forward to hearing him pressing the shutter again. We trudged across the undulating, slightly downward, névé into the increasing darkness. We had never roped together through this area other than the first time. I remembered where the few crevasses were and stepped carefully around them, half-asleep. Ath was about 50 metres ahead, still turning around and getting photos. The last light was like old, faded neon.

CAOILINN HUGHES

Avalanche

When the avalanche came down on us

it did not come down on us in a holy light,
flickering between this dimension and another

ultraviolet one. It did not shower its sermon upon us
in meaning-ful, vowel-less sounds like stalactites.
It did not come down on us at all. It came up, up, over

and around us; all around us in a pall. It met our bodies
in a hail, hail, hail, not a wall but heavier than water
if we were sitting at the bottom of the sea. We heard it crack
and sizzle on the ground. It filled the valley like a steam engine;

its clotted vapour urging forward to some terminus beyond us.
We watched it soar and could not inhale enough air between
the screams. Our lungs made fists. I thought of lips freezing shut
once and for all, the uncommon cold, no human fingers to close
the lids nor chance of rescuing the bodies, stiff as candy canes

striped red, white, red, white, grey. Your hands were fifty feet away,
your mind another hundred. My cries could not contend with this parade
of physics. You were wordless, as if the snow were slow motion surf
or a weir devouring its atmosphere. Was it fluid dynamics, glaciology
or meteorology you surveyed? There was something of the shock
wave about it, no doubt about that. The space between us

prolonged. I should never have collapsed in love with a physicist.
I saw the fort my brother built from bales of hay, whose tunnel
should never have been trusted. Oh, to make a hay citadel!
'When the fields are white with daisies,' my father would have said.
The ice wave rose and darkness fell. I doubted how well my elbows
would act as pick-axes, if it were to be a catacomb. I had once been told
that knowing which way is up is key: that the whiteness is homogeneous;
that people dig madly, burying themselves in the immortal white. I panicked:
would he have a better chance than I, with his gall; his practicality?
No, the snow was nothing like confetti. It would not applaud any small boys
or any small girls, no matter how insolent. We braced ourselves, finally.

Later, you described the form of a loose snow avalanche as a teardrop;
born of some great disparity between the tensile gift of snow layers
and their compressive heft. The angle of repose was soft, you allowed,
as we stood in the catchment area, making our observations and vowel sounds.

ANONYMOUS

A Solitary Climber (1906)

The temporary disappearance of Mr. R.S. Low, an Alpine enthusiast, in the Mount Cook ranges, is another painful tribute to the wisdom of the rule that places a discount upon solitary mountain-climbing. Happily, the high Alps of New Zealand have, thus far, claimed few victims among those who set out to 'conquer' them with axe and rope and pointed alpenstock. But every year an increasing number of people – chiefly Germans and English – are swept into eternity by the familiar dangers of high climbing in the Swiss Alps: thundering avalanches, showers of falling stones or ice, deep crevasses covered with thin and treacherous coatings of frozen snow. And such deaths! In 1865, for instance, Lord Douglas fell 4000 feet. His three guides turned somersaults down through the air for four-fifths of a mile. In August, 1895, Professor Schmidt dropped from the highest point of Iriglar. He never stopped falling till his remains made their final bump against the earth 9000 feet below. When you drop from one of those dizzy heights, you generally bang a few times against jagged projecting points of an ice or stone precipice, and leave something on each to feed the eagles with. But it is doubtful if that does any good to the climber. Even with good guides or other skilled companions and the aid of alpenstocks, ropes, ladders, snow-goggles, veils, hob-nailed shoes, ice-axes, wraps, and all the rest of the paraphernalia, high mountain climbing is a dangerous amusement, that requires great nerve and endurance. The Swiss mountain-guides know this. So they demand (and bank) their fees in advance. Solitary high-climbing is practically a funeral march.

Why do people go a-climbing? You might as well ask why they get cholera morbus or German measles. It's epidemic in alpine regions. It is the summer disease in Switzerland, and sundry colonies of its microbes have, during the past few summers, squatted among the Cook and other ranges in New Zealand. For scientists, mountain-climbing has a purpose that justifies the taking of reasonable risks by skilled alpinists. It is said to be very useful in the early stages of consumption – and in every stage of corpulency. It likewise affords a certain number of unskilled and foolish

people a great many different ways of breaking their foolish necks. But the ordinary or garden variety man would do well to remain 'way down below, where safety lies. Or if he must climb, let him do it as Mark Twain did, by deputy.

J. WALTON

A Pioneer Phase (1963)

Ten years ago I was a 'common labourer' on the Pioneer Hut site, and somehow I never got back to enjoy the fruits of my labours. Last Christmas I eagerly accepted an invitation to join a party which proposed to fly in from the Hermitage, have a look around, 'nothing spectacular you know', and walk out via Graham's Saddle. The flying in was something in itself that I had not done before, so my return to Pioneer commenced with the thrill of a flight on a glorious morning. We crossed the Divide through a slot near Graham's Saddle to a grand traverse of the névés that I had plodded over with Neil Hamilton after climbing the Minarets and De la Bêche so long ago. It was good to be back and such a wonderful day for sitting around and soaking in the beauty of that wonderful setting once again. I had not seen the hut before but every rock seemed familiar – the built-up platform a testimony to good workmanship (not mine!), and the towering pinnacles above as threateningly secure as ever. The old bivi above nestled on its shelf as safe a refuge as when it was built in 1937. ('Safest place on the ridge,' someone remarked.)

With the arrival of two more by surface from De la Bêche the hut complement was eight. Two, who were already in the hut, moved up into the Maori bunk and with all the others 'bunked'. I found my rope mate had also gone aloft and so I took the spare space up there too. One of the few occasions when I've been the last to grab a bunk!

Now the weather was putting a question or two and we had doubts that climbing was going to be 'on' the next day. However, although there was no doubt next morning that we were going to be in for something later it seemed to be 'later' enough to warrant an excursion. We all set off in various directions for the peaks of our choice. Four of us climbed Von Bulow and Halcombe and we had a most enjoyable climb of it too arriving back at the hut about fourteen hours later, burnt and happy.

'Alarms' the next morning were almost drowned by a gale, the weather had broken and the hut was enveloped in cloud and rain.

One day's rest even in a fairly crowded hut can be pleasant – was pleasant, – but next day when the weather showed no improvement or

promise the feeling of confinement in cramped quarters with little to do inclined to suggest we were waiting for 'something' instead of just the weather to clear.

We had thunder and lightning too close to count the seconds between. We spent that second day mostly sitting, all eight of us, on the top bunk, swapping yarns, reading, singing and playing guessing games with the 'sixty-four' dollar one, 'What's the weather doing now?' put to any unfortunate who had to go outside. Visibility was zero. The hut radio receiver was practically useless as it could not receive the Hermitage, and we were only able to get 3ZR with poor reception. We had quite a lot of fun really and finally settled down to sleep at about 10.30 p.m. – as if we needed it!!

At two a.m. a rock avalanche started from above the old bivi completely demolishing it and sweeping it with the out-house down the south side of the ridge on to the névé far below. Three large boulders (over a ton each) took off at a tangent from the main avalanche line and struck the Pioneer Hut 'on the full' (snow immediately behind the hut was unmarked) at the level of the top bunk. The end of the hut was smashed in, the top bunk being completely demolished and the boulders and wreckage came to rest well inside on top of the bottom bunk and its four occupants. It was still raining.

Asleep in the top bunk I was awakened by the starting rush of the avalanche and instinctively cringed into my pillow. The boulders seemed to hit simultaneously for there was an 'explosion' and then a sensation of being swept down a long chute. I ended up at the end of the bunk space clear of the wreckage and free to stand up in the cooking area which was undamaged. The bunk end of the hut was not there and beyond, a ghost of snow mistily silhouetted the mound that was the wreckage, boulders – and the others.

A body lay at my feet. Dead? Unconscious? – at least not buried – 'must uncover the others – throw things out the hole, dig!' I seemed to have thrown a lot of the matchlining and shattered timber that had made up the top bunk and end wall, before someone joined me – the only able-bodied survivor of the bottom bunk. It seems quite fantastic how long a minute or two can be for we seemed to have done quite a lot of chucking out of wreckage before a body reared its head from the heap of debris right in the line of our fire. We were joined in quick order by this body (not really able

– cuts and bruises) and another unscathed survivor. There were now four of us active but little had been said; we were still collecting our wits. Cries were heard from below. The dying man called but a few times and we had to leave him and turn our attention to the more continual, vigorous calls of the trapped living.

We manhandled a boulder out of the hut (later we had to use rope on double purchase to move it), and soon had another man free. An injured ankle, however, relegated this survivor to the 'sideline'. Immediately after we had uncovered another – if you can 'uncover' a man who is trapped under a rock from chest to ankles!

The boulder was about two feet thick and three feet wide and was, although pressing hard upon him, miraculously supported by the debris of the bottom bunk which had collapsed under him a few inches on to the rock platform.

It was still raining, cold with a thick mist that occasionally allowed us glimpses by torch light of the now more threatening rocks above. We were lucky (very lucky all round of course) that we found torches quickly and that the lantern was undamaged so that soon we had quite good lighting.

There is no point in going through all the agony of raising that monstrous rock the six inches or so necessary to get the injured man out. By sheer good fortune a timber jack had been 'left on the job' from ten years ago and without this we would have failed. We could only raise one corner of the boulder a notch at a time, hold it up whilst timber was wedged in and then lower it down. It always seemed to sink further down. Whilst it was up feeling seemed to return to the numbed body. We were glad when the trapped man's feet 'hurt' for the sheer guillotine-like end of the rock appeared to have settled down so deeply into his ankles that it seemed impossible that they were still 'attached'. All the time our 'victim' assisted us by passing pieces of wood (his arms were free) and by helping to build the shores.

Eight hours later we carried him in a blanket to the 'safe' end of the hut. The rock, as solid as ever, shored on doubtful looking wedges of shattered timber. The injured man (numerous breaks and internal injuries) by his fantastic stoicism 'lead' us in our efforts, and only one such as he could have survived such a terrible ordeal. Earlier in the 'piece' the unconscious body (broken shoulder) had come to and had been made comfortable.

So at 10.30 a.m., still in the fog and rain all that could be done had been done, the dead man was as he died still under a ton or so of rock and wreckage. The injured were reasonably safe and comfortable. Three of us set off for help.

Our trip down the névé was easy and we arrived at the Chancellor Hut full of hopes of getting out that night. We were a trifle angry at finding the hut in such a state (just as I remembered it from ten years ago!) that we were unable to heat up some soup that we had with us, as the stoves were unserviceable. We might have done better that night if we had been able to have something other than water and biscuits for we were pretty exhausted by that time.

Apparently ten years is quite a while in New Zealand glacier transformation, as I found out when we reached the glacier snout. Which way off? The right which led on to river flats seemed obvious, but looked a very doubtful proposition for us; light was fading rapidly, and so after a 'recce', we decided on the left. Off the ice we were bluffed in about 100 yards and rather than gamble time on the ice we started up the glacier wall with the intention of sidling behind the Cones.

We slept under a large rock after ensuring it was secure – it was the size of a small pub! It was wet and foggy. We had arranged that the others should listen in to 3ZR five minutes to each hour, when, once out, we would have a message broadcast. We felt bitter at not having made it that night and more than sorry for the listeners-in. Paschendale eroded all night in great crashing rumbles of falling rock. One wondered what Pioneer Ridge was doing.

At first light, we were off upon the bush and after four hours of bush-bound, fog-bound blundering, arrived at the Fox Glacier Hotel.

I will not write much more (enough surely!), but I cannot finish without saying how much I was impressed – deeply impressed – by the whole-hearted, all-out effort of all the available locals in the subsequent rescue operation. Particularly must I mention the pilot of the only available ski plane (Hermitage was fog-bound); without his untiring efforts there is little doubt that the seriously injured man would not have been got out in time. A surface party would have been too late.

We did not participate in the actual rescue operations, and as this was well covered by the newspapers at the time, I will not report it fully here. Due to the weather, (which was at least improving), landing near the hut

was out until later in the day, with the result that by the time the seriously injured man was lowered to the névé and installed in the aircraft, it was too dark (9.45 p.m.), to take off. This meant yet another night in the hut for the others and a night out in the snow for the rescue team. The aircraft engine was run every two hours for warmth and it is doubtful if anyone slept much.

We certainly did not, even in our comfortable 'base' accommodation, and some of us were airborne in the Dominie at first light to see what was doing, as we had not heard from the rescue plane since the previous evening. Radio silence was kept by the rescue aircraft to conserve batteries, but an all-night radio watch was maintained at base in case of an emergency. We arrived over the névé just as the ski plane took off and though we turned back immediately and dived for base, they were there before us. The rest of the day saw an air shuttle service (still the one aircraft) bring everyone out.

The following day four of us flew over to the Hermitage in glorious weather – the weather we had waited for.

The mountains so resplendent in their imperturbability that all seemed as it was in the beginning.

Footnote: Gilbert Murray's body was reburied nearby a fortnight later by an Alpine Club party which also demolished the remains of the hut.

PAUL HERSEY

from *High Misadventure: New Zealand mountaineering tragedies and survival stories*

In January 1977 a group of around 20 members of the Wanganui Tramping Club (WTC) gathered in the Hopkins Valley, south of Aoraki Mount Cook, to explore, tramp, fish and climb. Generally the WTC didn't organise official gatherings, preferring an informal approach of encouraging groups to meet for trips such as the one to the Hopkins.

Tom Luff, who was a member of the WTC at the time, went on this club trip to Hopkins Valley. Luff recalled the club as being 'full of keen outdoors people'. Many of the club trips were family-based. 'On the 1977 trip to the Hopkins, there were about the same number of adults and children,' he said. 'Everyone had travelled down to the South Island in various groups to do their own thing during the holidays. We'd all talked about meeting at the Hopkins beforehand, but weren't entirely sure how many of us would turn up.' Luff and his family met up with the rest of the group at Monument Hut in the lower Hopkins Valley, and then moved up into Huxley Valley.

Hopkins Valley is sweeping and expansive. Cattle and sheep meander along open grassy terraces near the valley's entrance, and sure-footed thar whistle to each other from the craggy outcrops overhead. The braided Hopkins River filters down through the boulder fields, the fingers of the river eventually merging into the opaque depths of Lake Ohau to the south. Here, time is measured by the sun sweeping across distant mountain tops, clouds riding ridgelines and the shadows of the hills lengthening down the valley.

The valley is framed on the east side by the constant rise of the Neumann Range, while to the west alternate valleys branch up towards the Main Divide of the Southern Alps. Glen Lyon and Rabbiters' Peaks, in the lower Hopkins, are gently sloped mountains around 2000 metres high. But further up-valley the mountains become steeper. Seen from the valley floor, the Dasler Pinnacles rock spires are impressive, and the southern flank of Ward has a dark, almost frowning, countenance. Huxley Valley, which sneaks off to the west opposite Mount Glenmary, is somehow comforting in its hidden confinement. Lined with bush and guarded by a barrier of

high peaks on all sides, and far from the trappings and worries of home life, the Huxley feels like a lost world.

Luff and the other WTC members set off to explore the countryside, which many of them had not visited before. 'Different people wanted to do different things,' Luff recalled. 'Some wanted to climb and tramp, but others just wanted to fish and stay near the huts.' The larger group split into smaller parties, and one party, including Luff, headed up into the North Huxley Valley to hopefully climb Mount Strauchon.

At Huxley Forks, the valley branches off into two. Luff and his companions followed the narrow stream north to Brodrick Hut. Winter avalanche paths had carved rubble runways down the mountain slopes, and the group picked their way over broken limbs of dead trees and around boulders disturbed from their perch. Above Brodrick Hut, some of the party, including Luff, climbed further up western slopes covered with alpine grasses and mountain lilies to Brodrick Pass. They then attempted to traverse south along the broken ridgeline to Mount Strauchon. 'The snow conditions weren't that pleasant on the ridge,' Luff recalled. 'No one made it to the summit that day, but we got some pretty good views down into the Landsborough.'

On their descent the group rested near Brodrick Pass. Luff remembers a band of local kea 'trying to cause mischief' among the climbers. 'The birds took a liking to one of the younger guys, Rob McLean. One even landed on his shoulder. The group retraced their tracks back down Huxley Valley to the beech forest at the valley entrance, where they met up with the others and then continued on into the heart of the Hopkins. Another two hours up the valley they reached Elcho Hut. Here they camped, and explored the lower reaches of the Elcho Stream. Some headed up through a steep and narrow track to the tiny Dasler Bivouac that overlooked the Hopkins Valley. 'We were amazed at the beauty of the place,' Luff said. 'There was so much to do, so many areas to explore and peaks to climb.'

After a number of days in the valley, where they enjoyed settled weather, most of the WTC group decided to head back to civilisation. A small group wanted to trek and climb further up the valley and on towards Aoraki Mount Cook 'We studied the map, and it looked like a pretty exciting route,' Luff said. 'My oldest boy John, who was 15 at the time, wanted to go because some of his friends were going. We thought he was a bit young and said no.'

In the end, four club members decided to attempt the trip. Craig Benge, the club's president, at 25 years of age was considered by others to be a very experienced tramper and climber. Fenella Druce, also 25, had just qualified as a doctor. Druce had recently moved to Wellington with her husband, but she was still an active member of the WTC. And teenagers Bill Bennett and Rob McLean, who were working towards jobs with the National Parks Board, tramped and climbed as often as they could.

Benge, Druce, Bennett and McLean left Elcho Hut, in the Hopkins Valley, on Thursday 27 January. They forded Elcho Stream and followed stock trails across the grasses of Apricot Flat. A few kilometres from Elcho Hut, Hopkins Valley narrows and travel becomes more confined, especially after Thomson Stream. The best way to get through is to find a route along the boulder edge of Hopkins River. In this part of the valley, the river is less braided and more of a focused torrent. Above Dodger Hut the four would likely have stuck to the true left of the river, and eventually reached Erceg Hut, nestled on the edge of a thick band of alpine scrub. Here, the mountains are very close, and because they are viewed from directly beneath, appear to be rather steep also. Immediately opposite Erceg Hut, the snowy eastern aspects of Mount Williams and Mount Percy Smith rise over glacially worn terraces of rock and rubble. Both rewarding climbs in themselves, their summits provide amazing views back down the Hopkins Valley and also over into the upper reaches of the Landsborough Valley.

It is unclear whether the climbers spent the night at Erceg Hut or carried on an extra hour to the Richardson Rock Bivouac. But to reach Barron Saddle, they would likely have first crossed over into the Dobson Valley the following day via Tragedy Col. To reach the col from the west is reasonably straightforward. Low-angle slopes lead up the Neumann Range to reach a height of just over 2000 metres. The descent into the Dobson is precipitous, involving deep snow and eroded bluffs, and has claimed lives in the past. The key is to traverse towards a prominent rocky outlier, and from there locate and angle down a vague spur to the valley floor. This crossing would have taken Benge, Druce, Bennett and McLean most of the day, and they may have elected to spend the night at Waterfall Hut immediately after crossing the Dobson River.

On Sunday 30 January, the four climbers headed north towards Barron Saddle, crossing beneath the Hour Glass Glacier on the eastern slopes of Mount Hopkins, and then scrambling up easy snow and scree slopes

to reach the saddle. The saddle was first crossed this way in 1914 by Jack Clarke, Peter Graham, Frank Milne, George Rose and Samuel Turner – some of New Zealand's most prominent pioneering mountaineers and explorers. On the day that Benge, Druce, Bennett and McLean crossed the saddle, the weather had deteriorated, with cloud building and strong winds blowing from the north-west.

That night the Wanganui climbers reported in to the 7 pm Mount Cook Village radio schedule from Three Johns Hut. They said they intended to continue on to the village once the weather improved. A severe storm lashed the national park that night. Wind gusts of over 200 kilometres per hour tore off roofs and damaged buildings in the village. The weather was still bad on the Monday, with gale-force winds and rain. The following day the storm abated somewhat, but the mountains were shrouded in cloud and whipped by strong winds.

Benge, Druce, Bennett and McLean failed to report in during the scheduled radio checks on Monday and Tuesday night. Senior ranger Stewart Irwin was not overly concerned. He figured that the four might have retraced their steps back into the Dobson Valley rather than carrying on to the village. But when there was still no response from the Three Johns Hut's radio on Wednesday 2 February, Irwin decided to send two rangers up to investigate.

Hugh Logan was one of the two rangers who went up to Three Johns Hut to look for the missing WTC party. At that time Logan was 23 years old. He had just finished his summer student job as a ranger with the Mount Cook National Parks Board and moved back to his parents' home in Christchurch to prepare for another year of studying. When his father suggested an inland fishing trip, Logan jumped at the opportunity. 'As was typical of my father, we got off to an early start,' Logan recalled. 'We left Christchurch at two in the morning, towing the caravan and heading south.' Logan remembered a 'pretty rugged storm brewing in the mountains' during their car trip. The wind got so bad that they had to leave the caravan on the side of the road. 'We reached the Mount Cook Village and the weather had lifted a little. Stewart Irwin asked if I'd mind doing one more job for the summer.' Irwin asked Logan and another ranger, Mal Clarbrough, to check Three Johns Hut for any sign of the four WTC members.

There are two options to reach Barron Saddle from Mount Cook Village

– either the Sealy Range or Mueller Glacier. 'Initially we climbed up onto Sealy Range,' Logan said. 'There's a spot on the range where you could see the hut if the weather was clear enough. But it was still raining, and we couldn't see anything.' Logan and Clarbrough decided to drop down to the Mueller Glacier and walk up the glacier to investigate further. 'Normally Mal was quicker than me,' Logan said, 'but for some reason I was ahead of him that day. As we reached the head of the glacier, just below the hut site, I called back to him that I'd go and put a brew on.'

Logan climbed up the last slope to the hut at just before 6 pm, but when he got to the Barron Saddle he became disoriented. 'I'd been to the hut only a few months before so I knew its location. But I got to where I remembered the hut to be, and it wasn't there.' Logan thought he must have been mistaken about the hut's location, and started to search the surrounding terrain. 'Then I looked down at my feet and saw bits of wire sticking out of the ground.'

Logan was standing directly on the hut site. 'What had happened took a moment or two to sink in,' he said. 'I looked over the edge but couldn't see anything. There was this suspension of belief. The whole hut had been completely blown away.'

Clarbrough reached Logan a few minutes later and radioed through to National Park Headquarters. Irwin arranged for more rescuers to be flown to the site. With the weather worsening, the two hunkered down and waited for the others. 'The helicopter came in right on dusk, and we quickly rigged a rope so I could abseil down the cliff,' recalled Logan. He managed to reach the hut debris on abseil but he did not find any survivors. Then Logan, Clarbrough and the other rescuers who had flown in on the helicopter dug in for a bleak night as another storm pushed through. 'The next day the weather was so bad that we decided to walk out,' Logan recalled.

Later in the day the weather cleared up, and the helicopter took the rescuers around to the Dobson side of Barron Saddle. Logan, Clarbrough and the other rescuers climbed up a gully to the hut debris, and continued to search for survivors through the snow. Eventually they found two bodies a short distance from the hut wreckage, and a few days later the other two bodies were also found.

Logan recalled that most of the debris was in a concentrated area of the slope, indicating that the hut had been lifted as a solid unit, rather than

blown away piece by piece. Most of the guy wires had been ripped from the ground and the rest were sheared off at ground level. Rescuers reported that the bodies of Benge, Druce, Bennett and McLean were fully clothed, suggesting that the four might have been preparing to leave the hut when it finally blew away.

It is difficult to imagine what they must have experienced in the minutes before the hut disintegrated. With his experience of alpine hut construction, Derek Chinn believes that the four climbers would likely have had plenty of warning but nowhere else to shelter in the atrocious weather conditions. 'The hut would have started to get pretty lively,' he said. 'It would have vibrated with each new gust, and then begun to bounce against the guy wires. This could have gone on for some time, depending on the strength of the wire and attachment points.'

Derek figures that the wires must have eventually given against the strain and begun to fail. 'There would have been a cyclic jumping of the hut as the guys slackened. More slack would have meant an increase in the intensity of the structure jumping.' Some wires would have sheared off, and then extra strain would have been placed on the remaining wires with each progressive wind gust. Eventually they would have been broken or pulled from the ground, and nothing would have been holding the hut down. It could have been blown away more or less intact.

Given the strength of the wind, the four friends had no hope of leaving the hut.

'They would have been blown away,' Derek reasoned. 'Maybe if they had dug a snow cave earlier, they could have sheltered there, but there was probably no indication beforehand that the hut was about to completely blow away.'

In the end there were no other options for the climbers. They had chosen to wait out the storm in Three Johns Hut – a structure that should have been able to withstand the storm – and this decision cost them their lives.

Members of the Wanganui Tramping Club were devastated when the news reached them. 'They were such careful climbers. What occurred was not a reflection on them,' Luff said. 'When you get to a hut you should be safe.' But the tragedy could have been much worse. Originally, more WTC members had hoped to go on that trip, but they had to return to work. Otherwise, more people could have been caught up in this accident.

It took many years for the Wanganui tramping community to recover. 'No one wanted to venture to the outdoors for a while,' Luff said. 'The club kind of petered out, but eventually we started up again.'

Some years later WTC members decided to set up a trust to commemorate the four friends. 'The trust was to help others in their love and enjoyment of, and respect for, the New Zealand outdoor life,' Luff explained. The trust was initiated to create financial support to others in the local community who wished to further their experiences in the outdoors. 'Looking back over the years we can be satisfied that the memory of these four fine people has been kept in front of us,' Luff said.

Tony Druce decided to build a memorial hut – Fenella Hut – in the Cobb Valley in Kahurangi National Park, for his daughter. Along with others, he led the fundraising for the project. Also, there is a well-used stone seat in front of the Mangaturuturu Hut in the Tongariro National Park. A bronze plaque set into the stone of the seat reads: *Remember here four friends killed Mount Cook January 1977.*

A new alpine hut was built in the Barron Saddle region in 1981, but this time further away from the saddle itself, and on a more sheltered site. Barron Saddle Hut is also more securely anchored to the ground beneath it.

BRIAN WILKINS

from *Among Secret Beauties*

A Shorter Life

10 January 1958. School holidays. I am at Unwin Hut near the Hermitage, Mount Cook, waiting to fly by ski-plane next day, with some of the best climbers in the country, up to the Pioneer Hut high among the snowfields of the Fox Glacier, to climb some of the highest peaks.

11 January 2 am. We are woken by the sound of talking, quiet but urgent. A climber is telling us that his two companions are in trouble just over the far side of the Tasman Saddle. He has walked from beyond the head of the Tasman Glacier, 25 miles away. One of his party, Tristram Hall, has fallen about 10 yards into a crevasse while roped, but they could not pull him out. Leaving the third, a young woman, on vigil above the spot, with two packs her only shelter, he has come for help. She is unable to dig in because both of the ice axes are being used to anchor the rope to Hall. He tells us that Hall is not injured, but we are worried when we hear that they were not carrying sleeping bags, having been travelling between the Murchison Hut and Malte Brun Hut, both of which have blankets. The ski-plane attempts to land there at daylight but the wind is too strong. This flight by John Hunter-Weston with some rather shaken climber-observers was a heroic effort. We cancel our plans and set off on foot, to help, along with others.

Hall is a member of our club, as is his father. The 10 of us get to the Ball Hut late in the afternoon, having walked the whole way because the Hooker Bridge has been damaged by floods and the road is closed to vehicle traffic. Others have gone ahead of us. Two young Scottish climbers reach the site and pull Hall out of the crevasse. A long day for those two, from the Hooker to the head of the Tasman and a climb of 7000 ft in 11 hours, and a good result. They wrap Hall up in one of their own down-filled jackets and place him along with Bartlett in a small snow cave they build for shelter from the cold wind, rain and sleet that night. He immediately vomits the hot soup they make for him.

12 January. The others of the advance party go towards the accident site with a stretcher, while the rest of us move up to wait at Malte Brun Hut. Some of us carry on to meet the rescue party coming down with Hall and deliver to

them a sledge we had brought up with us. All of us are needed to manhandle the sledge, to which he is strapped, up over 150 yards of loose moraine and steep tussock, to the hut. He is delirious, crying, 'Help. Please.' Now, as ropes strain on the sledge, hail beats on our faces and thunder reverberates from the slabs of Malte Brun. Most of the advance party are at their limit. We pull the stretcher in and begin to take off Hall's wet clothes which are under the down jacket he has been given. I untie his laces, preparing to rub his feet. He had been waving his arms around while on the stretcher, but just as I finish taking off his boots he lies back limp. 'I think he's gone,' says Harry Stevenson. We wrap him in warm blankets and try artificial respiration. 4.20 pm.

I know of no death of a mountaineer that is so painful to recall as that of Tristram Hall. We returned sad, and frustrated by the long list of decrements that had combined to kill him. The bridge being out, and the road cut off, making the time to get to him twice as long as it should have been. The ski-plane being unable to land. His own mistake in trying to jump a crevasse when, as implied in the report on the accident, he could have gone around it. The attempt, on the part of his two companions, to pull him out on the uphill side of the crevasse instead of the easier downhill side. Nor did they apply known techniques for crevasse rescue. His choice to wear mainly cotton clothing. The report implies that the clothing lowered to him by his companions could not offset this deficiency. Even near the end he may have survived had medically informed help been available. The advance rescue party, especially the two Scots who stayed the night with him, high on the glacier, working under extreme difficulty, in freezing rain and wind, were at the end of their tether. In the published report written by one of the advance party, describing the return journey of the larger group bringing him down, we read, 'Under these unpleasant conditions everyone started to walk down slowly to Malte Brun Hut. Hall managed to walk unaided for a good distance and was then supported by the Scots until the Ball Hut party arrived with the sledge at Darwin Corner.' Death was given too many opportunities to enter the bunkroom at Malte Brun Hut.

I spoke of none of these things in the classroom when I returned to Naenae College where I taught high-school science. I didn't feel capable of bridging the gap between their experience and mine. To them I was Elvis, and I had climbed with Hillary. That would do me too as I began my second year with them.

MARK WHETU

Summit of Dreams

Everest, North Face

I was surprised how late it was, being wheeled through well scrubbed corridors from Ward 5 and into Theatre No. 2. The day had finally arrived, a decision made. It had been three and a half months of waiting, thinking and wondering … how could things have been different? … regrets.

The trolley wheels had that kind of wobble as if they knew the way along these ancient corridors. Lights, ceiling, masks over faces, averted eyes.

Why won't he turn around, so fucking slow. This is insane, it's 5 o'clock, we're at 8700m and he wants to keep going! Gas must be low. God, it's 13 hours since we left Camp 6. The sun's low, too low, getting dark soon.

'Hey Digger, this is it mate. We've got to turn around – now!'

'How far to the top?'

'What?'

'Which way up?'

'Shit, it's too late, c'mon, it will take us all night to get back to six!'

'We'll bivvy.' My mind reeled at the word.

'Bivvy where?'

He follows me slowly.

Slowly the anaesthetic enters my brain. I sense a warm, feminine hand caressing mine. Blackness, heaviness that seems to drill through all thoughts, spiralling, spinning …

There's a lot more shit on the summit this time. Flags, bottles, even some sort of transmitting aerial.

Mike dived onto the summit.

Christ, he's finally done it, his gas mask hides the elation, but I can feel the vibes and he looks so at peace sitting there. The sunset, making him glow. I let the video just run and try to capture this ol' Digger taking in all those efforts over the years. After all this is his seventh attempt and he did it.

It's late, it seems so weird to be on top of the world watching the sun disappear behind Shishapangma. So far we've been there two minutes, too long!

'Let's fuck off!'

Descending at last. What a joke, we walk 50 metres. It's dark, the moon'll be up soon. Headwall's too steep to downclimb in the dark.

'This is it, mate, we'll dig in here.'

As I turn around to check the wind direction, I can still see the summit. Shaking my head, it's close and we're gonna dig a hole here!

Got to keep moving. Isometrics. That's the trick to circulation and avoiding frostbite.

Mike's wheezing and coughing, he doesn't sound good.

It's cold, so cold.

Thoughts of Edie, she's not far really – Kathmandu now, just over there … warm, sleeping in a bed. Another anniversary missed, apart again. Got to work on this, eight years and still together …

Lovers of the past wander through my mind, warmth, heat, special.

Moon's up, silvery white, the cold's so thick I can taste it, numbing.

Lovers, sex, stay warm. Friends, faces – good times. Each face so special, god I miss them.

Mike brings me back, he's cold, out of breath and trying to cough.

He's not good.

'Turn up your flow rate, when you're out we'll get going, okay?'

He's mumbling and not happy.

'Hey Digger, you did it mate, you did it.'

I hold Mike across my lap and embrace him, attempting to get some warmth. Sleep.

Stunned by the sunrise I realise I've been out to it for several hours. I can't believe I actually slept. My feet! Again, cold, numb, boots feel like they're full of mercury. Toes are dead. Fuck it!

We're outta here.

Mike raps the headwall as I downclimb beside him. Slow, so slow.

Slowly coming to in the recovery ward. Awake and feeling good. It smells chemical – recycled air. Sleeping bodies, warm eyes, smiles, friendly nurses, 'Are you okay?'

Sitting up, body check, sigh – relief, no skin grafts.

Holy shit, left foot's so small, short. It feels so light.

I hope they saved the meditarsus, god I hope I can run again. What about rock shoes. What the hell's going to fit?

Mind still thick with sleep.

My feet are asleep, edging on flakes, crampons hooking for a hold.

North Face below, Camp 6 so far away.

The third step goes by, and it's easy ground for a while. Where's Digger? We've got to get to Camp 6 today at least. Waiting.

I'll wait at the second step. It's windy, cold. Getting tired. Where are you, Digger? Waiting.

'How's it going, mate? You're doing well, but we've got to keep moving. I'll rap first so I can film you coming over.'

Waiting. The epic begins, tangled ropes, Mike's spinning in space, off route.

Time is running out.

Now Mike's blind, and we're just at the beginning of the technical stuff. Great, how the hell can he do the traverse!

Looking at the sun, it's getting late, we're not going to make it back to Camp 6 tonight. Christ, he won't make it through another bivvy. I lose a down mitt, flicking jammed ropes – real bummer. Almost instantly my fingers are wooden.

'Digger, just listen, I'll describe the moves to you. Let's keep it moving.'

Luckily I clipped him into some very tattered fixed line, two steps and he's airborne, limp and hanging from his harness. Unbelievably the rope holds. Hanging in space, Mike is oblivious to his fatal exposure.

Opting to guide him, I clip a sling from my Petzl ascender to Mike's Petzl which is attached to his harness by his own sling. This puts us in short-rope mode. Warning him that I am unattached, other than holding my Petzl, I know that I can hold him. Three steps and Mike's flying, almost ripping me towards the Central Rongbuk. Time is racing by, and we seem days from Camp 6.

6:00am, lights in my face. It's medication time. Just another start to the day in Ward 5. I've got to get out of here!

Sally, my specialist, she's kind, she'll understand. She'll let me go.

Chris turns up, after a sumptuous breakfast of rice bubbles, white toast and see-through coffee.

'How's the feet?'

'Great, fine. Want a dance?'

'Want to go home, don't you?'

'Absolutely.'

'Sally won't let you out, not till after the weekend.'

Layers of bandages, cotton wool, crepe pads, adaptic, meat!

Chris is impressed and Sally seems happy.

'Looks like I'll be home for the weekend,' I said hopefully.

The hope of getting to Camp 6 dissolved when I looked at my watch. I was stunned. Already 5:00pm and we're still on the traverse.

We had moved about 80 metres in two hours.

Mike falls a third time on me and the impact blows his suit zipper open. While yelling at him to get his weight off my arm, I spot the radio aerial sticking out of his inside pocket. Hauling Mike back up to the ledge, I grab the radio but suspect flat batteries. I try the radio.

'This is Whetu, anyone listening?'

'Go Mark, what the hell's going on up there man?' Simo sounds pissed off.

'Mike's blind, we're nearly at the ridge above the old camp 7 spot.'

'Mark, you listen to me, this is tough, you've got to live, you have to save yourself. If Mike can't get down, then you have to leave him now and save yourself!'

I think: fuck you arsehole. 'I can't leave my mate.'

Simo informs me there's gas at the first step and Jason is coming up from Camp 6. If I wait there for him we could bring the bottle back up to Mike together.

Mike is semiconscious. I tell him the plan and tie him off to a couple of pins and fixed line.

'Hey Digger, I'll be back soon.'

It's dark as I slither down the ropes on the first step. My headlamp still works. I find the oxygen bottle and put it in my pack as Jason arrives. His embrace is very comforting. Jason's radio is dead, so I tell him the plan and give him my radio, as I've had enough of Simo at this point.

He calls Base Camp, that we're heading back up to Mike together.

'I'm getting cold, I want to get going.'

'Mark, you have to go down, not up.'

'I just can't imagine leaving the man up on the mountain.'

'Mark, I can't imagine telling Edie you're not coming home.'

That really did it, hearing Edie's name made me realise that if I did go back up I probably wouldn't make it home.

'Mark, I want you to go down to Camp 6 now.'

Following Jason down the ropes to six seemed to go on and on.

Getting there around midnight, I was totally trashed, the boys wanted to get food and liquid into me straight away. I lay down in the tent corner with my Walkman, thinking, wondering …

My favourite track came on – Guns N' Roses, 'Don't Damn Me' …

Sally said I could go home, so it was a race across town to the airport to make the afternoon jet to Queenstown.

I hobbled up the steps to the plane.

'Skiing accident?' the hostess enquired.

'No, snowboarding.'

EDITH SEARLE GROSSMAN

from *The Heart of the Bush* (1910)

The Return to Light

Dennis came back from Mount Rangatira in boyishly high spirits, singing a negro song and whistling. At last he had stood on the summit where no man had been before, and he had seen a great kingdom of mountains, peak beyond peak, long valleys with their glacial streams, crags and ice-falls, away to where the forest trees seemed small as plumes of moss, and the western ocean came in sight. Now he was coming back to his love in the hour of sunset. She had not been quite happy at his going he knew, although she had told him to go. He had not been altogether blind to the little shadow that crept into her eyes, and the slight strain about the lips that she yielded to him. It was the merest fancy on her part and not reasonable, but – 'Darling!' he interjected half-aloud – he was not going to blame her for excess of fondness. Now he had had his own pleasure, and he would make it up to her tenfold. His own mood was hearty and fond enough to vanquish any mists and clouds. He had gathered some edelweiss for her, and as he carried an axe, a stick and a rope, the rare blossoms decorated his wide-awake and his belt.

As he and the Tohunga approached the place below the ice-cave where he had left Adelaide, he bounded forward, calling 'Aidie!' then stood astonished. She was nowhere to be seen. 'Of course,' he exclaimed aloud, 'what an ass I am. I couldn't expect her to sit still here for five hours.' Then he said to the Tohunga that his wife had taken a short walk, and that they had better sit down and wait until she came back. But his mood had received a check, and he could hardly contain his impatience as the minutes passed. The Tohunga sat and talked of the rivers that issued out of the Alps, and of the valleys that they flowed through. He said that there were rubies and emeralds and garnets amongst the grey shingle of their beds, and that he often wandered amongst their courses and picked up precious stones, but everybody laughed at him, so now he hid them in a secret place in his old house and showed them to no one. Then he began to speak of enormous reefs of pure gold on the west coast that they had seen from the Rangatira, and he talked of gold seekers who explored the

hills but always missed the reef. Dennis dug his axe vigorously down amongst the loose stones, and began to be half angry with Adelaide, half anxious, as the whole valley shone with gold, and then flushed red even to the stones. What could have happened? Her feeling of solitude among these moraines was an incomprehensible fancy to him. The very air of the Alps exhilarated him. These mountains had familiar voices and familiar looks. He had known them from childhood, and loved nothing better than wrestling with their hundred dangers, forcing their secrets from them and triumphing on their summits. That had been his chief idea of a holiday and its joys. But Adelaide astray amongst them! The Tohunga talked on and on, self-absorbed, as solitary people will do when once they have started. Dennis had ceased to pay any attention. The glow went out from atmosphere and valley, and the mountains turned spectral. Dennis astounded the Tohunga by leaping to his feet with a burst of profanity, meant for his companion or the scene around, or for fate in general. His face looked strained in the twilight as he stood collecting his powers. 'Stay here,' he said briefly, 'and light a bonfire.' And he went to search in the short space of daylight that remained. At first there seemed no clue as to what direction to take. If Adelaide and Tane had walked over the earth, there would have been footprints, or if over grass it would have been trodden down, but these accursed stones gave no indication. Soon he had got beyond swearing or uttering a syllable that was not necessary. The most probable thing was that she had gone back through the bush to the house, and he followed the course of the river back the way that they had come in the morning, and soon came to fern and loose soil. There were footmarks, but they all went towards the glacier. Except along the watercourse the bush was impracticable for one so inexperienced as she was and it was certain she and Tane had not returned. Indeed, it would not have been like Adelaide to go back alone. Where else, then? The valley of the Cascade? No! And he almost smiled when he thought over that chance. Adelaide enjoyed it at a distance, but she would never go near enough to get her pretty clothes wet with the spray. She would not be likely to climb such mountains alone, and if she had been on the terminal moraine he would have seen her. MacDiarmid returned to the spot where the Tohunga sat, now dumb and helpless in an emergency, and for some time he stood looking first in one direction, then in another, thinking. Then he went towards the ice-cave. It had fascinated her, and perhaps she

had gone nearer to see it. Daylight was over, and the moon did not rise till late, though in the unearthly clearness of this atmosphere there was no absolute darkness; two planets and a multitude of stars shone with white points of flame, too remote to be effectual, but the bonfire blazed up and threw flame on the leaping torrent and the ridges of stone. She was not there, and though he searched he found no trace. Adelaide, unlike most heroines, never dropped anything about, not even her gloves. Utterly at a loss, he scrambled up the unsound rocks above the cave on to the glacier. It was a perilous undertaking in the dark, and he felt cautiously with his stick or with bare hands as he went. Once he found himself on the very edge of a crevasse, but recovered his balance instantly. Then he knew what had happened, and sat down overcome. 'Adelaide! Adelaide!' he called with all the force of his breath across the frozen snow, and heard distinctly the howling of a dog. That ended the terrible blankness of uncertainty. Still feeling every step before him, and often creeping along on his knees, he followed in the direction of the sound, calling at intervals from the powerful lungs of a mountaineer accustomed to send his voice into the distance. Many a time in his life he had found his way into the bush or among the hills guided by the barking of a sheep dog. Hearing no sound from Adelaide he shouted 'Tane, Tane!' and with astonishing quickness the dog found its master, fawned at his feet, half mad with joy, looked for a stick, and in default picked up a stone by way of doing something or other. MacDiarmid wasted no time over him. 'Find her. Go on,' he said. Tane whined, he had a singular reluctance to return. MacDiarmid thrashed him as he had never done before, then repeated his command. Tane crawled dismally over the stones until they reached the yawning gap. 'God!' ejaculated MacDiarmid, and then, 'My Adelaide!' For a while he lay looking over the edge into the blackness of the hollow without being able to distinguish anything. From time to time he called down into the depth, but only the echo of his voice came back.

In the starlight he fancied at last that he saw something glimmering against the side of the gap. It might be snow. He considered the possibility attentively and reckoned that it was unlikely that there would be a single patch at that depth. Still watching intently, he seemed to see a slight movement of wind from above touching something moveable, he fervently prayed, some drapery. If it were Adelaide's dress she was probably stunned. That she was dead he refused to believe.

With his clasp knife he peeled and split the ends of his stick, dipped it in the spirits he carried and setting it alight made a rough torch. This he held over the hollow, and by its flame made out dimly the light summer gown Adelaide was wearing. When MacDiarmid saw it he clenched the nails hard into the palm of his hand. His wife seemed to stand before him as he had seen her standing by the cave early that morning; he remembered how pretty the dress was, so incongruously pretty in these wilds that he had pretended to ridicule it, 'woollen muslin' he called it, she said it was delaine; he had played with the ribbons at her wrists. 'Aidie, Aidie,' he cried now to himself, and lay for a few moments broken. There was no time to lose. MacDiarmid held the flaming stick over the hollow to see if the boulder against which Adelaide lay would support both of them. It would at least give him a footing. The danger was lest he might loosen it by the additional weight of his descent, but this was a risk that would not bear considering. There was a rock a few yards away. Round this he fastened his rope which he had used when mountaineering that morning. The other end he fastened round his own body, and with the axe on his shoulder and the torch in one hand he descended slowly, not resting his weight on the rope but sliding and using it merely as a support until his feet were on the boulder. Finding that it bore his weight, he tried to attach the end of the rope to it, but from its shape it afforded no hold. With his axe he chipped notches in the stone, breaking off crumbling lumps with his hands, until he had formed a groove deep enough to be secure. Then he stooped over the heap of drapery and lifted his wife in his arms, turning her face full to the light, but not speaking one word. She stirred slightly; her breath came naturally. She was not even stunned. A strange thing had happened to Adelaide, she had fallen into a profound sleep while her eyes were fixed on the sky, questioning it. An immense tender-ness possessed MacDiarmid, and his breath went out in great sighs over her. He looked up at the clear sky as children look up for God. But the trial was prolonged. The light of the moon now filled the upper atmosphere, but all below the mountains, moraine, glacier and their pit, were in shadow. His torch burnt out. It was useless to try the ascent in darkness. In daily life Dennis was often impatient and angry over little things, but somewhere in him, before the inevitable was inexhaustible patience. He sat down on the narrow ledge with Adelaide upon his knees and waited, watching for the dawn. Inutterable love filled his heart. Every girlish charm of hers came freshly

before his mind, as she lay still in the darkness, not yet rescued – her enchanting smile, her delicate reserves and her complete surrenders, her various pretences and half transparent unrealities. Adelaide's sleep was exhaustion, and she was too faint to help herself or to comprehend what had happened. The moon rose higher, but still an oblique shadow was thrown across the hollow. Adelaide opened her eyes and gazed with a long look at Dennis. 'You have come. It seemed such a long time waiting.' She sighed, but not in complaint. 'Have you been frightened, love?' he asked. Both spoke below their breath, as if in the presence of some mystery. 'Oh no, not really frightened. I knew that you would come.' Then after a pause, 'Must we wait here?' 'For more light, my love.' 'For how long, Dennis?' 'An hour or two.' He laid his hand upon her eyelids and kept them closed. 'Don't open your eyes until I tell you. It will be over soon. Can you sleep again?' 'Yes, I think so.' 'Then do.' She slept peacefully.

The first glimmering of dawn crept down amongst the stones. There was no more time to linger. MacDiarmid took off Adelaide's blue sash, and fearing she might lose her hold he bound her to his own body. Then grasping the rope, he made his way upward, toilsomely and slowly. One arm still supported his wife, who was now awake, but too faint to clasp him securely. Often he was obliged to use both hands. For a few yards the ascent was over bare rock, and farther on the loose stones kept slipping from under his feet. The sweat broke out in great drops, and his eyeballs were strained unnaturally. But he never once lost his footing. Extraordinary force and certainty entered into him. This one thing had to be done, impossible or not, and he could not fail in doing it. At last he struggled to the top.

As they emerged from their stony sepulchre, 'Look up, Adelaide,' he said. There was exultation in his voice and it thrilled her. The moon still shone, and there were stars high overhead, but the far off approaches of the day had blanched their light into mysterious paleness. One might have imagined a voice from the sky announcing some glorious manifestation at hand which should quench the Pleiades and the Milky Way, Orion and the Southern Cross. Absolute solemnity was throned on the summits of snow, rock and ice, but now they looked benignant and no longer cruel. It might have been the Resurrection dawn.

Still in the solemn veiled light, the man carried his wife over the glacier and back to the ice-cave; then down the terminal moraine to the shingle

banks of the river, now coloured like broken heaps of copper. The Tohunga was there and he looked at them wistfully. He could not quite understand these human happenings, but he vaguely remembered a girl whom he had loved half a century ago in a world that had no atom in common with this. 'Get us some food,' said MacDiarmid, not rudely but sparing of words. The old man disappeared in the gloom of the bush.

Adelaide was glad that she and her husband were alone again. They seemed to have something to say to each other, or better still, something secret to share. The bonfire had burned low into a heap of white powder and black wood, with only gems of scarlet. Dennis took off his jersey which he wore at night over his shirt, and spreading it on the stones he made Adelaide lie on it, keeping her head against his knee. 'Now you rest,' he said. She lay quite still with her eyes closed, not sleeping but letting thought and feeling pass through her as they would. The solemnity of escape was in the minds of both, and at some moments possessed them entirely, but there began to be a welcome return of everyday sensations. Adelaide remembered with a curious pleasure that he had not given her one kiss or caress since they met, and that she had not missed either. There was no longer any need of endearments. Seeing that her forehead was still bleeding, he pressed his handkerchief to it. 'Does it show much, Dennis?' she asked with a blush. He laughed that she should think of such a thing just then, and yet because it was Adelaide it was somehow sweet.

'Does it pain you? It is bleeding.' 'Oh, do wipe the blood away, please, Dennis dear,' she begged. He laughed again but obeyed, and going to the river rinsed her handkerchief out, then bathed the wound. 'Are you hurt anywhere else?' 'Not particularly.' 'Are you hurt?' he insisted with impatience. 'My shoulder and my foot – a little.' She spoke reluctantly. Dennis crouched down and drew off the small shoe and the worked silk stocking, that seemed to him so absurdly and yet delightfully pretty. The leg was bruised above the ankle where it struck the rock, and the soft flesh was broken. He bandaged it with a strip torn from his handkerchief, then pushing up her sleeve found a bad bruise on her shoulder, and pressed the cold leaf of a lily to the swelling. Adelaide lay quite still, but her lips and closed eyelids quivered. She had been adored, her husband had not touched her before, except after wooing, or in one of his overwhelming outbursts. 'I am disfigured. Don't look at those bruises, Dennis,' she said plaintively. 'Aidie.' He spoke with deep feeling. 'If you knew how I love you,

you would not mind anything.' 'I do know – my Dennis.' She looked up at him a moment with wide open happy eyes, as blue as the sky.

The dogs had eaten the remains of the meat, but Dennis had with him some hard bread and some of Emmeline's home-made wine, brought for an emergency, because Adelaide would not taste alcohol. She would eat nothing that he did not share, so she broke the bread and gave half to him. Then Dennis poured the wine into a horn goblet and they drank in turn. While they were eating and drinking, it struck Adelaide with a sense of awe that the meal was sacramental, and that somehow God was near, too near to them. They had never before so utterly worshipped each other as when they sat alone again simply sharing their food together. The body of the sun was itself invisible, but its spirit filled the upper atmosphere. In lower regions we see light through a cloudy medium of vapour, but here they were face to face with light itself, perfect light. Adelaide rose to her feet, and bride and bridegroom stood side by side to watch the sunrise. Dennis laid his hand on her shoulder. 'Look.' A long line of serrated crags of ice and rock glowed like knobbed brass in the blaze of a furnace, and the snow-peaks shone like new-wrought gold. The Alps dazzled their eyes, and they turned to look at each other, and each was beautiful to the other. Then came a long embrace and kisses and simple words. The Alps were nothing, they themselves were all in all. 'I am sorry, Dennis; I have given you so much trouble. You look tired.' Thinking of her awakening in the dark to feel his hand on her, her heart beat extravagantly. 'You have had scarcely any food, and you have not slept.'

'Don't, love. As if that mattered. I wish I had not left you in this wild place. I meant to take care of you, and now you've been frightened and hurt. I have quite spoiled your honeymoon, Aidie.'

'Oh no, Dennis, don't say that.' She put up a light hand to smooth his hair, disordered with the wind and clotted by the sweat of exertion. 'Last night and this have been much the loveliest part of all. Don't you understand?'

For some time Dennis studied with serious intentness her vivid face, weary but delicately flushed and illumined.

'Why, yes. Of course,' he answered finally.

IDA CORRY

Climbs at the Head of the Franz Josef (1933)

That night Mark set the alarm for 2 a.m., and we decided to climb only if the weather was still perfect and the snow hard. Since it was, we left the [Almer] hut at 3.30 a.m. to try the ascent of Goldsmith, but did not carry skis with us as we had a long way to go. We saw a cloudless dawn and watched the morning star and crescent moon paling above the silhouette of peaks and snowfield. Over Westland the sky flushed purple, then rosy pink, changing to gold. Mt. Cook and Tasman greeted us with a glorious sunlight on their tops, and it seemed a perfect morning for our objective. As the sun appeared over the mountains, we were well on our way, wearing crampons, and using our old tracks up the slopes of Matenga.

Goldsmith lies to the N.E. of the Minarets, and from the snowfield is concealed by these peaks. We ascended the first rock spur by a steep snow couloir and descended again to a snow plateau between the two spurs. The descent had to be made down steep snow for about 100 feet and then over slabby rocks which sloped the wrong way and gave us very little hand or foot-hold. This was one of the worst places on our return. While crossing the plateau we had a magnificent view of the hanging glaciers and steep ice-slopes of the western face of Elie de Beaumont which falls so abruptly into the Spencer Glacier. This has always been to me the most beautiful mountain in the Alps, as viewed from the West Coast side, and I was very happy when we climbed Elie this March.

We had no difficulty in getting up the second rock spur by another steep snow couloir, and on the crest of the spur we had a good view of our mountain and could make out what seemed a practicable route to the top. We avoided ascending the steep snow-face above us by traversing across it to the lip of an enormous schrund whose walls extended to the sky-line. Inside this schrund was like being inside a crystal palace; the most glorious shades of blue were reflected in the ice, and long icicles hung down over the entrance to a mysterious cave.

Climbing up through this schrund to the sky-line, we found ourselves in a snow basin, with the summit ridge of Goldsmith about 400 feet above us. The only remaining obstacle was a narrow schrund running nearly

the whole circuit of the basin and about half way up it. There was a snow bridge on the left hand side where the schrund ended against a rock ridge. But this bridge was not too good as the rocks over which it lay were steep and smooth. However, once across, we were soon on the summit ridge and then away like lightning to the top.

We had an imposing view of the steep corniced ridge leading up to the North peak of the Minarets, and decided to leave it severely alone and to return by the way we had come. In the opposite direction we had a splendid view along the Main Divide over Meeson and Coronet to Elie de Beaumont. It was too cold to stay long on top so we started down at 11.45 a.m. As the sun was so hot, Mark thought the snow-bridge over the schrund would not be too safe, so suggested we should jump across nearer to the centre of the basin. I readily agreed as we had only to jump downward four to five feet. Mark anchored while I jumped and landed knee-deep in soft snow. He followed me, but in landing pitched violently forward head first down the slope until held up by the rope around my axe. The shock sent me sliding off too, and I called out to Mark, 'Thank goodness the axe held us.' He called back faintly 'my leg's broken.'

At first I simply couldn't believe it, and then the gradual realisation of it seemed to spell disaster to us both. We can only suppose now that as he landed his right crampon struck a buried stone or a hard surface of ice a short distance beneath the snow. His right foot was hanging out to the side limply, twisted at the ankle and already very swollen by the time I had lowered him on the rope to a place where he could sit more comfortably in a hastily scooped-out hollow.

By marvellous good fortune Mark had that morning cut two wooden pitons about three feet long from a split ski and put these in his rucksack. These two pitons saved his leg from further injury and made it possible for him to get down. We kept the boot on and tried to pull the leg out and straighten it as much as possible.

Then with our four puttees and a leather belt of mine his leg was kept absolutely firm in these splints. Mark nearly fainted with the pain and shock, and I could see him struggling not to let go, and he asked for the coffee in his flask. We had no other stimulant. Then we had some food, and while we ate determined then and there that we were going to get back to Almer Hut. We didn't know how or when, but as Mark said, it would be 'some time to-morrow.' After lunch we had left a packet and a half of

ginger-nuts and some raisins and chocolate. Fortunately the pain in Mark's leg seemed to become partly numbed or he could never have achieved the long descent. From the moment that the accident happened, until we were safely back at the hut Mark showed the same fine courage and a marvellous endurance. He was all the time inspiringly calm and cheerful in a situation that was very far from reassuring, and not once did he complain about the pain in his leg.

We had to avoid the big schrund and instead descend the steep snow-face sloping at an angle of over 60 deg. The snow was hard and icy underneath a thin layer of fresh snow which had been frozen hard in the morning, but was now soft and treacherous. Descending and traversing this slope to the top of the couloir was anxious work and took us four and a half hours. Mark would lower himself, sitting on the snow and using his axe and good crampon leg as a brake until I had paid out the full length of the rope. Then he had to wait long intervals while I cut steps down to him, and this we did over and over again. When we were low enough to traverse he had to swing himself into the roughly made spoon-shaped steps, hopping upon his leg which was nearest to the slope and driving his axe hard into the icy surface. There was no fear of an avalanche upon the slope that we were descending, but two big avalanches thundered off the slopes immediately on our right, filling the abyss below us with a thick cloud of snow dust. When at last we reached the soft snow ridge, Mark could straddle this, and worked himself along it fairly easily till we reached the snow couloir. This seemed gloriously safe too, and again he did a series of sitting glissades the full length of the rope while I could run down from above in the soft snow.

We had our first spell at the bottom of the couloir about 5 p.m., and were by then terribly thirsty so drank some more coffee and refilled the flask with snow. Going across the plateau towards the other spur we sank into the snow over our knees. Desperately we tried every method of getting along, but both soon became exhausted, and then Mark hit on the idea of using the two axes as crutches, heads downwards in the snow. He got on much better this way and hobbled bravely along while I trailed behind him with the rope and rucksack. Fortunately on all the traversing back to Almer, until we were below Teichelmanns Corner, the upward slope was on our left so that Mark's broken right leg could hang down freely. Going up the rocks was less difficult than we had anticipated, and even here Mark

needed little assistance, but climbed up on his hands and knees behind me. He climbed the steep snow also on his knees in the steps, while I could get a safe anchor in the soft snow to help him with the rope. We safely descended the other side, crossed some nasty schrunds, and then had a second spell.

It was 7.30 p.m. and a strong south-west wind was blowing storm-clouds over the Divide. For about an hour we had been in a thick mist and expecting snow. Fortunately the wind dropped quite suddenly and the night was clear and starry. But the sunset was wild and stormy, the sinking sun turned the snow peaks blood-red, and flaming colours were reflected in the clouds. I remember thinking how very beautiful it was, and if only the weather held we should be fairly safe now, for there were only the long snow slopes to traverse below Matenga before we should reach the snowfield. Once there it would be only a matter of time, and of schrunds, before reaching Almer Hut, but it wouldn't do to think too far ahead.

At 10 p.m. we had to light one of two small stumps of candle to negotiate some schrunds, but we were already in our old tracks below Matenga. The final slopes, being well-frozen again, were excellent for sliding, and we landed upon the snowfield in utter darkness about midnight.

Mark suffered badly from cramp in the left thigh, but insisted upon carrying on with short rests only, for there was no shelter on the snowfield, and it was bitterly cold. Our teeth were chattering violently, and we were both yawning our heads off whenever we stopped, so to keep us awake I began to sing. In the middle of a rather shaky 'It's a Long Way to Tipperary' there was a thundering chorus from a huge rock avalanche which came off Matenga. It seemed to be making straight for us, though we could only see the sparks flying in the darkness as the rocks crashed together. Fortunately none reached us for, much as we wanted to run away, we couldn't.

Another dawn discovered us about 1½ miles from the hut, and putting on crampons again to descend the steep slopes above Teichelmanns Corner. Once safely down, I left Mark (still hobbling slowly along, for he never gave in) and ran ahead to get ski-sticks to take the place of the axes as crutches. I hoped to find someone at the hut, and bursting in, found Joe sound asleep in his bunk. He was splendid. We went back to Mark and helped him down the last stage, reaching the hut finally about 8 a.m. Wednesday. The accident had occurred just about noon on Tuesday, only

a few minutes after we left the top of the mountain. From that time until we reached Almer we were out 20 hours, and had to descend about 5,000 feet in covering the ten miles back to the hut. Since leaving after 3 a.m. breakfast on Tuesday, we had seen two dawns and kept going all through the night, but had only eaten a few biscuits and raisins. No wonder then that we were rattling inside with hunger! Joe had put the billy on before following me back, and we drank cup after cup of hot coffee and dived into all the food we could find. We finished up in great style on four or five fried sausages apiece, and still didn't feel too full!

Joe made three good splints from old skis, and we took off the old splints and the boot, and cut away the sock. The broken leg was terribly swollen and discoloured around and above the ankle. The X-ray showed later that the tibia was chipped at the ankle and the fibula fractured three inches above. We padded the splints with kapok from one of the pillows, and bandaged them on firmly with strips of sugar-bag, for we had no idea when Mark would see a doctor. Joe left us at 10 a.m. and was right through to Waiho in 2¾ hours! By the most amazing good fortune he met Dr. Cyril King on the glacier with Guide Jack Pope going to Defiance Hut. Dr. King put on Joe's crampons and came straight on up though he had never been on the ice before.

From the hut we could see nothing of the glacier below us as it was hidden in mist all day. About 6 p.m. the billy was boiling again, and I was trying to sweep up the loose kapok which was all over the hut, when there was a step outside and Jack Pope appeared in the doorway saying 'I've brought a doctor.' Dr. King was just behind him, a little bit puffed after his exertions up the ridge, but still infectiously full of a real 'joie de vivre.' He restored our confidence and good spirits as no one else could have done. In no time Mark was laid out on the table, and Jack was making new splints under the doctor's directions. Dr. King himself was ruthlessly tearing up hut blankets for padding, and soon had Mark and I roaring with laughter at his jokes. The mist had cleared off the glacier now, and Jack announced that a party of three men were coming up. They arrived at 8.30 headed by the indefatigable Joe, and the seven of us had a cheerful supper and turned in early.

By 7.30 a.m. next morning, Thursday the 26th, seven more men had arrived from Defiance Hut, bringing with them additional supplies of provisions, medical equipment, and a stretcher. The helpers from Waiho do

not arrive empty-handed. They were led by Peter and Alec Graham. With their arrival all my fears about the descent vanished. They gave confidence to the whole party because of their years of experience and the quiet determined way in which they set about preparing for the return journey. There were now twelve men arrived; it seemed quite a crowd, but every man in the party was well needed, and every man tired out before Waiho was safely reached that night. Little was said that day, but much was done.

GRAEME DINGLE

from *Two Against the Alps*

Avalanche

On 4th August the weather had deteriorated as we had anticipated. Cloud had closed in from the northwest. To the east, Hopkins, the Black Tower and McKerrow reared up like Himalayan giants against the ominous sky.

After a leisurely breakfast and an early morning radio sched. I went down to the river unhopefully to attempt to find the billy. Slowly I worked my way downstream until I came to a large pool. There was something dark on the bottom. I joined two ski poles together and stripped off my clothes to wade into the water. A tentative probe showed that it was our billy all right, so I carefully flipped it over and, catching it on the end of the ski poles, flicked it into the air with a cry of triumph. And from the top of the boulder Jill and some keas joined in. She was marking the airdrop site with our orange bivvy sack and the keas watched with destructive designs on the light nylon.

With the bad weather we did not expect the drop that day, but suddenly we heard an engine and soon saw a little Mount Cook Cessna. We surmised it might be John Tovey or Jerry Savage. In actual fact it was Robbie Hansen. Down valley he went and we waited excitedly for the noise to return. We could soon hear it again but could not see him. Then low over the moraine wall he swooped in, pulling the little plane into a tight turn, and out came a package – our snowshoes! The second loud cheer for the morning reverberated round the valley walls. The drop was spot on. Once more he came in and out came another little sack, our billy and sugar.

We rushed about like kids on Christmas morning. Jill quickly put on her snowshoes and began parading round like a spastic duck, then waddled off to the river to fill our new billy. What a ridiculous sight when she came back. The billy was spouting water like a watering can. 'The poor thing must have ruptured in the drop,' she giggled.

After lunch we packed up and headed up valley to find another home. We had heard of a large boulder shelter 400 feet above the Spence River and soon it appeared on the sky-line. When we arrived at the shelter we found the floor was covered with about three inches of thar dung. 'At least we

might be able to burn it,' Jill remarked, always looking on the brighter side. We started into the place, excavating out a sleeping platform and fireplace with our ice axes and soon had to agree that despite the smell it was our nicest little bivvy yet.

Next day the weather was even worse, with heavy rain from the north and snow on the tops. We woke early as usual, but just turned over when we saw the rain streaming across the valley. From below we could hear the swollen rivers roar. After a leisurely mid-morning breakfast we went for a looksee at Fyfe Pass. Through gaps in the cloud we saw what looked like an appallingly steep 2,000ft snow wall rising up abruptly from the head of the Spence Glacier. It did not look too encouraging, but we knew how slopes look so much steeper when viewed straight on.

We hurried back to the bivvy, scavenging bits of wet scrub from under the snow as we went, but were beaten by a heavy shower. At 7 p.m. the forecast from Cedric was gloomy, and in return we told him the pass looked OK, but prone to avalanche. It looked as if we would be lucky to get to Ashburton for my lecture to the Erewhon Club.

On the 6th I had the fire crackling by 3.30 a.m. We had decided that, despite all the cloud about, it would be better to try the pass and fail than not to try. A brew and a small dish of porridge went down easily and we left at 5.30.

As we climbed up the ridge a startled kea made a ridiculous fuss from the top of his rock and from somewhere in the darkness a thar whistled a warning as we approached. I could not imagine what they found to eat up here.

By the time it got light we had had enough of sinking into the snow up to our knees so we put on our snowshoes – rather sceptically. Despite the uneven ground they worked fantastically well and we continued at a great pace until we reached the lumpy cones of avalanche debris at the top of the glacier. Soon we swopped snowshoes for crampons and continued up a narrow gully after a brief discussion about what might be 'Hardie's Gut'.

What we surmised was Fyfe Pass looked pretty straight forward, so we cramponed up the steep slope quickly and confidently. We were actually moving up avalanche debris: once avalanched, the slope was not likely to go again, and the debris was compacted enough to make climbing much easier than in the soft undisturbed snow.

At about 6,000 feet and 10 a.m. we climbed out of the gully to begin up a long, steep slope and immediately we were struggling through knee-deep

snow. I ploughed ahead making the track, always looking for an easier line or better snow, but nowhere did there seem to be any better going. It was all knee deep and complete drudgery, except for the mystery of what might lie ahead. I reached a short ridge and wind scoop, where I could have waited for Jill, but cloud was slowly building up on the pass which was now only 300 feet above, and at all costs we must get a look over the other side before visibility became too bad.

As I climbed I began to think about the other passes we had crossed. Five so far. We had taken two attempts to cross two of them; each one we had crossed in bad or deteriorating weather.

That calculating took me one hundred feet up the slope, and then I began to count the steps. To begin with I could only get up to eighteen before I had to stop, but I improved on this to fifty-three. Only fifty feet above me a strong wind whipped long plumes of snow off the ridge. My excitement began to mount and I stopped counting steps.

With no warning, the slope around me collapsed. I was in an avalanche and helpless.

I was cartwheeling backwards, my mind working at an incredible pace, like a computer sorting out everything I knew about avalanches and attempting to put the information to use. I was screaming uncontrollably, the kind of cry when someone kicks you in the stomach. I tried to fight my way to the surface. It was impossible. The force of the thing was like a raging flooded river going over a waterfall. It all seemed a terrible nightmare, my body being twisted and limbs wrenched and flipping over and over like a rag doll.

I soon realised my biggest danger was suffocation, as the snow was packing into my mouth, and once it started there was nothing I could do to stop it. When I tried to put my hand over my face it was torn away.

The avalanche crashed over a drop – I don't know how high – and this seemed the final blow to drain my remaining strength. For the first time in my life I was resigned to death.

Next moment I realised my downward plunge was slowing as I flipped over a final time. I saw a form rushing down in the avalanche below and my thought switched to Jill. 'God, she must be in it, too,' I thought. The mass of snow stopped moving and I sat up and looked up the slope. Thank God, there was Jill, a tiny dot seemingly miles above. Above me I also saw the red blob of my pack. I had not even realised it was gone. I had stopped halfway down the face on top of a spur after a fall of at least 1,000 feet. To my right

and left the avalanche had crashed down two steep gullies and had roared out on to the Spence 1,000 feet below.

Slowly I stood up and tested my limbs. Apart from feeling that I had been through a mangle I was OK. My clothes were all but off me and snow was packed inside my jersey and trouser legs, my mitts had been torn off and my ice axe was lost although I had had a loop attaching it firmly to my wrist. I cleared the snow from my mouth and went stiffly about collecting all my gear which was strewn everywhere. Some was buried.

A piece of wire served to mend my broken pack, and I began the terrible ordeal of climbing back up the slope. As I went I was wondering, 'Will I go on climbing?' but it was only a lingering thought in a moment of weakness. I was almost too dazed to be frightened as I climbed back towards Jill, but I climbed fairly quickly because the going was much easier now that all the soft snow was swept away.

I began to think about the fall. Immediately after the avalanche had ceased I felt completely grateful to be alive, and the thought that most of my gear was lost, in itself quite serious, seemed quite trivial. Now that I was climbing again I was annoyed at the loss of minor items such as one snowshoe and my ice axe.

A hundred feet below where Jill stood I found myself confronted by an overhanging snow wall about eight or nine feet high. It was the break at the top of a secondary avalanche started by the first and higher avalanche. Whereas usually I would have clambered over it with reckless abandon, now, in my shocked state, its problem was just too much for me and I began to scream at Jill to let the rope down. I was almost hoarse from swallowing the copious quantities of snow and Jill did not hear a thing. I cursed silently and began stamping along the bottom of the wall. Then Jill's head appeared over the side and I shouted once more for the rope.

Even pulling violently on the rope I had trouble getting up. As I reached Jill I mumbled stupidly, grinning: 'If at first you don't succeed –', then had second thoughts about the rest and continued, 'give up!'

Jill buttered and honeyed me a biscuit and tried to shelter me from the cold wind. I was miserable and disheartened and no longer felt like taking the upper hand, so fell in behind Jill as she bravely started up the slope again. We were now in thick cloud and could not see fifty feet.

The slope under us still seemed unstable to me, but I thought maybe the Bank of England vault would be feeling a mite unsafe to me right then.

However, my fears were soon confirmed by Jill and I didn't need a further opinion to make me go scampering back down the slope.

The lower we got the less serious the last two hours seemed to have been, and I began to chatter excitedly. As we passed the enormous piles of avalanche debris I quipped, 'Imagine how embarrassing it would be if that happened in Lambton Quay – I mean all those people looking at you and you standing there wiv' your knickers down around your knees in all that snow.' On a slightly more serious note Jill said, 'Yeah, I wonder how all those people are enjoying their safe little offices today?' And by the time we had sat down by the glacier lake for lunch we were laughing and chattering as usual.

I imagined that going back up that slope to the pass was like going into a gunfight with a man whom you knew was just a little slower on the draw than you. The uncertainty and chance was still there, and you were frightened about it, but you knew that you had better than a 50/50 chance of coming out alive.

The moon was slowly being obscured as we made our way once again away from the bivvy rock. As the stars got brighter in the darkness Jill began pointing out some which were unknown to me, Pleiades, Sirius, Orion and so on. The seeds of one more of life's lessons were being planted in my mind.

We made better time up the glacier and when it came to the familiar avalanche face I bolted up, leaving Jill way behind.

Limbo Thompson and Keith McIver in a display of friendship had agreed to try to meet us on Fyfe Pass that day and, if necessary, drop a rope down the final few unknown feet. There had even been talk of a helicopter landing on the pass for an on the spot scoop interview. I had said sternly over the radio, 'You keep that helicopter off the pass; if you are going to bring one in, land it in the Spence, but keep off that pass. We don't want another avalanche down our necks.'

At the wind scoop, in comparative safety, I sat down to wait for Jill and set the radio up for a chat with Cedric and Ron Kingston. The day was perfect, although we had reason to expect a change because there had been some high cirrus about at dawn. Jill arrived at about 11 a.m. and we sat about leisurely eating lunch and occasionally shouting to Limbo, who we imagined was not far away. A terrific strain had been lifted from our minds by the knowledge that Limbo and Keith would soon be on the pass, and there seemed every chance that by evening we would be living it up at the

Hermitage, possibly that we might make the dinner-lecture at Ashburton. I was even raving about drinking wine and eating several-course meals. I sat there holding my bowl of brew like a glass of wine, with my little finger rampant, and imitating polite conversation.

About midday I called Cedric again. Came the friendly reply: 'Limbo called shortly after 10.30 and said he'd be on the pass by 12, over.'

The mountains echoed again to my cry of 'L-I-M-B-O', but an echo was the only reply. I decided to test the dangerous slope up to the pass. The surface was perfect for cramponing where the avalanche had been, but under the deceptive hard surface layer the slope was about as safe as a starved tiger. It made an ominous, hollow sound as I climbed, so that after 200 feet I was becoming definitely uneasy. I prodded the snow nervously and my shattered nerves shrieked that it was about to avalanche again. I didn't wait to see if it would, but climbed quickly down to Jill.

It must have been after 1 p.m. by now, and we were beginning to doubt if Limbo and Keith would make the pass at all. Meanwhile the weather had been brewing a nor'wester and before I knew it the forward divisions were upon us. The wind suddenly sprang up and a great layer of grey cloud began to curl around all the surrounding jagged peaks. I estimated thirty minutes before visibility would be nil. Jill was the one to take the initiative. Obviously not liking the devil we knew either, she waved an arm to our right across an evil looking steep snow slope which hung precariously above some great cliffs and said, 'Let's have a look into that gully'.

We could not face the idea of going back to the valley again and we realised that we must get a look into the Mueller Glacier and our descent route before the weather got too bad to see anything. I tied the rope haphazardly around my waist and took off quickly across the steep slope. The traverse was soft and dangerous and I was happy to reach the comparative safety of the gully, where the snow was hard wind-pack.

The weather seemed to be mock challenging me. As the cloud got thicker, cutting down visibility, I climbed with lungs, heart and muscles straining to their maximum, but the weather was just keeping ahead of me.

For a hundred feet or so the climbing in the gully remained good, but the angle steepened abruptly, and once again we began struggling up deep, ready-to-avalanche snow. The feeling was becoming just too familiar.

It was real 'heart in the mouth' progress, climbing at its worst – that is, dangerous with nothing we could do to make it safer. I could almost

feel the sickening lurch of the slope as it collapsed and the claustrophobic tumbling down in tons of snow. Jill was a hundred feet below me. She was not tied on to the rope which I trailed, because there were no places to anchor it – this problem had proved to be one of the big dangers of winter climbing.

Two hundred feet below the comparative safety of the main ridge cornices, the going got so bad that it became impossible to make any progress in the conventional way. The snow was so deep and the slope so steep that when I kicked a step and transferred my weight up, the snow beneath would collapse and I would be back to square one. I was soon near despair. However, necessity forced me to work out a method which, although slow, would get us to the top some time as long as we did not get avalanched.

The technique was to lie against the slope so that our weight was distributed and we would, therefore, not break through the thin crust. We would then squirm slowly upward, using hands, knees and toes to make progress. When the slope became too soft for this I would smash out a step above me with my hands, then struggle up onto it and repeat the manoeuvre until the surface became crusty again; then it was back into the slug crawl position.

The whole business repelled me, and it was only after an eternity that I reached the wind-swept ridge and peered over the cornice down a breath-taking, seemingly vertical drop on the eastern side. The cloud swirled around below, but through a gap I saw a small glacier and valley running south east. Hell! The Mueller was a huge glacier running north. After all this we had come up in the wrong place by misinterpreting our all too vague map. However, for the meantime we were safe, or at least safer, our only dangers being freezing to death or falling through a cornice.

I got up off my hands and knees from where I had been staring downwards and turned into the westerly which shrieked over the ridge blowing stinging ice crystals into my face. I went cautiously back into the gully from which I had just escaped and yelled down to Jill to 'tie on to the rope'. I made a firm anchor and she was soon up.

I broke the bitter news to her with a few sympathetic words: 'Sorry Jill, we're nowhere near Fyfe Pass.' She mumbled a disappointed 'Oh, no!' We pulled on all our windproofs and worked out our best course. What a change from an hour ago when we had been basking in the sun in our

windscoop. The situation was now serious, and in our minds we prepared for a bad night out.

There was really only one course open to us and that was to head north. A return down the gully seemed like suicide and visibility was too bad to find a safe alternative. The only worry in my mind was that we might be on a side ridge and not the Main Divide.

We set off along the seeming knife edge, not daring to go too far down on the west for fear of avalanches, and attempting to keep a safe distance from the cornices which hung over the east. Despite the uncomfortable conditions the climbing along the wind-sculpted ridge was exhilarating. Ahead cornices and icy bulges curled aesthetically into the mist. I was filled with a kind of worried excitement, and strained on the rope ahead of Jill like a greyhound eager for a run. Speed seemed to me now to be safety, with the weather deteriorating so quickly.

As we neared a summit I strained to see into the mist, and suddenly through a tiny gap I had a glimpse of a high pass with a dot on it that with luck might be a hut. It could only be Barron Saddle and Three Johns Hut, but the view had been so fleeting that I did not let my fears of a cold night out dissolve completely; besides we still had to get down to it.

If that was the hut the summit we were approaching could only be Scissors. We quickly took out the radio to call Cedric as it seemed that someone may have become alarmed at our mysterious disappearance from Fyfe Pass. Out in the mist ski planes were zooming about like big hornets and one in particular seemed to be almost clipping the crags with his wing tips. The atmosphere had become kind of circus-like. We could only assume that out there the cloud was not so thick, because we knew how cautious the Mount Cook pilots are. We later found that while we were saying, 'Look at those silly buggers up there', Keith Wakeman and an N.Z.B.C. cameraman were flying around us saying, 'Fancy climbing all over those things.' And when they swooped down under the cloud and saw the avalanche debris, Keith said, 'I must meet these kinky people.' Earlier in the day there had been some mention of various news people landing on the Mueller Glacier to scoop our story, but the weather had now put this out of the question.

To call Cedric I threw one end of the aerial over the cornice while Jill held up the other. Amazingly, contact was made with the help of Ron Kingston in Dunedin. I told Cedric that we would attempt to reach Fyfe

Pass and our two friends. He told me that the Erewhon Club in Ashburton were still hoping for my lecture and would turn on a plane from Pukaki (forty miles from Mount Cook) if necessary. The seriousness of our situation suddenly evaporated. Here we were, on a storm-swept summit at just under 8,000 feet and eight miles from the Hermitage, while 100 miles away some people were still hopeful that I would be giving one of my slide lectures to them in the evening.

We packed again quickly, and began along the ridge towards Fyfe Pass. We had only gone 200 feet when some pinnacles sprang out of the mist blocking our path. The wind was beginning to chill us and the pinnacles looked so intimidating that we smartly about-turned and climbed back to the top of Scissors. We ducked over on to the east side to peer down a steep ridge which seemed to fall in the direction of where I thought I had seen the hut. Out of the wind we felt much more comfortable and decided to climb down the plunging ridge below. The rock, which in summer would be easy climbing, was plastered with six inches of ice, which in turn had a thick layer of powder snow over it, but climbing down in relative safety we were beginning to enjoy ourselves. Belays were good, so we made our way down steadily, ropelength after ropelength, until we reached a flattening in the ridge. We now saw that the dot was definitely a hut and we knew for the first time since leaving Wanaka that we would be spending the night in the warm and dry.

I set the radio up again and called Limbo and Keith. It was 3 p.m. and they had just reached Fyfe Pass.

'IB6 this is IB2, how do you read Limbo? Over.'

'Oh – loud and clear, Ding. Where are you?'

I was surprised he sounded his usual cheery self. Not the least bit annoyed that we had not arrived at the pass.

'Limbo, we are one hour from Three Johns on the east ridge of Scissors. Over.'

'Mighty. I think you came up in the right place. We've just looked over Fyfe Pass and what's not vertical is overhanging. Over.'

Both Jill and I felt a flush of relief.

'See you back at the hut then. We'll have a hot brew on for you. Sorry we missed you, but thanks. IB2. Out.'

We plunged down through the deep snow, over the mounds of Barron Saddle and down to the hut. It seemed like the ultimate luxury to be able to

spread out our gear and stand up while we cooked without smashing our heads against some bivvy rock. The most simple things of life were now the most appreciated, and with our simple demands we were fully content.

Limbo and Keith arrived just before dark and we thrust steaming mugs of tea into their hands followed by heaped plates of stew. It was our last food, supplemented heavily with some rice found in the hut.

At 7 p.m. we had the Mount Cook Park radio sched. Barry Thomas, the cheerful head ranger, was calling, and it was heartwarming to hear his 'Welcome to the park'.

We radioed the Erewhon Club our condolences and wished them 'a mighty rave-up'. Then we all lay back in our bunks and talked far into the night about mountains and life while the nor'wester rocked the hut and screamed through the anchor wires.

Next morning it was difficult to make a start with the storm swirling snow about the hut. Eventually we all got away about 10.30, Jill and I on snowshoes and Limbo and Keith on skis. Limbo had brought me up a pair to replace those lost in the avalanche.

For Jill and I it was pretty frustrating plodding along at walking speed while the others glided down effortlessly. I don't think I have ever seen such an easy large glacier. No icefall, scarcely a crevasse, so it was rather boring travel. Our two friends waited for us below the climb up to the Mueller Hut. It was a thousand feet or more which none of us could face in the soft snow, so after sharing a tin of sardines we continued down the glacier.

We were glad that we had not followed the conventional route over the top when we found the glacier really easy. We skirted round the mighty cliffs and avalanche cones of Mount Sefton and were not forced to take skis and snowshoes off until we were only an hour from the Hermitage. The descent beside the moraine wall was as horrible as ever to tired, wobbly legs. I have a way (after years of practice) of smashing myself in moraine. This day was no exception. I tried to leap between a three-foot-wide gap with three-and-a-half-foot wide snowshoes on my pack and got a nasty fright as well as skinning my hands.

However, all things end – even loose moraine – and before long we had crossed the grassy flats to the Hermitage.

Once again the hotel staff made our transition from roughing it to the lap of luxury smooth and efficient. No shower ever felt so good. Moraine dust and blood alike swilled down the plughole.

PENNY GODDARD

Under the Mountain: An ascent of La Perouse from the Cook River

Afterwards, the thing that struck me as odd was the jealousy. An open-eyed, secretly whispered sort that slivered out of people's mouths before they realised what they were saying. It really wasn't the sort of thing to be proud of, but strangely people wanted to have been there with us. Just to have a story to tell, I suppose.

27th March: All dressed up, nowhere to go. Tim and I were standing on the bridge over the Cook River, a week's worth of food on our eager backs, gaiters pulled up high to our knees, resplendently ready in our fresh clean thermals. But there was no denying it. The river was a fat brown beast, urging keenly up against both banks and charging furiously towards us, only to slide smoothly underneath and rush importantly out, out, out to sea. Despondent, we put our packs back in the car, unzipped our gaiters, and turned back to Fox.

The next day we were unstoppable as a blue sky hung above us and the Cook River's boulders began disappearing behind our happy feet. We were glad we had waited out the previous day's frustration, as even now the river pushed against the bank, licking at our plastic boots and forcing us either into the thick slow hug of the bush, or to leap committingly from tiny rock islands and arrive with a desperate trot onto the quicksand shore. It was a certain recipe for wet boots and I was soon to soak my socks.

Travel was excitingly good in the beginning and once past the first bend in the river, we were gone. Any memory of a road, tourists, buses and cafés was absorbed into the still dark bush and swallowed without a word by the tumbling bouldery river. Soon a gorge forced us high into the bush, amongst overgrown rotten roots and logs. We stumbled and bumped with our heavy packs and marvelled that there had once been a stretcher rescue all the way down this river from high on La Perouse. Suddenly we were amongst an amazing jumble of huge erratic boulders, separated by sickeningly deep dark drops. We began some tense chasm-leaping and down-climbing manoeuvres, clinging on to whatever fern or creeper was

at hand. After a tiring period of absorbed concentration, we escaped and navigated back to the river. We found a small beach with soft sand, perfect for pitching our tent fly. Soon we fell asleep, lying on our packs, to the gentle sound of the river tumbling.

The river was beautiful the next day, sliding milky grey through deep drops and pools. The boulders in the riverbed were massive and required some strenuous moves to surmount. At one stage Tim reached down and pulled me up like a pack, leaving me feeling useless with my feet dangling below. At times we grovelled, crawling underneath boulders, our big packs trying to push our heads into the sand. Sometimes we were forced back up into the bush, which was just as slow.

Our first glimpse of La Perouse came as we rounded a bend in the river. She looked big, wintry and imposing, shrouded in a chilly-looking cap of south-east cloud and sitting staunch under a heavy coat of new white snow. As I jostled for my half of the sleeping bag that night (a questionable weight-saving tactic), her image persisted. Scratches from the bush on my arms and legs burned, and my back was aching.

The weather was crisp and beautiful again as we began up the final section of the river the following day. By late morning we were free from the narrow gorge and had broken out onto the flatter upper section of the river. The temptation to break into a gallop was soon tempered by our arrival at thick sections of tree fuschia the height of our shoulders. We tried to traverse the tops of them with an ungainly springy wobble, only enhanced by our unbalancing packs.

Ahead, the mountain was tauntingly close and we strode eagerly forward past the Balfour Glacier's large terminal lake. We began climbing a steep scree slope to eventually reach a beautiful tarn-side camp, loosely hemmed in by large blocks of rock. Mount Tasman's Hidden and Balfour Faces were so spectacular that all I could do was keep looking as the dropping sun cast a new glow over the mountainsides. I had a feeling of immense luck, and an overwhelming sense of gratitude that I could be there, that my life allowed me to do this.

That night the half-moon was too bright to let me sleep, and I shivered my way to 3am, when the alarm quietly beeped alive. I forced down some peanut butter and crackers, silently packed up, and we began the slog up moraine slopes in the dark to gain the ridge. I felt sick, sleepy and low on energy.

Soon the beams from our headlights were bouncing off steep flaky shale and precariously upwards we climbed. Another steeper buttress inspired us to pitch. With Tim leading off into the gloom, I felt subdued, but happy to be underway with the Strauchon Glacier now falling away below us to the right. With the help of a few tricky boulder moves we sidled past more spires, stopping every now and then to sip on water. Eventually we thought we'd found a link onto the glacier we were aiming for, but alas! As I stepped across a narrow void, I found myself on a sickeningly overhanging block. Forced to abseil, we finally found ourselves on the snow, and standing in the daylight.

I felt truly exhausted and dehydrated as we climbed up through a small icefall and up the long ice slopes to gain the crest of the ridge towards the summit. With every step I forcibly hauled myself. I began counting footsteps as a motivation: 'just another hundred.' I needed to drink, but there wasn't enough water. I needed to sleep, but we had to keep going. It was, however, an amazing day, with inversion cloud puffing up and covering the Cook River and spilling over the coast out to sea, now fallen so far below us.

The final ridge to the summit was dramatic, a great sweeping apex that joined with two more ridges at the top to form a white arrow, pointing to the heavens. This was the ridge I had looked at longingly all summer from my home in Mount Cook village, and here I was, feeling lucky again. On the summit we smiled and gazed around, happy in our bubble of perfect blue weather, the National Park empty of noise, on a crisp still autumn day.

I sat up, horrified. We were sliding towards the abyss, aided by the slippery yellow pack liners we were lying on. In a fluster of panic, we untangled ourselves from the damp sleeping bag, got into our wet boots, and started chopping out our platform again.

All we were doing now was surviving. Unable to move, we were simply shivering and waiting, three metres down a crevasse that opened up just wide enough for us to carve a platform and lie down, before dropping away again into an indefinite blackness. We didn't question the thickness of the floor we were lying on – with no other options the question was silently ignored. The single sleeping bag and tent fly we were wrapped in was a pathetic attempt at insulation and was slowly becoming limp with every blast of spindrift that came down the tunnel and covered us in a damp spray. The snow wall I'd

painstakingly created to block off the entrance had blown down twice and the effort of fixing it seemed more immense each time. Exhausted, I just wanted to sleep.

After many attempts we created a thick wall that held out the weather completely. Our sleeping ledge was flat and we felt safer. We tucked ourselves up and hung our soaking wet clothes from ice screws on the walls around us. In sad mockery of our attempt at drying them, a sheen of ice slowly formed. We fired up the cooker and made some hot soup. The howling of the storm was gone, and we lay down. We began to sing as a substitute for warmth, a duet of Neil Young echoing off the close ice walls. When we stopped, the cold silence enfolded us.

Suddenly the glacier shifted its giant weight, and groaned. Quietly frightened, we huddled together and shivered, now just like little animals sheltering. I had a memory of finding a tiny bird in a storm, its feathers sticking out in brave sodden clumps as feeble defense from the cold. I felt like that now, at the complete mercy of this giant mass of ice we were inside, desperately shivering but unable to keep warm.

Eventually we slept, and the space we were in became warmer. The next morning all was quiet and still. Tim got out of bed and uncomplainingly draped his wet salopettes, jacket and gloves on to check the weather. We were reluctant to break the wall we had so carefully created, but we needn't have worried. The more Tim chipped at the wall, the more it became apparent that it was no longer just a wall. The whole three meters of tunnel we had slid down to enter the crevasse was now completely full of snow. A terrible image of inescapable burial enthused us quickly into action and we started frantically digging. Eventually Tim was at the surface and broke through with his ice axe. Suddenly an icy blast of spindrift came swirling down onto us and confirmed that the storm was still in full swing. He sealed the top of the tunnel, and we slid back down to the platform and rearranged the soggy bed for another day.

We spent the day shifting around on aching hips and knees, making soup, shivering and snoozing. Whenever I moved, the wet down sleeping bag slapped me in the face. Later a wet bundle of polypro collapsed off the wall onto us unpleasantly. We felt alright though, pleased at our relative comfort. That afternoon I went to check the weather. I pulled on wet clothes and wriggled up the tunnel, then burst my ice axe through the roof above me. A torrent of spindrift landed in my eyes and down my neck and up my sleeves

all at once. In desperation I grabbed handfuls of snow and thrust them above my head to re-block the hole, cursing spindrift. The slide back down was quite an amusement, as I got some speed and plopped onto the sleeping bag. How confined, it seemed, our life had quickly become.

On the third day things felt different. It felt colder, crisper; it felt like high pressure. As Tim wriggled up the hole, I started getting ready too. Once he got to the top, all I could see were his legs. There was no response when I asked about the weather and I began to prepare myself for another stormy day. After a while he called down 'I can't break through.' He kept chipping and finally made a small hole, enough to see blue sky through. Excited to move and escape, we packed up and bid our crevasse farewell. Tim made a hole just big enough for us to squeeze through, and we popped out blinking in the sunshine.

Outside, I was astounded. What had been a large, deep, horizontal crevasse when we arrived was gone. All that remained was the tiny hole we had come out of. We thought how funny it would have been for someone to be walking past just as Tim's ice axe broke through, and to see us popping out like moles. All the peaks were plastered in heavy snow and Empress Hut was embarrassingly close.

We had spent three nights inside the glacier, had been swallowed by it, and now regurgitated. Happily we wandered across to Empress Hut, reaching it in forty-five minutes.

Up on the summit, we had hesitated. Thinking the weather to be bombproof, we bivvied up high that afternoon. Given my exhausted state, I preferred to stop, melt water and rest, and to have the entire next day for the descent into the Hooker. Overnight, however, a brisk westerly wind picked up, which quickly turned to gale force in the morning as we began our descent. To escape its fury, we elected to drop onto the eastern slopes of Mounts Low and Jellicoe and traverse our way towards the head of the Hooker.

The wind started screaming as we climbed, tiptoeing across steep icy slopes on our frontpoints, long slopes dropping away below our toes. The spindrift spilling down was so intense that we could not see where we were placing our ice axes or our feet, which were enveloped in a constant shower of whiteness. We didn't talk much as shouting into the wind was futile, instead concentrating on moving. Steep sideways climbing started to seem

endless, and was very tiring. My focus narrowed to thinking of a rhythm and trying to stick to it, in-between bouts of peering into the storm and trying to make out where we were, and where we were going. We ended up on some very steep ground and began downclimbing a gully system to try and reach some better slopes below. The climbing ended in a drop and we abseiled off an ice screw, leaving it behind uncaringly, far more concerned about whether the rope would reach.

We were still climbing at the end of the day, uncertain about where we were, as navigating from the map on such steep ground was difficult and the visibility was atrocious. We were tired, soaking wet and beginning to get clumsy. It was dark. How far from the hut we couldn't tell. All we could see were crevasses as they came looming up, with no idea which direction to turn to pass them. We started to look for an escape. And that was when Tim found the tunnel.

In Empress Hut I took off my inner boots, still wet from the river, for the first time in four days. My feet were fascinatingly unrecognisable. Deep gorges crisscrossed my soles and my toes were blistered and showing disturbing shades of purple, grey and white. After a couple of days procrastination, I ashamedly agreed to call in a SAR chopper.

Suddenly we were in the DOC first aid room, me feeling foolish in my bare feet as the medical team made their inspections. Released to freedom, Mt Cook village was stark. A bitterly cold winter's day was struggling to warm the land. The road remained in shadow while the sun weakly peeped onto the far hillsides. The flat that had been my home just weeks before was empty, furnitureless and locked against intruders.

Feeling humbled, we began the long hitch home.

PETER GOUGH

Never Let the Facts …

Climbing accidents are never funny, but after a few years, the humour of the situation often exerts itself so that the story becomes enlarged, slightly exaggerated and only vaguely based on the truth. With this caveat in mind, the following recounts the funniest accident I've ever had.

Early in 1975 after finishing my engineering degree, we moved from Christchurch, New Zealand, to Rochester, New York; one of those awful decaying industrial slum cities where everyone wants to leave to go almost anywhere else. Within a month or so, I found some climbers in the next city some 90 miles away and over the phone organised a weekend's ice climbing in the Adirondacks 300 miles NE into the mountains. We had arranged to meet in a café on the State Thruway about 100 miles from home and only two hours late they indeed arrived. Ken Martin was a slightly crazed half New Zealander with a passion for style, and with him was Tony Patane, your average second generation NY Italian. Ken had a flair for the faintly ridiculous and his car was a perfect example. He went down to the local car auction to buy a small economical car to get to work. However, it had snowed and everything was covered with a mantle of dirt-covering snow. Ken brushed some snow off the bonnet of an anonymous shape: he liked the colour. He wiped some more off a window: he liked the upholstery, so in a fit of inspired madness he bought the car. Consequently he now commutes in a 7.5 litre Trans Am, probably the worst designed, and, at 8 mpg, the most uneconomical car in the USA. What's more, he loves it.

We had decided to climb the ice cliffs above Chappell Pond, not far from Lake Placid, the site of the 1980 Winter Olympics. Chappell Pond has a few advantages, one being that, as it's only 100 yards from the road, access is not a problem; second being, the climbing is not too difficult. Subsequently, I found out that much smarter climbers than I had come to grief here and one of the more amusing stories concerns Yvon Chouinard and Jim McCarthy. Jim was one of the original Vulgarians, who, like many, ends up a wealthy lawyer. However the story goes, after a successful climb they were descending the easy route sliding on their bums. As Jim found himself going

a trifle too fast, he sticks a foot out to slow down. His foot and crampon get impaled on a tree and stop; the rest of him does not, thus breaking his leg. Now Jim is fairly solid and Yvon is all of 5′6″ and the snow was deep so after splinting his leg, Yvon tows him through the snow with a length of rope tied around his middle. Jim assisting by backstroking with his arms. At this stage, they meet a group of Appies – Appalachian Mountain Club members – a cross between the Salvation Army and the Tararua Trampers. 'What are you doing,' they inquired.

'Practising rescues! What does it look like,' was the supposed retort as they plunged on.

It was one of those rare perfect super-cold days when after a few moves you just know it's going to be a great climb. Movement; stretching, flowing, pitch after pitch, the vertical ballet. The pleasure of an absolutely perfect placement, followed by a little twostep with the feet. Eat your heart out, Nureyev.

The last pitch was our undoing. The whole damn ice slope fell off. I recall a desperate self arrest – which was pretty silly as the entire cliff was collapsing around us. This is what it is like to die. The blocks of ice smashing around you, the momentary pain as some part of you breaks. The weird reverse flight of the cliffs upward. The total detachment of imminent non-existence. Blackness and Pain.

We stop. Holy shit, we're alive. I'm hanging fifty feet off the deck. I wonder who this girl is next to me. 'Gidday,' I say in broad Kiwi, 'my name's Peter. What's yours?'

'Cut the rope!' That's a funny name I thought and noticed that I was still tied on and the rope went from me up around the girl's neck, down her back and a loop was caught around her foot. She looked like a devotee of some weird eastern religion. Since Tony Patane was hanging from me and I was hanging from the girl's foot, if she cut the rope we'd all fall off.

'No. No! Don't cut the rope' I pleaded. I lay there for a bit.

'I wonder where the hell Ken is?' The rope went from Tony back up over a small ridge and out of sight. A pathetic groan came from that direction.

'You OK Ken?'

'Ohh, I think I've broken my back.' Oh well, that's him kissed off.

'Tony. How are you?' There was no answer but he was still alive because I could just see him moving on the end of the rope. He had blood all

over his face and chest and more would gush out every time he coughed. Obviously a smashed rib cage and a punctured lung. His leg was at a weird angle too. As I watched he slumped over into unconsciousness. Well, that's him kissed off.

'Cut the rope,' she pleaded.

'No! No! Don't cut the rope,' I countermanded.

Just in case she did manage to cut the rope I hitched my bum up onto a tiny ledge and whipped in an ice screw. Nothing like insurance. In the course of this manoeuvre, I did notice that only a majority of me pointed in the same direction. One foot refused to do anything but flop around, so I reached down with the end of my ice axe and flicked it round so it pointed frontwards. Some time later I recovered and managed to splint it to my other foot and the ice axe – a very slow and increasingly painful task.

'Cut the rope.'

'No, no. Don't cut the rope.' This chorus was beginning to get boring. Ken was still moaning about his back and Tony would stir and cough occasionally. I began to wonder what had actually happened. Why did we stop at all? A fall of five hundred feet or so to stop just before we hit the ground. Who were these other three people anyway? What had transpired was a trifle hard to believe.

A rope of three relative beginners were just on the first pitch of an easy climb directly below the finish of ours. The first thing they knew was the scream of snow and ice blocks beating down on them. The second thing they knew was that as we fell past, a stray loop of rope caught around the girl's foot and neck, bringing the three of us to a rapid halt. The third thing they knew was

'Cut the rope.'

'Oh shut up!'

Well, at least it was going to be easy to be rescued. Just whistle at my wife who was reading a book in the pick-up parked on the road and she'd slip off to get the face rescue team. They do have a face rescue team I supposed. No doubt the book Janet was reading was fascinating. We yelled ourselves hoarse and watched as she turned over the pages. A group of Canadian tourists stopped, got out, waved back at us and, so help me, drove away.

'Bloody Frenchies.' Eventually Janet finished the exciting part of her book and noticed some other tourists pointing and gesticulating. A word in

her defence: the party we had got tangled up with did make a tremendous noise as they started up their climb. How was she to know that this was different.

After explaining our predicament, she drove off down to Keene Valley to get an ambulance and the face rescue team. Some time later the ambulance and the park ranger arrived.

'Where's the face rescue team,' I enquired.

'I'm it,' the ranger replied and was able to prove it too as he'd brought an antique pair of ten-point crampons with him. A couple of French Canadian climbers also turned up and were roped into the posse. Of course, like all true Frogs they refused to speak, or even understand, English. Perhaps I'm being ungrateful, after all they were there to rescue us.

'Cut the rope,' her voice was becoming faint.

'Hit her over the ear,' I told her companion.

Which ear was the problem. Her right foot was twisted up behind her back and planted firmly in her left ear.

Gradually the rescue team evacuated the dead and dying. The ranger had asked me how I felt and in true stiff-upper-lip tradition I said I was OK. He then proceeded to rescue everyone else first. On reflection, I should have screamed bloody murder since I was hanging around for about four hours at 25–30° below zero and by the time I was carried to the ambulance, I was in bad shape. I do remember taking my gloves off to zip up my duvet and then finding I was incapable of the mental resolve to get the gloves back on again.

Once inside the doctor's little clinic at Keene Valley, my troubles really started. In tottered this extremely ancient, rather obviously half blind man who had been drinking heavily.

'Doctor Gough,' he said. Rather puzzled I asked him how he knew who I was.

'No, No. I'm Doctor Gough,' he said.

'How confusing, so am I,' I replied, rather thankful that we were not related. He lurched over, poked around, ordered the staff to cut my clothes and boots off and went out for a restorative. (Ken and Tony had meanwhile been evacuated by helicopter to the nearest big hospital in Vermont).

Until now I had given up climbing for good. Never again, ever. Nice little house in the suburbs, thousands of screaming children – heaven. They started to cut down the inside of my boot.

'Don't do that, they're worth $200. I might need them again.' I'm as weak-willed as they come. The happy amateur surgeons chivvied my boots off. It was not a pretty sight – my leg was definitely badly broken. The other Doctor Gough (the one with the medical rather than engineering degree) returned. He was not a pretty sight either so Janet went off to ring my boss in Rochester to find out what she should do.

My boss, one B.J. Thompson, was a very big wheel in the scientific world in the US. Four-star generals in the Pentagon have been known to touch their fetlocks when he entered but despite that, despite even being a pommie from Manchester, he was OK.

So Janet rings Brian up. The conversation must have gone something like this.

'Er, Brian Thompson? This is Janet Gough speaking. You know, we met you the other night at dinner. Remember us, we speak with a funny accent? Well, we have a problem. We're 300 miles from home, it's 30 degrees below zero, Peter's broken his leg, the doctor's 80 years old, decrepit and possibly drunk. What do I do next?'

Brian who normally doesn't bother with problems under a few million dollars solved ours right away.

'Load him in the back of the pickup and drive home. I'll meet you at the hospital.'

We stayed at the Keene Valley clinic overnight. By we, I mean I slept inside and Janet outside in the car park. Rather cold night too, I recall, but we must economise where we can. The next day the nurses rolled me down the corridor, slotted me into the back of the pickup, gave me a bottle of painkillers and a bottle to piss in, covered me with all our clothes and sleeping bags and we left for home. The cold and the painkillers numbed me into insensibility.

The university hospital in Rochester is a grand place dedicated to making money as well as curing the sick. Janet drove until she found the emergency entrance where she stopped. An orderly leapt out,

'Oi, you can't park there, this is an emergency entrance.'

We swore at him for a bit until he indeed decided that we constituted an emergency and went inside to rustle up some help with a stretcher. I lay around in the admitting room for what seemed like hours trying to prove that we could indeed pay the bill. Where's your insurance card, social security card, credit card, etc. Brian Thompson arrived, sorted this problem out and Janet went off for some coffee.

That was the very moment they decided that a next-of-kin signature was needed. Brian pretended to be my father for a few seconds but they rumbled that ruse. There was nothing for it but to wait. I had run out of painkillers hours before so it was with some relief to me that Janet returned, signed on the dotted line and they thrust the needle home into my battered body. I had been admitted.

As a postscript, both Ken and Tony survived. My leg healed. In fact, well enough for me to go on an expedition only 9 months later. Ken spent years in a back brace and Tony's smashed thigh finally healed. He did indeed puncture his lung but they got him to a hospital in time to prevent any permanent damage. I never did find out who the girl was, but I'm sure she is OK.

REFLECTION

PAT DEAVOLL

from *Wind from a Distant Summit*

I find failing on a mountain hard to cope with and usually dread going home afterwards, building up the criticism I feel I'm bound to receive to almost unbearable levels. This was particularly bad after my second failure on Beka Brakai Chhok; so bad, in fact, that I mentioned my misgivings in an article for the *New Zealand Alpine Journal 2008*. I was devastated – to the point of not wanting to return home because of the reaction I thought I'd get from friends, family and sponsors. Friends who read the article reassured me that of course they didn't judge me, and that what was most important was that I got home safely. In their opinion, the only people who might judge are those who don't matter. They were right of course. Judgement would come from those who knew little about me, or about climbing in the Karakoram, or who were jealous of my achievements.

In my view, mountaineering is an occupation that is largely impossible to fake. From watching someone in everyday life, it's impossible to gauge how they will act in the mountains; I've seen people who appear strong and tough in daily life fall to pieces at the first hardship, while others discover previously unrecognised reserves of strength. Some climbers put aside future discomfort when planning a climb, but give up when the hardship is actually experienced. Those climbers who are successful may have a particularly strong drive to complete a task. Essentially, the only reason mountaineering reveals character in climbers is because it's hard. Maybe the desire to test oneself, combined with a poor memory for misery, explains why the toughest or most uncomfortable trips often produce the best memories. Pain and discomfort become, to some degree, the point of the trip.

A lot of older climbing literature emphasises the solidarity of the team and the depth of the relationships forged by hardship as a primary reason for why the alpinists involved went on expeditions. More recent literature often conveys a different story, however, emphasising the true loneliness and isolation of mountaineering, and the feeling of separation alpinists experience, even from their climbing partners. Being roped to another is not necessarily a bonding experience, and can even create enemies ... In

his book *K2: Triumph and tragedy*, Tim Curran reported that during the 1986 climbing season on K2 intense squabbles broke out in the British expedition before the climbers had even left base camp, and that two members of a small French team lugged an extra tent up the mountain so they wouldn't have to sleep together. When Bruce Normand and I climbed together in India in 2007, an antagonism existed between the two of us, and many times I was on the verge of going home. We seemed to be at loggerheads about everything: I was struggling with injury and limped everywhere; he had just summited K2 without oxygen and was supremely fit. Our isolation from one another was exacerbated by an empathy gap, which rendered Bruce unable to appreciate my disability or the fact that our first ascent of a 6500m peak, which meant little to him, was important to me. He thought he'd been lumbered with a lemon for a partner.

According to American climber Steve House, part of the reason why mountaineers climb mountains is 'that they can do it – they are good at it'. Joe Simpson said the same: 'There is a perverse delight in putting oneself in a potentially dangerous situation knowing that your experience and skill make you quite safe.' When Marty Beare and I survived our (comparatively small) epic on Mt Unicorn, we had the same sense of satisfaction in knowing that, although all sorts of things had gone wrong, our skill level, experience and ability to concentrate on the job at hand had enabled us to keep in control of the situation.

I find that my mastery of the sport is, and always will be, securely hitched to my self-esteem. I'm good at mountaineering, and knowing this and putting my skills into practice buoys my ego to such an extent that I've always been reluctant to make any life decisions that might stymie my plans for the next climb or the next expedition. This has included turning down jobs that, however enticing and well paid, don't allow me time off for expeditions, and committing to relationships when my partner doesn't understand, appreciate or give me the time I need to fulfil my compulsion. It's my drug, and regardless of the hardships I can't do without it.

GRAEME DINGLE

from *Wall of Shadows*

The Worst Day in the Life of a Himalayan Climber

The day after the discussion, Limbo and Don went back to Camp Three to collect some of the valuable equipment. Then everyone moved down to base. Once back at base camp we pilfered all the little bottles of whisky, gin and brandy from the high-altitude food boxes and had a good old-fashioned booze-up. This culminated in the collapse of several people.

I found Keith draped over a boulder at about 1 a.m. making an unbelievable noise. Ian John and I dragged him to his tent and then Ian went off to get the doctor to suggest that maybe Keith should be given oxygen. The doctor unfortunately was found to be in a similar condition so we decided to let nature take its course and went to bed.

No one wanted to return to the mountain to recover equipment but Brian Fearnley and Ian volunteered and the rest of us drew straws. The shortest straws were drawn by Pete and me.

The last day on Jannu was a crazy, heart-breaking pantomime.

It began with breakfast. While we stood around eating and waiting for the sun to reach base camp some of the Tibetans who had come up from Gunsa to begin the carry out were seen heading off across the glacier.

Pete asked Sikku: 'Hey, Sikku! Where are those guys going?'

'Oh, yaks getting,' Sikku lied. His answer was not too unlikely though because there were some yaks grazing in some amazing places on the mountainsides, and with a quizzical look Pete shrugged and went off to his tent. Soon we saw the Tibetan men, together with a shaggy, bearlike dog climbing up the lower slopes. Where the rock buttress reared up in front of them they traversed across to our fixed ropes and disappeared from sight in the first gully.

We followed confident that we would find the men and the dog near the start of the ropes, but when we got there the dog was sitting in the snow alone. There was no sign of the Tibetans.

We clipped on to the ropes and began up, figuring that they would surely go no further than Wayatt's Hole. But at Wayatt's Hole there was just rock and rope. The Tibetans had apparently continued on across the Hinterstoisser and up the ropes hand over hand.

Pete was doing a minor panic considering all the insurance on dead Tibetans. When we passed Da Tensing on his way down he cocked his head on one side and said: 'Today many men dying.' He closed his eyes and poked out his tongue out to demonstrate the point.

We crossed the Hinterstoisser marvelling at the Tibetans' courage, then we continued up the buttresses beside the icefall. The chaotic mass of ice bore no resemblance to the icefall of six weeks before as sérac collapses and avalanches had flattened out the surface.

One hundred feet below Half-way House we finally met the Tibetans on their way down. They were loaded up with food and knick-knacks pinched from the camp and their terror showed how valuable the stuff was to them. They clung desperately to the ropes and around their smooth shoes they had tied rope to give them more traction on the icy rock. One old fellow became so terrified that he eventually left his sack of loot on a ledge. Because of their efforts and because the stuff would probably have been wasted anyway we said nothing.

At Half-way House we were greeted by an unholy mess. It looked as if a pack of gorillas had just completed a picnic of our ration packs. The contents had been strewn over hundreds of feet. Badly-molested *Playboy* centre-folds, punctured cans of meat, whole fruit cakes and dozens of other items littered the snow.

Pete picked up a bundle of fruit rolls and said: 'This lot cost us six hundred bloody dollars!'

The clean-up was one of the most depressing jobs I have ever done. We piled it all together and set fire to it. The waste made me feel sick.

There was no shortage of lunch but none of us felt very hungry. As we sat beside the smouldering heap of food trying to choke down fruit cake I tried to remember Lionel Terray's words about man's litter on mountains: *'The seasons with their storms passed over, the ropes turned to straw and one day the mountain was clean again as in the beginning of the world.'*

As a gesture to the Japanese who would attempt this face during 1976 we left a little cache of luxuries under the big rock, and then, as the snow that had threatened for a week began to fall from a leaden sky, we began down for the last time.

Brian Fearnley and I went ahead to take all the ropes and pitons from the Hinterstoisser traverse and Engineers' Row while Ian and Pete began taking everything out as they came. By mid-afternoon we had a heap of

gear that would make the most dour gear-freak shout for joy – hexentrics, moacs, stoppers, lost arrows, angles, blades, karabiners, ropes, piton hammers, a winch, cable, and so on. We began to lower it down the cliff to Wayatt's Hole but the first item, a drum of cable, caught on a projection.

Brian volunteered to go down and clear it and with him he took most of the other stuff. I jammed the winch into the top of his huge pack for good measure. He abseiled gamely over the first overhang and found to his horror that his pack was heavier than his legs whereupon he tipped upside down. On the ledge above I could only conjure up a picture of disaster from his strangled cries followed by an incredible jangle as everything emptied from his pack and made its own way down to the Jannu Glacier.

Brian completed the abseil in the upside-down position.

Pete and Ian arrived to find me chuckling like an idiot.

'Good thing we cleaned all the gear off the mountain though,' I said thinking of all the equipment spread down the face.

Pete was loaded like a mule.

'I think *I* had better lower this lot,' he said.

I abseiled down to Wayatt's Hole, then Pete began lowering his pack. The operation went quite smoothly until, when about 50 feet above me, the pack suddenly broke away from the rope and hurtled down. It almost wiped me off the ledge before bounding down in the wake of all the other stuff.

We collected the four or five ropes below Wayatt's Hole, hurtled the aluminium ladders into space, and then, thoroughly fed-up we shambled down the lower slopes and across the glacier in the last light. We had very little to show for a hard day's work.

As we stumbled across the moraine I hated Jannu as I had never hated anything before.

RACHEL BUSH

Never

Look I think we can order
mountains arranged with
their crisp edge to the sky
their blue serrations.
They are on the menu with
their bulges and improbable
geometry, the intensity
of their new snow.
You could devour them.

These fearful mountains,
and I will never go again
into their extreme whiteness
which is broken by angular rock
that interrupts the agile light.
I will not stand on the ridge
and look down at my big boots
on stone or snow, will not see
the slips on the access road, nor
farms with foxgloves, thistles, thin cattle
and far off, the sea.

AAT VERVOORN

from *Beyond the Snowline*

How could we have foreseen that such a magnificent day would end in death? A blue day under the crystalline sun of mid-winter, on which the mountains were carved precisely by the frost out of light and shadow and the air did not become mild until midday. The ice of Mount Sefton soared above us, leaping forward through the transparent atmosphere as the car rounded the last bend in the road: pure whiteness, the upper slopes blazing light, momentarily framed between the black cliffs of Sebastopol and the bulk of Mount Wakefield.

Bruce Jenkinson's van was not parked outside the house when we drove up. Nor was he inside, although his gear was still spread about the house. That was surprising. He was due to meet the clients on his instruction course at Unwin Hut an hour later, but obviously had not packed yet. Still, he could be anywhere. We unloaded the car, put the skis away and made some tea, expecting him to turn up any minute. Afternoon cloud was drifting through Copland Pass; high cloud above the upper Hooker Valley was beginning to catch light from the sinking sun.

When it was almost time for his meeting I decided to look for him: I wanted to know if anything had developed during the past few days, and whether he would need a second instructor on the course. On the way back down the road to Unwin I kept my eye on the cliffs of Sebastopol lining the valley, for I knew that one thing he had had to do before the course started was to find a place suitable for rockclimbing instruction.

Sure enough, there was the van, parked on the track under the cliffs. He must be there, making some last-minute investigations. When I pulled up behind the van I could see nothing, for the cliffs were already deep in shadow. But there were voices: several. Soon I could make out figures climbing on the steep slabs to the right. Yet surely Bruce would be on his own? Elsewhere there was nothing to be seen, except an orange-coloured spot on one of the scree slopes to the left, not far from the base of the cliff. A rucksack perhaps, left behind by one of the climbers or by Bruce. I waited in the lengthening shadows. Eventually the people on the slabs stopped climbing. They came down the slope and walked across the valley floor to a car parked by the main road. So he was not with them.

Half an hour. Still no sign. The valley was completely in shadow now. There was no sound in the cold air. He would be late for his meeting. The orange object was still there.

Uneasy, I strained my ears and eyes against the approaching twilight. Only that unmoving patch of colour. Three-quarters of an hour. Something must be wrong. Filled with anxiety and growing fear, I walked towards the scree and its coloured patch, then up the broken rocks, closer and closer, with dread, staring ahead yet wanting desperately not to see. Oh no, no, not Bruce. I broke into a staggering run up the scree, slipping, falling, clawing at the rubble with my hands.

It was Bruce. He was lying on his back down the slope, his left arm curved as if to guard his head against a fall, right arm out-stretched, its fist clenched in pain. He had been wearing his orange singlet to catch some afternoon sun. On the rocks above, just out from the cliff, lay his watch, its glass broken: it had stopped at twenty to three.

That night the stars froze against the silhouettes of the mountains. Cold fell on the stones of the valley and the leafless thickets of ribbon-wood, until water congealed and the air shattered into fragments; needle ice pierced the earth. Over the glaciers a wind sprang up. It picked up the dust of the rocks ground fine by the ice and swirled it, clouds of darkness in darkness, above the fast-flowing waters braiding their way to the sea. Only the sound of the river echoed through the silence, rebounding from the cliffs and valley walls to lose itself in the inaudible hum of the slow-turning galaxy.

The enormity of the event forbids words which might trivialise it. That Bruce should die was almost unthinkable and, just as in life he had inspired veneration, so now his death filled us with awe. Perhaps Sue Miller expressed the feeling best, rhetorically distancing the event to make it bearable:

A mighty tree of the forest has fallen.

Yes. O Tane Mahuta. That the sky should collapse upon the earth in darkness, crushing every living thing. How could we have foreseen his death, he who epitomised strength and the possibility of survival? That death should take so much, the best we had, and leave behind such emptiness. An icy wind of total devastation blew around us, numbing the senses and the mind with an insidious foreboding of chaos to come.

Yet Bruce had accepted death as a normality of our lives, something as much part of the scene as the avalanches off Mount Sefton or the nor'wester threatening to take off the roof. That his death should occur on Mount Sebastopol, with Mount Cook gleaming at the head of the valley and wisps of cloud streaming through Copland Pass from the West Coast, would have aroused in him the response that, well, if you've got to die, it might as well be in a place you know and like, if only because that makes death a natural event in your familiar life, part of your everyday surroundings rather than something which reaches out from the other edge of the universe to grab you by the scruff of the neck.

For death was always imminent in the rhythm of our days, in a dangerous move or a falling stone, waiting to touch us on the shoulder. It was, in a sense, the reference point which gave our actions significance: not through morbid fascination, but through an awareness of its presence as the ultimate measure of the value of existence which cannot be cheated; the limit of human possibility which lies so dangerously close, yet at times recedes miraculously.

So we, too, must accept it; that the year will renew itself without Bruce, that in the summer again the white ourisia flowers will quiver above the green of their leaves in the clefts on Sebastopol. We must not look for reverberations throughout the natural world, for the tragedy is ours alone; there is no tragedy in nature. And we must not reduce his death to a pretext for philosophising, for stringing together a few slick phrases about the meaning of life and death. No wise words, only the pattern of life itself, in which death is one event like any other, and Bruce's life flows through mine and Dave's, through Vicky's and Herbie's and so many others, meeting and dividing like the streams of the Tasman River.

It is this pattern of meetings and departures which formed the structure of our world, a structure of friendships which bound us together despite being scattered around the globe. We were not united by some accident of geography, by habits tying us to a particular patch of ground, but by a common search for values which found expression in shared activity. Seeking a goal, some ultimate purpose? No, not that, not that illusion that life leads somewhere or serves some higher purpose in a teleological universe. What we searched for was no great mystery, just something more than mere existence or day-to-day animal survival. It was a search for what can give value to wanderings which lead nowhere, a humanity which can be shared as the wing of death passes over us.

FLEUR ADCOCK

Flight, with Mountains

(in memory of David Herron)

1

Tarmac, take-off: metallic words conduct us
over that substance, black with spilt rain,
to this event. Sealed, we turn and pause.
Engines churn and throb to a climax, then
up: a hard spurt, and the passionate rise
levels out for this gradual incline.

There was something of pleasure in that thrust
from earth into ignorant cloud; but here,
above all tremors of sensation, rest
replaces motion; secretly we enter
the obscurely gliding current, and encased
in vitreous calm inhabit the high air.

Now I see, beneath the plated wing,
cloud edges withdrawing their slow foam
from shoreline, rippling hills, and beyond, the long
crested range of the land's height. I am
carried too far by this blind rocketing:
faced with mountains, I remember him

whose death seems a convention of such a view:
another one for the mountains. Another one
who, climbing to stain the high snow
with his shadow, fell, and briefly caught between
sudden earth and sun, projected below
a flicker of darkness; as, now, this plane.

2

Only air to hold the wings;
only words to hold the story;
only a frail web of cells
to hold heat in the body.

Breath bleeds from throat and lungs
under the last cold fury;
words wither; meaning fails;
steel wings grow heavy.

3

Headlines announced it, over a double column of type:
the cabled facts, public regret, and a classified list
of your attainments – degrees, scholarships and positions,
and notable feats of climbing. So the record stands:
no place there for my private annotations. The face
that smiles in some doubt from a fuscous half-tone block
stirs me hardly more than those I have mistaken
daily, about the streets, for yours.
                                        I can refer
to my own pictures; and turning first to the easiest,
least painful, I see Dave the raconteur,
playing a shoal of listeners on a casual line
of dry narration. Other images unreel:
your face in a car, silent, watching the dark road,
or animated and sunburnt from your hard pleasures
of snow and rock-face; again, I see you arguing,
practical and determined, as you draw with awkward puffs
at a rare cigarette.
                        So much, in vivid sequence
memory gives. And then, before I can turn away,
imagination adds the last scene: your eyes bruised,
mouth choked under a murderous weight of snow.

4

'When you reach the top of a mountain, keep on climbing' –
meaning, we may suppose,
to sketch on space the cool arabesques of birds
in plastic air, or those
exfoliating arcs, upward and outward,
of an aeronautic show.
Easier, such a free fall in reverse,
higher than clogging snow
or clutching gravity, than the awkward local
embrace of rocks. And observe
the planets coursing their elliptical race-tracks,
where each completed curve
cinctures a new dimension. Mark these patterns.
Mark, too, how the high
air thins. The top of any mountain
is a base for the sky.

5

Further by days and oceans than all my flying
you have gone, while here the air insensibly flowing
over a map of mountains drowns my dumbness.
A turn of the earth away, where a crawling dimness
waits now to absorb our light, another
snowscape, named like this one, took you; and neither
rope, nor crumbling ice, nor your unbelieving
uncommitted hands could hold you to living.
Wheels turn; the dissolving air rolls over
an arc of thunder. Gone is gone forever.

JONATHAN SCOTT

from *Harry's Absence: Looking for my father on the mountain*

Dark Blue Light (with Apricots)

> *Tutorial passed pleasantly enough tonight – they got onto premonitions of death and similar pleasant phenomena, so I told them a few climbing stories.* – Harry Scott to Margaret Scott, 1952

> *The two survivors ... scanned the line of fall through field glasses, and called out. A high westerly wind was raging, and nothing was seen or heard.* – Christchurch *Press*, 2 February 1960

The loneliness of an island may lie bleached and exposed. It is a particular place, husbanding abnormality. Yet it is strong, its aloneness connected and composed. It is not only limited, but rendered unlimited by water. We must not equate an island solely with its land. It is made what it is also by the sea in which it stands.

New Zealand lies southerly in the greatest ocean in the world, high-sided under dark blue light. In Britain the light is fragile, tactile. In Greece it is clear and hard. In Tahiti, where the sun connects the sea and air into a single glass, it is bright blue. Five thousand miles southwest that hue has changed. Blue-black is the colour of the land. Yet no less bright: no ozone, no shelter, by thousands of miles of ocean on every side light is collected, reflected. Nature is a power which New Zealanders can deface but which they cannot, and do not particularly wish to, tame.

It is in the Mackenzie country of the South Island that we find this country's spectacular blue heart. Here the dramatic powder-blue lakes are given their colour by the glacial mastication of stone. Here, as if the general light were not enough, drawing colour and power from the sea, stone in water throws colour at the sky.

To the southwest are the forested mountains of Fiordland. No less extraordinary, these are the primary site of New Zealand's religion. Ask any British historian what is special to them about their geography – country or city; dry stone-walled upland or walled town – they will tell you that it has been inhabited for thousands of years. It has a history beyond the reach

of human knowledge. Ask a New Zealander the same question and they will tell you that in Fiordland there are places where no human being has ever set foot. It is this truth, in the minds of hundreds of thousands of New Zealanders, who have not set foot in Fiordland either, which establishes a virginity cult as powerful, if not as ancient, as that of Rome. This is the southern religion of the unput foot.

On the eastern shore of Lake Tekapo there is a famous small chapel. Through the western window one sees in microcosm the alpine view which spans the lake. Over an impossible blue, in the lightest air on earth, under perpetual snow, the Southern Alps stand like minted teeth. At their centre, and highest, is Mount Cook. To say that on a sunny sharp day it is one of the most beautiful sights on earth may be to mis-state the case. It is unearthly, and climbers regularly abandon sea-level to seek it.

It was in Tekapo that my mother last saw my father. This sight occurred, appropriately enough, in a rear-vision mirror. Preparations for the ascent finished, Harry had bought apricots. As Margaret drove away, the bag burst. Her last glimpse of her husband was of a man ducking and weaving through traffic to retrieve apricots.

Two evenings later there was a knock at the door. A policeman asked to speak to my grandfather. The following morning (2 February 1960) Margaret read in the Christchurch *Press* under the headline 'TWO MOUNTAINEERS KILLED: 6,000ft Fall Off Ice Cap of Mount Cook':

> *Two of a party of four climbers fell 6,000ft to their deaths off the ice cap of Mount Cook's high peak yesterday afternoon. The accident occurred near the Zerbruggen ridge, a well known landmark near the summit. The dead men were: MELVILLE JAMES PITT GLASGOW, married, with four children … and DR. T.H. SCOTT, married, senior lecturer in psychology at the University of Auckland.*

That evening, 'CLIMBERS BODIES NOT RECOVERED: Bad Weather Prevents Search on Mt. Cook':

> *The bodies of the two climbers who yesterday … slipped on the ice and plunged off the east face of Mt Cook … have not yet been recovered. Conditions today were impossible for searching, and the search parties were confined to the Haast Hut … Chief Inspector C.H. Reardon, of the Timaru police, said today that after making their way in bad weather to the Haast Hut the two survivors … Messrs Bruce Young and Jack*

Woodward ... were badly shaken ... the climbers, victims of a tragedy which had shocked everyone from Christchurch to the Hermitage, were roped in pairs.

It was raining in the search area and visibility was bad ... Mount Cook National Park Board chief ranger Mr H. Ayres said that there was 'only a 50-50 chance of recovering the bodies' ... Mr Reardon said 'I want the search party to go in and come out as quickly as possible ... Conditions are extremely dangerous.'

The following day (3 February): 'Search For Bodies on Mount Cook Abandoned':

Announcing this evening that the search had been abandoned, Chief Inspector Reardon said any further search would involve too great a risk ... Snow conditions are anything but safe.

In cloudy, overcast but calm weather a strong party left the Haast Hut at 8 a.m. today ... The route taken under the leadership of Mr Ayres ... was over the Glacier Dome (8047ft) [and] ... the Linda Glacier ... to the snow shelf on the northwest side of the Zerbruggen ridge ... a ski-equipped Cessna aircraft assisted ... A comprehensive search was made ... and at times the east face above them was shrouded in mist ... the bodies were not on any of the known routes ... It was impossible to scale the face to look for them ... and on two occasions while roped together and wearing crampons members of the party had to run for shelter because of avalanches coming down.

Without a body, there was no funeral. At the inquest on 24 May Harry Ayres stated:

There were five ropes of two men each, which meant that a fair area could be searched. The line of search made eliminates the possibility of the bodies being on the shelf. This means that the bodies are high up on the east face of Mount Cook, possibly caught on rocks or broken ice.

'Life is inside – what we have done,' Harry had written. 'Death is present before it has come.' As a family we were broken by it; hooked on rear-vision, and scattered like the apricots from his hand.

The Significance of Living Dangerously

Death comes easily now, in this loneliest part
of the ascent … Death crawls crabwise
… time's exit, presented spaciously,
In the best traditions of statesmen and frontiers
Arguing for untimely exits …

Ask me what, now that the dark curves
Dangerously … In a sharp canyon
… Ask me what serves
the issuing day and its sharp companion
… we go
Impaled on laughter in a long embrace
With death in our wind and limp lips moving
At this mountainous sepulchre of pain
All death begins. The thrush is lost in
My heart's edge. I am dead in these men.

– Harry Scott, 'Pursuit'

I was high on the east face, surrounded by rocks and broken ice.

In Ashford in December the snows came. Drifts gathered in the streets as I arrived home, and all night it snowed. In the morning I heard the silence.

Later I attempted the round walk. Snow lay waist-deep against the walls. By halfway up it was chest-high and level across the wall-tops. I took to the fields, circling drifts to reach the dale-head four hours later.

Below stretched the valley of Wye, not green but a knitting of black through white. To the right the limestone escarpments of Monsal head rose sheer from the river and scattered toward Wardlow. Across the valley the close-walled fields of Litton were visible on their high plateau. Behind me the land fell from Longstone edge across white wall, white stone village and skeletal tree. Nothing stirred.

Now the world curves here beneath us
And we touch it, reaching down as
Children, hollow-footed.

My mother said, without apparent irony, 'It is in the past. You must put it behind you.'

A year later, I returned to live in Cambridge. It was from there that, the following year, I finally visited New Zealand. It was my first trip there alone for ten years.

Midway across the Pacific the plane turned a tight arc over the island of Rarotonga. Two years earlier Lawrence Millman had written:

> *For my taste, there are few approaches anywhere on this planet more exhilarating than when your plane sweeps down out of the clouds and, suddenly, miraculously, you see the lush green mountains of Rarotonga rising out of the sea like a landscape from a childhood fairy tale, like a lost world.*

We came down onto a runway glassy with water. There were palms, rainbows, and the smell of vanilla in the rain. In the shops New Zealand groceries reminded me of childhood. In the motel laundrette I met Anne, with her mother, Jane. We drank James Cook beer on my balcony and watched the sunset for *le rayon vert.*

Then I was descending into Wellington between houses ranged steeply around Evans Bay. Cocoa-coloured seagulls wheeled above a harbour of steel blue in air washed clean by wind and rain. I rang Brian and we walked on the hill, hesitantly throwing up jumpers.

At home Margaret and I argued. When I became angry and said: 'We had 30 years of your grief. I now have my own,' she replied: 'You are mad. You are not my son.'

I travelled to Christchurch, where Rachel now lived. There I walked alone on the Port Hills. On one side they plunged sheer to Lyttelton's harbour. On the other lay Sumner, and beyond it the Southern Alps.

Labouring across that dark sky, with its many layers, I learned stabilisation, then navigation of a kind. Behind each absence there appeared another. It was at this time, quite suddenly, that I stumbled upon Harry.

He had been on the mountain, in January 1960, searching for two other climbers. Tony Evans and James Board fell on 22 January. On the 31st the search was abandoned.

The following day, Harry, Jim, Jack Woodward and Bruce Young left Haast Hut at 2.30 am. They were to climb to the summit by the Linda

Glacier route. The morning was clear, with a light northerly wind. The summit rocks were reached about 9 am and the ice above them at midday. Woodward later told the inquest:

> *The party was roped in pairs, Glasgow and Scott on one rope, and Bruce Young and myself on the other. All the party were wearing crampons. Until we reached the schrund on the ice, Glasgow and Scott were leading. At this point they elected to ascend a short, steep ice gully hard against the ridge, and proceeded to cut steps up to it. Young and I chose a different route, a little to the right, which brought us above Glasgow and Scott. Some 100ft to 150ft further on, the leader of the second rope, Glasgow, was seen to slip, and he either knocked Scott off his belay, or the belay failed to hold, and the two men slipped down the gully and towards the east face of Mount Cook.*

That is how Harry died. But why? Charles asked in 'The Estate' ('To Harry Scott'):

> What draws you …
> To blind altars of rock where man cannot linger
> Even in death?

And James Bertram remarked upon what he called that 'strange paradox of human behaviour':

> *why should a man who refuses to kill on orders, and invites the charge of cowardice from his fellow men, choose to risk his own life on the high peaks of the Southern Alps?*

James (how can I break the news?), this is not a paradox. Unless you think that the charge of cowardice is the same as the real thing. We have seen Harry explain that the courage of the pacifist, and of the climber, were the same. 'I wished to be sure that the tenderness I felt for men was born of strength, not weakness.'

But life and death: there is a paradox. My father had a 'childish preoccupation with the importance of life'. What about his own?

Throughout his story we have observed this proximity of life to death. So in 'Pursuit' he wrote of climbing and death: of one as the risk, confrontation and containment of the other. Every ascent carried the possibility of 'time's exit … untimely exit'. It was 'presented spaciously, in the best traditions of statesmen and frontiers'. Harry compared it to the

murder of young men in war. For it was above all war, in 1914–18 and 1939–45, that collected life and death together and packed them close.

The key passage occurs in 'A Citizen and the War':

> *Many [pacifists] realise the significance and challenge of living dangerously. They know the feeling and teaching of Jesus centres on the words*
>
> > *whoso loveth his life loseth it; whoso loseth his life for my sake finds it.*
>
> *This is the opposite of conservatism and timidity … The heroic virtues I … see as very real in experience and commendable in society … I cannot subscribe to them when they are turned against other men in warfare … [But] the person who is timid about life … especially about losing it, loses it anyhow for he lives narrowly and realises himself less than fully. Ultimately he should fear to cross the street … It is unseemingly trite to point [out] the paradox that in order to live we must risk death. Nevertheless, it is very true … Further too, the kind of perspective on life gained by narrow escape from death is real. Especially the risking of premature death in living. Life has a new significance. It is these considerations which make it possible for men to desert safety and comfort to go out into peculiar places and do difficult and dangerous things.*

A high westerly wind was raging.

SIR THOMAS HUNTER

Gifford, Talbot and Grenfell

If you wish to know men, explore with them in the wilds of Fiordland. Where all supplies have to be carried on the back, where the weather is usually wet, where food is limited and strictly rationed, where the conditions of travel are difficult and four men and their supplies must find what accommodation they can in a 6 x 8 tent – these are conditions that show the real fibre of men and expose their very souls. Looking back on my explorations in the Te Anau–Milford area I find in my memory, even after the lapse of half a century, sharply defined pictures of my companions: Gifford, Grave, Grenfell, Talbot, Tennent. Of these Grave and Talbot went on to much greater exploits and have left their mark on alpine achievements in this Dominion. Unfortunately both Talbot and Tennent lost their lives in World War I.

For me there were three major trips: the first, from the Glaisnock River to Bligh Sound; the second, from the Worsley River to Bligh Sound and the third from the Worsley to Sutherland Sound. Grave and I went on all these trips, Gifford on the first only and Talbot only on the second, while Grenfell travelled with us on the first and third occasions. At the time we explored the Glaisnock, Gifford and Grave had already had some experience in the bush and a certain measure of bushcraft. Gifford, the oldest member of the party, was then about forty years of age, while the infant of the group was in his early twenties. Gifford made friends easily and firmly. He was the good companion. His special studies were in mathematics and astronomy and he left his mark on science by his advocacy and proof of Bickerton's partial impact theory of the origin of the solar system. But his interests were at once wide and deep. He possessed great knowledge of and skill in photography. To decades of boys at Wellington College he was affectionately known as 'Uncle Charlie' and many of them, who like Stalky were 'as the beasts that perish' in mathematics, were fascinated by Gifford's skill in making real to them the wonders of photography and of the heavens.

For these trips of exploration we trained assiduously, and this preparation culminated in a journey on bicycles from Oamaru to Lake Te

Anau before the days of the 'free-wheel' and the bitumen road. We picked up Grenfell at Gore and completed the journey up the North Arm and through the 'Narrows' by rowing boat hired for the occasion. By the time we landed at the mouth of the Glaisnock, therefore, we knew a good deal of one another and were ready for the steady discipline ahead of us.

Gifford was tall, loose-limbed, fair with a sandy, thin, beard and fair hair that was worn somewhat long and on this trip had a habit of thrusting itself triumphantly through a hole in his felt hat. He reminded us so vividly of the picture of the hero of Daniel Defoe's popular work that he was promptly and inevitably dubbed 'Crusoe' by which name, almost as affectionate as his pupils' 'Uncle Charlie', he was known through the weeks that followed. A person of more even temper it would be hard to find. No matter how difficult the road and how frequent the punctures, no matter how awkward the pack or uncomfortable the camp, no matter how dreary and disagreeable the weather or how short the food supplies, Crusoe made no complaints but was always cheerful and ready to help a comrade in difficulty. Naturally he was the 'official' photographer and even in the very difficult circumstances of this journey produced photographic work that earned high praise when it was exhibited. These were the days before films and in addition to his quarter-plate camera, its stand with telescopic legs, and slides, Crusoe carried six dozen quarter-plates. It also fell to his unkindly lot to wait till his fellows were snugly in their sleeping bags before he doused the fire and, retiring to a most uncomfortable position in his blanket bag, proceeded to change the plates. But so patient and self-sacrificing was Crusoe that one hardly realised the work that fell on him until, a few weeks after our return, each member received a set of beautifully finished prints that have remained a joy for life.

Grave and I made our own swag bags, as big as an out-size in pillowslips, with broad carrying straps so placed as to give a well-distributed and balanced load. We saw to it, too, that our blankets and spare clothes provided a pad that protected our backs from the tins we had perforce to carry. For this trip Crusoe had bought a large, elaborate and very expensive rucksack with which we on occasion experimented. But we soon dropped it. But Crusoe never complained and carried the uncomfortable rucksack cheerfully from daylight to dark. Once coming back from a visit down Bligh Sound at low water we were compelled by the incoming tide to take to the bush and Crusoe, with his hands fully engaged

with his camera, had a nasty fall; indeed we thought he had broken some ribs. But he refused our offer to relieve him of some of his load though weeks afterward he confessed that for some days he suffered a good deal of pain. Gifford was also very cautious; perhaps this was necessary to offset the rashness of some of the newcomers. He did not like us to cross the river even when we got better conditions by so doing for he feared that sudden flooding might prevent our return. On subsequent trips when we threw caution to the winds and took risks, we often laughingly asked ourselves what Crusoe's reactions would have been if he had been with us.

What an interesting companion he was! His knowledge of astronomy, chemistry and botany, his wide human interests ensured that if we were compelled by adverse conditions to spend a day in camp – four men and their effects in a 6 x 8 tent – Gifford could while away the hours by interesting and informative talk, given with a simplicity and a modesty that were added charms. As a member of such an expedition as ours he had all the virtues: kindliness, friendliness, humour, consideration, sympathy, courage, capacity for hard work, persistence. For the many who knew and loved him his soul goes marching on in their own lives.

Whenever I think of Arthur Talbot there flash into my mind two incidents: one on the lower reaches of the Worsley and the other on the Worsley Pass and its approaches. The first trip up the Worsley was unique in our experience because the weather was continuously fine. Grave and I had tried to prepare our new companions (Talbot and Tennent) for the hardships of the journey by vivid descriptions of pouring rain, wet bush, and even wetter clothes. When the skies remained blue the school-master in Talbot, never doubting the word of his companions, sought in science the reasons for the difference. Again and again he proved to his own satisfaction, if not to ours, why this was a dry valley among all the other wet valleys. If he had gone with us the following year he would have had great difficulty in explaining the very different weather we experienced. The second incident might be called 'the romance of a railway ticket'. On this occasion, shirking the long bicycle ride, we went by train to Lumsden and thence by bicycle to Te Anau. At the Lake Hotel we changed into our bush clothes and left our town effects with the proprietor. Through the absence of mind that Talbot often showed, he found himself well up the Worsley Valley with his flimsy paper return-ticket in his pocket. Worse was to follow, for half-way down the Pitt River he discovered one morning

that he had lost it. He jumped to the conclusion that he had left it at a most uncomfortable camp we had had on a slip that had come down into a small lake that we called 'Bernard's Hole', after Bernie Tennent. Coming back we decided to avoid these difficulties by keeping high up above the lake side. Unfortunately, in a somewhat difficult place, Talbot slipped and fell about 30 feet down a steep bank. His swag fortunately caught in some young beech trees and this saved him from a fall of some 300 feet on to the rocks below. Though he was considerably shaken by this accident he insisted, when we came to the lake side, that he must go back to the old camp to get his ticket. Grave went with him but the journey proved fruitless. Arriving in camp late at night Talbot in the dark spilled a big billy of boiling water on his legs. One leg was considerably burned and must have been very painful. As our supplies were on the other side of the pass we could give him but one day's rest. Then dividing his load among us, we by means of rope helped him up the steep climb to the pass. It must have been a gruelling experience for him. We arrived at the pass before dusk, and here, walking slowly and painfully with a stick through the sparse scrub (believe it or not), Talbot picked up his ticket that must have been carried from our camp (some distance away) by an inquisitive weka. This accident put an end to further exploration, and as soon as he was able, we brought him back to Te Anau. He showed real grit in what must have been a very painful passage. This was Talbot's first venture in these fields, but under Grave's tuition he went on to become one of New Zealand's great climbers and with Grave the discoverer of the Grave–Talbot Pass.

Talbot was tall and dark with a good figure and carriage. In these respects he had advantages over Grave in climbing, for the latter was shorter and thickset. But what Grave lacked physically he more than made up in determination and thoroughness. This was the age of moustaches. Tennent was the only one to begin a trip clean-shaven; no one ended it without the fruitful beginning of a full beard.

Talbot, like Gifford and Grenfell, had qualities that made him a worthy companion on such trips. He had neither the great gift for friendship of Gifford nor the humour and banter of Grenfell. But he had courage and fidelity. He would not let a companion down. All these men could be trusted to the full. One would have to seek far and wide before one could find better companions for the hardships, difficulties and the many frustrations of these exploring ventures at the beginning of this century.

EDMUND HILLARY

A Tribute from Ed Hillary

For a few years from 1947 I was actively involved in climbing in the Mount Cook region. During this period the dominant figure in the New Zealand mountaineering world was unquestionably Harry Ayres. Of medium build but incredibly tough and sinewy, Harry was renowned for his remarkable ability with his great iceaxe and his flair for finding routes through shattered crevasse areas that were impassable to most of us.

I think the first time I saw Harry in action was on a climb of Aiguille Rouge. Allan Odell and I were in the Malte Brun hut and Harry was also there with Susie Sanders. The weather hadn't been particularly good but in the few days we were hut bound I built up a warm friendship with Harry. Finally a reasonable morning emerged and we set off up the mountains behind the hut – Harry heading for Malte Brun and Allan and myself for Aiguille Rouge. We climbed up cheerfully together but the weather was deteriorating so Harry suggested that he and Susie join us on the lower Aiguille Rouge. Allan and I were very happy to agree.

Aiguille Rouge is not a difficult mountain but a reasonable challenge for Allan and me – both enthusiastic climbers of modest technical skill. I was enormously impressed with the ease with which Harry met the few problems we struck on the mountain. Obviously his abilities were far beyond anything we aspired to. When he went calmly off to sleep on the summit rocks with a complete disregard for the descent and changing weather I was even more impressed. Later the same group of us climbed Haidinger together and I observed Harry's tremendous skill with the iceaxe as he hewed a path up the steep ice slope to the summit. I resolved that come what may I would spend some part of each year with Harry and try and gain a little of his skill and technique.

And so for a number of years I climbed with Harry and we did some good ascents together. I learned to appreciate his gift for route finding in difficult terrain; his strength and endurance to cut steps for a thousand feet or more up hard green ice; his ability to inspire a modest companion into efforts that seemed beyond his capacity. And I admired, too, Harry's willingness to carry out mundane tasks around the hut. He was no prima

donna – cooking, washing up, tidying a hut neglected by other parties – Harry did it all, not without a grumble or two, but with a firm sense of responsibility.

Although his companions were usually far below his own high standard of skill, Harry led them up innumerable ascents of the great peaks of the Southern Alps. His lightning reaction in moments of danger was often needed and never failed him. He seemed to have an instinctive knowledge when someone slipped and his iceaxe would belt to the hilt to form a sound belay.

We were tremendously pleased when Eric Shipton invited Harry to join the 1953 Everest Expedition and bitterly disappointed when the invitation was withdrawn with the change of leadership. As a technical climber Harry was far ahead of any member of our Everest Expedition and if he had acclimatised well I have little doubt that he would have been one of the first to set foot on the summit of the world.

PETER GRAHAM

Letter to Jim Glasgow, 1954

Dear Jim

Thank you for your letter of the 18th inst and for so kindly sending me the information about St James Church, that you have been able to extract from the files at Church House. The details of which have been very helpfull, and has enabled me to complete the historical records, which have been ask for by the Alexander Turnbull Library,

In reply to your earlier letter of the 15th inst, in reference to the £1000, that had been made to the N.Z Alpine Club by the relations of the late W.G.S. Brooks, and the Clubs Committees proposal, that the funds might be used to assist my brother Alex and I to jointly publish our 'memoirs', in book form, of our mountaineering experiences.

We would be dull indeed if we did not consider it a great honour, in having such a proposal made to us, I personally do appreciate very deeply that you and your committee should consider such a proposal being made. In considering the matter myself, the £1000 seems a lot of money for the club to expend when one feels that such an amount could be more usefully expended on more worthy purposes for the club as a whole.

My own climbs, except for the Mt Tutoko expedition with Mr S. Turner, have all been in the confines of the Mt Cook area, while Alex has had a more varied experiences in Pioneer expedition into different valleys with Dr. Teichelman and also with the Rev. Newton. Such as the Wanganui Valley, Franz Josef, Fox Glacier, Cooks River, Copland, Waiatoto, Arawata and the Matukituki Valleys and Mt Aspiring etc, each of these expeditions would be of great interest as separate articles for the N.Z. Alpine Journal without being in book form, if Alex can be persuaded to write them up.

For myself I have I fear a very low opinion of my own qualities and ability in being able to express in writing what I really feel about our mountains and what they have meant to me.

In any case most of my major climbs have been written up by Miss Du Faur and Mr Turner, which books the club will have in its library and will no doubt be available to all its members.

All I was able to do in those early years at the Hermitage have been

accomplished so many times since by club members and others, and would not have the same interest now, as those expeditions in the more remote valleys on the West Coast.

In any case I will be very pleased to come and see you when we are next in Christchurch, and talk it over – I can't at the moment say just when that will be. We are hoping it won't be much longer delayed, the final meeting of our company. When the date has been fixed I will let you know when to expect us and arrange a time when it will be most convenient for you that we may call on you.

Thanking you again for your letters and help, and in the mean time, with kind regards

Yours sincerely
Peter Graham

JOHN PASCOE

from *Great Days in New Zealand Mountaineering*

A Westland Memory: Mount Evans

North of the Rakaia Divide and wholly in Westland rises the rocky mass of Mount Evans, whose triple peaks are, at the highest point, 8,612 feet. This mass feeds hanging, shelf and valley glaciers, the sources of three great Westland rivers, the Whitcombe, the Waitaha and the Wanganui. The rock is greywacke, seldom rotten but split by cracks. It has been handled by few men, and its occasional quartz seams have never been seen by gold prospectors. Its ridges are four, serrated, steep and snow cleft. Until New Year's Day 1934 Mount Evans was a big unclimbed chunk, Mecca of young and self-trained mountaineers in the New Zealand tradition of having fun where they found it.

Because I was implicated in the attempts and in the first ascent and traverse of Mount Evans and have already written fully of them, I consider some apology is necessary for this postscript version some twenty-three years later. My original accounts were laconic and tensely exuberant as befitted the approach of a young man, and perhaps my chapters on Mount Evans gave cause to complain that much was left out for which the layman could rightly wish.

Elsewhere in this book I have tried objectively to give the flavour of alpine days and nights based on the contemporary narratives of other men. Now I do the same for some of my own. With the passage of time I can see events in a wider perspective and can include some vivid personal backlighting that at the time seemed irrelevant to a young fellow who wrote fast, as he tried to climb, gaily heading for the next horizon, without having time to stop and contemplate the cause of it all.

My generation was primarily concerned with new country. We were intolerant of tourist climbers, had no money for guides in those depression days, and deliberately chose virgin peaks away from the delectable field of the highest central Southern Alps. Mistakes in route finding were inevitable and defeat was routine. Hope shone bright through both errors and reverses, and once in a while persistence bumbled through to deserved success.

In the course of traverses and walks to the tops of the outer ranges, occasional views of the Rakaia mountains were tantalising for what was hidden. Glimpses from peaks in the Waimakariri and the Mathias were more impressive, and the closer we reached the new objectives in the Rakaia, the more realistic were the sound effects of avalanches. In my second season there was a break in the clouds from the top of Louper Peak that showed a tough-looking bunch of ridges; obviously Mount Evans. This documentary memory was salutary in comparison with a 'glamour shot' from Cave Camp in the Whitcombe, showing faces, ridges and glaciers framed in a bush setting.

If my friends and I had climbed Mount Evans the following Christmas (1931) we should have been free to wander into other monkey business farther south. As it was, Mount Evans did not take kindly to intruders. Not that it was the mountain's fault. It was our lack of experience in snow camps that made us attempt the mountain from a height of 2,600 feet and a distance of 7 miles as the kea flew. From our camp under Jim's Knob at the end of the Rakaia River bed it was a walk of some 10 miles to the foot of the east ridge, by the time we had weaved a trail through the Ramsay moraine, by-passed the Ramsay Icefall, crossed the Erewhon Col and high-tailed it for the Full Moon Saddle. We reached a height of 8,200 feet on the ridge on what my romantic approach called 'the golden road' with recollections of Flecker's Pilgrim Chorus in *Hassan*. There was a deal of mountaineering on the golden road, too much for us in spite of the brilliance of our engineering-student leader, the ambitions of my law-clerk self or the loyalty of our accountancy clerk third man. We learnt how to belay to save our lives. Avalanchy snow and loose pinnacles were something of an experience for the three of us and we were very conscious of being a long way from base.

When we had returned to that base after an absence of sixteen hours with few spells we had covered 20 miles and made and lost 5,600 feet of altitude. This experience quite startled me out of any idea that I could get new peaks easily; somewhat of a contrast to the previous season in the Mathias when we had cleaned up thirteen virgins in two days. I absorbed the necessary humility, and my imagination, already a susceptible one, fired a love for a grim mountain that has not died even today. Whether Mount Evans gave us mercy, kindness or hardship did not concern me much. All I knew was that I must climb it.

DOREEN MURIE (URQUHART)

Speech presented at 'Summits for Suffrage', 10 February 1993

Fellow climbers and friends …

I hope I am not here under false pretences in this year of celebration. The decades of the 40s and 50s were golden years in N.Z. society. Reading Clive James recently I observed his statement that regarding class distinctions in Australia, some people knew that they were superior but the majority did not know that they were inferior so it did not affect them. I submit that women were in that position after the war, and also, I strongly suspect, our ethnic minorities. Women and the Maori Battalion had made such a contribution during the war that their mana was on an all-time high. Coming from a farming community where roles of men and women were determined by the fact they must work as a team to survive, and coming from a family dominated by two strong matriarchal grand-mothers, I was 22 years old before I even suspected some people thought men were better than women. Other N.Z. women my age and younger have agreed that this was also their experience. Fifty years into women's suffrage, post war and post-depression, living in a N.Z. of full employment and low crime rates we can perhaps be excused for thinking the battle had been won.

Before our climb of Mt. Cook the first all-woman climb of a 10,000 ft. peak had been made in the 30s by Betsy Blunden, Rosamund Harper and Lella Davidson. An outstanding climb of Sefton from the west where the women climbed in a remote region completely independent of support, responsible for carrying in all their gear and completely responsible for their own safety at least two days' hard tramping from any other human. They climbed with the very basic equipment we were still using in the fifties; a rope, an ice axe and their crampons. They had no helmets, no harness, no pitons or karabiners and no radio contact. Two Japanese asked me recently who organised you and who sponsored you? Such concepts were undreamed of. We thought of going, we saved from the small funds we earned and we went. Jim Wilson has made the point in 'Aorangi' that women climbers tended to be all-round mountaineers with a genuine commitment to and love of the mountains, not just peak-baggers and this

was certainly true of the three of us on Mt. Cook, and of the many women climbing at the same time and before us. I like to think it is true today.

During the war, Junnee Ashurst and Betsy Blunden broke new ground as the first women guides at Mt. Cook, filling in for the men overseas. Junnee was an outstanding climber who very nearly beat all the men to be the first to climb all the 10,000 ft. peaks. She worked at the Hermitage so her climbing companions were the guides, but she did not climb with them as a client but as an equal. Harry Ayres said of her that there were only a handful of men he would rather climb with.

The three of us who formed the first all-woman party on Mt. Cook did not feel we were there to prove a point – we felt we were there to meet a challenge. Mt. Cook is one of the most beautiful peaks in the world and must have special significance in any climbing career. Mavis, Sheila and I had taken part in many N.Z. expeditions and climbs and we were all used to leading through on the rope. I had been in several all-woman climbs in the Arthur's Pass region and had got a greater enjoyment and a greater freedom from climbing with women friends. I have always been the ideas person and have been lucky enough to be able to involve people with special strengths in my many undertakings. Late in 1951 I contacted Mavis and Sheila, whom I had met but not climbed with, and suggested a climb of Cook up the Linda route. They were as enthusiastic as I and we spent that year brushing up, during our climbs, on our techniques and skills. At this stage I must point out that our method of keeping fit was to climb, tramp and ski at every opportunity. Our packs and gear were cumbersome and the big loads we carried certainly contributed to our fitness.

We met at the Hermitage early in January and proceeded as planned to carry food for a week and all our equipment up the Haast ridge. The forecast was good and we had plans to make some training climbs before our attempt. Two thirds of the way up the ridge we found that a rock had badly crushed the foot of Earle Riddiford, a member of another team. Without hesitation, we cached everything we could and taking our basic gear, we started to assist two members of his team to take him down the ridge. I carried his gear on top of my own while Sheila and Mavis who were taller than I helped support him. The Haast ridge is not easy for such a manoeuvre, but in those days when the ceiling for helicopters was 6,000 ft. and they were extremely rare, every mountaineer knew that in an emergency they only had each other to rely on. Equality within the

mountain world carried responsibilities as well as privileges and not for one minute was it thought we would not do an equal share with the rescue, carrying and helping as much as the men. We reached the bottom of the ridge before others from Haast Hut reached us to help.

After a sleepless night in Ball Hut we climbed back to Haast Hut, at that time deciding that we must take advantage of the exceptional weather by making the climb the next day. We were away at 1.00 a.m. on January 6th, 1953 on a clear windless morning when the moon was so bright we hardly needed our torches. We tied ourselves to our 100 ft. nylon rope which with our ten-point crampons and our ice axes were our only equipment. The snow on Glacier dome and the Grand Plateau was crisp and firm but the Linda was badly broken with huge seracs poised under the Silberhorn ridge. There were four other ropes on the mountain and by the top of the summit rocks we were right behind them. Like most amateur parties we climbed as a group, no particular person leading throughout and on this climb we moved together with Mavis as our most experienced rock climber leading the summit rocks. On the ice cap it was very hot and breathless and we tended to climb towards the edge of the ice cap above the eastern face in the hope of catching a breeze. On the ice we made a couple of pick belays moving through on the rope to share the lead.

We sat on the summit with the other ropes content to stay for two hours taking in the view from the breakers on the west coast seemingly at our feet, to the rather hazy ocean to the east. The descent took longer than hoped. Some of the seracs had collapsed across our upwards tracks adding urgency to our flight down the Linda and some of the snow bridges looked fragile in the afternoon heat, but what caused us the most distress was the long plod over breakable crust on the Grand Plateau. We reached Haast Hut after a twenty hour climb just as the last of the sun was sliding off the wonderful red rock of the Malte Brun range.

And so we completed our set task. The climb had been a happy one with a confidence in each other and a shared unity of purpose which could not have been greater if we had made other climbs together. We received great encouragement from the guides, particularly Mick Bowie and Harry Ayres who some of us had climbed with in the past. That year Ed Hillary climbed Everest and suddenly climbing became in the eyes of the populace not a sport for the slightly crazy, but almost a respectable pastime and endeavour.

Looking back I remember that the C.M.C. did not accept women members saying their club modelled itself on the English Alpine Club. We women in Canterbury treated it as a game. One Easter they gave three of us a lift in a truck they were using to take 40 men into the mountains. The women climbed Mt. Harper and were the only ones to complete a peak. The C.M.C. men were given to asking you to sleep in the woodshed if you were using their huts, but it could only be a game when they kept coming out to offer you food and drink and inquire about your welfare. Men like Andy Anderson of Otira were incredibly generous to all young mountaineers, not only at sharing their skills but at letting you lead on difficult routes.

Given the calibre of women climbers of this era it was only a matter of time before they would choose to climb together on more and more difficult peaks, not to prove anything to the mountaineering world – all the taboos there had long been broken, but because of the bonds of sisterhood that were forged and strengthened when difficulties and challenges were met with people of similar physical strength and mental outlook.

There is a fashion at present, to denigrate the climbs of Freda du Faur because she climbed with guides, but she was climbing within the boundaries of mountaineering attitudes of her time as much as we were within ours. At that time men with wealth climbed with guides by tradition, and Freda, as a woman without husband or brothers, had no other avenue through which she could express her love of the mountains. There can be no questioning her commitment and her all-round ability. For the five years she climbed she was the most outstanding woman climber in the world.

Let us not lose sight of some of the other outstanding women climbing during her times and whose stories have not been written. I refer in particular to Mrs. Jane Thompson who was the first N.Z. woman to traverse Cook aged 56 and the first woman to climb Mt. Rolleston when she was aged 70. She made many outstanding climbs not only in the Central Alps but also around Arthur's Pass. We must be very careful to preserve our history, not only as a true record but as an inspiration to women following us.

In more recent times, women have moved on to a mastery of techniques undreamed of in my day. They have taken part in many overseas expeditions and have formed all-woman parties to climb in the highest mountains in the world. We who went before salute you.

Mountains have always been a visible symbol of earth's reaching towards heaven – which was thought to be above us. The Bible says 'I will lift up mine eyes to the hills from whence doth come mine aid.' It is fitting therefore in this year in which women celebrate their suffrage, which was basically a freeing of their spirits from an insufferable injustice made explicit in the right to vote, that we should climb higher to expand our spirits in a symbolic gesture of celebration. Let us think as we do so of the challenges ahead. Let us ponder the injustices of poverty, prejudice and ill-will that beset all mankind. Let the next century be a time when all humanity works together to free themselves as women in this century have worked to liberate themselves.

Within the mountain world I felt I experienced true fellowship. On February 13th let us vow to extend that fellowship to all who would enter it. To the disabled and the disadvantaged and the poor in spirit who were born to make only one step forward at a time. Let us say to men that we know now you are not the enemy. The enemy lies in a society that breeds people, both men and women, who tolerate injustice. For the banner we would pass on is not a new one but it is one that would cure all the ills of the world. It is a message which mountaineers, of all people, are well qualified to expound.

It was best expressed by a poet of the fifteenth century in the words:

> *Fellowship is heaven, and lack of fellowship is hell, and the deeds that ye do on earth it is for fellowship's sake ye do them, and the good that is in it, that shall go on and on, and each one part of it so long as ye all shall live.*

LYDIA BRADEY with LAURENCE FEARNLEY

from *Going Up Is Easy*

It is March 2014, and in a few days' time Lydia will leave New Zealand for Mount Everest. But for the moment she has climbed into my bed and snuggled under the covers, drinking coffee as she flicks through the pages of a *Vogue* magazine. She appears oblivious to my discomfort and has failed to acknowledge my suggestion that we might be happier at the kitchen table. Perhaps, after a lifetime of cramped alpine tents, the closeness of our bodies seems perfectly natural – to her. Despite having known Lydia since the late 1980s, I don't find the intrusion on my personal space entirely welcome. Yet Lydia is like a sister to me – the closest I have to a sister – so I try to relax, telling myself to stop being so uptight.

Lydia is immersed in the fashion pages, dismissing a tailored, knee-length skirt as 'bogus' while admiring an exquisite lace bra that costs upwards of £150. Turning to me she asks, slyly, if we might go shopping for underwear later? I think of all the famous mountaineers who have attempted or climbed Everest since 1922 and wonder how many, if any, have made similar requests of their friends. Somehow I doubt that George Mallory, Edmund Hillary or Reinhold Messner were thinking about G-strings in the days leading up to their departure for the Himalaya.

But here is one of the interesting facts about Lydia. As well as being a committed high-alpine climber, and a respected mountain guide, she spends a lot of time thinking about clothing – from a design and style point of view. I know she does because we spend hours underwear shopping every time she visits, and because I have seen her go to extraordinary lengths to get bought garments – often short, sleeveless shift dresses – tailored to fit. I also recall a speech she made to the Dunedin branch of the New Zealand Alpine Club where she spent several minutes describing the colour and fit of a jacket, and the choice and style of her sunglasses, and how uncomfortable (or bored) the majority of the male audience appeared until she moved on to describing the more technical aspects of the climb.

So why are clothes and, by extension, image, so important? In a largely male world, does she want to emphasise her femininity, or her sexual attractiveness? Or, perhaps, her dress sense announces her creativity and

non-conformity? 'It's taken me a very long time,' she says, 'to achieve what other women – young women – have dialled into within minutes of being born, and that's to enjoy my femininity. This transition is partly about accepting that some traditions are okay, and even enjoyable. So it's about my being able to stop resisting conformity to feminine ideals. Once I was able to ditch my fear of conformity I realised it was okay to shave my legs, or colour my hair, or pluck my eyebrows. It didn't mean I was giving up my feminist beliefs, or giving in to 'beauty' stereotypes. It was about me feeling good about myself, and as I've got older and become more serious about guiding, I think it's important that I present myself well. It's about professionalism. I could make a pair of soft-shell pants last another season, for example, but if they're baggy I don't look pulled together and it affects the response clients have towards me. If I feel good about how I look, I am more confident personally and professionally. Same with my body. I need to be in condition, and appear fit and strong. It gives me a feeling of self-respect.

'Colour is super-important to me. I think that when I look at certain shades of colours I release endorphins. I have clear memories of the first women-specific Thermarests that came out. I never had one but they were a beautiful shade of cerise and when a friend laid her orange sleeping bag out on her cerise mat I couldn't stop looking at it. The colour gave me a strong feeling of pleasure. I currently own a pair of Gore-tex overtrousers in a soft mustard colour, and I wear them all the time because the colour makes me feel good. I'm certain I have a large percentage of cone cells in my eyes.

'For a long time I was living a fairly minimalist life: living in tents or out of cars, or in rented apartments with little furniture. So one of the few ways I could assert myself, creatively, was through my clothing. But back when we were climbing at Yosemite everyone spent time going to charity stores looking for patterned shirts. I had a favourite shirt that was white with big green daisies. I liked sewing as well and that's because I liked creating things and I'm attracted to colour and texture. I wasn't dressing in order to be sexy but once I got my head around it I liked being feminine, and I liked being attractive, it was part of the fun.'

PAUL HERSEY

from *Protection*

Rope length after rope length measured off the climb. The passing sun and an arch of cloud gathered over mountains to the west, shadows stretching across the rock buttress and conspiring to keep the three of us in the cold while, a few metres away, warm sunlight reflected off the snow.

At the start of the climb we had chatted at belays as if this was little more than a sunny afternoon at our local crag. But that seemed ages ago. A different life perhaps. Now, we exchanged the shoulder-sling of protection with barely a word of encouragement to whoever was next to lead. We didn't talk about how far we had climbed or how close the summit of Maunga O Hine might or might not be.

But it was on all of our minds. We were utterly committed.

It was Duncan's lead. My brother had just traversed across a scoop of rock with a narrow split through the middle of it. Then he disappeared around a steep corner, the two ropes slithering from my belay device with reluctance.

'Must be another hard bit,' Brian said beside me. He had tried to sit on our narrow ledge but managed only half a butt cheek. He looked exhausted.

'Yeah,' I replied.

Brian stared back down towards our starting point, and I could guess what he was thinking. Everything felt like it was conspiring against us. The route was more difficult and taking much longer than we had anticipated. And then there was the weather – the cloud and the increasing wind. None of these things needed to be highlighted through conversation.

I followed Brian's line of sight back down the buttress, to where we had spent last night in relative comfort on a flattish scree shelf. Eating freeze-dried stew from the warmth of our sleeping bags and imagining the climb ahead. The unknown had felt so intoxicating. Everything – *anything* – seemed possible.

And now we were, quite literally, on the edge of things. To descend from this height and down this aspect of the mountain would be impossible, the number of abseils required to reach flat ground far greater than the amount of protection we had. Continuing up this bloody buttress was the only option.

Eventually both ropes came tight. A muffled cry echoed across the void. I started to dismantle the belay, flicking two poorly placed wires from the flared crack that had been our pretence for security.

Brian stood slowly and tightened his pack straps. He turned to the rock. 'See you on the other side.'

I forced a smile, appreciating that despite his fatigue he was still attempting a bit of humour.

'If you get there before me can I have your car?'

He laughed. 'Fuck off. Dunc said he's got first dibs.'

The tightness in my muscles took a few moments to ease as I followed Brian across the scoop. The rope led the way, pulling against my harness, a small and insistent comfort that everything would work out all right.

For a short time the wind eased. I could hear a faint rasping as my rope drew across the rock. The sound was hypnotic, causing me to notice other weird details, like the colour and shape of a small blob of lichen a few inches from my face. I reached out and brushed it lightly with my fingertips.

A grasshopper with really long legs boinged from somewhere. *Where the hell did that come from?* Then came the realisation that I was being consumed by trivia.

Shit I must be tired! Sort it out Jase.

Somewhere ahead but out of sight, Brian muttered like he did when tackling the harder sections. The sound of his voice carried across the still air, helping me refocus on what needed to be done. I wondered what he might be dealing with that was causing him to talk to himself so much.

Shaking my head, I told myself it didn't matter. We – or more specifically Duncan and I as the strongest members of the team – could cope with whatever the mountain had left for us. There was no other choice.

Then Brian swore.

'You all right?' I yelled, but he didn't reply. My rope had stopped moving for a few moments, and I waited for Duncan to take in the slack. The previous confidence I had felt evaporated. *What was around the corner? What new challenge waited? Had we finally reached a section of rock that was impossible to climb? Fuck, what now?*

It took me a few moments to commit to the next moves, and when I reached the others I smiled. Brian's swearing had been due to surprise

rather than fear. Finally, and quite suddenly, we had climbed to the top of the buttress. Hidden beyond the corner that Duncan and then Brian had passed before me was a platform of rock the size of a small house. The summit of Maunga O Hine was only a short snow slope away.

Duncan was sitting on coils of rope, huddled over the last of the water from his bottle. Despite his fatigue he looked relaxed, giving me one of his goofy, lopsided grins.

'Never had a doubt,' he said confidently, a remark which left no doubt how close to his limit the climb had pushed him.

Brian let out a small '*whoop*'. He tried to do a little dance but it looked more like the steps of a drunk. I realised, again, that I really didn't like the guy very much.

I walked a few metres away from the others, closer to the edge and where I could look back over the valley. At the abyss. The clouds to the west had gained bulk, swallowing the last of the sun. Another gust of wind could be heard approaching.

I felt nothing.

* * *

After finishing a climb, and despite the physical exertion and mental satisfaction and even relief that the risk is over, I often carried an empty feeling. It was something I never understood about myself. Perhaps a sign of weakness or inadequacy, or a dissatisfaction with my so-called normal life. At the very least, a detached melancholy. *What is wrong with me?*

Sometimes, I interpreted the feeling as a sadness in the realisation that what we had experienced couldn't last. And even the memory of something that had felt so critical and intimate would fade in time. All that was left was swallowed by the nothingness, as if reaching the actual summit was an anticlimax rather than achieving a goal. For me, and despite the angst while in the act of doing it, the will to climb only ended because there was nothing more to climb.

Inevitably I would be left with an overwhelming sense of *what do I do now?*

Later in the cold dark the ice of the glacier penetrated my mat and sleeping bag. I scrunched onto my side to lessen my contact with the ground. The three of us were bivouacked under the lip of a crevasse. Through a slit in

the ice I could see stars twinkling like fool's gold and then disappearing as dark blotches passed close by. Beneath our bodies, the glacier groaned.

The slow insistence of the approaching weather meant the storm would likely be a doozy. Digging in was not a good option but it was the only choice. Brian had been almost dead on his feet.

The storm hit sometime in the morning. I had been snoozing, and was awakened by ice shards rattling against the fabric of my bivouac bag. The wind was a cacophony, and my legs lifted by the force of it rushing into the crevasse. Beyond our shelter it sounded like a full-scale war.

The others were already awake. I turned on my head torch and leaned towards Duncan, shouting to be heard. 'What's the time?'

He removed a gloved hand from the depths of his sleeping bag, and held it up with his fingers curled and his thumb extended.

Nothing else was said.

RICHARD THOMSON

Incantation

There are the big walls you now about. Routes you've walked under or looked across at and thought, *Yes, I have to climb that.* The classics. Some are close to home: Sabre's blunt grey North Buttress. Others are farther away: the stern exfoliations of the Cassin Route on the Piz Badile. Articles in magazines and journals recall the taste of sweat and fear on first ascents, and then they tell you where to go, what to take, the order of the pitches. You've committed the topo to memory.

Then there are the last great problems. Talked up between bursts of winter effort on a plywood wall. Speculated about after untying from a summer's evening at the crag. The magazines offer these up too: pictures of immaculate stone architecture turning the colour of honeyed skin in dusky light.

Next, there are the walls you've never seen. But you look at the topographic blur of Google Earth and think, *There's something there.* One year, from far down in a valley, you catch a glimpse amid a kaleidoscope of unclimbed faces. The wall heads a north-facing cirque shaped like a giant throne, or a cormorant drying its wings. Then the mist hides everything, leaving a wisp of memory.

Finally, there are the walls you never knew existed: panning across a mighty gash of grass-infested cliff, the eye of the imagination takes a higher sweep of red-streaked iron-hard rock. Its rumpled facets look as if they were shaped with a giant club hammer.

In 2008 Rich Turner, Dave Vass and I hiked in to climb the North Face of Te Wera, the highest peak in the central Darran Mountains. You push up the valley for a day through a forest protected by thorns, rotten logs and wind-throws. Commit your weight to short tussocks on slippery bluffs. Dodge ice shrapnel thrown down wide slabs from rotten seracs. Find refuge from westerly gales in a cave – an eyrie – near the top of Karetai.

After a night in that grotto, we shuffled onto the slabs beneath the face as the sky lightened, and we took in the compact seams and the massive blocks that make up Te Wera's summit pyramid.

'Look over there,' Rich said, and he pointed at rumpled, ruddy facets on the adjacent peak that formed the cirque's eastern perimeter: Ngaitahu,

climbed and named in 1959 by Mike Gill and Phil Houghton. It was the last of the big Darrans peaks to be summited, and like so much else there, it was promptly forgotten. Gill would make the first ascent of Ama Dablam two years later, while Houghton headed down-valley, built a hut in the dense, waterlogged Fiordland bush and wrote a history of Europeans' failed attempts to settle the area.

Rich was from Britain. It was hard to imagine his intense, restless energy finding a home there. He once told me that everyone who came to live in New Zealand had to make a big, deliberate, life-changing decision. Now the sun lit the top of Ngaitahu's north wall. Where Te Wera was grey and fissured, Ngaitahu was flushed, smooth, soaring above us. Five hundred meters of unanticipated joy. 'Shall we try that?' Like dogs distracted by a pungent new odour, we forgot all our imagination and doubt, our plans and ambitions for Te Wera. There was nothing to decide. We started climbing.

Darrans Diorite has been heated, twisted, squeezed, crystallised, cracked, faulted. You can see the pain. You learn to trace the angles, to lean this way or that, embracing and resisting the tension in the body. Hold too tight and the crystals will slice your fingertips. You must keep on your toes.

Several pitches up, Dave danced sideways off a belay, making complex step-through moves on a holdless hanging slab. He grinned and chuckled above the emptiness. This was the moment he'd come for: forgetting thought; finding dynamic balance. Far below him, the cirque floor ran off into bluffs and grassed montane flats, just before the stream pitched into a dismal chasm and emerged again, sluggish amid the temperate swamp forest, to join the main river.

While Rich and I hung at the belay, the cracks closed in and the gaps between runners grew longer. Higher up, the spaces between the holds and gear placements stretched out even farther as Rich climbed across runnels and ripples of implacable, slabby stone. Despite the scale of the Darrans, you seldom encounter big features – few perfect cracks or unremitting dihedrals. You can spend hours mapping out a route only to find that the wall is nothing like what you expected. Back home looking at your photos, trying to figure out which line you took, you can only shrug. All you remember are those instants of motion, energy and grace, of touching rock and climbing.

On the upper wall, the afternoon mist rose up from the valley to hide us. Dave took pictures of toes dangling over a ledge, framed in cloud. I

tried to head toward the great red shield, but the mountain resisted: the only gear I could find tempted me the other way. And it wasn't much. Pitch followed pitch over a vertical maze of ramps and overlaps, the rock's secrets decrypted slowly with each grasping hand. As happens so close to the sea, the mist soon parted.

From the summit, the dark towers on Te Wera's east ridge still rose ahead. Gill and Houghton had climbed that way after their Ngaitahu ascent. We were intimidated, and it was too late to follow in their footsteps. We began rapping from the col to the far side of the mountain. In the deepening blackness, we made a final abseil into the gaping bergschrund and swung wildly to snatch the snowfield. By the time we crossed the neve to Karetai Col, the moon was up and almost full, illuminating the low clouds on the other side as they rose to fill the valley. The two great ice mountains, Tutoko and Madeline, rode the horizon. Before long, we were enveloped in mist again and lost on tussock bluffs until we emerged below the clouds to find the bivy by the lake. I slept until the sun was hot on my face.

Magick, said Aleister Crowley, imbues objects with the power of their owners. A pipe that's sucked on for half a century; a favourite pair of boots or a knife taken along on every expedition. But do the mountains also own us? As we return to this place, year after year, do we begin to absorb a little of its power? I'd like to think so. Next time on Ngaitahu we'll go left, we think. We'll climb the last honeyed pitch to the summit as the sun descends to the sea. Next time. The face has a name now, a picture, and a line. It exists in the imagination. All future action has become premeditated. If anyone remembers.

But no one has been back.

TOM RILEY

West on Sunset

I

I got off the bus at the top of the hill. It was hot, and the air smelled of eucalyptus. The leaves under my feet split into small pieces, all of their moisture gone.

I walked beside the highway for a while, then turned towards the sea, towards La Jolla far below. A knot of people were standing around a green car, inspecting it, sizing it up.

I decided I had to investigate.

The green car was parked outside a long, low house. The garage door was wide open, and I could see there were more people inside. It was some kind of estate sale. A woman behind a table in the garage was taking money, handing out change from plastic containers.

The house was very airy and open, with oiled wood panelling and bare floors. There were wholesome looking hangings on the wall, all textured wool. Clear yellow light flooded the rooms and the hallway. In one room, there was an enormous billiard table. The kitchen looked out on a parched garden.

On my way out, I stopped in the garage to rummage through a box of tools. I found a pocket knife made of mottled dark steel and yellow wood, and I gave my money to the woman behind the table. The knife seemed to me to be more than just a knife. The way it looked told me that someone had looked after this knife for a long time, keeping it oiled and sharp.

I took the knife with me, along with everything else, back across the Pacific to Wellington.

II

I left Wellington in a fever dream. I hadn't managed to sleep very much. The hot wind rattled at my door, and I waited for my alarm to ring.

Richard and I landed in Christchurch and waited. When the first plane arrived, we went to Queenstown.

The first thing we needed to do was to find James' car. He'd had some kind of adventure, and had had to get the locks changed. We were to make

our way to the Subaru dealer to collect the new set of keys. The car was parked around the corner in a street, with a view of the lake. When we opened the doors, the car smelled like James.

It felt vaguely illicit driving away in a car we'd never seen before. But we did. We drove into Queenstown proper to get the boots Richard had ordered. Then we drove to Wanaka to find Dave and John.

We loaded the car at Dave's house and headed off into the bright afternoon.

When we reached the roadend, the light had almost gone. We packed quickly, and it was at this point that I realised I'd brought the wrong pocket knife. In the confusion of the morning, I'd grabbed the good knife, the one that I've treasured. I didn't have another one, so I didn't have a choice. I hoped for the best as I put it in the lid of my pack.

We started off up the Moraine Creek track with our headtorches on. The bush was dusty, hot and oppressive. My movements felt brittle and imprecise after the long drive, the long day. The bogs had all dried up and there were no streams to jump.

We climbed up into the bush on the side of a slip, climbing over stacked piles of trees brought low by the storms. I managed to get separated from everyone, and I had to listen carefully for the voices of the others in order to find my way back.

Some time later we arrived at a kind of bivvy rock, and collapsed. I arranged myself on the moss, and worried about the weather.

III

The next morning I could tell that it was going to be another sweaty day. I'd hoped for a day with clarity, a gin-and-tonic, crystal-clear, silver-and-cool kind of day. Instead, the dust prevailed.

We made our way up the track towards a slash-wound of a gully which ran all the way from a point out of sight, somewhere high above, down to a point somewhere in a notional space in front of my toes.

We followed the path of least resistance straight up, over rocks covered in orange lichen, through more treefall, and over greasy slabs to a broad shelf. We climbed a headwall covered in shrubbery, the kind of thing that would usually feel quite secure. Moisture seems to at least give the impression of structural integrity. But it all felt so marginal. The ferns and herbs seemed like skeletons, sketchy representations of their usual selves.

We rediscovered water when we reached the top of the gully and worked our way around into the basin that holds Rainbow Lake. We went for a swim, and I finally felt connected to the deep, wet world. We basked for a short time, then began the climb to the pass which would take us over into the Te Puoho. Sidling around the lake took us to a small col, with a scree fan to descend below.

Dave hurt his knee in a fairly important sort of way, so we decided to stay in Boulder Basin for the next day or so, just to see how it went.

IV

I see Dave take off down a ramp on the edge of the icefall. He runs quickly, crab-like, crampons tick-ticking in the blue ice. He comes to a small crevasse about halfway down. He plants his axe on one side, then uses it as a fulcrum to perform a neat pirouette. He lands on the other side, safe, poised. He doesn't seem to stop, and lets his momentum carry him through and on down. In that series of connected motions, I imagine that I can see everything that led to that point, all of the small errors at the beginning of the learning process, the constant refinements, the experience and pain that taught him which bits to get rid of, which actions to pare away.

V

After more than a week of running about on the rock, my feet feel like they could stick to anything. I can't make a wrong move as we move down a long series of slabs. It's when we have to perform actions that rely on objects that aren't made of rock that things get interesting. There's a brief connecting move which involves a short vertical jump with a really big tussock for a handhold. The mechanics of the thing seem sound, but I have trouble suspending my disbelief for long enough to pull it off.

When we reach the bottom of the slabs, we're standing in Chasm Creek. When I turn around, the way we've come looks infeasible. It's as if we're the victims of some kind of scam, intended to make us believe that such things are possible. But the memories of tussock and the friction of skin against stone are too good not to be true.

James leads us on a tour of likely-looking bivvy rocks, the outline of his ponytail standing out starkly against the black, grey and green of the valley. Most of them aren't really that flash, but there's a cavern in the very head of the valley which looks very good indeed: a commanding position, an excellent view and even a kind of floor.

VI

I run around the boulders, springing, making things work, propelled by joy. When I stop, my heart is pounding. The others are in the distance now, and I feel a shock of solitude.

I take a deep breath and begin again. When I catch up, it's time to start descending towards the Hollyford, picking our way across down the side of a fan to get to the first fragment of bush, far below. Sunshowers sweep across the upper valley, like a lawn sprinkler in macrocosm. They aren't very big, but they are very frequent. I'm soaked when we reach the bush. The trees are all curled around each other, like a Turkish knot. We sit in their branches.

The sun comes out for a while, but stronger this time. I see Richard lower his hood and turn his face to the sky. He half-smiles, and his hair steams.

VII

I've lost my knife. I remember using it to cut up a roll of salami when we were having lunch. But now it's gone. I look everywhere I can think of, trying to nut out all of the possible trajectories of a falling knife. My knife is down there, somewhere, but I'd need to deconstruct a good part of the moraine wall to find it. I imagine picking up each rock, placing it aside, making neat piles. I would do this until the rocks were too big for me to lift by myself and then I would need to fabricate a lever. It would be difficult, here, to find anything longer than my ice axe. At least there would be lots of fulcrums. I would work diligently, carefully undoing the work of millennia to find my pocket knife.

I don't do this, of course. I think about my knife and the things that it represents for me, the things I've gained and lost. I think of the sun, and the eucalyptus leaves.

Boulder Basin is a great place to leave behind special objects from your past. As well as, perhaps, the past itself.

KERRY POPPLEWELL

Quail Flat, 1960

(for Brian)

Five of us slept that night on the stone floor
of an old cob hut, close by the Clarence River –
our ears ringing still from the silence
of high screes, our eyes still burning
from hot snow, the bright shimmer of bugloss
and briar rose on the parched valley flats.

When I woke, cold, in that monochrome time
before colour seeps in, I saw you sprawled
quite motionless, eyes closed. Rough stubble
darkened planes of shadow on your face.
You could have been a nameless casualty,
you looked so spent, so vulnerable and young.

But you weren't called upon to fight and die
at twenty, under unfamiliar stars.
The sun came up. We took the river route,
then climbed a pass that led us down
to adulthood – terrain as yet empty,
brilliant as sea-dazzle; as sun-strike.

BRIN WILLIMAN

Passing Generations in the Hopkins

Nearly twenty years ago I had ventured up the Hopkins Valley on my first attempt on the mountain of the same name. The day was showery with a cool breeze to deny that it was January. The others in my party had their heads down, bums up, going up the valley in the most direct route, for we only had a long weekend for our attempted ascent.

Jo and I diverted to the shelter of Elcho Hut for our lunch. At the door of this comfortable refuge we were welcomed by the friendly faces of Tom Barcham and Fred Hollows who thrust cups of tea into our hands. Tom and Fred I had read of in Alpine Club journals of the 1950s. Now as older men they were taking a two-week break from their responsible jobs in Sydney to revisit the alpine valleys of their youth.

Their eyes full of laughter, they talked mountain yarns of old. They were loving being back in the New Zealand mountains and Mt Ward was their objective. The weather was not good; they were in no hurry to get to grips with the peak. Elcho Hut was an adequate objective for the moment.

Jo and I finished our lunch and set our reluctant legs on the walk up valley after the rest of our party, heading for a bivvy on the Richardson Glacier. Despite our perseverance the weather was not kind and Mt Hopkins did not yield its summit to me that trip. Nor was it to on two subsequent attempts in the 1980s.

February 1993. With five others of greying beards like mine I was wandering up the tussock and beech-flanked flats of the beautiful Hopkins. Our association stemmed from university tramping club days a generation earlier. Stu Allan and Neil Kane I had climbed with since our days at Canterbury; Geoff Todd (Victoria University) I had been with in the Andes in 1976; Brian Smith (Auckland University) I was with on Mont Blanc in 1975; and Dave Tapp (Auckland University) had done trips with my wife Jo in their university days.

Our trip up the valley was unhurried. The havens of Elcho and Erceg Huts were graced by us. This progress was determined as much by our relaxed frames of mind as the patchy weather. On the fourth evening we lay in our sleeping bags on warm rock ledges of Faith Col. We watched the

sun set over Humphries and the sky fill with stars. The echoes of Dave's recorder reverberated off the cliffs of Prudence above.

At 4.30 in the morning drizzly rain set in. At 4.40 Stu came to share my two-man bivvy bag. It reminded me of home: being joined in the middle of the night by my small son when he had nightmares, for there was a similar shortage of space in which to roll over.

Nevertheless, come daylight the drizzle eased, and we decided to give the mountain a go, albeit with a 9.30 am start. Soon we were enveloped in the cloud and visibility was down to a rope length. My previous knowledge of the snowface up to the ridge proved of little value due to its broken crevassed nature. Route-finding, complicated by the odd steep snow wall, became the challenge. Seracs seemed to tower above us in the mist, only to shrink as the rope snaked out to put them into perspective. Neil put a nice lead up a rotten snow wall, Stu slid down a crevasse wall on to a dubious snow bridge, Dave snapped photos from the back. Oddly enough, as things became more difficult our resolve to climb increased.

This new-found enthusiasm was dampened as rain set in again. At least the rain improved the visibility to three rope lengths and the route to the ridge was clear. Stu front-pointed on. Soon his voice was calling down, telling of wind-driven rain on the ridge. It was already after 1.00 pm, and while we might reach the top we were in no mood for an epic. Retreat was agreed on, and Erceg Hut was reached at dusk.

We still had one more day for another attempt but there were no takers next morning. We lay on our bunks talking and laughing, while the drizzling rain eased down outside. We caught up with each other's careers and family fortunes. Responsible jobs and young families were over-riding occupations for most of the year, here in the mountains they could be put in a different perspective.

As we wandered back down the valley next day I reflected that this was one of the least successful trips in terms of peaks climbed that I had ever done – not even Prudence as a consolation peak. But it was one of the most relaxing and enjoyable trips to the mountains I had experienced.

I thought of Fred Hollows and Tom Barcham who I had met in this valley a generation earlier. It seemed we had inherited their attitude of love of the mountains. I felt privileged to have met them and to have been influenced by them.

PAT DEAVOLL

from *Wind from a Distant Summit*

But why do I want to go back to the mountains? To the cold and discomfort, the danger and the potential for another failure? Obviously there is something more than the satisfaction and kudos gained from making a summit that's been drawing me to climbing for thirty-five years. True, there have been lapses, when I've strayed towards kayaking and rock climbing, but I've always come back to alpinism as the thing that's determined the way I've led my life. Why?

Importantly, it keeps me in touch with the outside world. Few countries share our enviable lifestyle, and living in New Zealand it's all too easy to ignore the troubles of countries less fortunate than our own. I love Pakistan, and not just for its mountains. I'm fascinated by its politics and history, but most of all I admire the Pakistani people for their enduring fortitude in dealing with a tumultuous political and social agenda and the everyday problems this throws at them. Their lives keep mine in perspective.

I love the whole expedition process – researching the unclimbed peak, raising the funds, flying out of Christchurch with that sense of joyous anticipation, knowing I've got a day in Bangkok or Singapore to relax by the pool before arriving at my destination, sorting last-minute bureaucracy and travelling to the mountains in a jeep with all the gear. I love to look through the windows as we drive along, observing people going about lives so very different to my own. The walk into base camp with my climbing mates, our cook, porters, sirdar, liaison officer, goats and chickens is a chance to relax and socialise before the acclimatisation period. And finally there's the summit. It's like a wonderful, if short-lived, vocation.

I love the way the petty problems of my everyday life fade to the background, regardless of whether I'm on a six-week expedition to the Himalayas or a weekend climb at Mt Cook. Work problems, unpaid bills, and family and relationship dramas dissolve the moment I start the walk up the valley towards the mountain. Problems and anxieties resume their rightful place, my mood lifts, and my psyche begins to find a peace.

And I have nurtured a skill few people have. Over thirty-five years I've

developed the technical ability to climb in the greatest mountain ranges of the world, and this in itself is tremendously satisfying. I've made ascents of previously unclimbed mountains. I can join other elite mountaineers in their exasperation at the public perception of Everest as the pinnacle of alpinism. Everest is for guided 'tourons', as Bruce would say, with pots of money, who flock to the summit in their hundreds every season.

But more than that, my skill has offered me such wonderful experiences. Sometimes I have to pinch myself when I think, was it *me* who reached the summit of the unclimbed peak in India in a gathering storm on dusk, with lightning flashing on the horizon? Was it *me* who made the first female ascent of one of the greatest ice climbs in the world? Was it *me* who drove the famous Karakoram Highway and who drank tea with a nomad in a smoky tent on the Tibetan Plateau? Was it *me* who walked the length of the longest glacier in the Himalayas?

There are negatives, of course, the most painful being the loss of a dear friend on a lonely mountain in the wilds of Alaska. I've given away long-term partners and a marriage, a permanent home and financial security to pursue what I'm just beginning to accept has been my only path. There have been defeats and failures, but anyone who climbs mountains will have failures; I accept this now. It's the journey and the trying that matter; the heart that goes into the attempt rather than the summit. My body is wearing thin but even that isn't all bad. By default, it has added another string to my bow – it has given me the time and patience to write this book. For the past three decades I've been first and foremost a climber. Now I'm not just a climber – I'm also a writer.

SHARRON CAME

Many Happy Returns

Dawn is drawing near when I wriggle into the warm cocoon of my sleeping bag. The icicles hanging in my hair melt and drip down my neck, soaking my silk liner. The air in Blyth Hut reminds me of my grandfather's coolstore where he kept the apples harvested from his orchard. I dream I'm helping grade apples when a wolf enters the coolstore. Desperate to avoid being eaten I hide inside an apple, but the wolf is no idiot and works out there is only one place of concealment. He takes a bite out of the nearest Granny Smith. A bright light in my face jolts me awake. Someone is signalling via head torch that it's time to get up.

Kitted out in my tramping boots, oversized yellow raincoat, baggy red over-trousers and blue bike helmet, I join the rest of the group as we open the coolstore door and follow David into the void. I met David at my local tramping club. He always arrived at the last minute and attempted to sit unobtrusively at the back of the hall. With his long hair, large tinted glasses that hid half his face, worn trainers and old wilderness raincoat he stood out. It was rumoured he'd been on multiple of expeditions to climb 8000m peaks. I was sceptical. He looked more like a vagabond than an alpinist. After I completed the club alpine climbing course I asked him if I could join one of his trips. He stared at me for a long time then nodded.

Outside it is difficult to discern ground from air; there is light and shadow but no tangible landmarks or defined edges. In the absence of a visible horizon, where the clag stops and the sky starts is a mystery. The precise location of the ground beneath me is also a puzzle. Sometimes my feet land where I expect the ground to be, and other times the earth turns out to be closer or further away than I anticipate. In my confused and disorientated state I could be walking anywhere. 'This must be what sleep walking is like,' I think.

It dawns on me the silence is not due to the lack of visibility discouraging conversation; it's down to an absence of wind. My pack is coated in sticky frost which comes off when I scrape it with my glove, only to be replaced by more frost. 'It must be snowing,' I think, although I can't see any snow. I can see my breath though as it condenses in white puff-balls

in front of me. The cold air causes my nose to run, the mucus freezing to my face. My eyelashes are coated in crunchy snow-crystal mascara. My raincoat grows heavy and hard till I can only see a pale version of its yellow shade in the creases. I squint through fogged-up sunglasses in a vain effort to identify the silhouette in front of me or footstep impressions in the whiteness underfoot.

Inside this cloud world it's not only my spatial awareness that's haywire, I've lost all track of time, as my watch is buried under four layers of clothing. I stop to avoid bumping into the person in front of me. We huddle together over a map and I understand that we have been going around a basin in a circle. In my distracted dream-like state the revelation – that the people whose judgement I'm relying on to get me back to shelter safely might not be infallible – fazes me only slightly.

We continue our ascent through increasingly thick soggy snow. When there is no more snow above us we halt and I realise that this time we are at the top. I'm cold, wet and pleased. For a brief period before I hurry down after the others I catch a glimpse of blue sky and the shape of what I recognise as clouds.

When my brother asks me how my first alpine climb went I tell him Girdlestone was scary, disorientating and exhilarating. Like going to the moon in a spaceship and climbing a giant lemonade popsicle. Everything was white, our space suits leaked a bit and we communicated mostly via sign language.

After 18 months of climbing North Island peaks and those at the top of the south I think I've convinced David I'm nearly ready to climb a 3000m peak. My first glacier, the Bonar, is stripped bare of loose snow leaving even small crevasses easy to spot. Nevertheless I walk cautiously, stepping in old footprints left by other climbers, and carefully keeping the rope tensioned. The slots may not be wide or deep but I can see down their throats to blue ice and I have no wish to fall into one.

Sunlight sparkles on the milky massif of Aspiring, which dwarfs the little red shed known as Colin Todd Hut perched on the plateau below. Close up I struggle to comprehend the scale and steepness of the columns of rock at the bottom of the north-west ridge. Aspiring is Gulliver compared to its Lilliputian-sized cousins further north. David suggests we undertake a reconnaissance of the lower part of the route. Scrambling up a couple of hundred metres of slabs mostly avoiding the pockets of ice and

old snow, I struggle with the exposure and some of the moves, especially when it comes to reversing them to get back down. 'Maybe I'm not ready for this', I think.

That evening the coolstore world fails to appear. Instead I lie awake listening to the roar of wind and sleet lashing the vibrating hut. I understand why there are big steel cables attached to it and to the toilet. The storm continues throughout the long day. David sleeps while I listen spellbound to the guides shouting tales of climbing in Europe, Alaska and New Zealand over the racket outside. When dawn finally arrives clear and quiet I'm dying to leave the confines of the cramped, smelly hut but David insists there is no point getting up early. His lethargy irritates me till I venture outside.

Where there used to be bare rock the mountain is now white. 'Verglas', David pronounces. The guides agree. 'The season is over,' says one as he dials up a chopper to take his clients back to Wanaka. We head across to the rock and I touch the icy coating. It's cold, glossy and frictionless. David explains that the autumn daytime temperature will be too low and the heat of the sun too weak to melt the ice for long enough for us to complete the climb. My disappointment dissolves into relief. We are stardust with delusions of grandeur, I reflect, as we wander past Stargazer Peak simply enjoying being in the mountains. Bad weather is no guarantee you can't climb a mountain, pleasant weather is no guarantee you can. What matters is the memories you make.

Another three years pass before I return to the Aspiring region. After a family wedding we stop off in Wanaka and head up the West Matukituki to camp at Cascade Saddle. Framed by the Isobel and Dart glaciers and offset by the supine blue and white striped wiggles of Cascade Stream, the saddle is popular with cheeky kea and ravenous sandflies, as well as the occasional gypsy camper. It also serves as a perfect tussock-carpeted viewing platform for Mt Aspiring.

Lying on our Thermarests in front of our tents, resplendent in our stripey polypropylene pyjamas which smell of insect repellent, stale perspiration and camping gas, we sip our hot chocolates and watch the sun set over the mountain. Viewed from a distance, Aspiring looks more alluring than intimidating. The sunset coupled with the tight-rope walk up the summit ridge of Mt Liverpool the following morning reignites my desire to climb it.

For my second attempt I select late spring when snow conditions are more likely to be favourable. I'm joined by David and John. The trip across the Bonar is John's first time on a glacier. His cautious progress and obvious wonder mixed with fear at the sight of the big mountains surrounding us echo my previous visit. In Colin Todd Hut my easy-going, self-deprecating brother immediately befriends the Australian pair who return to the hut shortly after we arrive, tired from a practice climb on a nearby peak. When they ask whether he will be climbing the mountain the following day (they have been told by their guide that they need another day of practice), John feigns astonishment and replies, 'Oh no, I've got two young children!' Worried looks cross their faces before we all burst into fits of laughter. Their guide is less amused.

Everyone is asleep when I prise David out of his sleeping bag pre-dawn. I want to minimise the risk of encountering soft snow while descending the ramp. We're lucky to have a full moon, and despite mild temperatures the snow is firm enough to enable rapid progress back onto the Bonar where we follow the easy crevassed slopes to the base of the route.

Our route of choice involves ascending a 600-metre moderately steep snow slope to join the north-west ridge. This is the fastest and most straightforward way to climb the mountain before the warmer weather causes the bergschrund at the base to melt and open like a drawbridge preventing access to a castle. This drawbridge route is also the quickest way to descend Aspiring but is easy to underestimate, particularly if you are fatigued or unfamiliar with the route having ascended by the more popular and technical south-west ridge. Our ascent is straightforward, the perfect conditions allowing us to leap the bergschrund and proceed quickly up the slope using two tools. We pause briefly at the ridge to shake out our hands before continuing up the broad, relatively flat upper third of the north-west ridge.

As my crampons scrape and squeak across the last chunk of sastrugi-coated ridge the sky is lightening with the promise of dawn. In the stillness of a fine, calm morning snowy peaks stretch out below us in every direction, while cloud froths atop the valley floors below.

Sunlight begins to smudge the horizon, brightening the sky and colouring the snow icing pink, tangerine and yellow. One by one, like a series of candles on a birthday cake, the white frosted peaks are ignited by the soft dawn light.

David's grin is worth a thousand words. This is his third ascent and the best conditions he has encountered here. He gestures to where the south-west ridge joins the summit ridge. The chunky shape of Aoraki is easily identifiable in the distance reminding me of the zoomed-in version that delighted and temporarily distracted me from the terror of perching on the tiny, precarious summits of Sefton and the Footstool. Closer to home the twin peaks of Mt Earnslaw jog memories of a couple of roller coaster ascents to Esquilant Biv followed by quick descents with bad weather hard on our heels. Mt Brewster, a mountain that I will always associate with a broken crampon and a long, exposed summit ridge, is sticking its neck up above the clouds. It took a second attempt to summit that one, too.

I point to the pink reflection of Aspiring's summit triangle on the western horizon. The silhouette begins tiny but grows in definition before fading as rapidly as it appeared as daylight flexes its muscles, evicting the moonlight. I've seen this type of shadow only once before, while ascending Mont Blanc at dawn. Like a rainbow or a brocken spectre it's a poignant reminder of fleeting moments of bliss experienced in alpine places, the ephemeral nature of life.

Back at the rocky outcrop beside the hut John waves to us. He's been anxiously awaiting our return the entire morning though he feigns nonchalance. Tomorrow David and I will escort him across the glacier to French Ridge Hut, but for now we have an afternoon to enjoy munching chocolate, cheese and crackers and exploring the lower reaches of Shipowner Ridge. Just me, John, and my other brother, the vagabond alpinist I met eight years ago and who, through mountain journeys, has become part of my family.

In the mountains what matters is food and warmth, taking care of your mates and not falling off; everything else is unimportant. We experience intense highs and lows, forge a strong connection with the environment and learn what we are capable of. We endure some hardship and are bewitched by the sublime. Mountaineering is both an addiction and, ironically, a test of what you can give and give up. The intrinsic value inherent in the opportunity to spend time with close friends in beautiful mountain landscapes, the dual gifts of perspective and connection, these are the things that drive me to climb.

CHRISTOPHER JOHNSON

Letter from Nigeria, 1942

For some days I've been engrossed in Geoffrey Winthrop Young's book, *On High Hills*, and oh, what a surge of nostalgic longing these tales bring out. This last week I've done more climbing than ever before I think. As I lie in bed – day or night – I reclimb old peaks – it is quite a strenuous job – the reluctant lazy fluctuating brain must be forced like a jibbing horse, to stick to the road and not skip a few hours. For example, climbing the Minarets last night, I must have spent five minutes cudgelling before I reluctantly admitted that I couldn't remember what we had for breakfast. Then the long bit between the schrund at Teichelmanns Corner and the Mackay Rocks – a long plod in what might have been harder snow – that had to be filled in with detail sufficient to its temporal length – sunrise on Tasman – standing on tiptoe to see if we were coming and blushing when it saw us looking – an erudite discussion on angles of attack of crevasses so that we could find our way home in fog – and so on.

And the strange thing was that today I have vivid memories of a climb as of last night – yet my memories are first-hand, not last night's rehash. It was wonderful. My recollections have always been so blurred before that I thought it was natural to me, not merely the result of lazy thinking in the past. Winthrop Young describes how the return to scenes of happiness is so seldom successful in recapturing the old emotion – except in the mountains, where the opposite seems to apply. Away from them you can remember being happy, but not the happiness itself.

All that survives of such a climb is seldom more than this sediment of small interest. From the constant companionship of the scenery and from the continuity of the action, the human interests stood out a little at the time and they endure as the clearer impressions because they were incongruous. In our less exalted valley humour we find them less in our glass of memory, and stir them diluted into a tale; but our vivid and day-long consciousness of the mountain, of each other, and of the drama which we and the mountain played out and at length together, cannot be reproduced faithfully. It has escaped all but our general recollection. The mountaineer returns to the hills because he remembers always that he has

forgotten so much. Of one thing alone he is certain, that he will pass one more such irreproducible day somewhere among the mountain source of unspoiled pleasure.

HONE TUWHARE

Man in the Landscape

Far off
the sea beckons
to the mountains.

Austerely
the mountains ponder
the cacaphonic river tossing
white-splintered mane to the
mist's swirl.

Here
alien sounds are struck.
Nowhere is there greater fuss
to tear out the river's tongue.

Blue hiss and crackle
of the welding rod,
compressed sigh of air
and the whump and whoof
fuse to the rising clamour
of the rivet gun.

Cursing
scuffing the earth with massive
boots, men are walking away:
and from the smoke-wreathed shoulder
of a crouching hill a gigantic fist
of sound unfolds – shattering the clouds.
Coaxed into staccato life
a tractor nonchalantly puffs
perfect rings into the startled air.

Exulting men
as skilled as spiders thread
a skyline of steel crucifixes.

The sea beckons
again and again
to the mountains. Unmoved
the austere mountains ponder
a silence as profound as stars.

NOTES ON EXTRACTS

Eleanor Adams was born in Lawrence, Otago, in 1876. In 1889 she joined the survey party led by her father, Charles William Adams, on a three-week trip from Milford Sound to Te Anau via Mackinnon Pass (Omanui). The overland crossing from Te Anau via Omanui had been used by Māori gathering pounamu/greenstone from the area around Anita Bay in Milford Sound; Quintin McKinnon made the first European crossing in 1888. Using her married name, Ella Spicer, Adams became a watercolourist specialising in botanical and landscape paintings.

Fleur Adcock is a New Zealand-born poet and one of this country's most distinguished writers. Raised in both New Zealand and Britain, she gained a MA in classics and was a lecturer in the subject at the University of Otago in the late 1950s. She also worked at the university library until 1961, and it was during this period that she met mountaineer David Herron. 'Flight, with Mountains', written in memory of Herron, appeared in her 1967 poetry collection *Tigers*, and was later included in *Poems 1960–2000*, published in Britain by Bloodaxe Books. Adcock has lived in England since 1963 where she has worked as a librarian, translator and freelance writer. She has published many collections of poetry and was editor of *The Oxford Book of Contemporary New Zealand Poetry* and *The Faber Book of 20th Century Women's Poetry*. She has won several literary awards, including the New Zealand Book Award for Poetry in 1984 and the Queen's Gold Medal for Poetry in 2006. In 1996 she was awarded an OBE for her contribution to New Zealand literature, and in 2008 was named a Companion of the New Zealand Order of Merit for services to literature.

David Herron was born in 1926 and studied history at the University of Otago, gaining his PhD in 1959. By the time he left New Zealand in late 1959 he had climbed all but two of New Zealand's 10,000ft mountains. His 1955 first ascent of Mt Magellan with Sir Edmund Hillary, Harry Ayres and Bruce Gillies is his most notable climb from this period. He planned to join Hillary's 1960–61 'yeti expedition', but was killed by an avalanche on Aiguille d'Argentière near Mont Blanc in 1960.

David Baguley was introduced to the wilderness from a young age in both New Zealand and Switzerland. Through the Auckland University Tramping Club he ventured into mountaineering and went on to complete a number of seasons at Aoraki/Mount Cook and Mt Aspiring National Parks. Ascents include the south faces of Cook, Aspiring and Mt Hicks. He has also climbed in South America on a New Zealand Alpine Club expedition. Baguley is married with two children and now lives in Northland. He works as a real estate agent and visits the South Island mountains once a year.

Lydia Bradey was born in Christchurch in 1961 and began tramping and mountaineering as a teenager, climbing Aoraki/Mt Cook at 18 and the Balfour Face of Mt Tasman during the 1980–81 season. During the 1980s Bradey took part in several Himalayan expeditions and became the first woman to climb Mt Everest without supplemental oxygen in 1988. A qualified international mountain and ski guide, she has taken part in more than 24 expeditions to peaks over 6000m in Europe, Asia, Antarctica and New Zealand. She is one of the first two women to successfully guide Mt Everest, and has climbed it four times. She lives in Lake Hawea with her partner and fellow guide Dean Staples. Her autobiography *Going Up Is Easy* was published in 2015 and was a finalist at the Banff Mountain Book competition.

Bradey's autobiography was written with Laurence Fearnley; the narrator 'I' of the second selection is Fearnley.

Rachel Bush was born in 1941 and grew up in Hawera. She lived much of her life in Nelson and was a keen tramper and explorer of New Zealand's national parks. She walked many tracks up and down the country, often more than once. A brisk walk over Nelson's Centre of New Zealand hill was a daily ritual until just a few months before she died in 2016.

Sharron Came grew up on a dairy farm in Northland. 'We passed time reading and roaming the hills while inventing stories. I discovered my first mountain when I was 15. It was love at first sight. At university I fell into tramping and, soon after, climbing. My interest in the outdoors has been an important constant in my life, and writing a great way of attempting to create order out of chaos, a type of therapy. In Aotearoa we are fortunate:

there are plenty of beautiful, wild places to visit to find solace and inspiration and regain a sense of perspective. You can choose a challenging journey or something more relaxing. From challenge comes growth, but nature is equally valuable for its restorative qualities.'

Derek Chinn has been a self-confessed 'spectacularly average' climber for decades. His career started in Christchurch in the late 1970s and involved walking up peaks in Arthur's Pass and shaking his way up various rock climbs on Castle Rock. Sadly, most of these climbs collapsed in the Canterbury earthquakes. Chinn progressed to classic and moderate routes in the Mount Cook area during the golden age of the 1980s, a time when 'big hair' was considered fashionable. Later, he participated in a variety of expeditions to greater mountain ranges including in Alaska, South America and the Himalaya. He achieved a number of first ascents around the world, but says the only peak that anyone ever wants to hear about is Mt Everest.

Carol Diamond Christie's most prolific mountaineering years were 1991–2006. Drawn to mountains for fun, a pared back existence, challenge and adventure, she accumulated ascents of over 160 peaks. The list reads like a dossier of some of the world's highest and most famous mountains. From the 46 countries she travelled to, ascents include the Eiger, Mont Blanc, Matterhorn, Elbrus, Alpamayo, Kilimanjaro, Huascaran and Aconcagua. Aoraki/Mt Cook features twice alongside many lofty New Zealand summits. A passion for wild places is something she and husband Richard now share with their two boys, Edmund and Scott, through tramping, skiing and mountain scrambles.

Thom Conroy is author of two novels, *The Salted Air* and *The Naturalist*, both with Penguin Random House, and editor of the essay collection *Home* (Massey University Press). His short fiction has been recognised by *Best American Short Stories 2012*, and has won awards such as the Katherine Ann Porter Prize in Fiction and the *Sunday Star–Times* Short Story Award. Conroy is a senior lecturer in creative writing at Massey University.

Ida Corry was introduced to mountaineering by her father, Robert Corry, a member of the (British) Alpine Club. A member of the Ladies' Alpine Club (founded in 1907 for women mountaineers because the Alpine Club barred

membership of women until 1975), Corry spent several seasons climbing with local guides in the Mount Cook region in the 1930s, and scaled a number of high peaks including Aoraki/Mt Cook, Mt Sefton, Malte Brun and Elie de Beaumont. She is remembered for her first ascent of Mt Goldsmith (2905m) with guide Mark Lysons in January 1933. During the descent from the mountain Lysons broke his leg and Corry lowered him down, shepherding him towards Almer Hut where, to her relief, guide Joe Fleurty was present and able to assist. Veteran New Zealand mountaineer Arthur P. Harper praised the rescue, writing in the 1933 *Alpine Journal*: 'I consider this a very outstanding rescue, even had it been performed by an experienced man, and I think it will stand out as a record so far as a girl climber is concerned ...' Corry herself took little credit for the rescue, praising Lysons for his courage.

James Cowan was a journalist and historian and published more than 30 books in his lifetime as well as numerous newspaper and magazine articles. Born in 1870, his journalism career included a stint with the newly formed Department of Tourist and Health Resorts, writing handbooks and brochures to publicise the South Island's scenic areas. Cowan is best known for his writing about the New Zealand wars, but was also interested in Māori legend, history and culture. 'First over the Alps: The epic of Raureka and the greenstone' comes from his 1935 book, *Hero Stories of New Zealand.*

Jack Cox began his guiding career at the start of 1929 while working as a dish washer and porter at the Hermitage. He worked under guide Betsy Blunden before relocating to Franz Josef in November, where he was employed by Peter and Alex Graham. There he mastered climbing skills such as step-cutting from guide Joe Fleurty. With Fleurty and fellow guide Jack Pope, Cox made the first ascent of Mt Tasman from the West Coast in March 1932. Of all the clients he guided, Cox most enjoyed the trips he made with Marjorie Edgar-Jones from the mid- to late 1930s, including the first traverse of Mt Dampier (with second guide Syd Brooks) in January 1938. Suffering from a knee injury, Cox left guiding at the end of the 1938 season and took up farming near Whanganui.

Nick Cradock started climbing in 1975 at age 17 and has become one of New Zealand's top mountaineers, achieving a number of difficult first ascents. Born in Christchurch, he started guiding in 1980 and became a fully certified IFMGA climbing and ski guide in 1984. In 2010 he was made a lifetime member of the New Zealand Alpine Club. When asked what he likes most about climbing, Cradock replied, 'Getting down and having a shower.' These days he has a penchant for using two sleeping mats when in the mountains.

Ross Cullen is an emeritus professor of resource economics at Lincoln University. He scrambled up peaks and crags for over 40 years, including many fine trips and first ascents with Bill McLeod. Ross wrote two editions of the guidebook *Barron Saddle – Mt Brewster*. His autobiography, *Slice of Heaven*, draws on economics to chronicle his climbs and scrambles on seven continents.

Dora Hallenstein de Beer was born in Australia, grew up in Dunedin and made her first trip to the Southern Alps in 1915. From the 1920s she began guided climbing and spent six seasons mountaineering at Mount Cook before departing for London in 1932. From London she made trips to the French Alps, traversing Mont Blanc by the Peuterey Ridge in 1935 with Una Cameron and guides, the first women to do so. During this period she also travelled to the Dolomites, and her diaries describing her car journeys from London to the mountains of Italy in 1936 (in the Hocken Collections) make interesting reading. Back in New Zealand for the 1937 season, she climbed Mt Hamilton, Mt Pibrac, the Minarets, Malte Brun and Mt Hooker, as well as completing a traverse of Green and Walter and crossings of both Ball and Copland passes and Graham Saddle. In 1938 she was a member of the first New Zealand overseas expedition to Yunnan, China, with the goal of climbing Mt Satseto, the highest peak in the Sansato Massif. With her were Australian Marie Byles (the expedition leader), Marjorie Edgar-Jones, Fraser Radcliffe and guides Mick Bowie and Kurt Suter. They did not reach the summit, but her account of the trip, including the 400-mile approach, displays her enthusiasm for adventure.

As she grew older de Beer described the satisfaction of climbing 'round' rather than 'up' mountains, and wrote about the joy of climbing passes and the anticipation of seeing across to the 'other side'. She was a member of

the New Zealand Alpine Club for 50 years and was elected president of the Ladies' Alpine Club (Britain) in 1970.

James Robert Dennistoun

Born at Peel Forest, Canterbury, in 1883, Dennistoun began his mountaineering career with trips up Mt Peel before progressing to the Tasman Glacier and an ascent of Hochstetter Dome in 1907. His interest lay in the mountains at the head of the Rangitata River, which ran close to his home, and in February 1908 he made a 10-day trip exploring the Havelock Glacier area. March 1908 saw him back at Mount Cook, making a crossing of Ball Pass and climbing Glacier Dome with his sister Barbara. Further exploration of the Rangitata followed and in March 1910 Dennistoun, in the company of guide Jack Clarke and British mountaineer Lawrence Earle, made the first ascent of Mt D'Archiac (2875m), the highest peak between the Mount Cook region and the Kaikoura ranges. At Mount Cook for six weeks from November 1910 to January 1911, Dennistoun made seven ascents, including Elie de Beaumont, Malte Brun, Mt Aylmer, the Minarets and De la Beche, with Jack Clarke and Ada Julius – the latter a family friend and contemporary of Freda du Faur, and the first New Zealand woman to venture up high mountains.

Dennistoun made the first ascent of Mitre Peak (1692m) in March 1911, and left New Zealand at the end of that year to join Captain Scott's South Pole expedition aboard the *Terra Nova*. In February 1914 he was at the Haast Ridge bivouac when an avalanche on the Linda Glacier killed guides Darby Thomson and Jock Richmond and client Sydney King. Dennistoun joined the search party for what was the first fatality at Mount Cook.

World War I brought an end to Dennistoun's mountaineering career. Attached to the Royal Flying Corps, his plane was shot down near Arras in June 1916 and he died in a prisoner-of-war camp in August. His notebooks and letters have been collected by Guy Mannering and published in *The Peaks & Passes of J.R.D.* (1999).

Pat Deavoll was born in Canterbury and began mountaineering as a teenager in the 1970s. By 1980 she had climbed all the 10,000ft peaks in New Zealand, as well as making a first female ascent of Logan's Run on the South Face of Mt Hicks. Drawn to extreme, technical climbing, Deavoll

travelled overseas, mountaineering in Alaska, India, Tibet, China and Central Asia. In 1999 she won the Macpac/CMC Mountaineer of the Year award. For the past 20 years she has focused on expeditions to 6000–7000m peaks in Pakistan and Afghanistan, and in 2009 made the first ascent of Karim Sar in North Pakistan. An accomplished writer, Deavoll has written a memoir of her mountaineering life, *Wind from a Distant Summit: The story of New Zealand's top woman mountaineer* (2011), from which the extracts in this anthology are taken. Deavoll stopped climbing in 2016 and now channels her energy towards adventure motorcycling. She details her travels on her blog: patdeavoll.co.nz.

Sir Graeme Dingle was born in 1945 and is known for his adventuring, writing and humanitarian efforts. He has achieved over 200 mountaineering and adventure firsts worldwide, including first ascents in the Himalaya, the Andes and New Zealand. He has served as chairman of the Sir Edmund Hillary Outdoor Pursuits Centre and the Project K Charitable Trust, and was founding chairman of the New Zealand Outdoor Assembly. He was knighted in 2017 for his services to New Zealand. *Two Against the Alps* (1972) is an account of the first winter traverse of the Southern Alps made from south to north in 1971. Graeme Dingle and Jill Tremain completed the traverse in two months, from July to September. *Wall of Shadows: The New Zealand Jannu expedition* (1976) describes the New Zealand attempt to make a first ascent of Jannu (7710m) in Nepal via the North Face in 1975.

Freda du Faur was inspired to visit the mountains after seeing photographs of Aoraki/Mt Cook during a visit to the International Exhibition in Christchurch in 1906. Australian-born, she made her first trip to Mount Cook in 1909 and returned to make the first female ascent of the mountain with guides Peter and Alexander Graham during December 1910. Over the next few seasons she made ascents of Mts Tasman and Sefton, as well as making the first grand traverse of Aoraki/Mt Cook in January 1913. First ascents of Dampier, Pibrac, Cadogan and Nazomi were also achieved. She did not climb again after 1913 but recorded her mountaineering achievements in *The Conquest of Mount Cook and other climbs* (1915).

Rangi Faith (Kāi Tahu and Ngāti Kahungunu) is a poet who lives in the South Island. His recent works are included in *Poetry in Multicultural Oceania* (Vaughan Rapatahana, Essential Resources, 2017); *Night Burns with a White Fire: The essential Lauris Edmond* (eds Frances Edmond and Sue Fitchett, Steele Roberts, 2017); and *The Penguin Book of New Zealand War Writing* (eds Harry Ricketts and Gavin McLean, Penguin Random House, 2015). His latest volume of poetry is *Spoonbill 101* (Puriri Press, 2014).

Laurence Fearnley's parents, Brian and Wendy, were keen climbers in England and members of the Manchester-based Karabiner Club. As a child and first-generation New Zealander, Laurence was taken into the Canterbury hills on trips up Torlesse and low peaks in Arthur's Pass. While her father Brian and brother Dave became active mountaineers, Fearnley derived more pleasure from sitting and looking at the view and writing about it. Her novel *The Hut Builder* won the fiction award in the 2011 New Zealand Post Book Awards and was a finalist in the Boardman Tasker Prize for Mountain Literature.

Rhian Gallagher's most recent work, *Freda Du Faur, Southern Alps 1909–1913* was produced in collaboration with printer Sarah M. Smith and printmaker Lynn Taylor (Otakou Press, 2016). Gallagher's previous collections include *Salt Water Creek* (Enitharmon Press, 2003), shortlisted for the Forward Prize for First Collection; and *Shift* (Auckland University Press, 2011; Enitharmon Press, 2012), winner of the 2012 New Zealand Post Book Award for Poetry.

W. Scott Gilkison was born in 1912 and climbed extensively in the Otago mountains. With the establishment of the Otago Section of the New Zealand Alpine Club in 1930 (OSONZAC), mountaineering into the more remote areas of the southern South Island became increasingly popular. Gilkison was at the forefront of this trend, making 16 first ascents and the first grand traverse of Mt Earnslaw. He wrote several books during his lifetime, notably *Peaks, Packs, and Mountain Tracks* (1940), *Aspiring* (1951) and *Earnslaw* (1957). In 1948 and 1950 he collaborated with Arthur Hamilton to produce new editions of *Moir's Guide Book*. Gilkison was president of the New Zealand Alpine Club from 1963–65 and was instrumental in gaining support for the creation of Mount Aspiring National Park. He died in 1976.

Michael Gill grew up with a compulsion to climb trees and the papa cliffs of Auckland's Hobson Bay. While at the Otago Medical School in 1955 he transferred this passion to the larger arena of the granite ridges and walls of Fiordland's Darran Mountains. A further widening of mountain and human horizons took place in 1960 when he was invited to join Sir Edmund Hillary's Silver Hut Expedition to the Everest–Makalu Himalaya. He has published three books: *Mountain Midsummer* (1969), *Himalayan Hospitals* (2011) and *Edmund Hillary: A biography* (2017).

Penny Goddard is an IFMGA guide and avalanche forecaster. She has climbed and skied all over the world and currently resides in a mountain town in Canada. She makes better use of weather forecasts and navigation aids these days. Her home turf of New Zealand is still nearest to her heart.

Peter Gough started climbing on Mt Taranaki in 1963 while at high school in New Plymouth. On moving to Christchurch for university studies he joined the Canterbury Mountaineering Club, where he met and climbed with a range of local mountaineers, notably John Glasgow. After completing his degree in 1970, he travelled to Peru to climb in the Sierra Blanca. Back in New Zealand he and Glasgow achieved the first ascent of the Caroline Face on Aoraki/Mt Cook in November 1970. Among his other notable climbs are the second ascent of the Balfour Face of Mt Tasman (with Ian 'Foxy' Ross), the first ascent of the Central Gullies on the South Face of Hicks (with Bill Denz and Etienne Kumar), the first winter ascent of the Sheila Face of Aoraki/Mt Cook (with Bill Denz), along with some lesser known ascents – mostly in Aoraki/Mount Cook and Westland national parks.

Peter Graham was born in Okarito, Westland, in 1878. His introduction to the mountains took place on Franz Josef Glacier, followed by trips from Fox Glacier with mountaineers Ebenezer Teichelmann and Rev. Henry Newton. By 1903 Graham was the assistant guide at Mount Cook and from 1906–22 was chief guide. His most famous client was Australian Freda du Faur, who became the first woman to climb Aoraki/Mt Cook in 1910. The first New Zealand woman to climb New Zealand's highest mountin was Peter's wife Muriel Graham, guided by her husband, in 1915. In 1924 Graham led the first ascent of Mt Tukoko (2756m) in Fiordland. He died while writing his memoir in 1961.

Graham's letter in this anthology is addressed to Jim Glasgow, an active mountaineer and member of the New Zealand Alpine Club who was editor of the *New Zealand Alpine Journal* from 1952 until shortly before his death (with climbing companion Harry Scott) in an accident on Aoraki/Mt Cook in 1960. Glasgow was a devout member of the Church of England and was involved in establishing the Interdenominational Chapel at Arthur's Pass.

William Spotswood Green's love of 'wild sport' within sublime surroundings, coupled with an interest in natural science, first brought him face to face with the challenges of mountaineering in Switzerland in the late 1860s. In 1881 he was at the Jubilee meeting of the British Association at York when he happened to see photographs of the New Zealand alps – and Aoraki/Mt Cook. The image of the mountain was enough to persuade him to leave his post as a cleric in the south of Ireland and travel to New Zealand to attempt the first ascent. Green is largely responsible for introducing the sport of mountaineering to New Zealand in 1882, but the *idea* of climbing the mountain was already instilled in the local imagination. For example, in 1873 Governor Bowen made a week-long journey to the Hooker and Tasman glacier area and was so taken by his surroundings that he offered official aid to any member of the British Alpine Club should they wish to attempt the ascent of Aoraki/Mt Cook.

Edith Searle Grossman (1863–1931) was educated at Canterbury College, Christchurch, where she gained an MA in English, history and political science. She worked as a teacher, university tutor and freelance journalist, as well as publishing four novels between 1890 and 1910. Her final novel, *Heart of the Bush*, was written while she was resident in England, and is set in colonial South Island backcountry – although the location appears romanticised rather than real. The protagonist, Adelaide Borlase, is the well-educated daughter of a runholder. As a young woman she must choose between two suitors: the refined but dull Englishman, Horace Brandon, or the 'uncivilised' New Zealand station manager, Dennis MacDiarmid. She marries the latter, and on their honeymoon in the mountains she falls down a crevasse and almost dies. *Heart of the Bush* is a romance novel that explores themes of marriage, civilisation and the 'wilderness'. The full text is available online through the New Zealand Electronic Text Collection: nzetc.victoria.ac.nz

Norman Hardie was one of New Zealand's pioneering mountaineers and completed first ascents around New Zealand and abroad. Notably, Hardie was a member of the party that climbed Kangchenjunga (8586m), the world's third-highest peak, in 1955. He was also part of the 1954 NZAC expedition to the Barun Valley led by Sir Edmund Hillary, which completed 20 new climbs, including Baruntse and Pethangtse. In New Zealand Hardie and his friends – Bill Beaven, Earle Riddiford, Jim McFarlane and Bill Packard – made many first ascents in the 1940s, including the South Ridge of Mt Sefton with an approach from Fyfe Pass. He was also instrumental in the rescue of Ruth Adams from La Perouse down the Cook River, an outstanding effort of wide acclaim in New Zealand mountaineering history. He died in 2017.

Steve Hart has been involved with the mountains for over 35 years, starting with courses at Outward Bound and the Outdoor Pursuits Centre and moving on to climbs of Mt Aspiring and Aoraki/Mt Cook. Expeditions followed, to Peru, Pakistan, Alaska, Tibet and Nepal. He has always been in search of interesting projects rather than big names, climbing peaks like Dir Gol Zom in the Hindu Kush, Triglav in the former Yugoslavia, and intriguing routes in Europe and New Zealand.

Bernard Head was British, one of a number of well-off overseas climbers who travelled to Mount Cook at the turn of the twentieth century. Like Freda du Faur and Lawrence Earle, Head employed local guides to help fulfill his mountaineering ambitions. With Jack Clarke and Alex Graham as guides, he succeeded in making the first ascent of Mt Aspiring (3033m) via the West Face on 23 November 1909. During the following seasons he completed ascents of Mt Sefton from the west, Elie de Beaumont and Haeckel Peak, as well as the first crossing of Cascade Saddle from the Matukituki Valley to the Dart in 1911, and a first ascent of Mt Edward in 1914. Head intended to spend more time exploring and climbing in the Southern Alps but was killed by a sniper in Gallipoli in August 1915.

Paul Hersey

Surfing and a lack of any nearby mountains stopped Hersey really getting into climbing until his mid-twenties. Some 25 years later he still occasionally finds time to pander to his bent for attempting new routes

in obscure places, and grudgingly accepts his inability at high altitude. Hersey's book *Our Mountains* won the Adventure Travel section at the 2017 NZ Mountain Film & Book Festival.

Sir Edmund Hillary was born in 1919 and first travelled to the mountains during a school ski-trip to Mt Ruapehu in the mid-1930s. Following World War II he spent several summers at Mount Cook and in 1948 made the first ascent of the South (Hillary) Ridge of Aoraki/Mt Cook with Ruth Adams and guides Harry Ayres and Mick Sullivan. Expeditions to the Himalaya followed in the early 1950s, and on 29 May 1953 he and Sherpa Tenzing Norgay made the first ascent of Mt Everest (8848m). In 1958 he was a member of the Commonwealth Trans-Antarctic Expedition that reached the South Pole. Later, he established the Himalayan Trust and was committed to building hospitals and schools in Nepal. He died in 2008. In 2017 his friend and climbing companion Michael Gill published an in-depth biography, *Edmund Hillary.*

This anthology includes a letter written by Hillary to his future father-in-law, Jim Rose, who was president of the New Zealand Alpine Club. Hillary married Louise Rose in September 1953.

Caoilinn Hughes' debut novel *Orchid & the Wasp* was published in 2018 by Hogarth (US) and Oneworld (UK). Her poetry collection *Gathering Evidence* (Carcanet & VUP, 2014) won the *Irish Times* Shine/Strong Award and was a finalist for four other prizes. She has received fellowships from the James Merrill Foundation, the Bogliasco Foundation, the Centre Culturel Irlandais, the Tin House Workshop, Art Omi, as well as an Arts Council of Ireland Literature Bursary Award and the Ireland Funds Monaco Award. Her work has appeared in *POETRY*, *Granta*, *Tin House*, *Poetry Ireland*, *Best British Poetry*, *Best NZ Poems*, on BBC Radio 3 and elsewhere. Her PhD is from Victoria University of Wellington, where she lived for seven years and climbed a few mountains.

Sir Thomas Hunter (1876–1953) was invited by fellow Waitaki Boys' High School teacher William Grave to take part in several exploratory journeys to remote areas of Fiordland. In 1900 Hunter was a member of Grave's Glaisnock expedition, which travelled over Oilskin Pass to Bligh Sound before returning to Te Anau. ('Oilskin' was Hunter's nickname, and referred to the protective sun-oil he applied to his face.) A.C. Gifford was also on

this expedition. Hunter made several more trips with Grave, but is best remembered as an academic and educationalist at the University of New Zealand and Victoria College (later Victoria University of Wellington). Anita Crozier's *Beyond the Southern Lakes: The explorations of W.G. Grave* (1950) provides details of Grave's expeditions in the company of Hunter, Gifford, Talbot, Grenfell and Lyttle. Grave's original papers are in the McNab Archives at Dunedin Public Library.

Christopher Johnson (1913–1953) began climbing mountains as a student in the 1930s. His early explorations were mainly in the vicinity of the Hopkins Valley. These included first ascents of several peaks, notably Mt Fettes in the Landsborough Valley, the peak named by the early West Coast explorer Charlie Douglas after his uncle, Sir William Fettes, who had founded Fettes College in Edinburgh, where Johnson had part of his schooling.

Johnson gained an MA with honours in Latin and French from Otago University. After completing war service as a fighter pilot with the RNZAF in North Africa and the Mediterranean, he became a teacher at King Edward Technical College in Dunedin and was commanding officer of the Territorial Air Force Squadron at Taieri Aerodrome. He maintained a strong interest in mountains and mountaineering and was editor of *New Zealand Alpine Journal* from 1947–51.

Yodellings was a newsletter sent to members of the Otago Section of the New Zealand Alpine Club (OSONZAC) serving overseas during World War II. As well as providing information about New Zealand mountaineering at home, it published letters from mountaineers serving in Africa, Europe, Asia and the Pacific. Many of Johnson's letters were included. The one in this anthology, to his wife Jean in Dunedin, was written from Nigeria in June 1942. At the time Johnson was en route from Britain to Egypt: a circuitous journey by ship to South West Africa (now Namibia) then by flying boat from Nigeria to Cairo. Johnson died in January 1953 in a plane crash in the West Matukituki Valley while assisting in a search for two missing trampers.

Rob Kettels is an artist, climber and long-distance desert and bushwalker. He has climbed world-renowned peaks and crossed deserts – often solo – but now considers climbing a social activity. Kettels has recently graduated

with an honours degree in fine arts, which focuses on the philosophical history of climbing in Western culture by interrogating the Romantic sublime and neo-colonial beliefs latent in mountaineering.

Sara Knox teaches cultural studies and English in the School of Humanities and Communication Arts at Western Sydney University. Her research focuses on the cultural history of death and the representation of violence. She is author of *Murder: A tale of modern American life* (Duke University Press, 1998), and her novel *The Orphan Gunner* (Giramondo, 2007) was shortlisted for both the regional Commonwealth Writer's Prize and the *Age* Book of the Year. Her father Ray Knox guided at Mount Cook in the early 1950s and edited *A Thousand Mountains Shining: Stories from New Zealand's mountain world* (1984).

Andy Lindblade began climbing at the age of 15 at Mt Arapiles and the Grampians in Australia, and went on to climb in New Zealand, Patagonia, India, Nepal and Pakistan. With Athol Whimp he was awarded the international mountaineering prize, Piolet d'Or, for their 1997 first ascent of Thalay Sagar's North Face. In 2000 Lindblade and Whimp made an attempt on Jannu (7710m) by the unclimbed direct line on the North Face. When their portaledge bivouac was destroyed at 6100m they turned their attention to the Wall of Shadows route to the left of the face, and reached the summit. Lindblade currently lives in Portland, Oregon, with his wife and two children.

Kim Logan is of Ngāti Kahungungu decent. 'My only connection with Ngāi Tahu, other than sharing the same waka, Tākitimu, was that my father Rangi Logan was commander of D Company in the 28th Maori Battalion. D Company included Ngāi Tahu from the South Island. Most of the older kaumātua have heard of my father and know of D Company's exploits, and I'm sure they must think I should know better than to climb Aoraki, but having been taught very little of the customs of our people but only the customs of the European privileged at King's Prep at a very young age, my Māori side misses out. As my father said, "This is a Pākehā world, you must talk and think like them if you want to succeed." That was a sign of the times; in his later years he returned to his roots, I have to say, happier and more contented.'

Bob McKerrow has been tramping and climbing since his early teens. He has climbed and trekked extensively in New Zealand, Europe, Peru, Antarctica, Borneo, East Africa, Nepal, India and Central Asia, and has been a member of expeditions to the Arctic and Antarctic. McKerrow spent many years working in national parks and for the Department of Conservation, and in 35 years working for the International Red Cross he has been involved in many major conflicts and disasters. He is author of three books and has written extensively on mountaineering, polar regions, humanitarian aid and early Polynesian voyagers and exploration.

Karen McNeill was born in New Zealand and lived in Canada for much of her adult life. She was a particularly strong mountaineer who climbed a number of major routes in the Andes, Greenland, Alaska and the Himalaya. McNeill teamed up with American Sue Knott for many of her later climbs, including attempting Mt Shivling's difficult East Ridge in 2000. In 2004 they became the first women to climb the Cassin Ridge on Mt Denali. The pair went missing in 2006 when climbing the Infinite Spur on Mt Foraker in Alaska.

Doreen Murie (Urquhart), née Pickens (1926–2008), grew up in the North Island before taking up a teaching position in Springfield, Canterbury, in 1949. With a background in tramping, Murie began exploring the backcountry and peaks of the South Island, sometimes climbing in all-woman teams such as during ascents of Mts Murchison and Harper. The first female ascent of Mt Arrowsmith followed, and in 1953 she was a member of the first all-woman party to scale Aoraki/Mt Cook (with Mavis Davidson and Sheila MacMurray). Murie married station-owner Gerald Urquhart in 1953 and moved to Flock Hill, where she raised a family and spent the winters skiing. After Gerald's death she married ranger Bob Murie and moved to Arthur's Pass.

Summits for Suffrage was part of the 1993 celebrations to mark the centennial of women's suffrage in New Zealand. A co-ordinated event encouraging women to climb a mountain or hill was planned for the weekend of 13 February. Eight years earlier, in 1985, Women Climbing NZ was established. The first climbing meet bringing women mountaineers together was organised by Carol Nash and Marilyn Staite and scheduled to take place at Mount Cook. Only one person attended the initial event

but within months the organisation took off and groups were formed throughout New Zealand.

Joseph O'Leary was raised in Otago, a member of a family of eight. Like his brother William O'Leary (Arawata Bill), he spent much of his adult life prospecting for gold. His letter to W.J.P. Hodgkins (son of artist and mountaineer W.M. Hodgkins) describes the first ascent of Mt Earnslaw by women in 1894. In it he refers to Forrestina Ross, who had made an attempt on the mountain in 1892 but turned back before reaching the summit. Birley Glacier was named after Harry Birley, a local shepherd from Glenorchy who, in 1890, was the first to climb Mt Earnslaw.

John Pascoe (1908–1972) was introduced to mountaineering while a young man living in Christchurch. From the late 1920s he made many climbing trips to the Canterbury and Westland areas, focusing on unclimbed peaks rather than the more popular ranges around Mount Cook. He belongs to the generation of New Zealand mountaineers who climbed without guides (often for financial reasons), preferring the company of like-minded companions. Pascoe climbed over 100 peaks in his lifetime, a quarter of which were first ascents, but he is most closely associated with Mt Evans (2620m), a mountain he was drawn to and eventually summitted on his third attempt in 1934. Pascoe was a prolific writer and photographer, and his articles and books have entered the canon of New Zealand mountaineering literature. Notable among these are *Unclimbed New Zealand* (1939), *Land Uplifted High* (1952) and *Mr Explorer Douglas* (1957). At times his work was criticised for failing to include significant mention of mountains south of the Mount Cook region, but his writing reached a wide audience and helped popularise mountaineering in this country.

Kerry Popplewell began writing poetry after she retired from teaching in the mid-1990s. For many years she has been a keen tramper, and a number of her poems reflect her fondness for both the bush and the open mountaintops. 'Quail Flat, 1960' refers to a Victoria University Tramping Club trip made to the Kaikoura ranges at the end of 1960. The party she was in climbed Mt Tapuaenuku on Christmas Day. Two days later they crossed Muzzle Saddle and dropped into the Clarence Valley, where they received a warm welcome at Bluff Homestead. The following day they travelled upriver

to spend a night at Quail Flat before coming out over the Seaward Kaikoura Range.

Tom Riley lives at Port Chalmers on Otago Harbour and works as an archivist. He enjoys walking in the hills, especially in Fiordland.

Forrestina Ross was born in 1860 and trained and worked as a schoolteacher before marrying journalist and mountaineer Malcolm Ross in 1890. Throughout the 1890s she made trips into the Tasman Valley, climbing Hochstetter Dome in 1897 and again in 1900. She also mountaineered in the Otago–Aspiring region, climbing Mt Bonpland and almost reaching the summit of Mt Earnslaw in 1892. Although she did not become a leading alpinist, she enjoyed travelling in the mountain regions and became the first female member of the New Zealand Alpine Club in 1892. After marriage she worked as a parliamentary reporter and journalist and wrote several books, including *Mixed Grill* in 1934. She died in 1936.

Jonathan Scott is a professor of history at the University of Auckland. He explains: 'My father died when I was very young. I never knew him but there came a time in my adult life when I wanted to know more about him. I had by that stage completed a historical biography of a seventeenth-century figure and discovered that I had the skills to research and write a biography of my father that brought him back to life and gave me a relationship with him.' Two chapters from *Harry's Absence: Looking for my father on the mountain* are included in this anthology.

Thomas Henry (Harry) Scott was born in 1918. He was a writer, a lecturer in psychology and a mountaineeer. Interned as a conscientious objector during the war, Scott took up mountaineering in the 1950s and climbed throughout the South Island, often in the company of Jim Glasgow. His writing was published in the literary quarterly *Landfall*, and he made several tramping trips to the Matukituki Valley and Mt Sealy with poet and *Landfall* editor Charles Brasch. Brasch dedicated his long poem *The Estate* to Scott. Scott and his climbing companion Glasgow were killed on Aoraki/ Mt Cook in 1960.

Rebecca Smith is a veterinarian in Central Otago, a self-described 'farmer's wife and mother of two gorgeous girls'. 'It's been years since I've climbed;

at the moment I live my climbing dreams vicariously through my little brother Riley. That's not to say the passion's not still there … just the whole family and work thing took over for a bit. Being outdoors is still a huge part of my life. I have a wonderful job where I get to spend a lot of time out on farms, and in any spare time I get these days I like to head out into the hills to run. Trail-running is a kind of therapy for me, it clears my mind, helps me set goals and challenges my personal limits – I guess in a similar way that climbing used to. I think it's so important for everyone to find that in something they do – it keeps you sane!'

Reverend Richard Taylor, a Whanganui-based missionary, kept detailed notebooks of all his parish journeys, including those to the volcanic centre of the North Island during the period 1843–73. He accompanied Governor George Grey up the eastern slopes of Ruapehu to the summit ice fields on 30 January 1853, despite feeling unwell at the time. The following day they shifted camp as Grey wished to make an ascent of Ngāuruhoe (called Tongariro in Taylor's account), but for various reasons the climb was called off.

The first ascent of Tahurangi, the high peak of Ruapehu, was carried out in February 1879 by George Beetham and Joseph Prime Maxwell. Etheldreda Birch made the first female ascent in 1881.

Philip Temple moved to New Zealand from his Yorkshire home when he was 18. His interest in mountaineering and exploration flourished and he climbed throughout the Southern Alps. In 1962 he joined Austrian Henrich Harrer (of *Seven Years in Tibet* fame) on an expedition to West Papua, where they made the first ascent of the Carstensz Pyramid (Puncak Jaya, 4884m), the highest peak in Australasia and one of the 'seven summits'. An expedition to Heard Island and first ascent of Big Ben followed. Temple has worked as a full-time writer since 1972 and is the author of some of this country's classic mountaineering titles, including *Castles in the Air* and *World at Their Feet.* His fiction often responds to the mountain world, notably in *The Explorer* (based on the life of West Coast explorer Charlie Douglas and included in this anthology), *Beak of the Moon* and, more recently, *The Mantis.* Temple has been awarded many literary prizes and fellowships and currently lives in Dunedin.

Dorothy Theomin (1888–1966) was born into a wealthy merchant family in Dunedin and spent most of her adult life running the family home, Olveston. Her love of the mountains took root in 1914 and she spent many seasons based at Mount Cook, taking advantage of the clean air to manage her asthma. She was a prolific letter writer, and her letters to her family capture her wit and keen sense of observation. Theomin never married and often climbed with guides Alex Graham (whom she nicknamed 'The Philosopher'), Peter Graham, Jack Lippe and Frank Milne. In April 1916 she made the first ascent of Brass Peak (named after guide William Brass who had died at Gallipoli the previous year) with Peter Graham and Jack Lippe acting as guides. In 1919 she scaled the Minarets – the highest mountain she climbed. Theomin was not drawn to technical mountaineering, and preferred travelling over glaciers and alpine passes, such as the 'perfect camping trip', made in 1926 from the head of Fox Glacier to Franz Josef Glacier and included in this anthology.

Richard Thomson wrote: 'As a small child I was viscerally scared of heights. Now, peering over the edge of a cliff into the enormous void below has become a source of great pleasure. Somehow, the intensity of the response remains and has been transfigured. I first visited the Darrans in 1986 and immediately knew that I would be going back. But for various reasons, it took until I was nearly 40 for the climbs I did there (like the one in this story) to equal (and, actually, far surpass) the climbs that scurried about in my imagination.'

Jill Tremain was born in 1946, took up tramping in 1963 and was a member of the Hutt Valley Tramping Club. In 1965 she made the second ascent of Mt Aspiring via the West Face with Ian Jowett, a route that had not been repeated since 1909. She spent the 1966 season at Mount Cook, completing a first ascent of the East Face of Footstool, a grand traverse of Aoraki/Mt Cook, and ascents of Mt Tasman, Douglas and Dampier–Vancouver. With Graeme Dingle she completed a new route up Mt Dixon from Pioneer Pass, and in 1971 joined Dingle in making a complete 100-day winter traverse of the Southern Alps. This trip was documented in Graeme Dingle's *Two Against the Alps*, which was illustrated by Tremain and published in 1972. Tremain lost her life in an avalanche in 1974 during the Indian–New Zealand all-woman expedition to climb Hardeol (7151m)

in the Indian Garhwal region. Graeme Dingle wrote of Tremain: 'To be with her in the mountains and to share her philosophy was to know life better.'

A generation older than Tremain, Mavis Davidson (the recipient of the letter from Tremain reproduced in this anthology) rose to prominence as a mountaineer during the 1950s and was a member of the first all-woman team to reach the summit of Aoraki/Mt Cook in 1953. She was a vocal member of the New Zealand Alpine Club and became the first woman to be elected to the national committee in 1952. An author and world authority on sika deer, she continued to journey into the remote backcountry throughout her life. She was awarded an OBE for services to science and mountaineering in 1992.

Brian Turner (born 1944) is a poet, essayist, biographer and editor. His interest in outdoor sports such as cycling, fishing and mountaineering has been matched by his environmental activism and dedication to the conservation movement. Turner is recognised as one of New Zealand's leading poets and has been the recipient of many fellowships and awards, including the 2003 Te Mata Estate New Zealand Poet Laureate and the 2009 Prime Minister's Award for Literary Achievement in Poetry. Since the late nineteenth century, New Zealand poets such as botanist Arnold Wall, Charles Brasch, Denis Glover and James K. Baxter have ventured into the backcountry and found inspiration in the mountain world. But whereas some of these poets tend to romanticise their response, Turner writes with a sense of realism born from continued engagement with the natural environment.

Hone Tuwhare (Ngāpuhi, Ngāti Korokoro, Ngāti Tautahi, Te Uri-o-Hau, Te Popoto) was born in 1922 and grew up in Auckland. A qualified boilermaker and active in the trade union movement, Tuwhare began writing and publishing poetry in 1956. His first poetry collection, *No Ordinary Sun*, was published in 1964, and the initial print run of 700 copies sold out within 10 days. The book has since been reprinted 12 times and is one of the most widely read poetry collections in this country. Tuwhare has won many awards and fellowships, including being named Te Mata Estate New Zealand Poet Laureate in 1999. In 2003 he was included in a list of New Zealand's 10 greatest living artists. He moved to Kaka Point in Otago in 1992 and lived there until his death in 2008.

Allan Uren has been climbing and mountaineering in New Zealand and overseas for 34 years. While at Wanaka Area School in the late 1970s he started tramping in Mt Aspiring National Park. Wearing the same tramping boots he learned to rockclimb at Hospital Flat near Wanaka. For a few years in the late 1990s he went down the mountaineering rabbit hole, briefly becoming 'Allan in Wonderland', climbing difficult new routes that he believes are some of the best in the country. He feels blessed to have lived through that time and to have had so much fun with awesome people. Uren is a volunteer for the Wanaka Alpine Cliff Rescue team, and enjoys putting up new climbs on the cliffs around Wanaka and walking his dog.

Aat Vervoorn began tramping and climbing at an early age. His first climbs include a number of long routes on Mt Geryon in Tasmania, such as the first ascent of the East Face of the north peak in December 1961. Six months later an old friend from his Sydney club suggested he go to New Zealand to climb – and gave him the fare. Vervoorn's New Zealand climbing activity focused strongly on the Aoraki–West Coast glaciers alpine area. For a number of years he worked as a guide and mountaineering instructor in Aoraki/Mount Cook National Park, and was heavily involved in search and rescue work. In 1974 he moved to Canberra to study and teach at Australian National University. Thereafter his New Zealand alpine activities consisted primarily of long solo journeys on the western side of the Main Divide. In 2009 he moved back to New Zealand and now lives in Nelson.

Bill Whelen spent the 1960s and 70s climbing in Australia and New Zealand, and joined an expedition to the Ayacachi (Mamariti) group in Peru in 1971. He scaled back his climbing in the 1990s.

Mark Whetu, a Kiwi camera operator and professional mountaineer, was part of a team filming an Everest-based documentary, *The Summit of Dreams*, in 1994. Having reached the summit with Australian Mike Rheinberger, Whetu realised it was too late to return to camp before dark. They spent a freezing night just 50 metres below the summit then attempted further descent, but Rheinberger was stricken with cerebral edema. After a day-long struggle, Mark had to decide whether to stay on the mountain with his dying friend or save his own life. As a result of that

night at 8780m, Mark lost his toes to frostbite and entered a period of deep depression. He returned home to Queenstown and endured a long recovery and much emotional turmoil before eventually deciding to return to the Himalaya.

Brian Wilkins is a man of many parts: industrial chemist, high-school science teacher, academic pharmaceutical chemist, a better-than-average classical singer and leg-spin bowler, an author and researcher in cricket, science and mountaineering, and a New Zealand and Himalayan climber with a particular interest in backcountry and mountain safety. A few years ago he invented a safe technique for crossing rivers.

Tristram Hall (1934–1958), referred to in Wilkins' excerpt in this anthology, was introduced to mountaineering by his father, David Oswald William Hall. He climbed extensively in the Arthur's Pass–Waimakariri area, as well as making trips to the Mount Cook and Hollyford regions. He graduated from Otago University with a BSc in mathematics and physics. In 1975 the DOW Hall Publications Fund was established to provide support for the publication of mountaineering literature. Managed by the New Zealand Alpine Club, this fund has supported the publication of many books, including Brian Wilkins' *Among Secret Beauties: A memoir of mountaineering in New Zealand and the Himalayas* (Otago University Press, 2013), and this anthology itself.

E. Brin Williman was born in 1948 and educated in Christchurch, where he gained an MA in engineering from the University of Canterbury and later specialised in water resource engineering. Williman has mountaineered throughout New Zealand, making numerous ascents in the Mount Cook region (including Aoraki/Mt Cook, Sefton, Douglas and Magellan) and the backcountry areas of Fiordland, Aspiring and the Arrowsmiths. Overseas trips have taken him to the European Alps, Indonesia and the Andes, where he climbed several peaks including Lasunayoc in Peru (5960m). He remains a keen tramper and skier.

SOURCES

Acknowledgements for permission to reprint items included in this anthology are made to the following copyright holders and places of publication. Every effort was made to contact the copyright holders for material reproduced here. The publishers would be grateful to hear from any other copyright holders.

PART 1: APPROACH

Rangi Faith, 'Castle Hill, 2003', *Conversation with a Moahunter* (Wellington: Steele Roberts, 2005). Reproduced with permission of the author and Steele Roberts.

Rebecca Smith, 'Young, Short and Loving It!', *New Zealand Alpine Journal*, vol. 56, 2004, 51. Reproduced with permission of the author and New Zealand Alpine Club.

Eleanor Adams, 'Child Explorer on the Milford Track', in Sarah Ell (ed.), *The Adventures of Pioneer Women in New Zealand* (Auckland: Bush Press, 1992, 127–29). Reproduced with permission of the author and Bush Press. The original account by Eleanor Adams is in the Alexander Turnbull Library, Wellington, MS-Papers-3542.

Rev. Richard Taylor, 28–31 January 1853, in *Journals, 1833–1873*, MS-302, Auckland War Memorial Museum Tāmaki Paenga Hira. Reproduced with permission of Auckland War Memorial Museum Tāmaki Paenga Hira.

W. Scott Gilkison, *Peaks, Packs, and Mountain Tracks* (Auckland: Whitcombe & Tombs, 1940, 102–10). Reproduced with permission of Bruce Gilkison and Penguin Random House New Zealand.

Philip Temple, *The Explorer* (Auckland: Hodder and Stoughton, 1975, 57–63). Reproduced with permission of the author and Hachette New Zealand.

Forrestina Ross, 'Housekeeping on a Glacier', in Mrs. Malcolm Ross and Noel Ross, *Mixed Grill* (Auckland: Whitcombe & Tombs, 1934, 9–11). Reproduced with permission of Penguin Random House New Zealand.

Jack Cox, 'Guiding Memories at the Hermitage and Franz Josef 1929–1938', Personal Papers, New Zealand Alpine Club: Records (1864–2013) MS-1164-2/022/01, Hocken Collections Uare Taoka o Hākena, Dunedin. Reproduced with permission of Hocken Collections Uare Taoka o Hākena.

Michael Gill, *Mountain Midsummer: Climbing in four continents* (London: Hodder & Stoughton, 1969, 15–18). Reproduced with permission of the author and Hachette New Zealand.

Sara Knox, 'Climbing', *Sport 2*, April 1989, 115. (Wellington: Victoria University Press, 1989). Reproduced with permission of the author and Victoria University Press.

Lydia Bradey, *Going Up Is Easy* (Auckland: Penguin Random House, 2015, 47–54). Reproduced with permission of the author and Penguin Random House New Zealand.

Aat Vervoorn, *Mountain Solitudes: Solo journeys in the Southern Alps of New Zealand* (Nelson: Craig Potton Publishing, 2000, 27–35). Reproduced with permission of the author and Potton & Burton.

John Pascoe, 'The Reconnaissance of Mt. Evans', *New Zealand Alpine Journal*, vol. 15, no. 19, May 1932, 25–30. Reproduced with permission of Jonathan and Linda Pascoe and New Zealand Alpine Club.

Steve Hart, 'Alpine Reflections: A values-based approach to climbing', *New Zealand Alpine Journal*, vol. 54, 2002, 112–13. Reproduced with permission of the author and New Zealand Alpine Club.

Rob Kettels, 'Tokens of the Spirit: Exploring objectivity, emotions and fate in the Southern Alps', *New Zealand Alpine Journal*, vol. 61, 2009, 28–30. Reproduced with permission of the author and New Zealand Alpine Club.

Brian Turner, *Ancestors* (Dunedin: John McIndoe, 1981, 44). Reproduced with permission of the author.

Philip Temple, 'Fire and Ice', unpublished at time of printing, 2017. Reproduced with permission of the author.

PART 2: CLIMB

James Cowan, *Hero Stories of New Zealand* (Wellington: Harry H. Tombs, 1935). Reproduced with permission of Penguin Random House New Zealand.

Bill Whelen, 'The Climb of the Ancient Mariners', *New Zealand Geographic*, no. 40, Oct–Dec 1998, 18–21. Reproduced with permission of New Zealand Geographic.

Thom Conroy, *The Naturalist* (Auckland: Vintage–Random House New Zealand, 2014, 293–96). Reproduced with permission of the author and Penguin Random House New Zealand.

Joseph O'Leary, 'Letters to W.J.P. Hodgkins re an account of an ascent of Mt Earnslaw, 1894', New Zealand Alpine Club: Records (1864–2013), MS-1164-2/59/1, Hocken Collections Uare Taoka o Hākena, Dunedin. Reproduced with permission of Hocken Collections Uare Taoka o Hākena.

Bernard Head, Typescript account of expeditions up the Matukituki River, 1909 and 1911 (n.d), in Robert Pinney: Papers in ARC-0587, MS-3184/002, Hocken

Collections Uare Taoka o Hākena, Dunedin. Reproduced with permission of Hocken Collections Uare Taoka o Hākena.

J.R. Dennistoun, 'First to the Summit: Mitre Peak, Milford Sound', *New Zealand Alpine Journal*, vol. 16, June 1956, 406–11. Reproduced with permission of New Zealand Alpine Club.

Bob McKerrow, 'Maori Mountaineers of South Westland', *New Zealand Alpine Journal*, vol. 44, 1991, 164–70, centennial edition. Reproduced with permission of the author and New Zealand Alpine Club. This article uses an unusual referencing system, where each source has been assigned a single, individual number. For example, #8 is used for all material sourced from Trish McCormack's *The Maori in Westland*.

Rhian Gallagher, *Freda du Faur: Southern Alps 1909–1913* (Dunedin: Otakou Press, 2016, n.p.). Reproduced with permission of the author and Otakou Press.

Freda du Faur, *The Conquest of Mount Cook and other climbs: An account of four seasons' mountaineering on the Southern Alps of New Zealand* (London: George Allen & Unwin, 1915, 231–35).

Dorothy Theomin, Letter describing a five-day camping trip from Fox Glacier to Franz Josef Glacier, 1926. 'Letters from Dorothy Theomin to her family', New Zealand Alpine Club, MS-1164-2/77/6, Hocken Collections Uare Taoka o Hākena, Dunedin. Reproduced with permission of Hocken Collections Uare Taoka o Hākena.

Doreen Pickens, 'Karangarua–Landsborough', *New Zealand Alpine Journal*, vol. 14, June 1951, 77. Reproduced with permission of New Zealand Alpine Club.

Laurence Fearnley, *The Hut Builder* (Auckland: Penguin Books, 2010, 167–73). Reproduced with permission of the author and Penguin Random House New Zealand.

Rangi Faith, 'Cushioning the Blow', *Conversation with a Moahunter* (Wellington: Steele Roberts, 2005, 55). Reproduced with permission of the author and Steele Roberts.

Dora de Beer, *Yunnan 1938: Account of a journey in south-west China* (Oxford: Dora de Beer, 1971, 1–6).

Edmund Hillary, Copies of letters to Jim Rose, New Zealand Alpine Club, MS-1164-2/66/3, Hocken Collections Uare Taoka o Hākena, Dunedin. Reproduced with permission of Sarah Hillary, Peter Hillary and Hocken Collections Uare Taoka o Hākena.

Derek Chinn, 'The First Clyde Ascent of Mount Everest', *New Zealand Alpine Journal*, vol. 56, 2004, 81–83. Reproduced with permission of the author and New Zealand Alpine Club.

N.D. Hardie, 'Five Feet from the Gods: Kanchenjunga, 1955', *New Zealand Alpine Journal*, vol. 16, June 1956, 280–87. Reproduced with permission of the author and New Zealand Alpine Club.

Karen McNeill, 'A Ridge Too Far: The first female ascent of Denali's Cassin Ridge', *New Zealand Alpine Journal*, vol. 56, 2004, 64–67. Reproduced with permission of New Zealand Alpine Club.

Brian Turner, 'High Hopes', *Inside Outside* (Wellington: Victoria University Press, 2011, 133). Reproduced with permission of the author and Victoria University Press.

Michael Gill, 'The Ramsay Face of Whitcombe', in *Mountain Midsummer: Climbing in four continents* (London: Hodder & Stoughton, 1969, 159–67). Reproduced with permission of the author and Hachette New Zealand.

Anon., 'Ngauruhoe', *Heels*, 1965, n.p. (Wellington: Victoria University of Wellington Tramping Club, 1965).

Aat Vervoorn, 'Plateaunic Melodrama', *The Canterbury Mountaineer 1964–1965*, vol. 10, October 1965, 21–22. Reproduced with permission of the author and Canterbury Mountaineering Club.

Ross Cullen, 'Economic Man', *Barron Saddle–Mt Brewster: A guide for climbers* (Christchurch: New Zealand Alpine Club, 2002, 24–26). Reproduced with permission of the author and New Zealand Alpine Club.

Nick Cradock, 'Oh Where Have You Been my Blue-eyed Sons?', *The Canterbury Mountaineer*, no. 46, December 1977, 14–15. Reproduced with permission of the author and Canterbury Mountaineering Club.

PART 3: EPIC

W.S. Green, *The High Alps of New Zealand, or, A trip to the glaciers of the Antipodes with an ascent of Mount Cook* (London: Macmillan & Co., 1883, 244–51).

Kim Logan, 'Hongi's Track', *The Canterbury Mountaineer*, no. 50, October 1965, 7–9. Reproduced with permission of the author and Canterbury Mountaineering Club.

Jill Tremain, Letter to Mavis Davidson, 24 September 1971. Correspondence and other papers relating to Jill Tremain, MS–2985/268, Hocken Collections Uare Taoka o Hākena, Dunedin. Reproduced with permission of Pauline Tremain and Hocken Collections Uare Taoka o Hākena.

Allan Uren, 'White as a Sheet', *Alpinist*, no. 46, 2014, 63–65. Reproduced with permission of the author and *Alpinist* magazine.

Carol Diamond Christie and David Baguley, 'Ruapehu, 23 September 1995, 5.08pm', *New Zealand Alpine Journal*, vol. 48, 1995, 38–39. Reproduced with permission of the authors and New Zealand Alpine Club.

Andrew Lindblade, *Expeditions* (South Yarra: Hardie Grant Books, 2001, 150–57). Reproduced with permission of the author.

Caoilinn Hughes, 'Avalanche', *Gathering Evidence* (Wellington: Victoria University Press, 2014, 11–12). Reproduced with permission of the author and Victoria University Press.

Anon., 'A Solitary Climber', *New Zealand Tablet*, vol. 34, issue 10, 8 March 1906: paperspast.natlib.govt.nz. The authors of this anthology acknowledge the National Library of New Zealand in reproducing this material.

J. Walton, 'A Pioneer Phase', *The Canterbury Mountaineer 1962–63*, vol. 9, no. 32, October 1963, 205–07. Reproduced with permission of Canterbury Mountaineering Club.

Paul Hersey, *High Misadventure: New Zealand mountaineering tragedies and survival stories* (Auckland: New Holland Publishers (NZ), 2009, 55–61). Reproduced with permission of the author.

Brian Wilkins, *Among Secret Beauties: A memoir of mountaineering in New Zealand and the Himalayas* (Dunedin: Otago University Press, 2013, 179–81). Reproduced with permission of the author and Otago University Press, Dunedin.

Mark Whetu, 'Summit of Dreams', *New Zealand Alpine Journal*, vol. 47, 1994, 42–45. Reproduced with permission of the author and New Zealand Alpine Club.

Edith Searle Grossman, *The Heart of the Bush* (London: Sands & Co., 1910, 526–30).

Ida Corry, 'Climbs at the Head of the Franz Josef', *New Zealand Alpine Journal*, vol. 5, no. 20, June 1933, 210–15. Reproduced with permission of New Zealand Alpine Club.

Graeme Dingle, *Two Against the Alps* (Christchurch: Whitcombe & Tombs, 1972, 66–78). Reproduced with permission of the author and Penguin Random House New Zealand.

Penny Goddard, 'Under the Mountain: An ascent of La Perouse from the Cook River', *New Zealand Alpine Journal*, vol. 56, 2004, 47–50. Reproduced with permission of the author and New Zealand Alpine Club.

Peter Gough, 'Never Let the Facts …', *The Canterbury Mountaineer 1984*, no. 50, 1984, 46–48. Reproduced with permission of the author and Canterbury Mountaineering Club.

PART 4: REFLECTION

Pat Deavoll, *Wind from a Distant Summit: The story of New Zealand's top woman mountaineer* (Nelson: Craig Potton Publishing, 2011, 240–42). Reproduced with permission of the author and Potton & Burton.

Graeme Dingle, *Wall of Shadows: The New Zealand Jannu adventure* (Auckland: Hodder & Stoughton, 1976, 147–49). Reproduced with permission of the author and Hachette New Zealand.

Rachel Bush, 'Never', *Nice Pretty Things* (Wellington: Victoria University Press, 2011, 16). Reproduced with permission of Molly Nunns and Victoria University Press.

Aat Vervoorn, *Beyond the Snowline* (Wellington: Reed; Dunedin: McIndoe, 1981). Reproduced with permission of the author and Penguin Random House New Zealand.

Fleur Adcock, 'Flight, with Mountains', *Poems 1960–2000* (Newcastle upon Tyne: Bloodaxe Books, 2000, 15–16). Reproduced with permission of the author and Bloodaxe Books.

Jonathan Scott, *Harry's Absence: Looking for my father on the mountain* (Wellington: Victoria University Press, 1997, 16–19; 212–15). Reproduced with permission of the author and Victoria University Press.

Sir Thomas Hunter, 'Gifford, Talbot and Grenfell', in Anita Crozier (ed.), *Beyond the Southern Lakes: The explorations of W.G. Grave* (Wellington: Reed, 1950, 32–37). Reproduced with permission of Penguin Random House New Zealand.

Edmund Hillary, 'A Tribute from Ed Hillary', *The Canterbury Mountaineer 1979*, no. 48, 1979, 25. Reproduced with permission of Sarah Hillary, Peter Hillary and Canterbury Mountaineering Club.

Peter Graham, Letter to Jim Glasgow, 26 October 1954. Brooke Bequest and the Graham Memoir 1948–58, New Zealand Alpine Club, MS-1164-1/6/21, Hocken Collections Uare Taoka o Hākena, Dunedin. Reproduced with permission of Hocken Collections Uare Taoka o Hākena.

John Pascoe, 'A Westland Memory: Mount Evans', *Great Days in New Zealand Mountaineering: The rock and the snow* (Wellington: A.H & A.W. Reed, 1958, 59–61). Reproduced with permission of Jonathan and Linda Pascoe and Penguin Random House New Zealand.

Doreen Murie, Speech given at Turnbull House, Wellington, 10 February 1993, for 'Summits for Suffrage'. Women Climbing Inc., Summits for Suffrage, MS-3022/011, Hocken Collections Uare Taoka o Hākena, Dunedin. Reproduced with permission of Hocken Collections Uare Taoka o Hākena.

Lydia Bradey, with Laurence Fearnley, *Going Up Is Easy* (Auckland: Penguin Books, 2015, 78–80). Reproduced with permission of the author and Penguin Random House New Zealand.

Paul Hersey, *Protection* (Canmore: Imaginary Mountain Surveyors, 2018). Reproduced with permission of the author and Imaginary Mountain Surveyors.

Richard Thomson, 'Incantation', *Alpinist*, no. 46, 2014, 78–80. Reproduced with permission of the author and *Alpinist* magazine.

Tom Riley, 'West on Sunset', *New Zealand Alpine Journal*, vol. 65, 2013, 28–31. Reproduced with permission of the author and New Zealand Alpine Club.

Kerry Popplewell, 'Quail Flat, 1960', *Leaving the Tableland* (Wellington: Steele Roberts, 2010, 53). Reproduced with permission of the author and Steele Roberts.

Brin Williman, 'Passing Generations in the Hopkins', *New Zealand Alpine Journal*, vol. 46, 1993, 14–15. Reproduced with permission of the author and New Zealand Alpine Club.

Pat Deavoll, *Wind from a Distant Summit: The story of New Zealand's top woman mountaineer* (Nelson: Craig Potton Publishing, 2011). Reproduced with permission of the author and Potton & Burton.

Sharron Came, 'Many happy returns', unpublished at time of printing, 2017. Reproduced with permission of the author.

Christopher Johnson, Extract of letter to his wife, Jean Johnson, from Nigeria, 1942. *OSONZAC Yodellings*, no. 13, 30 October 1942. New Zealand Alpine Club Archives, MS-1164-2/009/11, Hocken Collections Uare Taoka o Hākena, Dunedin. Reproduced with permission of Peter Johnson and Hocken Collections Uare Taoka o Hākena.

Hone Tuwhare, 'Man in the Landscape', *No Ordinary Sun* (Dunedin: John McIndoe, 1977, 224). Reproduced with permission of the Estate of Hone Tuwhare.

ACKNOWLEDGEMENTS

We were very fortunate to receive the 2017 Friends of the Hocken Collections award and wish to thank the committee, and Peter Holland in particular, for their wonderful support of this project. We spent many happy hours in the Hocken and wish to acknowledge the valuable assistance of Anna Blackman and all the staff who helped source and copy archival material. Thanks to the Hocken Collections Uare Taoka o Hākena for permitting us to reproduce work included in this anthology.

Thank you to the staff of the McNab Collection at Dunedin Public Library, and Martin Collett at the Auckland Museum Library, for their professional and friendly help.

We would like to acknowledge the generous support of the New Zealand Alpine Club DOW Hall Fund and the Federated Mountain Clubs of New Zealand Mountain and Forest Trust. We are grateful also to New Zealand Alpine Club and Canterbury Mountaineering Club for allowing us to reproduce articles.

Thanks to all the people who offered help and information during the research of this anthology. In particular we would like to thank Graham Langton, Kennedy Warne, David Fearnley, Pat Deavoll, Rhian Gallagher, Sue Wootton, Jay Davison, Peter Johnson and Alison Ballance. Thank you to our families for their love, patience and encouragement.

Many thanks to Otago University Press: Rachel Scott for providing advice, encouragement and support, Imogen Coxhead for editing, Fiona Moffat for cover and design, and Victor Billot for publicity. Thanks also to Kathryn Tall for taking on a massive job and turning over 200 photocopied pages into a Word document. The superb cover image was taken by Tony Rae, and we acknowledge his generosity in making it available to us. Thanks also to Troy Mattingley for the use of his photos.

Especial thanks to all the contributors in this anthology. Your story-telling and writing has captured our attention and held us spellbound over many months. Thank you, too, to the families and friends of contributors who have generously given permission for us to include the work of loved ones in this anthology.

Finally, we would like to dedicate this book to all the people who have guided and shared days in the mountains with us. Without you this book would not be possible.